NEUTROSOPHIC SET IN MEDICAL IMAGE ANALYSIS

NEUTROSOPHIC SET IN MEDICAL IMAGE ANALYSIS

Edited by

YANHUI GUO
AMIRA S. ASHOUR

ACADEMIC PRESS

An imprint of Elsevier

Academic Press is an imprint of Elsevier
125 London Wall, London EC2Y 5AS, United Kingdom
525 B Street, Suite 1650, San Diego, CA 92101, United States
50 Hampshire Street, 5th Floor, Cambridge, MA 02139, United States
The Boulevard, Langford Lane, Kidlington, Oxford OX5 1GB, United Kingdom

Notices
Knowledge and best practice in this field are constantly changing. As new research and experience broaden our understanding, changes in research methods, professional practices, or medical treatment may become necessary.

Practitioners and researchers must always rely on their own experience and knowledge in evaluating and using any information, methods, compounds, or experiments described herein. In using such information or methods they should be mindful of their own safety and the safety of others, including parties for whom they have a professional responsibility.

To the fullest extent of the law, neither the Publisher nor the authors, contributors, or editors, assume any liability for any injury and/or damage to persons or property as a matter of products liability, negligence or otherwise, or from any use or operation of any methods, products, instructions, or ideas contained in the material herein.

Library of Congress Cataloging-in-Publication Data
A catalog record for this book is available from the Library of Congress

British Library Cataloguing-in-Publication Data
A catalogue record for this book is available from the British Library

ISBN: 978-0-12-818148-5

For information on all Academic Press publications
visit our website at https://www.elsevier.com/books-and-journals

Publisher: Mara Conner
Acquisition Editor: Tim Pitts
Editorial Project Manager: Peter Adamson
Production Project Manager: Nirmala Arumugam
Cover designer: Greg Harris

Typeset by SPi Global, India

Working together
to grow libraries in
developing countries

www.elsevier.com • www.bookaid.org

Contents

Part I Background on neutrosophic set in medical image analysis

Chapter 1 Introduction to neutrosophy and neutrosophic environment   3

Florentin Smarandache, Said Broumi, Prem Kumar Singh,
Chun-fang Liu, V. Venkateswara Rao, Hai-Long Yang,
Ion Patrascu, Azeddine Elhassouny

Part III Neutrosophic set in medical image clustering and segmentation

Contributors

Yaman Akbulut   Informatics Dept., Firat University, Elazig, Turkey

Thilaga Shri Chandra Amma Palanisamy   Department of ECE, College of Engineering Guindy, Anna University, Chennai, India

Amira S. Ashour   Department of Electronics and Electrical Communications Engineering, Faculty of Engineering, Tanta University, Tanta, Egypt

Varun Bajaj   Department of Electronics and Communication, Indian Institute of Information Technology Design and Manufacturing, Jabalpur, India

Said Broumi   Laboratory of Information Processing, University Hassan II, Casablanca, Morocco

Umit Budak   Electrical and Electronics Eng. Dept., Engineering Faculty, Bitlis Eren University, Bitlis, Turkey

Guanxiong Cai   School of Data and Computer Science, Sun Yat-sen University, Guangzhou, People's Republic of China

Weiguo Chen   Department of Diagnostic Radiology, Nanfang Hospital, Guangzhou, People's Republic of China

Azeddine Elhassouny   Rabat IT Center, ENSIAS, Mohammed V University in Rabat, Rabat, Morocco

Yanhui Guo   Department of Computer Science, University of Illinois at Springfield, Springfield, IL, United States

Ahmed Refaat Hawas   Department of Electronics and Electrical Communications Engineering, Faculty of Engineering, Tanta University, Tanta, Egypt

Mohan Jayaraman   Department of ECE, SRM Valliammai Engineering College, Kattankulathur, India

Murat Karabatak   Department of Software Engineering, Technology Faculty, Firat University, Elazig, Turkey

Deepika Koundal   Department of Computer Science and Engineering, Chitkara University School of Engineering and Technology, Chitkara University, Himachal Pradesh, India

Chun-fang Liu   College of Science, Northeast Forestry University, Harbin, China

Yao Lu   School of Data and Computer Science, Sun Yat-sen University, Guangzhou, People's Republic of China

Ion Patrascu Mathematics Department, Fratii Buzesti College, Craiova, Romania

Abdulkadir Sengur Department of Electrical and Electronics Engineering, Technology Faculty, Firat University, Elazig, Turkey

A.I. Shahin Department of Biomedical Engineering, Higher Technological Institute, 10th of Ramadan City, Egypt

Bhisham Sharma Department of Computer Science and Engineering, Chitkara University School of Engineering and Technology, Chitkara University, Himachal Pradesh, India

Prem Kumar Singh Amity Institute of Information Technology and Engineering, Amity University, Noida, India

Florentin Smarandache Department of Mathematics, University of New Mexico, Gallup, NM, United States

Erkan Tanyildizi Department of Software Engineering, Technology Faculty, Firat University, Elazig, Turkey

Krishnaveni Vellingiri Department of ECE, PSG College of Technology, Coimbatore, India

V. Venkateswara Rao Division of Mathematics, Department of S&H, VFSTR, Guntur, India

Hai-Long Yang College of Mathematics and Information Science, Shaanxi Normal University, Xi'an, China

Hui Zeng Department of Diagnostic Radiology, Nanfang Hospital, Guangzhou, People's Republic of China

Yuanpin Zhou School of Data and Computer Science, Sun Yat-sen University, Guangzhou, People's Republic of China

Preface

Medical images consist of imprecise and fuzzy information, which complicates the denoising, segmentation, feature extraction, and classification processes and analysis. To interpret this inherent uncertainty, vagueness, and ambiguity, different medical image analysis and processing procedures are explored and developed. Fuzzy sets are extensively used to handle the uncertainty and fuzziness in several domains. However, fuzzy sets have some limitations, owing to the unconsidered spatial context of the pixels due to the artifacts and noise. Consequently, unlike fuzzy logic, neutrosophic logic introduces an extra domain to deal with higher uncertainty degrees that are very challenging to handle using fuzzy logic. In medical image analysis, the neutrosophic set (NS), which is a generalization of the fuzzy set, becomes more prevalent in overcoming the restrictions of the fuzzy-based approaches. Neutrosophy is the foundation of neutrosophic statistics, neutrosophic logic, neutrosophic sets, and neutrosophic probability. Such methods are applied for intuitively performing diagnosis in terms of the neutrosophic theory for efficient medical image denoising, segmentation, clustering, and classification in numerous medical applications. Simultaneously, medical image analysis has a central role in all aspects of diagnosis and healthcare. Various researchers struggle with how to make their methods more accurate in handling medical images. To solve such challenges, several studies have been conducted on different medical modalities for different organs and diseases. Those studies established the effectiveness of NS in medical image processing and analysis.

This book is a cutting-edge contribution to fulfill the interests of engineers, researchers, and software developers for understanding the concepts of neutrosophic theory as well as for providing information on how to gather, interpret, analyze, and handle medical images using NS methods in different medical applications. The book involves numerous topics related to the role of neutrosophic theory in addressing medical image analysis in different healthcare applications due to the heterogeneous nature and rapid expansion of medical images from different modalities that pose challenges for medical image analysis. To face these challenges and achieve our goal, this book includes 15 *chapters,* starting with Chapter 1 by Dr. Florentin Smarandache, who proposed the theory of neutrosophical logic and sets in 1995. In Chapter 1, Smarandache et al. provide concepts with an overview on neutrosophy with its mathematical progress to make the readers aware of neutrosophy and the neutrosophic set (NS), the standard NS, the hesitant NS, and their extension to complex fuzzy environments. This chapter also reports on the neutrosophic algebraic structures, neutrosophic graphs, neutrosophic triplets, neutrosophic duplets, and the neutrosophic multiset as well as the extension of crisp/fuzzy/intuitionistic fuzzy/neutrosophic sets with their mathematical expressions. In Chapter 2, an advanced background on the neutrosophic set in different medical image analysis applications is introduced by Shahin et al., followed by a specific ultrasound image analysis using an advanced neutrosophic set in Chapter 3 by Koundal and Sharma. These three chapters are gathered in Part 1 in the book, followed by Part 2, which is made up of the neutrosophic set in medical image denoising in three chapters. In Chapter 4, Jayaraman et al. map the magnetic resonance image (MRI) to the neutrosophic domain for denoising using the NS of median filtering, the NS of Wiener filtering, and the nonlocal NS of Wiener filtering. The Brainweb database was used to evaluate the performance of these denoising approaches with respect to the quantitative/qualitative measurements. The results establish the superiority of proposed NS-based denoising methods compared to the traditional denoising methods, which proves the impact of NS in MR image denoising. Then, in Chapter 5, Ashour and Guo propose a new optimized indeterminacy filter (OIF) for dermoscopy image denoising, followed by Shahin et al. proposing a neutrosophic set-based denoising technique in optical coherence tomography images in Chapter 6.

Subsequently, five chapters in Part III are directed to the neutrosophic set in medical image clustering, which is followed by a survey on neutrosophic medical image segmentation in Chapter 7 by Sengur et al. In Chapter 8, *Hawas et al.* study the effect of the NS filter's type and size during the clustering of the skin lesion regions in dermoscopic images using the NS-based K-means (NKM) clustering method. In Chapter 9, Chandra et al. combine the NS with a fuzzy c-means clustering algorithm and a modified particle swarm optimization for automated segmentation of brain tumors in magnetic resonance (MR) images. Then, in Chapter 10, Ashour et al. detect the nuclei of the blood cells using a proposed neutrosophic Hough transform method. In the final part of this section in Chapter 11, Guo and Ashour proposed an NS-based dermoscopic medical image segmentation method. Then, three chapters in Part IV focus on the NS in medical image classification. Accordingly, Sengur et al. in Chapter 12 design a neutrosophic similarity score-based entropy measure for focal and nonfocal electroencephalograms for classification, followed by Guo and Ashour in Chapter 13 who implement a neutrosophic multiple deep convolutional neural network for skin dermoscopic image classification. Then, Cai et al. in Chapter 14 propose a deep learning network based on NS for segmentation and classification of mammogram images. Finally, Part V reports on the challenges with suggested future directions in neutrosophic set-based medical image analysis in Chapter 15 by Koundal and Sharma.

These five parts of the book together provide researchers from areas of neutrosophic theories, computer vision, machine learning, soft computing, and optimization as well as clinical researchers with the required knowledge to develop new medical image analysis and computer-aided diagnosis systems based on NS.

The Editors,
Yanhui Guo
University of Illinois at Springfield, Springfield,
United States

Amira S. Ashour
Faculty of Engineering, Tanta University, Egypt

Acknowledgement

All knowledge begins with an expression of curiosity pertaining to the unknown or unknowable. Expressions of uncertainty and a doubtful nature lead a person to useful discoveries.
Kilroy J. Oldster

Our endless indebtedness is directed to *our families* for their interminable support. No words can give them the right they deserve.

We highly appreciate the great efforts done by our wonderful, strong, highly skilled *authors* and their dedication and collaboration through our book journey to introduce it in this valuable form. We believe that this book would not have happened without their perfect blend of knowledge and skills.

Especially unlimited thanks are given to the Elsevier publisher team, who showed us the ropes and gave us their trust. Our sincere appreciation is directed to *Chris Katsaropoulos* (senior acquisitions editor, biomedical engineering) as well as *Tim Pitts* (senior acquisitions editor, electronic engineering, computer vision, and medical imaging), *Dr. Peter Adamson* (editorial project manager, Elsevier) and *Nirmala Arumugam* (project manager, S&T Book production).

Last, but not least, we would like to thank our *readers*, to whom we have worked hard to introduce such knowledge on neutrosophic theory in medical image analysis and applications. We hope they will find the book a valuable and outstanding resource in their domain.

The Book Editors,
Yanhui Guo
University of Illinois at Springfield, Springfield, United States

Amira S. Ashour
Faculty of Engineering, Tanta University, Egypt

Background on neutrosophic set in medical image analysis

Introduction to neutrosophy and neutrosophic environment

Florentin Smarandache*, Said Broumi[†], Prem Kumar Singh[‡], Chun-fang Liu[§], V. Venkateswara Rao[¶], Hai-Long Yang[‖], Ion Patrascu[#], Azeddine Elhassouny**

*Department of Mathematics, University of New Mexico, Gallup, NM, United States. [†]Laboratory of Information Processing, University Hassan II, Casablanca, Morocco. [‡]Amity Institute of Information Technology and Engineering, Amity University, Noida, India. [§]College of Science, Northeast Forestry University, Harbin, China. [¶]Division of Mathematics, Department of S&H, VFSTR, Guntur, India. [‖]College of Mathematics and Information Science, Shaanxi Normal University, Xi'an, China. [#]Mathematics Department, Fratii Buzesti College, Craiova, Romania. **Rabat IT Center, ENSIAS, Mohammed V University in Rabat, Rabat, Morocco

1   Introduction

The theory of fuzzy sets was introduced at the earliest by Zadeh (1965) for dealing with the uncertainty that exists in given datasets. In this section, a problem is developed that the FSs represents acceptance, rejection and uncertain parts via a single-valued membership defined in [0, 1]. It is unable to represent the indeterminacy independently. In 1995, the theory of neutrosophical logic and sets was proposed by Smarandache (1995, 1998). Neutrosophy leads to an entire family of novel mathematical theories with an overview of not only classical but also fuzzy counterparts. The reason is that a fuzzy set representing uncertainty exists in the attributes using single-valued membership. In this case, one cannot represent when win, loss, and draw match independently. To represent this, we need to characterize them lay in membership-values of truth, falsity, and indeterminacy. This makes it necessary to extend the fuzzy sets beyond acceptance and rejection regions using single-valued neutrosophic values (Smarandache, 1998; Ye, 2014). It contains truth, falsity, and indeterminacy membership values for any given attribute. The most interesting point is that all these three functions are completely independent, and one function is not

Neutrosophic Set in Medical Image Analysis. https://doi.org/10.1016/B978-0-12-818148-5.00001-1

affected by another. NS essentially studies the starting point, environment, and range of neutralities and their exchanges with ideational ranges. One of the suitable examples is that the win, draw, or loss condition of any game cannot be written independently using the properties of FS. Similarly, there are many examples that contain uncertainty and indeterminacy such as the opinion of people toward a leader and other areas shown in Ramot, Milo, Friedman, and Kandel (2002), Ye (2014b), and Torra and Namkawa (2009). In many cases, some people support a leader, some people reject a leader, and some people vote NOTA or they abstain. To approximate these types of uncertainties, the mathematics of neutrosophic theory are extended to several environments such as hesitant neutrosophic sets (NSs) (Ye, 2015), bipolar environments (Ali & Smarandache, 2015; Deli, Ali, & Smarandache, 2015; Broumi, Bakali, et al., 2019; Broumi, Nagarajan, et al., 2019; Broumi, Talea, Bakali, Smarandache, & Singh, 2019), complex NSs (Ali, Dat, Son, & Smarandache, 2018), rough sets (Bao & Yang, 2017; Bao, Hai-Long, & Li, 2018; Guo, Liu, & Hai-Long, 2017; Yang, Bao, & Guo, 2018; Yang, Zhang, Guo, Liu, & Liao, 2017; Liu, Hai-Long, Liu, & Yang, 2017), and cubic sets (Aslam, Aroob, & andYaqoob, 2013; Jun, Kim, & Kang, 2010, 2011; Jun, Kim, & Yang, 2012; Jun, Smarandache, & Kim, 2017) with applications in various fields (Broumi et al., 2018; Broumi, Bakali, et al., 2019; Broumi, Talea, et al., 2019; Singh, 2017, 2018a, 2018b, 2018c, 2019; Smarandache, 2017). In this chapter, we will try to provide a comprehensive overview of those mathematical notations.

To measure the future perspective of any given event, this chapter also discusses the properties of cubic sets as a new technique in the NS theory. Jun et al. (2012) introduced cubic sets in both FS and valued interval fuzzy sets. The author also has distinct internal (external) cubic sets and has studied some of their properties. The designs of cubic algebras/ideals in every Boolean Abelian group and commutative algebra with its implication, that is, BCK/BCI algebra, are also introduced in Jun et al. (2010). Jun et al. (2011) proposed the notion of cubic q-ideals in BCI algebras where BCK/BCI are the algebraic structure by applying *BCK* logic. This abbreviation is provided by *B*, *C*, and *K* and the relation of both a cubic ideal and a cubic q-ideal. In addition, they recognized conditions for a cubic ideal to be cubic q-ideal and the characterizations of a cubic q-ideal and a cubic extension property for a cubic q-ideal. The idea of a cubic sub LA-semihypergroup is considered by Aslam et al. (2013). The same authors defined some results on cubic hyper ideals and cubic bi-hyper ideals in left almost-semihypergroups. The reader can refer to Singh (2018a, 2018b) and Broumi et al. (2018) for more information about other types of NSs not included in this chapter. Some researchers tried to incorporate the algebra of NSs and its extension for knowledge-processing tasks in various fields. Recently, it was extended to n-valued neutrosophic context and its graphical visualization for applications in various fields for multidecision processes.

Other parts of this chapter are organized in the following way: The preliminaries are shown in Section 2. Sections 3–14 contains each distinct extension of a NS with its mathematical algebra for better understanding, followed by conclusions and references.

2 Preliminaries

This section contains preliminaries to understand the NS.

Definition 1 Crisp set

It defines any set ξ based on a given universal set U such that an element belongs to ξ or not. One of the examples is a student who is either present or absent in the class. It does not define the exact membership of whether an element belongs to the set.

Definition 2 Fuzzy set (Zadeh, 1965)

Let us suppose E is a universe, then the FS(ξ) can be defined as mapping $\mu_X(k):\xi \to [0,1]$ for each $k \in \xi$. In this case, each element is represented using the defined membership values μ_ξ within [0, 1]. It represents the degree of an element that belongs to the given set. In this method, it provides representation of any element in the given set via a soft boundary.

Definition 3 Intuitionistic fuzzy set (Atanassov, 1986)

The IFS is a generalization of FS. It represents the acceptation or rejection part of any attribute simultaneously. The IFS A can be defined by $A = \{x, \mu_X(k), \nu_X(k)/k \in \xi\}$ where $\mu_A(k):\xi \to [0,1]$, $\nu_A(k):\xi \to [0,1]$ for each $k \in \xi$ such that $0 \le \mu_A(k) + \nu_A(k) \le 1$. Here, $\mu_A(k):\xi \to [0,1]$ denotes degrees of membership and $\nu_A(k):\xi \to [0,1]$ denotes nonmembership of $k \in A$, respectively.

Definition 4 Interval-valued fuzzy set

The interval-valued fuzzy set is nothing but an extension of FS. It provides a way to represent the membership for belonging of any attribute. The interval-valued fuzzy set A over a universe ξ is defined by

$$A = \{[A^-(k), A^+(k)]/k \in \xi\}, \tag{1}$$

where $A^-(k)$, $A^+(k)$ represent the lower boundary and upper boundary for the given membership degrees within interval [0, 1].

Definition 5 Cubic set

The cubic set provides a way to represent the interval-valued fuzzy set with more predictive analytics. It can be defined with the help of an interval-valued fuzzy set $A(x)$ as well as a single-valued fuzzy set $\mu(k)$ as $\Xi = \{<x, A(k), \mu(k)> / k \in \xi\}$. It means one can also represent the cubic set as $\langle A, \mu \rangle$ for precise representation of any event.

Example 1 The set of NS A of ξ defined by

$$A = \left\{ \begin{array}{l} \langle [0.2, 0.32], [0.32, 0.42], [0.71, 0.91] \rangle / x_1^+ \\ \langle [0.12, 0.22], [0.51, 0.91], [0.12, 0.91] \rangle / x_2^+ \\ \langle [0.71, 0.82], [0.11, 0.11], [0.51, 0.42] \rangle / x_3^+ \end{array} \right\}$$

and a NS λ is a set of ξ defined by

$$\lambda = \left\{ \begin{array}{l} \langle 0.02, 0.21, 0.41 \rangle / x_1 \\ \langle 0.11, 0.02, 0.21 \rangle / x_2 \\ \langle 0.31, 0.11, 0.71 \rangle / x_3 \end{array} \right\}$$

then $\tau = \langle A, \lambda \rangle$ n is a neutrosophic cubic set.

Definition 6 Interval cubic set

The interval cubic set is nothing but an extension of the cubic set where the single-valued fuzzy set is replaced by interval-valued set, that is, $\Xi = \langle A, \mu \rangle$ where A(k) is the interval-valued fuzzy set and the $\mu(k)$ lies between them as:

$$A^-(x) \leq \mu(x) \leq A^+(x), \quad \forall k \in \xi. \tag{2}$$

Example 2 Let $\tau = \langle A, \lambda \rangle \in C_N^X$ where C_N^X is the set of cubic sets. $A(x) = \langle [0.1, 0.3], [0.4, 0.6], [0.7, 0.8] \rangle$ and $\lambda(x) = \langle 0.2, 0.5, 0.6 \rangle$ for every k in ξ. Then $\tau = \langle A, \lambda \rangle$ is an interval cubic set.

Definition 7 External cubic set

The external cubic set $\Xi = \langle A, \mu \rangle$ is a set in which the FS $\mu(k)$ membership values do not belong to the given interval set $A(x)$ meaning

$$\mu(x) \notin (A^-(k) \, A^+(k)) \quad \forall k \in \xi. \tag{3}$$

Example 3 Let $\tau = \langle A, \lambda \rangle \in C_N^X$ where C_N^X is the set of cubic sets. $A(k) = \langle [0.1, 0.3], [0.4, 0.6], [0.7, 0.8] \rangle$ and $\lambda(k) = \langle 0.4, 0.2, 0.3 \rangle$ for every k in ξ. Then $\tau = \langle A, \lambda \rangle$ is an external cubic set.

Definition 8 Neutrosophic set

The NS consists of reptile functions, namely truth, indeterminacy, and false, (T, I, F), independently. Each of these values lies between 0 and 1 and does not depend on them. The boundary conditions of the sum of these membership degrees are $0 \leq T+I+F \leq 3$. In this, 0 is hold for the universal false cases and 3 are the universal truth cases three memberships, that is,

$$\lambda = \{\langle x : T, I, F\rangle : x \in \xi\}. \tag{4}$$

Definition 9 Interval neutrosophic set

The interval-valued neutrosophic set consists of reptile functions, namely truth, indeterminacy, and false, (T, I, F). Each of these values is defined in the following form $[T^-, T^+]$, $[I^-, I^+]$, and $[F^-, F^+]$. All these values lie between 0 and 1, and we denote this as

$$A = \{\langle k : [A_T^-, A_T^+], [A_I^-, A_I^+], [A_F^-, A_F^+]\rangle : k \in \xi\}. \tag{5}$$

3 Neutrosophic set

Definition 10 Neutrosophic set (Smarandache, 1995)

This set contains triplets having true, false, and indeterminacy membership values that can be characterized independently, T_N, I_N, FN, in [0,1]. It can be abbreviated as follows:

$$N = \{k; T_N(k), I_N(k), F_N(k) : k \in ; \xi; T_N(k), I_N(k), F_N(k) \in \xi]^-0, 1^+[\}. \tag{6}$$

There is no restriction on the sum of $T_N(k)$, $I_N(k)$, and $F_N(k)$. So

$$0^- \leq + T_N(k) + I_N(k) + F_N(k) \leq 3^+. \tag{7}$$

Definition 11 Nonstandard neutrosophic set (Smarandache, 1995)

Let ξ be a nonempty set and its element is k, the NS N in ξ is termed by

$$A = \{\langle k; T_A(k), I_A(k), F_A(k)\rangle | k \in \xi\} \tag{8}$$

which is characterized by a TMF $T_N(k)$, an IMF $I_N(k)$, and an FMF $F_N(k)$, respectively, where

$$T_N(k) : \xi \to]^-01^+[$$
$$I_N(k) : \xi \to]^-01^+[$$
$$F_N(k) : \xi \to]^-01^+[$$

The functions $T_N(k)$, $I_N(k)$, $F_N(k)$ in ξ are real standard or nonstandard subsets of $]^-0, 1^+[$. The sum of $T_N(k)$, $I_N(k)$, $F_N(k)$ does not have any restrictions, that is

$$^-0 \leq \sup T_N(x) + \sup I_N(k) + \sup F_N(k) \leq 3^+. \tag{9}$$

Here $]^-0, 1^+[$ is named the nonstandard subset, which is the extension of real standard subsets $[0,1]$ where the nonstandard number $1^+ = 1 + \varepsilon$, "1" is named the standard part, and "ε" is named the nonstandard part. $^-0 = 0 - \varepsilon$, "0" is the standard part and "ε" is named the nonstandard part, where ε is closed to positive real number zero.

In this case, the left and right endpoints of the nonstandard fuzzy membership values represent ambiguity and uncertainty while describing the practical problems.

Definition 12 Standard neutrosophic set (Wang, Smarandache, Zhang, et al., 2010)

It is well known that the NS (N) in use contains a TMF $T_N(k)$, an IMF $I_N(k)$, and a FMF $F_N(k)$, respectively. Each of them can contain the membership values as given below in case of the standard format:

$$T_N(k) : \xi \to [0, 1]$$

$$I_N(k) : \xi \to [0, 1]$$

$$F_N(k) : \xi \to [0, 1]$$

Then,

$$N = \{\langle k; T_N(k), I_N(k), F_N(k) \rangle | k \in \xi\} \tag{10}$$

is termed an SVNS.

If the nonempty set ξ has only one element x, then we call the NS N the single-valued neutrosophic number (SVNN). We abbreviate it as $N = \langle k; T_N, I_N, F_N \rangle$.

Generally, if $I_N(k) = 0$, the SVNS A is reduced to the IFS $N = \{\langle k; T_N(k), F_N(k) \rangle | k \in \xi\}$. If $I_N(k) = F_N(k) = 0$, then it is reduced to FS $N = \{\langle k; T_N(k) \rangle | k \in \xi\}$. The FS, IFS, and NS relationships are shown in Fig. 1.

Definition 13 (Wang et al., 2010)

Suppose N and M are two SVNSs, N is contained in M, if

$$T_N(k) \le T_M(k), \quad I_N(k) \ge I_M(k), \quad F_N(k) \ge F_M(k) \tag{11}$$

for each k in ξ.

Definition 14 (Wang et al., 2010)

Suppose N is an SVNS, and its complement is termed as below:

$$N^C = \{\langle k; F_N(k), 1 - I_N(k), T_N(k) \rangle | k \in \xi\}. \tag{12}$$

Definition 15 (Wang et al., 2010)

Suppose $N = \langle T_N, I_N, F_N \rangle$ and $M = \langle T_M, I_M, F_M \rangle$ are two SVNNs, and $\lambda > 0$, then

$$N \oplus M = \langle T_N + T_M - T_N T_M, I_N I_M, F_N F_M \rangle; \tag{13}$$

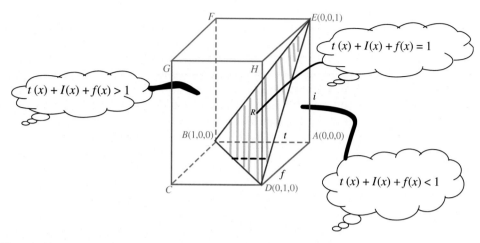

Fig. 1 The graphical visualization of a neutrosophic environment.

$$N \otimes M = \langle T_N T_M, I_N + I_M - I_N I_M, F_N + F_M - F_N F_M \rangle; \qquad (14)$$

$$\lambda N = \left\langle 1 - (1 - T_N)^\lambda, (I_N)^\lambda, (F_N)^\lambda \right\rangle; \qquad (15)$$

$$N^\lambda = \left\langle (T_N)^\lambda, 1 - (1 - I_N)^\lambda, 1 - (1 - F_N)^\lambda \right\rangle. \qquad (16)$$

4 Single-valued neutrosophic overset/underset/offset

Definition 16 Single-valued neutrosophic overset (Smarandache, 2007)

Let us suppose that ξ is a series of real number points presented by k, then the NS will be a subset of those points, that is, $N \subset \xi$ having $T_N(k)$, $I_N(k)$, and $F_N(k)$. It describes the TM degree, the IM degree, and the FM degree for the given element $k \in \xi$ with respect to the NS N. The overset of NS can be defined as follows:

$$N_{\text{SVNOV}} = \{(x, T_N(k), I_N(k), F_N(k)),$$

$$k \in \xi \text{ and } T_N(k), I_N(k), F_N(k) \in [0, \Omega]\}, \qquad (17)$$

where $T_N(k)$, $I_N(k)$, $F_N(k)$: $\xi \rightarrow [0, \Omega]$, $0 < 1 < \Omega$ and Ω are named overlimit, then there exists at least one element in N such that it has at least one neutrosophic component >1, and no element has a neutrosophic component <0.

Definition 17 Single-valued neutrosophic underset (Smarandache, 2007)

Let us suppose that ξ is a series of points (objects) with basic elements in ξ presented by k and the NS $N \subset \xi$. Here $T_N(k)$, $I_N(k)$, $F_N(k)$ ts are the TM degree, the IM degree, and the FM degree for the element $x \in \xi$ with respect to the NS N. In this case, the underset of neutrosophic values can be defined as:

$$N_{\text{SVNU}} = \{(k, T_N k, I_N k, F_N(k)), k \in \xi \text{ and } T_N k, I_N k, F_N(k) \in [\Psi, 1]\}. \tag{18}$$

In this case, $T_N(k)$, $I_N(k)$, $F_N(k)$: $\xi \to [\Psi, 1]$, $\Psi < 0 < 1$ and Ψ are named the lower limit. It shows that there exists at least one element in A that has one neutrosophic component value <0, and no element has a neutrosophic component value >1.

Definition 18 A single-valued neutrosophic offset (Smarandache, 2007)

Let us suppose that ξ is a series of points (objects) with basic elements in ξ presented by k and the NS $N \subset \xi$. Let $T_N(k)$, $I_N(k)$, $F_N(k)$ represent the TM degree, the IM degree, and the FM degree for the given element $k \in \xi$ with respect to the NS N. The offset can be defined as follows:

$$N_{\text{SVNOF}} = \{(k, T_N(k), I_N(k), F_N(k)), x \in \xi \text{ and } T_N k, I_N k, F_N(k) \in [\Psi, \Omega]\}. \tag{19}$$

In this case, $T_N k$, $I_N k$, $F_N(k)$: $\xi \to [\Psi, 1]$, $\Psi < 0 < 1 < \Omega$ and Ψ are named the underlimit while Ω is named the overlimit. It means there exists some elements in N such that at least one neutrosophic component >1 and at least another neutrosophic component <0.

Example 4 $N = \{(k_1, \langle 1.2, 0.4, 0.1 \rangle), (k_2, \langle 0.2, 0.3, -0.7 \rangle)\}$ because $T(k_1) = 1.2 > 1$, $F(k_2) = -0.7 < 0$.

Definition 19 Complement of overset/underset/offset (Smarandache, 2016)

The complement of an SVN overset/underset/offset N is abbreviated as $C(N)$ and is defined by

$$C(N) = \{(k, \langle F_N(k), \Psi + \Omega - I_N(x), T_N(k) \rangle), k \in \xi\}. \tag{20}$$

Definition 20 Union and intersection of overset/underset/offset (Smarandache, 2016)

The intersection of two SVN overset/underset/offset N and M is an SVNN overset/underset/offset (C) represented as follows: $C = N \cap M$ and is represented by

$$C = M \cap M = \{(k, <, \min(T_N(k), T_M(k)), \max(I_N(k), I_M(k)),$$
$$\max(F_N(k), F_M(k))), \quad k \in \xi\}. \tag{21}$$

The union of two SVN overset/underset/offset N and M is an SVN overset/underset/offset denoted C is abbreviated as $C = N \cup M$ and defined by

$$C = N \cup M = \{(k, < \max(T_N(k), T_M(k)), \min(I_N(k), I_M(k)),$$
$$\min(F_N(k), F_M(x))), k \in \xi\}. \tag{22}$$

To deal with interval-valued uncertainty and indeterminacy approximately the properties of NS theory are extended as IVNS.

Definition 21 Containment of interval neutrosophic set (Wang, Smarandache, Zhang, et al., 2005; Zhang, Pu, Wang, et al., 2014)
Suppose N and M are two INSs, N is contained in M,

$$\begin{aligned}
\inf T_A(k) &\leq \inf T_M(k), & \sup T_N(x) &\leq \sup T_M(x) \\
\inf I_N(k) &\geq \inf I_M(k), & \sup I_N(k) &\geq \sup I_M(k) \\
\inf F_N(k) &\geq \inf F_M(k), & \sup F_N(k) &\geq \sup F_M(k)
\end{aligned} \tag{23}$$

for every k in ξ.

Definition 22 (Wang et al., 2005; Zhang et al., 2014)
The complement of INS A is defined by

$$N^C = \{\langle k; T_{N^C}(k), I_{N^C}(k), F_{N^C}(k)\rangle | k \in \xi\}, \tag{24}$$

where $T_{N^C} = F_N(k) = [\inf F_N(k), \sup F_N(k)]$, $I_{N^C}(k) = [1 - \sup I_N(k), 1 - \inf I_N(k)]$, and $F_{N^C}(k) = T_N(k) = [\inf T_N(k), \sup T_N(k)]$.

Definition 23 (Wang et al., 2005; Zhang et al., 2014)
Suppose $N = \langle T_N, I_N, F_N \rangle$ and $M = \langle T_M, I_M, F_M \rangle$ are two INSs, and $\lambda > 0$. The operational laws will then be defined as below:
(1)

$$C = N \oplus M$$
$$\inf T_C(k) = \min(\inf T_N(k) + \inf T_M(k), 1)$$
$$\sup T_C(k) = \min(\sup T_N(k) + \sup T_M(k), 1)$$
$$\inf I_C(k) = \min(\inf T_N(k) + \inf T_M(k), 1)$$
$$\sup I_C(k) = \min(\sup I_N(k) + \sup I_M(k), 1) \tag{25}$$
$$\inf F_C(k) = \min(\inf F_N(k) + \inf F_M(k), 1)$$
$$\sup F_C(k) = \min(\sup F_N(k) + \sup F_M(k), 1)$$

(2)

$$N \otimes M = [\inf T_N \inf T_M, \sup T_N \sup T_M], [\inf I_N + \inf I_M - \inf I_N \inf I_M,$$
$$\sup I_N + \sup I_M - \sup I_N \sup I_M], [\inf F_N + \inf F_M$$
$$- \inf F_N \inf F_M, \sup F_N + \sup F_M - \sup F_N \sup F_M] \tag{26}$$

(3)

$$\lambda N = \{[\lambda \inf T_N, \lambda \sup T_N], [\lambda \inf I_N, \lambda \sup I_N], [\lambda \inf F_N, \lambda \sup F_N]\} \quad (27)$$

(4)

$$N^\lambda = \Big\{ \Big[(\inf T_N)^\lambda (\sup T_N)^\lambda\Big], \Big[1 - (1 - \inf I_N)^\lambda, 1 - (1 - \sup I_N)^\lambda\Big],$$
$$\Big[1 - (1 - \inf F_N)^\lambda, 1 - (1 - \sup F_N)^\lambda\Big] \Big\}$$

$$F_{N^c}(k) = T_N(k) = [\inf T_N(k), \sup T_N(k)], \quad (28)$$

where $T_N = T_N(k)$, $I_N = I_N(k)$, $F_N = F_N(k)$.

Ye (2015) has developed the concepts of interval neutrosophic linguistic sets (INLS) and interval neutrosophic linguistic variables by combining a linguistic variable with an interval neutrosophic set (INS).

5 An interval-valued neutrosophic linguistic set

Definition 24 An interval-valued neutrosophic linguistic set (Ye, 2015)

Let ξ be a series of points with basic elements in ξ presented by *k, then an interval neutrosophic linguistic set N (IVNLS) in ξ is* defined as

$$N_{\text{IVNLS}} = \big\{ \langle k, [s_{\theta(k)}, (T_N(k), I_N(k), F_N(k))] \rangle | k \in \xi \big\}, \quad (29)$$

where $s_{\theta(x)} \in \widehat{s}$,

$$T_N(k) = [\inf T_N(k), \sup T_N(k)] \subseteq [0, 1],$$
$$I_N(k) = [\inf I_N(k), \sup I_N(k)] \subseteq [0, 1],$$
$$F_N(k) = [\inf F_N(k), \sup F_N(k)] \subseteq [0, 1],$$

with the condition $0 \leq T_N(k) + I_N(k) + F_N(k) \leq 3$, for any $k \in \xi$. $s_{\theta(x)}$ is an uncertain linguistic term. The functions $T_N(k)$, $I_N(k)$, and $F_N(k)$ express, respectively, the TM degree, the IM degree, and the FM degree of the element k in ξ belonging to the linguistic term $s_{\theta(x)}$, which is another continuous form of the linguistic set $S.s_\theta, s_\rho, s_\mu, s_\nu$ are four linguistic terms, and $s_0 \leq s_\theta \leq s_\rho \leq s_\mu \leq s_\nu \leq s_{l-1}$ if $0 \leq \theta \leq \rho \leq \mu \leq \nu \leq l-1$, then the trapezoid linguistic variable (TLV) is termed as $\widehat{s} = [s_\theta, s_\rho, s_\mu, s_\nu]$, and $\widehat{s}$ represents a set of the TLVs.

Definition 25 Linguistics variable

Let $\overline{S} = \{s_\theta | s_0 \le s_\theta \le s_{l-1}, \theta \in [0, l-1]\}$ be the linguistic set in its continuous form $S.s_\theta$, s_ρ, s_μ, s_ν are four linguistic terms, and $s_0 \le s_\theta \le s_\rho \le s_\mu \le s_\nu \le s_{l-1}$ if $0 \le \theta \le \rho \le \mu \le \nu \le l-1$, then the TLV is defined as $\widehat{s} = [s_\theta, s_\rho, s_\mu, s_\nu]$, and $\widehat{s}$ represents a set of the TLVs.

6 Linguistic neutrosophic set

Definition 26 Linguistic neutrosophic set (Ye, 2015)

The concept of SVNLS N in ξ can be defined in the following form

$$N_{\text{SVNLS}} = \{\langle k, [s_{\theta(x)}, s_{\rho(x)}], (T_N(k), I_N(k), F_N(k))\rangle | k \in \xi\}, \quad (30)$$

where $s_{\theta(x)}, s_{\rho(x)} \in \widehat{s}$, $T_N(k) \subseteq [0,1]$, $I_N(k) \subseteq [0,1]$, $F_N(k) \subseteq [0,1]$ with the condition $0 \le T_N(k) + I_N(k) + F_N(k) \le 3$, for any $x \in \xi$. $[s_{\theta(x)}, s_{\rho(x)}]$ is an uncertain linguistic term. The functions $T_N(k)$, $I_N(k)$, and $F_N(k)$ express, respectively, the TM degree, the IM degree, and the FM degree of the element x in ξ belonging to the linguistic term $[s_{\theta(x)}, s_{\rho(x)}]$.

Definition 27 (Ye, 2015): Operations on linguistics neutrosophic set

For any given two SVNULVNs $\tilde{\alpha}_1 = \left\langle \left[s_{\theta(\tilde{\alpha}_1)}, s_{\rho(\tilde{\alpha}_1)}\right], (T(\tilde{\alpha}_1), I(\tilde{\alpha}_1), F(\tilde{\alpha}_1))\right\rangle$, $\tilde{\alpha}_2 = \left\langle \left[s_{\theta(\tilde{\alpha}_2)}, s_{\rho(\tilde{\alpha}_2)}\right], (T(\tilde{\alpha}_2), I(\tilde{\alpha}_2), F(\tilde{\alpha}_2))\right\rangle$, $\lambda > 0$ is a constant, and their operational rules are defined as follows:

$$\tilde{\alpha}_1 \oplus \tilde{\alpha}_2 = \left\langle \begin{array}{l} \left[s_{\theta(\tilde{\alpha}_1)+\theta(\tilde{\alpha}_2)}, s_{\rho(\tilde{\alpha}_1)+\rho(\tilde{\alpha}_2)}\right], (T(\tilde{\alpha}_1)+T(\tilde{\alpha}_2)-T(\tilde{\alpha}_1)T(\tilde{\alpha}_2)), \\ I(\tilde{\alpha}_1)I(\tilde{\alpha}_2), F(\tilde{\alpha}_1)F(\tilde{\alpha}_2) \end{array} \right\rangle, \quad (31)$$

$$\tilde{\alpha}_1 \otimes \tilde{\alpha}_2 = \left\langle \begin{array}{l} \left[s_{\theta(\tilde{\alpha}_1) \times \theta(\tilde{\alpha}_2)}, s_{\rho(\tilde{\alpha}_1) \times \rho(\tilde{\alpha}_2)}\right], (T(\tilde{\alpha}_1)T(\tilde{\alpha}_2)), \\ (I(\tilde{\alpha}_1)+I(\tilde{\alpha}_2)-I(\tilde{\alpha}_1)I(\tilde{\alpha}_2)), (F(\tilde{\alpha}_1)+F(\tilde{\alpha}_2)-F(\tilde{\alpha}_1)F(\tilde{\alpha}_2)) \end{array} \right\rangle, \quad (32)$$

$$\lambda \tilde{\alpha}_1 = \left\langle \left[s_{\lambda\theta(\tilde{\alpha}_1)}, s_{\lambda\rho(\tilde{\alpha}_1)}\right], \left(1 - (1 - T(\tilde{\alpha}_1))^\lambda, (I(\tilde{\alpha}_1))^\lambda, (F(\tilde{\alpha}_1))^\lambda\right)\right\rangle, \quad (33)$$

$$\tilde{\alpha}_1{}^\lambda = \left\langle \left[s_{\theta^\lambda(\tilde{\alpha}_1)}, s_{\rho^\lambda(\tilde{\alpha}_1)}\right], \left((T(\tilde{\alpha}_1))^\lambda, \left(1 - (1 - I(\tilde{\alpha}_1))^\lambda\right), \left(1 - (1 - F(\tilde{\alpha}_1))^\lambda\right)\right)\right\rangle. \quad (34)$$

It is well known that linguistics contains bipolar information, that is, positive and negative membership values simultaneously. To deal with these types of datasets, the NS is extended as a bipolar neutrosophic set (BNS).

7 Bipolar neutrosophic sets

Definition 28 Bipolar neutrosophic set (Deli et al., 2015)
Suppose ξ is a series of points (objects) with basic elements in ξ presented by x. A bipolar neutrosophic set N (BNS) in ξ is defined as in the following form

$$N = \left\{ \left\langle k, \left(T_N^+(k), I_N^+(k), F_N^+(k), T_N^-(k), I_N^-(k), F_N^-(k) \right) \right\rangle : k \in \xi \right\},$$

where T^P, I_N^+, $\mathrm{F}^P : \xi \to [1,0]$ and T^P, I_N^-, $F^P : \xi \to [-1,0]$ are the PMFs NMFs. We call $T_N^+(k)$, $I_N^+(k)$, $F_N^+(k)$ the TMF, IMF, and FMF of an element $k \in s$. The NMF degree $T_N^-(k)$, $I_N^-(k)$, $F_N^-(k)$ represents the TMF, IMF, and FMF of an element $x \in \xi$. If the set has only one element, then we call N a BNN and define it by

$$N_{BNS} = \left\langle T_A^+, I_A^+, F_A^+, T_A^-, I_A^-, F_A^- \right\rangle. \tag{35}$$

In case the uncertainty in the dataset fluctuates at given intervals of time, then the complex NS is defined.

8 Complex neutrosophic set

Definition 29 Complex neutrosophic set (Ali & Smarandache, 2015)
Suppose that ξ is a set of some points denoted as k. A complex neutrosophic set (CNS) is defined on the set ξ through the definition of three membership functions, $T_N(k)$, $I_N(k)$, $F_N(k)$, and we call them the TMF, the IMF, and the FMF, respectively. Here, we allocate a complex-valued grade of $T_N(k)$, $I_N(k)$, and $F_N(k)$ in N for any $k \in \xi$. All the values $T_N(k)$, $I_N(k)$, and $F_N(k)$ and the sum values of these three functions are all in the complex plane unit circle, and their forms are as follows.

$$\begin{aligned} T_N(k) &= \rho_N(k) \cdot e^{j\mu_N(k)}, \\ I_N(k) &= q_N(k) \cdot e^{jv_N(k)}, \text{and} \\ F_N(k) &= r_N(k) \cdot e^{j\omega_N(k)} \end{aligned} \tag{36}$$

Here $\rho_N(k)$, $q_N(k)$, $r_N(k)$ and $\mu_N(k)$, $v_N(k)$, $\omega_N(k)$ are real values, respectively, and $\rho_N(k), q_N(k), r_N(k) \in F_A(x) \in [0, 1]$ such that

$$^-0 \le T_A(x) + I_A(x) + F_A(x) \le 3^+. \tag{37}$$

The CNSN can be rewritten in a set form as

$$N_{CNS} = \{(k, T_N(k) = a_T, I_N(k) = a_I, F_N(k) = a_F) : k \in \xi\}, \tag{38}$$

where

$$\begin{aligned} T_N &: X \to \{a_T : a_T \in C, |a_T| \le 1\} \\ I_N &: \xi \to \{a_I : a_I \in C, |a_I| \le 1\} \\ F_N &: \xi \to \{a_F : a_F \in C, |a_F| \le 1\} \\ &|T_N(k) + I_N(k) + F_N(k)| \le 3. \end{aligned} \tag{39}$$

The complex grade of TMF is characterized by a truth amplitude term $\rho_N(k)$ and a truth phase term $\mu_N(k)$.

In addition, the complex degree of IMF is defined as an indeterminate amplitude term, and the complex grade of IMF is defined as an indeterminate term $q_N(k)$ and an indterminate phase term $v_N(x)$.

The complex grade of the FMF is defined by the false amplitude term $r_N(k)$ and a false phase term $\omega_N(x)$, respectively. It should be noted that the truth amplitude term $\rho_N(x)$ is equal to $|T_N(k)|$, the amplitude of $T_N(k)$. The indeterminate amplitude term $q_N(x)$ is equal to $|I_N(k)|$ and the false amplitude term $r_N(k)$ is equal to $|F_N(k)|$.

Definition 30 Union and intersection of CNSs

Suppose N and M are two CNSs in ξ, where $N = \{(k, T_N(k), I_N(k), F_N(k)): k \in \xi\}$ and $M = \{(k, T_M(k), I_M(k), F_M(k)): k \in \xi\}$.

Then the union of N and M is termed as $N \cup_{\text{CNS}} M$ and we denote it as

$$N \cup_{\text{CNS}} M = \{(k, T_{N \cup M}(k), I_{N \cup M}(k), F_{N \cup M}(k)): k \in \xi\}, \qquad (40)$$

where the TMF $nT_{N \cup M}(k)$, the IMF $I_{N \cup M}(k)$, and the FMF $F_{N \cup M}(k)$ are denoted by

$$
\begin{aligned}
T_{N \cup M}(k) &= [(p_N(k) \vee p_M(k))] \cdot e^{j \cdot \mu_{T_{N \cup M}}(k)}, \\
I_{N \cup MB}(k) &= [(q_N(k) \wedge q_M(k))] \cdot e^{j \cdot \nu_{I_{N \cup M}}(k)}, \\
F_{N \cup M}(k) &= [(r_N(k) \wedge r_M(k))] \cdot e^{j \cdot \omega_{F_{N \cup M}}(k)},
\end{aligned}
\qquad (41)
$$

where $\vee$ and $\wedge$ represent the operators max and min, respectively.

The phase term of the complex truth function, the complex indeterminacy function, and the complex falsehood function belongs to $(0, 2\pi)$ and the definitions of the phase term are as follows:

a) *Sum:*

$$
\begin{aligned}
\mu_{N \cup M}(k) &= \mu_N(k) + \mu_M(k), \\
\nu_{N \cup M}(k) &= \nu_N(k) + \nu_M(k), \\
\omega_{N \cup M}(k) &= \omega_N(k) + \omega_M(k),
\end{aligned}
\qquad (42)
$$

b) *Max:*

$$
\begin{aligned}
\mu_{N \cup M}(k) &= \max(\mu_N(k), \mu_M(k)), \\
\nu_{N \cup M}(k) &= \max(\nu_N(k), \nu_M(k)), \\
\omega_{N \cup M}(k) &= \max(\omega_N(k), \omega_M(k)),
\end{aligned}
\qquad (43)
$$

c) *Min:*

$$
\begin{aligned}
\mu_{N \cup M}(k) &= \min(\mu_N(k), \mu_M(k)), \\
\nu_{N \cup M}(k) &= \min(\nu_N(k), \nu_M(k)), \\
\omega_{N \cup M}(k) &= \min(\omega_N(k), \omega_M(k)),
\end{aligned}
\qquad (44)
$$

d) *"The game of winner, neutral, and loser"*:

$$\mu_{N \cup M}(k) = \begin{cases} \mu_N(k) & \text{if } p_N > p_M \\ \mu_M(k) & \text{if } p_M > p_N \end{cases},$$

$$\nu_{N \cup M}(k) = \begin{cases} \nu_N(k) & \text{if } q_N < q_M \\ \nu_M(k) & \text{if } q_M < q_N \end{cases}, \tag{45}$$

$$\omega_{N \cup M}(k) = \begin{cases} \omega_N(k) & \text{if } r_N < r_M \\ \omega_M(k) & \text{if } r_M < r_N \end{cases}.$$

For more details, we refer the readers to Ramot et al. (2002).

9 Bipolar complex NSs

Definition 31 Bipolar complex neutrosophic set (Broumi, Bakali, et al., 2019; Broumi, Talea, et al., 2019)

Suppose ξ is a set of some points with basic elements in ξ presented by x. A bipolar complex neutrosophic set A (BCNS) in ξ is defined in the following form

$$N = \left\{ \left\langle k, T_1^+ e^{iT_2^+}, I_1^+ e^{iI_2^+}, F_1^+ e^{iF_2^+}, T_1^- e^{iT_2^-}, I_1^- e^{iI_2^-}, F_1^- e^{iF_2^-} \right\rangle : k \in \xi \right\},$$

where $T^P, I_1^+, F^P : X \rightarrow [1,0]$ and $T^P, I_1^-, F^P : X \rightarrow [-1,0]$. The positive membership degree $T_1^+(k)$, $I_1^+(k)$, $F_1^+(k)$ represents the TM, the IM, and the MF of an element $x \in \xi$ corresponding to the given property, whereas the negative membership degree $T_1^-(k)$, $I_1^-(k)$, $F_1^-(k)$ represents the TM, the IM, and the FM of an element $k \in \xi$ to some implicit counterproperty. A BCNN can be abbreviated as follows:

$$N_{BCNS} = \left\langle T_1^+ e^{iT_2^+}, I_1^+ e^{iI_2^+}, F_1^+ e^{iF_2^+}, T_1^- e^{iT_2^-}, I_1^- e^{iI_2^-}, F_1^- e^{iF_2^-} \right\rangle. \tag{46}$$

Definition 32 Containment operations on bipolar neutrosophic sets (Broumi, Bakali, et al., 2019; Broumi, Talea, et al., 2019)

Suppose there are two BCNSs $BCN_1 = (T_1^+ e^{iT_2^+}, I_1^+ e^{iI_2^+}, F_1^+ e^{iF_2^+}, T_1^- e^{iT_2^-}, I_1^- e^{iI_2^-}, F_1^- e^{iF_2^-})$ and $BCN_2 = (T_3^+ e^{iT_4^+}, I_3^+ e^{iI_4^+}, F_3^+ e^{iF_4^+}, T_3^- e^{iT_4^-}, I_3^- e^{iI_4^-}, F_3^- e^{iF_4^-})$. BCN_1 is contained in the other BCN_2 detailed as $BCN_1 \subseteq BCN_2$ if

$$T_{1BCN_1}^+(x) \leq T_{1BCN_2}^+(x), I_{1BCN_1}^+(x) \geq I_{1BCN_2}^+(x), F_{1BCN_1}^+(x) \geq F_{1BCN_2}^+(x) \text{ and}$$
$$T_{2BCN_1}^+(x) \leq T_{2BCN_2}^+(x), I_{2BCN_1}^+(x) \geq I_{2BCN_2}^+(x), F_{2BCN_1}^+(x) \geq F_{2BCN_2}^+(x)$$

and

$$T_{3BCN_1}^-(x) \geq T_{3BCN_2}^-(x), I_{3BCN_1}^-(x) \leq I_{3BCN_2}^-(x), F_{3BCN_1}^-(x) \leq F_{3BCN_2}^-(x)$$

and

$$T_{4\mathrm{BCN}_1}^-(x) \geq T_{4\mathrm{BCN}_2}^-(x), I_{4\mathrm{BCN}_1}^-(x) \leq I_{4\mathrm{BCN}_2}^-(x), F_{4\mathrm{BCN}_1}^-(x)$$
$$\leq F_{4\mathrm{BCN}_2}^-(x) \forall x \in \xi. \tag{47}$$

Definition 33 Union and intersection of BCNSs

Suppose N and M are two BCNSs in ξ, where

$$N = \left(T_1^+ e^{iT_2^+}, I_1^+ e^{iI_2^+}, F_1^+ e^{iF_2^+}, T_1^- e^{iT_2^-}, I_1^- e^{iI_2^-}, F_1^- e^{iF_2^-}\right) \text{ and}$$
$$M = \left(T_3^+ e^{iT_4^+}, I_3^+ e^{iI_4^+}, F_3^+ e^{iF_4^+}, T_3^- e^{iT_4^-}, I_3^- e^{iI_4^-}, F_3^- e^{iF_4^-}\right)$$

Then, the union of N and M is termed as $N \cup_{\mathrm{BCN}} M$

$$N \cup_{BCN} M = \{(k, T_+^{N\cup M}(x), I_+^{N\cup M}(x), F_+^{N\cup M}(k), T_-^{N\cup M}(k) I_-^{N\cup M}(k)$$
$$F_-^{N\cup M}(k)): k \in \xi\}. \tag{48}$$

where PTMF $T^+{}_{N\cup M}(k)$, PIMF $I^+{}_{N\cup M}(k)$ and PFMF $F^+{}_{N\cup M}(k)$, NTMF $T^-{}_{N\cup M}(k)$, NIMF $I^-{}_{N\cup M}(k)$ and NFMF $F^-{}_{N\cup M}(k)$ is termed by

$$T_{A\cup B}^+(k) = \left(T_1^+ \vee T_3^+\right) e^{i\left(T_2^+ \cup T_4^+\right)}, T_{A\cup B}^-(k) = \left(T_1^- \wedge T_3^-\right) e^{i\left(T_2^- \cup T_4^-\right)}$$
$$I_{A\cup B}^+(k) = \left(I_1^+ \wedge I_3^+\right) e^{i\left(I_2^+ \cup I_4^+\right)}, T_{A\cup B}^-(k) = \left(I_1^- \vee I_3^-\right) e^{i\left(I_2^- \cup I_4^-\right)}$$
$$F_{A\cup B}^+(k) = \left(F_1^+ \wedge F_3^+\right) e^{i\left(F_2^+ \cup F_4^+\right)}, F_{A\cup B}^-(k) = \left(F_1^- \vee F_3^-\right) e^{i\left(F_2^- \cup F_4^-\right)} \tag{49}$$

Suppose N and M are two BCNSs in ξ, where

$$N = \left(T_1^+ e^{iT_2^+}, I_1^+ e^{iI_2^+}, F_1^+ e^{iF_2^+}, T_1^- e^{iT_2^-}, I_1^- e^{iI_2^-}, F_1^- e^{iF_2^-}\right) \text{and}$$
$$M = \left(T_3^+ e^{iT_4^+}, I_3^+ e^{iI_4^+}, F_3^+ e^{iF_4^+}, T_3^- e^{iT_4^-}, I_3^- e^{iI_4^-}, F_3^- e^{iF_4^-}\right)$$

and the intersection of N and M is termed as $N \cap_{\mathrm{BCN}} M$

$$A \cap_{BCN} B = \{(x, T^+{}_{A\cap B}(x), I^+{}_{A\cap B}(x), F^+{}_{A\cap B}(k), T^-{}_{A\cap B}(k), I^-{}_{A\cap B}(k),$$
$$F^-{}_{A\cap B}(k)): k \in \xi\} \tag{50}$$

where PTMF $T^+{}_{N\cap M}(k)$, PIMF $I^+{}_{N\cap M}(k)$ and PFMF $F^+{}_{N\cap M}(k)$, NTMF $T^-{}_{N\cap M}(k)$, NITMF $I^-{}_{N\cap M}(k)$ and NFMF $F^-{}_{N\cap M}(k)$ is denoted by

$$T_{N\cap M}^+(k) = \left(T_1^+ \wedge T_3^+\right) e^{i\left(T_2^+ \cap T_4^+\right)}, T_{A\cap B}^-(k) = \left(T_1^- \vee T_3^-\right) e^{i\left(T_2^- \cap T_4^-\right)}$$
$$I_{N\cap M}^+(k) = \left(I_1^+ \vee I_3^+\right) e^{i\left(I_2^+ \cap I_4^+\right)}, T_{A\cap B}^-(k) = \left(I_1^- \wedge I_3^-\right) e^{i\left(I_2^- \cap I_4^-\right)}$$
$$F_{N\cap M}^+(k) = \left(F_1^+ \vee F_3^+\right) e^{i\left(F_2^+ \cap F_4^+\right)}, F_{A\cap B}^-(k) = \left(F_1^- \wedge F_3^-\right) e^{i\left(F_2^- \cap F_4^-\right)} \tag{51}$$

The symbols $\vee$ and $\wedge$ represent the the minimim and maximum operators.

10   An interval complex NS

Definition 34 (Ali et al., 2018)

Suppose ξ is a series of points (objects) basic elements in ξ presented by k. An ICNS is defined on ξ, which is characterized through a function ITMF $\tilde{T}_N(k) = [T_N^L(k), T_N^U(k)]$, an interval IMF $\tilde{I}_N(k)$, and an interval FMF $\tilde{F}_N(k)$ that assigns a complex-valued membership grade to $\tilde{T}_N(k), \tilde{I}_N(k), \tilde{F}_N(k)$ for any $k \in \xi$. The values of $\tilde{T}_N(k), \tilde{I}_N(k), \tilde{F}_N(k)$ and their sum take some values within a complex plane unit circle. The forms of the functions are below:

$$\tilde{T}_N(k) = [p_N^L(k), p_N^U(k)] \cdot e^{i[\mu_N^L(k), \mu_N^U(k)]},$$

$$\tilde{I}_N(k) = [q_N^L(k), q_N^U(k)] \cdot e^{i[v_N^L(k), v_N^U(k)]}, \text{and}$$

$$\tilde{F}_N(k) = [r_N^L(x), r_N^U(k)] \cdot e^{i[\omega_N^L(k), \omega_N^U(k)]}. \tag{52}$$

All the amplitude and phase terms are real valued. And $p_N^L(k)$, $p_N^U(k)$, $q_N^L(k)$, $q_N^U(k)$, $r_N^L(k)$ and $r_N^U(k) \in [0,1]$, whereas $\mu_N(k)$, $v_N(k)$, $\omega_N(k) \in (0, 2\pi]$, such that the condition

$$0 \leq p_N^U(k) + q_N^U(k) + r_N^U(k) \leq 3 \tag{53}$$

is satisfied. $T_A(x)$ an ICNS $\tilde{A}$ can thus be termed in the defined form as:

$$\tilde{N} = \{\langle k, T_N(k) = a_T, I_N(k) = a_I, F_N(k) = a_F \rangle : k \in \xi\}, \tag{54}$$

where $T_N: \xi. \to \{a_T: a_T \in C, |a_T| \leq 1\}$, $I_N: \xi. \to \{a_I: a_I \in C, |a_I| \leq 1\}$, $F_N: \xi. \to \{a_F: a_F \in C, |a_F| \leq 1\}$, and also $|T_N^U(k) + I_N^U(k) + F_N^U(k)| \leq 3$.

Definition 35 (Ali et al., 2018)

For two ICNS N and M in ξ, the union of N and M detailed as $N \cup_{ICNS} M$ is abbreviated as:

$$N \cup_{ICNS} M = \left\{ \left(k, \tilde{T}_{N \cup M}(k), \tilde{I}_{N \cup M}(k), \tilde{F}_{N \cup M}(k) \right) : k \in \xi \right\}, \tag{55}$$

where $\tilde{T}_{N \cup M}(k), \tilde{I}_{N \cup M}(k), \tilde{F}_{N \cup M}(k)$ are given by

$$T_{N \cup M}^L(k) = [(p_N^L(k) \vee p_M^L(k))] \cdot e^{j \cdot \mu_{T_{A \cup B}}^L(k)},$$
$$T_{N \cup M}^U(k) = [(p_N^U(k) \vee p_M^U(k))] \cdot e^{j \cdot \mu_{T_{A \cup B}}^U(k)}$$

$$I_{N \cup M}^{L}(k) = \left[\left(q^{L}(k) \wedge q_{M}^{L}(k) \right) \right] \cdot e^{j \cdot \mu_{I_{A \cup B}}^{L}(k)},$$

$$I_{M \cup M}^{U}(k) = \left[\left(q_{N}^{U}(k) \wedge q_{M}^{U}(k) \right) \right] \cdot e^{j \cdot \mu_{I_{A \cup B}}^{U}(k)},$$

$$F_{N \cup M}^{L}(k) = \left[\left(r_{N}^{L}(k) \wedge r_{M}^{L}(k) \right) \right] \cdot e^{j \cdot \mu_{F_{A \cup B}}^{L}(k)},$$

$$F_{N \cup M}^{U}(k) = \left[\left(r_{N}^{U}(k) \wedge r_{M}^{U}(k) \right) \right] \cdot e^{j \cdot \mu_{F_{A \cup B}}^{U}(k)}. \tag{56}$$

The intersection of N and N detailed as M is abbreviated as:

$$N \cap_{ICNS} M = \left\{ \left(x, \tilde{T}_{N \cap M}(k), \tilde{I}_{N \cap M}(k), \tilde{F}_{N \cap M}(k) \right) : k \in \xi \right\}, \tag{57}$$

where $\tilde{T}_{M \cap M}(k), \tilde{I}_{M \cap M}(k), \tilde{F}_{N \cap M}(k)$ are given by

$$\tilde{T}_{N \cap M}(k) = \begin{cases} T_{N \cap M}^{L}(k) = \left[\left(p_{N}^{L}(k) \wedge p_{M}^{L}(k) \right) \right] \cdot e^{j \cdot \mu_{T_{A \cup B}}^{L}(k)} \\ T_{N \cap M}^{U}(k) = \left[\left(p_{N}^{U}(k) \wedge p_{M}^{U}(k) \right) \right] \cdot e^{j \cdot \mu_{T_{A \cup B}}^{U}(k)} \end{cases}, \tag{58}$$

$$\tilde{I}_{N \cap M}(k) = \begin{cases} I_{N \cap M}^{L}(k) = \left[\left(q_{N}^{L}(k) \vee q_{M}^{L}(k) \right) \right] \cdot e^{j \cdot \mu_{I_{A \cup B}}^{L}(k)} \\ I_{N \cap M}^{U}(k) = \left[\left(q_{N}^{U}(k) \vee q_{M}^{U}(k) \right) \right] \cdot e^{j \cdot \mu_{I_{A \cup B}}^{U}(k)} \end{cases}, \tag{59}$$

$$M(k) = \begin{cases} F_{N \cap M}^{L}(k) = \left[\left(r_{N}^{L}(k) \vee r_{M}^{L}(k) \right) \right] \cdot e^{j \cdot \mu_{F_{A \cup B}}^{L}(k)} \\ F_{N \cap M}^{U}(k) = \left[\left(r_{N}^{U}(k) \vee r_{M}^{U}(k) \right) \right] \cdot e^{j \cdot \mu_{F_{A \cup B}}^{U}(k)} \end{cases}. \tag{60}$$

We calculate the phase terms of the CTMF, CIMF, and CFMF union and intersection, respectively, by applying the following operations:
Sum:

$$\mu_{N \cup M}^{L}(k) = \mu_{N}^{L}(k) + \mu_{M}^{L}(k), \mu_{N \cup M}^{U}(k) = \mu_{N}^{U}(k) + \mu_{M}^{U}(k),$$

$$\nu_{N \cup M}^{L}(k) = \nu_{N}^{L}(k) + \nu_{M}^{L}(k), \nu_{N \cup M}^{U}(k) = \nu_{N}^{U}(k) + \nu_{M}^{U}(k),$$

$$\omega_{N \cup M}^{L}(k) = \omega_{N}^{L}(k) + \omega_{M}^{L}(k), \omega_{N \cup M}^{U}(k) = \omega_{N}^{U}(k) + \omega_{M}^{U}(k), \tag{61}$$

Max:

$$\mu_{N \cup M}^{L}(k) = \max \left(\mu_{N}^{L}(k), \mu_{M}^{L}(k) \right), \mu_{N \cup M}^{U}(k) = \max \left(\mu_{N}^{U}(k), \mu_{M}^{U}(k) \right),$$

$$\nu_{A \cup M}^{L}(k) = \max \left(\nu_{N}^{L}(k), \nu_{M}^{L}(k) \right), \nu_{N \cup M}^{U}(k) = \max \left(\nu_{N}^{U}(k), \nu_{M}^{U}(k) \right),$$

$$\omega_{N \cup M}^{L}(k) = \max \left(\omega_{N}^{L}(k), \omega_{M}^{L}(k) \right), \omega_{N \cup M}^{U}(k) = \max \left(\omega_{N}^{U}(k), \omega_{M}^{U}(k) \right), \tag{62}$$

Min:

$$\mu_{N \cup M}^{L}(k) = \min \left(\mu_{N}^{L}(k), \mu_{M}^{L}(k) \right), \mu_{N \cup M}^{U}(k) = \min \left(\mu_{N}^{U}(k), \mu_{M}^{U}(k) \right),$$

$$\nu_{N \cup M}^{L}(k) = \min \left(\nu_{N}^{L}(k), \nu_{M}^{L}(k) \right), \nu_{N \cup M}^{U}(k) = \min \left(\nu_{N}^{U}(k), \nu_{M}^{U}(k) \right),$$

$$\omega_{N\cup M}^{L}(k) = \min\left(\omega_{N}^{L}(k), \omega_{M}^{L}(k)\right), \omega_{N\cup M}^{U}(k) = \min\left(\omega_{N}^{U}(k), \omega_{M}^{U}(k)\right), \tag{63}$$

"*The game of winner, neutral, and loser*":

$$
\begin{aligned}
\mu_{N\cup M}(k) &= \begin{cases} \mu_N(k) & \text{if } p_N > p_M \\ \mu_M(k) & \text{if } p_M > p_N \end{cases}, \\
\nu_{N\cup M}(k) &= \begin{cases} \nu_N(k) & \text{if } q_N < q_M \\ \nu_M(k) & \text{if } q_M < q_N \end{cases}, \\
\omega_{N\cup M}(k) &= \begin{cases} \omega_N(k) & \text{if } r_N < r_M \\ \omega_M(k) & \text{if } r_M < r_N \end{cases}.
\end{aligned}
\tag{64}
$$

11 An interval-valued bipolar neutrosophic set

Definition 36 (Deli, Şubaş, Smarandache, & Ali, 2016)

Let ξ be a series of points with basic elements in ξ presented by k. *An interval-valued bipolar neutrosophic set N (IVBNS) in ξ is abbreviated in the following form*

$$\widetilde{A}_{\text{IVBNS}} = \{\langle k, t^p, i^p, f^p, t^n, i^n, f^n \rangle : k \in \xi\}, \tag{65}$$

where $t^p = [T_L^p, T_M^p]$, $i^p = [I_L^p, I_M^p]$, $f^p = [F_L^p, F_M^p]$, $t^n = [T_L^n, T_M^n]$, $i^n = [I_L^n, I_M^n]$, $f^n = [F_L^n, F_M^n]$, and $T_L^p\text{TP}$, $T_M^p I_L^p\text{TP}$, $I_M^p, F_L^p\text{TP}$, $F_M^p\text{FP}$: $\xi \to [0, 1]$ and $T_L^n\text{TP}$, $T_M^n I_L^n\text{TP}$, $I_M^n, F_L^n\text{TP}$, F_M^n: $\xi \to [-1, 0]$. The PIM degree where $T_L^p\text{TP}$, $T_M^p I_L^p\text{TP}$, $I_M^p, F_L^p\text{TP}$, $F_M^p\text{FP}$ denotes the LTM, UTM, LIM, UIM, and LFM, UFM of an element $k \in \xi$ corresponding to a BNS A and the NIM degree $T_L^n\text{TP}$, $T_M^n I_L^n\text{TP}$, $I_M^n, F_L^n\text{TP}$, F_M^n: denotes LTM, UTM, LIM, UIM, and LFM, UFM of an element $k \in \xi$ to some implicit counterproperty corresponding to an IVBNS A.

12 Neutrosophic rough sets and their extensions

For the study of fusion about SVNS and rough sets, (Liu et al., 2017; Yang et al., 2017) defined SVNRS.

Definition 37 Suppose S is a SVNR in ξ, $\widetilde{A} \in \text{SVNS}(\xi)$, the lower and upper approximations of $\widetilde{A}$ with respect to $(\xi, \widetilde{S})$, abbreviated as $\underline{S}(\widetilde{A})$ and $\overline{S}(\widetilde{A})$, are two SVNSs whose membership functions are defined as follows: $\forall k \in \xi, T_{\underline{S}(\widetilde{A})}(k) = \wedge_{l \in U} F_S(k, l) \vee T_{\widetilde{A}}(l),$

$$T_{\overline{s(\widetilde{A})}}(k) = \vee_{l \in U} T_S(k, l) \wedge T_{\widetilde{A}}(l),$$

$$F_{\overline{s(\widetilde{A})}}(k) = \vee_{l \in U} T_S(k, l) \wedge F_{\widetilde{A}}(l),$$

$$\overline{I_{\overline{SA}}}(k) = \wedge_{l \in U} I_S(k, l) \vee I_{\widetilde{A}}(l),$$

$$F_{\overline{SA}}(k) = \wedge_{l \in U} F_S(k, l) \vee F_{\widetilde{A}}(l). \tag{66}$$

The tuple $\left(\underline{s}(\widetilde{A}), \overline{s}(\widetilde{A}) \right)$ is termed a single-valued neutrosophic rough set (SVNRS).

Furthermore, Yang et al. (2017) and Liu et al. (2017) proposed SVNRS on two universes as follows.

Definition 38 Suppose S is an SVNR from ξ to ζ, $\widetilde{A} \in$ SVNS(ζ), *the lower and upper approximations* of $\widetilde{A}$ with respect to (ξ, ζ, S), abbreviated as $\underline{S}(\widetilde{A})$ and $\overline{S}(\widetilde{A})$, they are two SVNSs presented as follows: $\forall k \in \xi$,

$$T_{\underline{S}(\widetilde{A})}(k) = \wedge_{l \in \zeta} F_S(k, l) \vee T_{\widetilde{A}}(l),$$

$$T_{\overline{S(\widetilde{A})}}(k) = \vee_{l \in \zeta} T_S(k, l) \wedge T_{\widetilde{A}}(l),$$

$$I_{\underline{S}(\widetilde{A})}(k) = \vee_{l \in \zeta} (1 - I_S(k, l)) \wedge I_{\widetilde{A}}(l),$$

$$I_{\overline{S(\widetilde{A})}}(k) = \wedge_{y \in \zeta} I_S(k, l) \vee I_{\widetilde{A}}(l),$$

$$F_{\underline{S}(\widetilde{A})}(k) = \vee_{l \in \zeta} T_S(k, l) \wedge F_{\widetilde{A}}(l),$$

$$F_{\overline{S(\widetilde{A})}}(k) = \wedge_{l \in \zeta} F_S(k, l) \vee F_{\widetilde{A}}(l). \tag{67}$$

The tuple $\left(\underline{S}(\widetilde{A}), \overline{S}(\widetilde{A}) \right)$ is termed a SVNRS on two universes.

Next, Guo et al. (2017) proposed a rough set model based on a cut relation under single-valued neutrosophic information.

Definition 39 Suppose S *is an SVNR from ξ to ζ.* $\widetilde{R}_{\{(\alpha, \beta, \gamma)\}}$ *is the (α, β, γ) cut relation from ξ to ζ.* $Q \subseteq \zeta$, *and the lower and upper approximation of Q with respect to (ξ, ζ, S) and (α, β, γ) are given as* $\underline{S}_{\{(\alpha, \beta, \gamma)\}}(Q) = \left\{ k \in \xi \mid \underline{S}_{\{(\alpha, \beta, \gamma)\}}(k) \subseteq Q \wedge \underline{S}_{\{(\alpha, \beta, \gamma)\}}(k) \neq \varnothing \right\},$

$$\overline{S_{\{(\alpha, \beta, \gamma)\}}}(Q) = \left\{ k \in \xi \mid \underline{S}_{\{(\alpha, \beta, \gamma)\}}(k) \cap Q \neq \varnothing \vee \underline{S}_{\{(\alpha, \beta, \gamma)\}}(k) = \varnothing \right\}. \tag{68}$$

The pair $\left(S_{\{(\alpha, \beta, \gamma)\}}(Q), \overline{S_{\{(\alpha, \beta, \gamma)\}}}(Q) \right)$ is termed a rough set based on the single-valued neutrosophic cut relation.

Bao and Yang (2017) introduced SVNRRS.

Definition 40 Suppose S is an SVNRR p in ξ. $A \in \text{SVNRS}p(\zeta)$, the lower and upper approximations of A with respect to $(\xi;S)$ are *two p-dimension SVNRSs*, abbreviated as $\underline{S}(A)$ and $\overline{S}(A)$, are two SVNSs whose membership functions are denoted as follows: $\forall k \in \xi$

$$
\begin{aligned}
T_{\underline{S}(A)}(k) &= \tilde{\wedge}_{l \in \xi} F_S(k, l) \tilde{\vee} T_A(l), \\
T_{\overline{S}(A)}(k) &= \tilde{\vee}_{l \in \xi} T_S(k, l) \tilde{\wedge} T_A(l), \\
I_{\underline{S}(A)}(k) &= \tilde{\vee}_{l \in \xi} (\sim I_S(k, l)) \tilde{\wedge} I_A(l), \\
I_{\overline{S}(A)}(k) &= \tilde{\wedge}_{l \in \xi} I_S(k, l) \tilde{\vee} I_A(l), \\
F_{\underline{S}(A)}(k) &= \tilde{\vee}_{l \in \xi} T_S(k, l) \tilde{\wedge} F_A(l), \\
F_{\overline{S}(A)}(k) &= \tilde{\wedge}_{l \in \xi} F_S(k, l) \tilde{\vee} F_A(l).
\end{aligned}
\tag{69}
$$

The pair $(\underline{S}(A), \overline{S}(A))$ is termed as SVNRRS.

Yang et al. (2018) initiated GINRS.

Definition 41 Suppose S is an IVNR in ξ, $A \in \text{INS}(\xi)$, the *generalized lower and upper approximations* of A with respect to (ξ,S) are two INSs, abbreviated as $\underline{S}(A)$ and $\overline{S}(A)$ where $\forall k \in \xi$,

$$
\begin{aligned}
T_{\underline{S}(A)}(k) &= \overline{\wedge}_{l \in \xi} F_S(k, l) \underline{\vee} T_A(l), \\
T_{\overline{S}(A)}(k) &= \underline{\vee}_{l \in \xi} T_S(k, l) \overline{\wedge} T_A(l), \\
I_{\underline{S}(A)}(k) &= \underline{\vee}_{l \in \xi} ([1, 1] - I_S(k, l)) \overline{\wedge} I_A(l), \\
I_{\overline{S}(A)}(k) &= \overline{\wedge}_{l \in \xi} I_S(k, l) \underline{\vee} I_A(l), \\
F_{\underline{S}(A)}(k) &= \underline{\vee}_{l \in \xi} T_S(k, l) \overline{\wedge} F_A(l), \\
F_{\overline{S}(A)}(k) &= \overline{\wedge}_{l \in \xi} F_S(k, l) \underline{\vee} F_A(l).
\end{aligned}
\tag{70}
$$

The pair $(\underline{S}(A), \overline{S}(A))$ is termed GINRS.

Definition 42 Suppose S is an INR from ξ to ζ, $A \in \text{INS}(\zeta)$, the lower and upper approximations of A with respect to (ξ,ζ,S) *are two* INSs in ξ, abbreviated as $\underline{S}(A)$ and $\overline{S}(A)$, where $\forall k \in \xi$,

$$
\begin{aligned}
T_{\underline{S}(A)}(k) &= \overline{\wedge}_{l \in \zeta} F_S(k, l) \underline{\vee} T_A(l), \\
T_{\overline{S}(A)}(k) &= \underline{\vee}_{l \in \zeta} T_S(k, l) \overline{\wedge} T_A(l), \\
I_{\underline{S}(A)}(k) &= \underline{\vee}_{l \in \zeta} ([1, 1] - I_S(k, l)) \overline{\wedge} I_A(l), \\
I_{\overline{S}(A)}(k) &= \overline{\wedge}_{l \in \zeta} I_S(k, l) \underline{\vee} I_A(l), \\
F_{\underline{S}(A)}(k) &= \underline{\vee}_{l \in \zeta} T_S(k, l) \overline{\wedge} F_A(l), \\
F_{\overline{S}(A)}(k) &= \overline{\wedge}_{l \in \zeta} F_S(k, l) \underline{\vee} F_A(l).
\end{aligned}
\tag{71}
$$

The pair $(\underline{S}(A), \overline{S}(A))$ is called a GINRS on two universes.

Bao et al. (2018) proposed the (I, N)-single valued neutrosophic rough set.

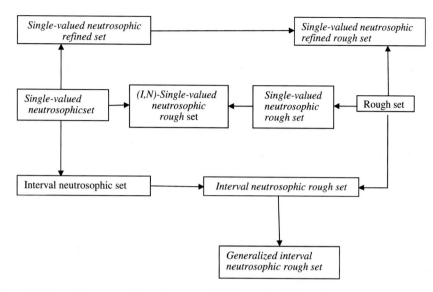

Fig. 2 The flowchart for various extensions of neutrosophic sets and their relationships.

Definition 43 Suppose (ξ, S) is a SVNAS and $A \in \text{SVNS}(\xi)$. Let N and I be *SVN-norm and SVN-implicator. N-upper and I-lower approximations of A* with respect to the approximation space (ξ, S), abbreviated as $\underline{S}_I(A), \overline{S}^N(A)$, are formed by

$$\underline{S}_I(A)(k) = \wedge_{l \in \xi} N(S(k, l), A(l)), \quad \forall k \in \xi,$$
$$\overline{S}^N(A)(k) = \vee_{l \in \xi} I(S(k, l), A(l)), \quad \forall k \in \xi. \tag{72}$$

The pair $(\underline{S}_I(A), \overline{S}^N(A))$ is termed an (I, N)-single valued neutrosophic rough set. The relationships among the above sets can be visualized graphically as shown in Fig. 2.

13 Neutrosophic cubic sets (Jun et al., 2017)

Fig. 2 shows the flow chart for various extensions among NSs, whereas Fig. 3 shows the relationship among neutrosophic and cubic sets.

Definition 44 Neutrosophic cubic sets (NCS)

Suppose ξ is a universe. Then a neutrosophic cubic set (NCS) is termed by τ of the form

$$\tau = \{\langle \xi : A(k), \lambda(k) \rangle : k \in \xi\}. \tag{73}$$

Definition 45 Internal neutrosophic cubic sets (INCS)

Let $\tau = \langle A(k), \lambda(k) \rangle$ be a neutrosophic cubic set (NCS) is termed to be internal neutrosophic if it follows the conditions $A_T^-(k) \le T(k) \le A_T^+(k), A_I^-(k) \le I(k) \le A_I^+(k)$ and $A_F^-(k) \le I(k) \le A_F^+(k)$ for every $k \in \xi$. Thus τ is an INCS.

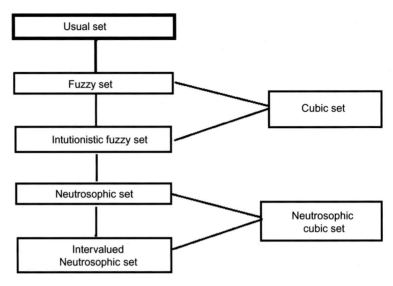

Fig. 3 The relationship among the cubic set and the neutrosophic set.

Definition 46 External neutrosophic cubic sets (ENCS)

Let $\tau = \langle A(k), \lambda(k) \rangle$ be a neutrosophic cubic set (NCS) termed to be external neutrosophic if it satisfies $T(k) \notin (A_T^-(k), A_T^+(k))$, $I(k) \notin (A_I^-(k), A_I^+(k))$, and $F(k) \notin (A_F^-(k), A_F^+(k))$ $\forall k \in \xi$. Thus τ is an external neutrosophic cubic set.

Definition 47 $^2/_3$ INCS or $^1/_3$ ENCS

Let $\tau = \langle A(k), \lambda(k) \rangle$ be a neutrosophic cubic set (NCS) said to be $^2/_3$ INCS or $^1/_3$ ENCS if it fulfilled one of the following conditions:

1. $A_T^-(k) \leq T(k) \leq A_T^+(k), A_I^-(k) \leq I(k) \leq A_I^+(k)$, and $F(k) \notin \left(A_F^-(k), A_F^+(k) \right)$. (74)

2. $A_T^-(k) \leq T(k) \leq A_T^+(k), A_F^-(k) \leq F(k) \leq A_F^+(k)$, and $I(k) \notin \left(A_I^-(k), A_I^+(k) \right)$. (75)

3. $A_I^-(x) \leq I(x) \leq A_I^+(x), A_F^-(k) \leq F(k) \leq A_F^+(k)$, and $T(k) \notin \left(A_T^-(k), A_T^+(k) \right)$. (76)

Example 5 Let $\tau = \langle A, \lambda \rangle \in C_N^X$ where C_N^X is the set of cubic sets. $A(k) = \langle [0.1, 0.3], [0.4, 0.6], [0.7, 0.8] \rangle$ and $\lambda(k) = \langle 0.2, 0.7, 0.72 \rangle$ for every k in ξ. Then $\tau = \langle A, \lambda \rangle$ is a $^2/_3$ INCS or $^1/_3$ ENCS.

Definition 48 $^1/_3$ INCS or $^2/_3$ ENCS

Let $\tau = \langle A(k), \lambda(k) \rangle$ be a neutrosophic cubic set (NCS) said to be $^1/_3$ INCS or $^2/_3$ ENCS if it satisfies one of the following conditions:

1. $A_T^-(k) \leq T(k) \leq A_T^+(k)$, $I(k) \notin (A_I^-(k), A_I^+(k))$, and $F(x) \notin (A_F^-(k), A_F^+(k))$.

2. $A_F^-(k) \leq F(k) \leq A_F^+(k)$, $T(k) \notin (A_T^-(k), A_T^+(k))$, and $I(x) \notin (A_I^-(x), A_I^+(x))$.

3. $A_I^-(x) \leq I(x) \leq A_I^+(x), F(x) \notin \left(A_F^-(x), A_F^+(x) \right)$, and $T(x) \notin \left(A_I^-(x), A_I^+(x) \right)$.

Example 6 Let $\tau = \langle A, \lambda \rangle \in C_N^X$ where C_N^X is the set of cubic sets. $A(x) = \langle [0.1, 0.3], [0.4, 0.6], [0.7, 0.8] \rangle$ and $\lambda(x) = \langle 0.2, 0.7, 0.9 \rangle$ $\forall k$ in ξ. Then $\tau = \langle A, \lambda \rangle$ is a $^1/_3$ INCS or $^2/_3$ ENCS.

Definition 49 Equality, P-order, and R-order
Let $\tau = (A, \lambda)$, $\tau^* = (A^*, \lambda^*)$ are two NCSs. Then

$$\text{Equality}: \quad \tau = \tau^* \Leftrightarrow A = A^* \text{ and } \lambda = \lambda^* \tag{77}$$

$$P-\text{order}: \quad \tau \subseteq_P \tau^* \Leftrightarrow A \subseteq A^* \text{ and } \lambda \leq \lambda^* \tag{78}$$

$$R-\text{order}: \quad \tau \subseteq_R \tau^* \Leftrightarrow A \subseteq A^* \text{ and } \lambda \geq \lambda^*. \tag{79}$$

Note: For our convenience, the notation for all neutrosophic cubic sets is C_N^X.

Definition 50 P-union and P-intersection
Let $\tau_j = \langle A_j, \lambda_j \rangle \in C_N^X$, where $j \in < \{1, 2, 3, \ldots, n\}$.

$$P-\text{union}: \quad \bigcup_{j=i}^{n}{}_P \tau_j = \left\{ \left\langle \left\langle k, \left(\underset{j}{\cup} A_j(k) \right), \left(\underset{j}{\cup} \lambda_j(k) \right) \right\rangle \mid k \in \xi \right\rangle \right\}, \tag{80}$$

$$P-\text{Intersection}: \quad \bigcap_{j=i}^{n}{}_P \tau_j = \left\{ \left\langle \left\langle k, \left(\underset{j}{\cap} A_j(k) \right), \left(\underset{j}{\cap} \lambda_j(k) \right) \right\rangle \mid k \in \xi \right\rangle \right\}. \tag{81}$$

Definition 51 R-union and R-intersection
Let $\tau_j = \langle A_j, \lambda_j \rangle \in C_N^X$, where $j \in < \{1, 2, 3, \ldots, n\}$.

$$R-\text{union}: \quad \bigcup_{j=i}^{n}{}_R \tau_j = \left\{ \left\langle \left\langle k, \left(\underset{j}{\cup} A_j(k) \right), \left(\underset{j}{\cap} \lambda_j(k) \right) \right\rangle \mid k \in \xi \right\rangle \right\}, \tag{82}$$

$$R-\text{intersection}: \quad \bigcap_{j=i}^{n}{}_R \tau_j = \left\{ \left\langle \left\langle k, \left(\underset{j}{\cap} A_j(k) \right), \left(\underset{j}{\cap} \lambda_j(k) \right) \right\rangle \mid k \in \xi \right\rangle \right\}. \tag{83}$$

Definition 52 Complement of NCS
Let $\tau = \langle A, \lambda \rangle$ is a NCS. The complement of NCS $\tau = \langle A, \lambda \rangle$ is termed by

$$\tau^C = \langle A^C, \lambda^C \rangle. \tag{84}$$

Definition 53 Distance between two NCS
Let $\tau_1 = \langle A_1, \lambda_1 \rangle$, $\tau_2 = \langle A_2, \lambda_2 \rangle$ are two NCSs. The distance between two NCSs is

$$d(\tau_1, \tau_2) = \frac{1}{9n} \left\{ \sum_{i=1}^{n} \left(\begin{array}{l} \left| A_{1,T}^-(k_i) - A_{2,T}^-(k_i) \right| + \left| A_{1,I}^-(k_i) - A_{2,I}^-(k_i) \right| + \left| A_{1,F}^-(k_i) - A_{2,F}^-(k_i) \right| + \\ \left| A_{1,T}^+(k_i) - A_{2,T}^+(k_i) \right| + \left| A_{1,I}^+(k_i) - A_{2,I}^+(k_i) \right| + \left| A_{1,F}^+(k_i) - A_{2,F}^+(k_i) \right| + \\ \left| T_1(k_i) - T_2(k_i) \right| + \left| I_1(k_i) - I_2(k_i) \right| + \left| F_1(k_i) - F_2(k_i) \right| \end{array} \right) \right\}. \tag{85}$$

Definition 54 Neutrosophic cubic distance is metric

Let $\tau = (A, \lambda)$, $\tau^* = (A^*, \lambda^*)$, $\tau^{**} = (A^{**}, \lambda^{**})$ be three NCS. The distance function satisfies the following conditions:

- ➤ NCS distance is always positive, that is, $d(\tau, \tau^*) \geq 0$.
- ➤ NCS distance between the same points is zero, that is, $d(\tau, \tau^*) = 0$ if $\tau = \tau^*$.
- ➤ NCS is symmetric, that is, $d(\tau, \tau^*) = d(\tau^*, \tau)$.
- ➤ Triangular iniquity $d(\tau, \tau^*) + d(\tau^*, \tau^{**}) \geq d(\tau, \tau^{**})$.

Algorithm for the decision-making attribute by using NCS distance function reorganization:

Step 1: Build a specific NCS $\tau^* = \langle A^*, \lambda^* \rangle$ on X.

Step 2: Contract NCS $\tau_k = \langle A_k, \lambda_k \rangle \in C_N^X$ where $k = 1, 2, 3, \ldots, n$ for pattern reorganization.

Step 3: Compute the NCS distance between every pair, that is, $d(\tau^*, \tau_k)$ where $k = 1, 2, 3, \ldots, n$.

Step 4: If $\begin{array}{l} d(\tau^*, \tau_k) \leq 0.5 \text{ is recorganization.} \\ d(\tau^*, \tau_k) \geq 0.5 \text{ is not recorganization.} \end{array}$

14 Plithogenic set

Definition 55 Plithogenic set (Smarandache, 2017)

Let ξ be a universe of discourse, P be a subset of this universe of discourse, "a" be a multivalued attribute, V the range of the multivalued attribute, "d" the known (fuzzy, intuitionistic fuzzy, or neutrosophic) degree of appurtenance with regard to some generic of element x's attribute value to the set P, and c the (fuzzy, intuitionistic fuzzy, neutrosophic) degree of contradiction (dissimilarity) between attribute values.

Then (P, a, V, d, c) is called a plithogenic set (PS).

A PS is a set P whose element x is characterized by many attribute values.

A generic element $x \in P$ is therefore characterized by all attribute values in $V = \{v_1, v_2, \ldots, v_n\}$, for $n \geq 1$.

For a better design of the plithogenic operators, a contradiction (dissimilarity) degree function $c(., .)$ between the attribute values is implemented. Each plithogenic operator is a linear combination of the fuzzy t-norm and the fuzzy t-conorm:

$$c : V \times V \to [0, 1]$$

is the contradiction degree function between the values v_1 and v_2, noted as $c(v_1, v_2)$, and satisfying the following axioms:

$$c(v_1, v_1) = 0,$$

$$c(v_1, v_2) = c(v_2, v_1), \text{commutativity.}$$

Into the set V, in general, one has a dominant attribute value (the most important attribute value in V) that is established by each expert upon the application needed to solve.

The PS is a generalization of the classical set, fuzzy set, intuitionistic fuzzy set, and NS because in all these four types of sets, a generic element x is characterized by one attribute only (appurtenance), which has one single attribute value (membership—in classical and fuzzy sets), two attribute values (membership and nonmembership—in an intuitionistic fuzzy set), and three attribute values (membership, indeterminacy, and nonmembership—in a NS).

15   Conclusions

In this chapter, the authors give an overview on each of the neutrosophic environments, its definitions, and its operations. The paper contains SVNS, IVNS, bipolar NSs, CNS, BCNS, interval complex neutrosophic, neutrosophic rough sets, neutrosophic cubic sets, and PS definitions and their operations. It will be helpful for researchers who want to work on this topic for applications in various fields.

References

Ali, M., Dat, L. Q., Son, L. H., & Smarandache, F. (2018). Interval complex neutrosophic set: Formulation and applications in decision-making. *International Journal of Fuzzy Systems, 20*(3), 986–999. https://doi.org/10.1007/s40815-017-0380-4.

Ali, M., & Smarandache, F. (2015). Complex neutrosophic set. *Neural Computing and Applications, 28*(7), 1817–1834. https://doi.org/10.1007/s00521-015-2154-y.

Aslam, M., Aroob, T., & andYaqoob, N. (2013). On cubic-hyperideals in left almost-semi hypergroups. *Annals of Fuzzy Mathematics and Informatics, 5*(1), 169–182.

Atanassov, K. T. (1986). Intuitionistic fuzzy sets. *Fuzzy Sets and Systems, 20*(1), 87–96.

Bao, Y. L., Hai-Long, Y., & Li, S. G. (2018). On characterization of (I;N)-single valued neutrosophic rough approximation operators. *Soft Computing.* 1–20. https://doi.org/10.1007/s00500-018-3613-z.4.

Bao, Y. L., & Yang, H. L. (2017). On single valued neutrosophic refined rough set model and its application. *Journal of Intelligent & Fuzzy Systems, 33,* 1235–1248. https://www.doi.org/10.3233/JIFS-17094.

Broumi, S., Bakali, A., Talea, M., Smarandache, F., Singh, P. K., Uluçay, V., et al. (2019). Bipolar complex neutrosophic sets and its application in decision making problem. In: *Studies in Fuzziness and Soft Computing: Vol. 369. Fuzzy multi-criteria decision making usingneutrosophic sets* (pp. 677–702). https://doi.org/10.1007/978-3-030-00045-5_26.

Broumi, S., Bakali, A., Talea, M., Smarandache, F., Uluçay, V., Sahin, M. Dey, A., Dhar, M., Tan, R.P., Bahnasse, A., Pramanik, S. (2018) 'Neutrosophic sets: An overview', In book: New trends in neutrosophic theory and applications, Edition: Vol. 2, Publisher: Pons edition, Editors: Florentin Smarandache, Surapati Pramanik,pp. 403-434

Broumi, S., Nagarajan, D., Bakali, A., Talea, M., Smarandache, F., & Lathamaheswari, M. (2019). The shortest path problem in interval valued trapezoidal and triangular neutrosophic environment. *Complex & Intelligent Systems*, 1–12.

Broumi, S., Talea, M., Bakali, A., Smarandache, F., & Singh, P. K. (2019). Properties of interval valued neutrosophic graphs. In: *Studies in Fuzziness and Soft Computing: Vol. 369. Fuzzy multiriteria decision making using neutrosophic sets* (pp. 177–302).

Deli, I., Ali, M., & Smarandache, F. (2015). Bipolar neutrosophic sets and their application based on multi-criteria decision making problems. In: *International conference on IEEE advanced mechatronic systems (ICAMechS)* (pp. 249–254).

Deli, I., Şubaş, Y., Smarandache, F., & Ali, M. (2016). Interval valued bipolar neutrosophic sets and their application in pattern recognition. In *2016 IEEE international conference on fuzzy systems (FUZZ-IEEE)* (pp. 2460–2467).

Guo, Z. L., Liu, Y. L., & Hai-Long, Y. (2017). A novel rough set model in generalized single valued neutrosophic approximation spaces and its application. *Symmetry, 9*, 119. https://doi.org/10.3390/sym9070119.3.

Jun, Y. B., Kim, C. S., & Kang, M. S. (2010). Cubic subalgebras and ideals of BCK/BCI-algebras. *The Far East Journal of Mathematical Sciences, 44*, 239–250.

Jun, Y. B., Kim, C. S., & Kang, J. G. (2011). Cubic q-ideals of BCI algebras. *Annals of Fuzzy Mathematics and Informatics, 1*(1), 25–34.

Jun, Y. B., Kim, C. S., & Yang, K. O. (2012). Cubic sets. *Annals of Fuzzy Mathematics and Informatics, 4*(3), 83–98.

Jun, Y. B., Smarandache, F., & Kim, C. S. (2017). Neutrosophic cubic sets. *New Mathematics and Natural Computation, 13*(1), 41–54.

Liu, Y. L., Hai-Long, Y., Liu, Y. L., & Yang, H. L. (2017). Further research of single valued neutrosophic rough sets. *Journal of Intelligent and Fuzzy Systems, 33*, 1467–1478.

Ramot, D., Milo, R., Friedman, M., & Kandel, A. (2002). Complex fuzzy sets. *IEEE Transactions on Fuzzy Systems, 10*(2), 171–186.

Singh, P. K. (2017). Three-way fuzzy concept lattice representation using neutrosophic set. *International Journal of Machine Learning and Cybernetics, 8*(1), 69–79.

Singh, P. K. (2018a). Complex neutrosophic concept lattice and its applications to air quality analysis. *Chaos, Solitons and Fractals, 109*, 206–213.

Singh, P. K. (2018b). Interval-valued neutrosophic graph representation of concept lattice and its (α, β, γ)-decomposition. *Arabian Journal for Science and Engineering, 43*(2), 723–740.

Singh, P. K. (2018c). Three-way n-valued neutrosophic concept lattice at different granulation. *International Journal of Machine Learning and Cybernetics, 9*(11), 1839–1855.

Singh, P.K. (2019) 'Three-way bipolar neutrosophic concept lattice, In: Iremotay et al. Fuzzy multi-criteria decision making using neutrosophic sets', Studies in Fuzziness and Soft Computing, Springer Vol. 369, https://doi.org/10.1007/978-3-030-00045-5_16.

Smarandache, F. (1995). *Neutrosophy, neutrosophic probability, set, and logic.* Ann Arbor, MI: American Research Press: ProQuest Information and Learning.

Smarandache, F. (1998). *A unifyingfields in logics: Neutrosophiclogic, neutrosophy, neutrosophic set neutrosophic probability and statistics.* Available at: http://fs.unm.edu/eBook-Neutrosophics6.pdf.

Smarandache, F. (2007). *A unifying field in logics: neutrosophic logic. Neutrosophy, neutrosophic set, neutrosophic probability and statistics* (pp. 92–93). Ann Arbor, MI: ProQuest Info & Learning. http://fs.gallup.unm.edu/ebookneutrosophics6.pdf (First edition reviewed in ZentralblattfürMathematik (Berlin, Germany). https://zbmath.org/?q=an:01273000.

Smarandache, F. (2016). *Neutrosophic overset, neutrosophic underset, and neutrosophic offset: Similarly for neutrosophic over-/under-/off-logic, probability, and statistics* (p. 170p). Brussels: Pons Editions.

Smarandache, F. (2017). *Plithogeny, plithogenic set, logic, probability, and statistics*: (p. 141p). Brussels, Belgium: Pons Publishing House. https://arxiv.org/abs/1808.03948.

Torra, V., & Namkawa, Y. (2009). On hesitant fuzzy sets and decision. In *The 18th IEEE international conference on fuzzy systems* (pp. 1378–1382). Korea: Jeju Island.

Wang, H., Smarandache, F., Zhang, Y. Q., et al. (2005). Interval neutrosophic sets and logic: Theory and applications in computing. *Computer Science, 65*(4), 87–90.

Wang, H., Smarandache, F., Zhang, Y. Q., et al. (2010). Single valued neutrosophic sets. *Multispace Multistructre, 4*, 410–413.

Yang, H. L., Bao, Y. L., & Guo, Z. L. (2018). Generalized interval neutrosophic rough sets and its application in multi-attribute decision making. *Filomat, 32*(1), 11–33. https://doi.org/10.2298/FIL1801011Y.

Yang, H. L., Zhang, C. L., Guo, Z. L., Yiu, Y. L., & Liao, X. W. (2017). A hybrid model of single valued neutrosophic sets and rough sets: single valued neutrosophic rough set model. *Soft Computing, 21*(21), 6253–6267. https://www.doi.org/10.1007/s00500-016-2356-y.

Ye, J. (2014). A multi-criteria decision-making method using aggregation operators for simplified neutrosophic set. *Journal of Intelligent & Fuzzy Systems, 26*, 2459–2466.

Ye, J. (2015). Multiple attribute decision making based on interval neutrosophic uncertain linguistic variables. Neural computing and applications. *International Journal of Machine Learning and Cybernetics, 8*(3), 93 pp. https://doi.org/10.1007/s13042-015-0382-1.

Zadeh, L. A. (1965). Fuzzy sets. *Information and Control, 8*, 338–353.

Zhang, H. Y., Pu, J., Wang, J. Q., et al. (2014). Interval sutrosophic sets and their application in multicriteria decisionmaking problems. *The Scientific World Journal, 2014*, 645953. https://doi.org/10.1155/2014/645953.

2

Advanced neutrosophic sets in Microscopic Image Analysis

A.I. Shahin*, Yanhui Guo†, Amira S. Ashour‡

*Department of Biomedical Engineering, Higher Technological Institute, 10th of Ramadan City, Egypt. †Department of Computer Science, University of Illinois at Springfield, Springfield, IL, United States. ‡Department of Electronics and Electrical Communications Engineering, Faculty of Engineering, Tanta University, Tanta, Egypt

1 Introduction

Whole slide imaging and digital pathology have had great impact in transforming diagnostic pathology from human observation to completely automatic processing and diagnosis (Mukhopadhyay et al., 2018; Pantanowitz et al., 2011). Each slide can carry a blood smear or any tissue from the human body. Each tissue differs in its structure, according to the acquired specimen from a specific organ in the human body. The automated microscopic image analysis (MIA) systems assist the pathologist to reduce the diagnosis time, achieve accuracy, and increase the quality of disease treatment. Such systems play an imperative role in enhancing the diagnosis of several diseases (Wilbur et al., 2009). MIA systems are concerned with the application of different image processing techniques on microscopic digital slides, such as image enhancement, segmentation of specific components in the microscopic image, or classification of some cell structures to investigate certain diseases (Ashour et al., 2018; Byun et al., 2006; Chakraborty et al., 2017; Dey, Ashour, Ashour, & Singh, 2015; Dey et al., 2016; Ghosh et al., 2015; Hore et al., 2015; Kotyk et al., 2016; Sadeghian, Seman, Ramli, Kahar, & Saripan, 2009; Selinummi, Seppälä, Yli-Harja, & Puhakka, 2005; Shahin, Guo, Amin, & Sharawi, 2019; Vasiljevic et al., 2012).

Microscopic images can be characterized by fuzziness, inconsistency, ambiguity, indecisiveness, indeterminacy, and imprecise information as well as uncertainty due to the acquisition process. To overcome such uncertainty, several techniques have been

Neutrosophic Set in Medical Image Analysis. https://doi.org/10.1016/B978-0-12-818148-5.00002-3

employed, including fuzzy set theories (Sezgin & Sankur, 2004; Sonka, Hlavac, & Boyle, 2014; Sulaiman & Isa, 2010). Nevertheless, such theories can handle only fuzzy and vague information without managing any incomplete problems. On the contrary, neutrosophic approaches have recently been used to handle uncertainty, inconsistency, and incompleteness in one framework (Aggarwal, Biswas, & Ansari, 2010; Smarandache, 2003; Sodenkamp, 2013). Smarandache introduced neutrosophy as one of the most interesting philosophy theories. It is considered an extension of the intuitionistic fuzzy sets and the fuzzy set (Smarandache, 2010; Tu, Ye, & Wang, 2018). In real-world applications, the nonstandard intervals method has several applications (Eisa, 2014; Leng & Shamsuddin, 2010; Ye, 2014a, 2014b; Yu, Niu, & Wang, 2013; Zhang, Wang, & Chen, 2014). Ye introduced the NS in terms of its truth, indeterminacy, and falsity subsets within a real interval (0, 1), which have contributed to its wide use in different applications (Ye, 2014a).

Typically, neutrosophy theory is considered the basis of neutrosophic logic, which identifies the indeterminacy to solve practical problems using a specific model called ⟨Neut-A⟩ (Zhang, Zhang, & Cheng, 2010). Intuitionistic fuzzy logic and neutrosophic logic commonly represent the indeterminacy percentage compared to all other logics by defining each neutrosphic subset (T, I, F) that is overflooded over 1 or underdried under 0 to make a difference between relative and absolute truth cases, along with between relative and absolute falsity (Ansari, Biswas, & Aggarwal, 2013; Smarandache, 2010). Recently, NS was applied in decision-making problems under certain criteria (Biswas, Pramanik, & Giri, 2014; Broumi & Deli, 2015; Broumi & Smarandache, 2013; Chi & Liu, 2013; Hanafy, Salama, & Mahfouz, 2012, 2014; Peng, Wang, & Yang, 2017; Peng, Wang, Zhang, & Chen, 2014; Tian, Zhang, Wang, Wang, & Chen, 2016; Ye, 2013a, 2013b, 2014b; Zhang, Ji, Wang, & Chen, 2015; Zhang et al., 2014). A neutrosophic set (NS) similarity measure provides significant details about the NS interval and the similarity degree between each of these intervals (Ye, 2014a). Moreover, the neutrosophic similarity score (NSS) is considered a promising indication that can be used in different applications (Guo, Şengür, & Ye, 2014). It was applied in several computer vision applications on images, such as thresholding (Guo et al., 2014), edge detection (Guo et al., 2014), segmentation (Guo, Şengür, & Tian, 2016), and classification (Amin, Shahin, & Guo, 2016). Consequently, neutrosophic systems outperform their fuzzy counterparts in several applications (Bhattacharyya, Dutta, & Chakraborty, 2015; Mohan, Krishnaveni, & Guo, 2014).

Generally, neutrosophic methods are considered indiscriminate logic/sets, which can retain all the compulsory attributes to encode the medical/microscopic information. Hence, NS offers a new foundation to link the break between the fuzzy systems and innovative medical applications. It is independently described by three subsets, namely the truth, indeterminate, and false components, which are suitable to reduce the effect of the artifacts and noise in microscopic images. Several artifacts can affect the captured microscopic images due to the staining procedure, the imaging procedure including the effect of the charge-coupled device camera, and other noise sources (Chang, Sud, & Mycek, 2007; Tek, Dempster, & Kale, 2009).

This chapter includes different NS-based MIA techniques with prior clarification of the NS definitions. Section 2 contains the concept of NSs and different models, followed by Section 3, which reports on different MIA processes based on an NS environment with related preceding studies for different microscopic tissues. Finally, Section 4 concludes with details on challenges and new perceptions.

2 Neutrosophic sets

A NS plays an imperative role in numerous medical image analysis systems and applications (Nguyen, Son, Ashour, & Dey, 2017). It is an extensive context of the classic, fuzzy, dialetheist, intuitionistic fuzzy, and the interval-valued fuzzy set. Image analysis requires NSs in the case of ambiguous, vague, indeterminate, unknown, and incomplete data within the microscopic images. In digital pathology, NS theory has been applied to different microscopy images at different image-processing stages. NS contributed in the enhancement of microscopic images (Guo, Ashour, & Sun, 2017; Sayed & Hassanien, 2017; Shahin, Amin, Sharawi, & Guo, 2018; Shahin, Guo, Amin, & Sharawi, 2018). Numerous definitions of NS are introduced as follows, including Definitions 1–6, which describe the image in the NS domain, the NSS, the NSS under multicriteria, the adaptive NSS, the enhanced neutrosophic true subset, and the NS with shearlet transform, respectively.

Definition 1 Image in the neutrosophic domain

For a universe U, and a B_P bright pixel set in U (Guo et al., 2014) defined an image I_m in the NS domain producing a neutrosophic image I_{NS}. This I_{NS} is deduced using three subsets, namely T, I, and F, which have values within the range [0 1]. A pixel in I_{NS} is denoted as $P_{NS}(T, I, F)$. Accordingly, a pixel $P(x, y)$ is interpreted in the NS domain using the following expression:

$$P_{NS}(x, y) = \{T(x, y), I(x, y), F(x, y)\} \tag{1}$$

where $T(x, y)$, $I(x, y)$, and $F(x, y)$ are the three memberships representing the bright pixel set, the indeterminate set, and the nonbright pixel set, respectively. In terms of the intensity criterion, the three subsets are:

$$T(x, y) = \frac{g(x, y) - g_{min}}{g_{max} - g_{min}} \tag{2}$$

$$I(x, y) = 1 - \frac{G_d(x, y) - G_{d_{min}}}{G_{d_{max}} - G_{d_{min}}} \tag{3}$$

$$F(x, y) = 1 - T_{c_g}(x, y) \tag{4}$$

where $g(x, y)$ is the gray level intensity value in an image at the (x, y) position, and $G_d(x, y)$ is the gradient magnitude value on the grayscale image at the same position, where $G_{d_{min}}$ and $G_{d_{max}}$ are the minimum and maximum gradient magnitude values, respectively.

Afterward, the neutrosophic image entropy is defined to measure the similarity and the imperfection of information, which are indicated by a set. The entropy measurement has a significant role in the NS to model the indeterminate cases and to assess the gray level distribution within the image (Nguyen et al., 2017). Typically, if the intensity values have equal probability, the entropy will have maximum value, whereas small entropy values refer to nonuniform intensity distribution. Let E_T, E_I, and E_F represent the entropy value of T, I, and F, respectively. Thus, for an image, the neutrosophic entropy is expressed as follows:

$$E_{NS} = E_T + E_I + E_F \tag{5}$$

$$E_T = -\sum_{i=\min\{T\}}^{\max\{T\}} \text{Pr}_T(i) \ln \text{Pr}_T(i) \tag{6}$$

$$E_I = -\sum_{i=\min\{I\}}^{\max\{I\}} \text{Pr}_I(i) \ln \text{Pr}_I(i) \tag{7}$$

$$E_F = -\sum_{i=\min\{F\}}^{\max\{F\}} \text{Pr}_F(i) \ln \text{Pr}_F(i) \tag{8}$$

where for the elements of i values, $\text{Pr}_T(i)$, $\text{Pr}_I(i)$, and $\text{Pr}_F(i)$ are the probabilities of the three neutrosophic subsets, respectively.

Then, in an image, to calculate the I degree of the element of probability $\mathrm{Pr}_{NS}(i,j)$, the values of $I_{NS}(i,j)$ are used, where the subset I will be correlated with T and F if the changes in them affect the element distribution in I and vary E_I. Thus, the entropy can be measured in an image to evaluate NS performance by evaluating the gray level distribution.

Definition 2 Neutrosophic sets similarity score

The NSS is defined by Guo et al. (2014) to calculate the similarity degree between any different elements. In image processing, the NSS is widely used, owing to its capability for describing indeterminate information, including vague boundaries and noises in an image. In NS, for a set of alternatives $A=\{A_1, A_2, \ldots, A_m\}$ and a set of criteria $C=\{C_1, C_2, \ldots, C_n\}$, then the NS can be expressed under different criteria (Guo et al., 2014). The alternative A_i at the C_j criterion can be given by:

$$\left\{T_{C_j}(A_i), I_{C_j}(A_i), F_{C_j}(A_i)\right\}/A_i \tag{9}$$

where $T_{C_j}(A_i)$, $I_{C_j}(A_i)$, and $F_{C_j}(A_i)$ are the membership values of the T, I, and F subsets at the criterion C_j. Subsequently, the similarity measurement between two different sets of alternatives A_m, and A_n is used to calculate the similarity between two elements in the NS under multicriteria (Zhang et al., 2015) as:

$$S_{C_j}(A_m, A_n) = \frac{T_{C_j}(A_m)T_{C_j}(A_n) + I_{C_j}(A_m)I_{C_j}(A_n) + F_{C_j}(A_m)F_{C_j}(A_n)}{\sqrt{T_{C_j}^2(A_m) + I_{C_j}^2(A_m) + F_{C_j}^2(A_m)}\sqrt{T_{C_j}^2(A_n) + I_{C_j}^2(A_n) + F_{C_j}^2(A_n)}} \tag{10}$$

This definition is then used in the following definition to identify the ideal element concept, which is used to find the best alternative.

Definition 3 Neutrosophic sets similarity scores under multicriteria

In a multicriteria situation, the ideal element model employed to determine the best ideal alternative A^* is represented as:

$$\left\{T_{C_j}^*(A_i), I_{C_j}^*(A_i), F_{C_j}^*(A_i)\right\}/A_i^* \tag{11}$$

The similarity to A^* is measured using the following expression (Guo & Şengür, 2014):

$$S_{C_j}(A_i, A^*) = \frac{T_{C_j}(A_i)T_{C_j}(A^*) + I_{C_j}(A_i)I_{C_j}(A^*) + F_{C_j}(A_i)F_{C_j}(A^*)}{\sqrt{T_{C_j}^2(A_i) + I_{C_j}^2(A_i) + F_{C_j}^2(A_i)}\sqrt{T_{C_j}^2(A^*) + I_{C_j}^2(A^*) + F_{C_j}^2(A^*)}} \tag{12}$$

To take the weights of each element into account (Amin et al., 2016) defined weighted correlation coefficient vectors, which are given by:

$$w_k = [w_1, w_2, \ldots, w_n] \tag{13}$$

These weighted correlation coefficients are used to determine the score of an element A_i with respect to the ideal element A^* using the following expression:

$$S_{C_j}(A_i, A^*) =$$
$$\frac{w_k\left[T_{C_{j_i}}(A_i)T_{C_j}(A^*) + I_{C_j}((A_i)I_{C_j}(A^*) + F_{C_{j_i}}(A_i)F_{C_j}(A^*)\right]}{\sqrt{w_k\left(T_{C_j}{}^2(A_i) + I_{C_j}{}^2(A_i) + F_{C_j}{}^2(A_i)\right)}\sqrt{w_k\left(T_{C_j}{}^2(A^*) + I_{C_j}{}^2(A^*) + F_{C_j}{}^2(A^*)\right)}} \tag{14}$$

Thus, the similarity score for a pixel $P(x,y)$ is measured as follows:

$$S_{C_j}(P(x,y), A^*) =$$
$$\frac{w_k\left[T_{C_j}(x,y)T_{C_j}(A^*) + I_{C_j}(x,y)I_{C_j}(A^*) + F_{C_j}(x,y)F_{C_j}(A^*)\right]}{\sqrt{w_k\left(T_{C_j}{}^2(x,y) + I_{C_j}{}^2(x,y) + F_{C_j}{}^2(x,y)\right)}\sqrt{w_k\left(T_{C_j}{}^2(A^*) + I_{C_j}{}^2(A^*) + F_{C_j}{}^2(A^*)\right)}} \tag{15}$$

where w_k represents the weight of criteria with predefined values, which controls the NSS output.

Definition 4 Adaptive neutrosophic sets similarity scores

The preceding NSS measure ignored the weights of each criterion throughout the similarity calculations. Hence, for adaptive similarity measures with different criteria (Shahin, Amin, et al., 2018), the NSS algorithm is modified to be adaptive according to the intensity variation with the input image diversity. Thus, the weights coefficients w_{k1} can be given by:

$$W_{k1} = \frac{1}{t \times u}\sum_{i=0}^{t-1}\sum_{j=0}^{u-1} P(i,j) \tag{16}$$

The weights coefficients w_{k1} values are deduced from the mean intensity values of each criterion, where u and t signify the image width and height, respectively. In addition, $P(i,j)$ represents the pixel intensity value at point (i,j).

Definition 5 Neutrosphic true subset enhancement

For an input colored image, the true subsets are extracted for each color channel T_R, T_G, and T_B in the neutrosophic domain (Sayed & Hassanien, 2017). The truth subset was converted into a binary set by applying an adaptive thresholding. These enhanced T subsets were used to obtain the binary image using the following rule:

$$S(x, y) = \begin{cases} \text{True} & \text{if } (T'_R = 1 \cap T'_B = 1 \cap T'_G = 1) \\ \text{Flase} & \text{otherwise} \end{cases} \quad (17)$$

Definition 6 Neutrosphic subsets with shearlet transform

The shearlet transform entails an association of localized patterns at different locations, scales, and orientations. Thus, Guo and Labate (2009) transformed the input image into the shearlet framework, and then mapped the shearlet image into the neutrosophic subsets. In addition, an α-mean operation is applied to remove indeterminacy. The powerful characteristics of the shearlet environment along with the NS can be well employed in MIA systems for finding the region of interest (ROI) location along with capturing the orientations.

Shearlets are nonadaptive, where the shearlet transform can be described in terms of the composite wavelets, which can be expressed as (Guo & Labate, 2009; Shan, Cheng, & Wang, 2012):

$$\xi_{AS}(\xi) = \left\{ \xi_{j,l,k}(x) = |\det A|^{j/2} \xi \left(S^l A^j x - k \right) \right\} \quad (18)$$

where $j,\, l \in Z$, $k \in Z^2$, $\xi \in L^2(R^2)$ and A and S are invertible matrices of $|\det S| = 1$. The shearlet is measured as a specific example of $L^2(R^2)$, when $A = A_0 = \begin{pmatrix} 4 & 0 \\ 0 & 2 \end{pmatrix}$, and $S = S_0 = \begin{pmatrix} 0 & 1 \\ 1 & 1 \end{pmatrix}$, where $A = A_0$ represents the anisotropic dilation matrix, and $S = S_0$ signifies the shearing matrix, which is employed for controlling the directionality of the shearlet transform. Generally, the shearlet transform is given by (Jayanthi, 2016):

$$\xi_c^0 = \left\{ \xi_{j,l,k}^{i,0} \right\} \quad (19)$$

$$\xi_c^1 = \left\{ \xi_{j,l,k}^{i,1} \right\} \quad (20)$$

$$\xi_c^2 = \left\{ T_{ck\phi} \right\} \quad (21)$$

For $\xi_0^1, \dots, \xi_0^L, \dots, \xi_1^1, \dots, \xi_1^L \in L^2(R^2)$, $U'\{\xi_{j,\,l,\,k}^{i,\,0} : j \geq 0,\ -2^j \leq k \leq 2^j\}$, and $U'\{\xi_{j,\,k,\,l}^{i,\,1} : j \geq 0,\ -2^j \leq k \leq 2^j\}$, where $\xi_{j,l,k}^{i,1} = D_{Al}^{-j}{}_{Sl}^{-k} T_{ck}\xi_l^i$ for $l = 0, 1$ and $i = 1, \dots, L$, and if ξ_c^p denotes a frame for $L^2(R^2)$, then the function $\xi_{j,l,k}^{i,m}$ is in the ξ_c^p shearlets' system. Afterward, by using the shearlet transform, the features are extracted and transformed into the neutrosophic domain to reduce the indeterminacy as follows:

$$T(x, y) = \frac{ST_L(x, y) - ST_{L_{\min}}}{ST_{L_{\max}} - ST_{L_{\min}}} \quad (22)$$

$$I(x,y) = \frac{ST_H(x,y) - ST_{H_{\min}}}{ST_{H_{\max}} - ST_{H_{\min}}} \tag{23}$$

where T and I are the NS true and indeterminate subset values, also at the current pixel $P(x,y)$, and $ST_L(x,y)$ represents the low-frequency component of the shearlet features. Furthermore, in the whole image, $ST_{L_{\max}}$ and $ST_{L_{\min}}$ are the maximum and minimum values of the shearlet feature's low-frequency component, respectively. Also, at the current pixel $P(x,y)$, the shearlet feature's high-frequency component is $ST_H(x,y)$, where in the whole image, $ST_{H_{\max}}$ and $ST_{H_{\min}}$ represent the maximum and minimum of the shearlet feature's high-frequency component, respectively. To reduce the NS indeterminacy, the α-mean process was applied on subset T as follows:

$$T'_{\alpha(x,y)} = \begin{cases} T(x,y) \\ \dfrac{1}{w \times w} \left(\displaystyle\sum_{m=x-w/2}^{x+w/2} \sum_{n=y-2/2}^{y+w/2} T(m,n) - T(x,y) \right) \end{cases} \tag{24}$$

where w is the local window's size. By applying the α-mean process, the entropy of T is reduced and the distribution of the elements in I becomes more uniform. This process is iteratively performed while the T subset's entropy becomes unaffected. The entropy of T was used to evaluate the element distribution in the neutrosophic domain:

$$E_{nT} = \sum_{i=\min\{T\}}^{\max\{T\}} PT(i) \ln PT(i) \tag{25}$$

where $PT(i)$ is the element probability in T having I value. Lastly, for segmenting the glomerular basement membrane (GBM), the K-means clustering method was applied on the NS image. The objective function of the K-means can be given by:

$$J_{TC} = \sum_{j=1}^{b} \sum_{i=1}^{nj} \left\| T'_{\alpha}(i) - Z_{Tj} \right\|^2 \tag{26}$$

where b is the number of clusters, n_j is the number of cases, $\left\| T'_{\alpha}(i) - Z_{T_j} \right\|^2$ is the distance function, and the centroid of the cluster Z_{T_j} is:

$$Z_{T_j} = \frac{1}{n_j} \sum_{T(i) \in C_j} T(i) \tag{27}$$

where n_j is the number of elements of cluster C_j.

3   NSs in MIA systems

There are several medical imaging modalities that have been processed using NS, such as ultrasound images (Shan et al., 2012), CT images (Guo et al., 2013; Jayanthi, 2016; Sayed, Ali, Gaber, Hassanien, & Snasel, 2015), and MRI images (Elnazer, Morsy, & Abo-Elsoud, 2014). In the literature, NS algorithms can be used with different types of microscopic images (Ashour, Guo, Kucukkulahli, Erdogmus, & Polat, 2018; Ashour, Hawas, Guo, & Wahba, 2018; Guo, Ashour, & Smarandache, 2018; Guo et al., 2017; Sayed & Hassanien, 2017; Shahin, Amin, et al., 2018; Shahin, Guo, et al., 2018). For blood smear microscopic images, the NS algorithms were utilized to enhance the image and segment white blood cells (WBCs). For kidney tissues, the NS algorithms were utilized to segment the glomerular basement membrane. For breast tissue, the NS algorithms were utilized to detect mitosis. Also, for dermoscopy images, the NS algorithms were employed to segment skin lesions with melanoma. In the next sections, these neutrosophic algorithms related to microscopic images are discussed.

3.1   NSs for microscopic image enhancement

Usually, for different types of microscopic images, variations exist in the image quality, such as contrast, color, brightness, appearance, and resolution. These lead to weak robustness of automated MIA systems. For blood smear image enhancement, Shahin et al. proposed an enhancement algorithm as shown in Algorithm 1, based on NS and its similarity under specific criteria (Shahin, Amin, et al., 2018).

Algorithm 1   Neutrosophic sets for blood smear image enhancement

Read RGB microscopic image
Apply circular averaging filter
For z:=1:3 **do** For each channel in input smoothed image
Calculate T, I, and F subsets for each pixel
Calculate NSS under homogeneity Criteria A
Calculate NSS under intensity and homogeneity Criteria B
End
Calculate neutrosophic scaling coefficients ($TS^Z = HS_{C_j}{}^z + DS_{C_j}{}^z$)
Obtain final enhanced image be scaling the input image by Neutrosophic scaling coefficients

---

The input blood smear image is first smoothed with a circular filter according to the circular component. Then, the NSs T, F, and I are calculated for each pixel for each smoothed input channel. Neutrosophic similarity score under criteria A, which represent homogeneity criteria for ideal alternative $A = [0\ 0\ 1]$. The NSS under criteria B represents dual criteria (intensity and homogeneity) for the ideal alternative $A = [1\ 0\ 1]$. Subsequently, the scaling coefficients are obtained by adding the neutrosophic similarity score for both criteria A and B. These coefficients were multiplied by the input image to enhance it.

In Shahin, Guo, et al. (2018), the results were obtained using different blood smear image datasets, including 3327 blood smear images from three different benchmark datasets. The quantitative evaluation metrics used to validate the algorithm were the absolute mean brightness error, light distortion, the multiscale structural similarity index, the contrast enhancement index, and the color difference metric ($\triangle E$). The results established the robustness of the applied enhancement algorithm. The cost time with different resolution was also calculated compared to the other enhancement methods. A comparative study was proposed to compare the proposed enhancement algorithm with the previous enhancement methods, such as histogram equalization, adaptive histogram equalization, RG Chroma, and luminance correction. The processing time of this method was also investigated and it was increased within the range of 0.276–0.96 s with the increasing input image resolution. This method improved the efficiency of the K-means clustering algorithm compared to other enhancement methods.

3.2 NSs for WBC segmentation

In Shahin, Amin, et al. (2018), Shahin et al. implemented a two-step segmentation method on the WBC dataset. This method reduced the processing time and the error rate. The WBC ROI was primarily localized using Algorithm 2.

Afterward, each WBC was cropped, and the segmentation process was performed to obtain the WBC nuclei using Algorithm 3.

Additionally, the segmentation of the WBC cytoplasm is reported in Algorithm 4 as follows.

Consequently, the input image is first smoothed with a circular filter according to the circular component for the blood smear image. An adaptive neutrosophic approach has been introduced to tackle the different color components used in the algorithm (Shahin, Guo, et al., 2018). The adaptive weight coefficients were calculated for the previous color components, then the NSs

---

Algorithm 2 Neutrosophic sets for WBC localization

Read RGB microscopic image
Apply circular averaging filter
Extract b,H,Y color components
For each color component
Calculate T, I, F subsets for each pixel
Calculate *weights coefficients*
End
Calculate Neutrosophic sets similarity score
Apply multi-Otsu's thresholding
Extract WBCs Regions

Algorithm 3 Neutrosophic sets for nuclei segmentation

Extract G,C,M,H,S color components
For each color component
Calculate T, I, F subsets for each pixel
Calculate weights coefficients
End
Calculate Neutrosophic sets similarity score
Apply Otsu's thresholding
Extract segmented nuclei mask

Algorithm 4 Neutrosophic sets for WBC segmentation

Extract b,H,Y color components
For each color component
Calculate T, I, F subsets for each pixel
Calculate weights coefficients
End
Calculate Neutrosophic sets similarity score
Apply Otsu's thresholding
Extract segmented cell mask
Obtain cytoplasm mask by subtracting cell mask–nuclei mask

---

similarity score algorithm was calculated to detect and segment the WBCs.

The quantitative evaluation metrics used to validate the algorithm were the segmentation performance metric (SPM), the correctly detected WBCs in the total number of detected WBCs (A_1), and the number of detected WBCs in the total number of WBCs in all the dataset images (A_2). A comparative study that proposed reflects high system efficiency. The segmentation algorithm was applied on five different WBCs and compared to the previous results in the literature. The segmentation of different cells–basophil, eosinophil, lymphocyte, monocyte, and neutrophil-achieved high segmentation performance accuracy values of 96.2%, 98.6%, 98.8%, 97.2%, and 94.2%, respectively. The results indicated high precision rates of $A_1 = 96.5\%$ and $A_2 = 97.2\%$ using the NS-based method. The average segmentation performance accuracy reached 97%.

3.3 NSs for mitosis detection

A mitosis detection algorithm was proposed by Sayed and Hassanien (2017) based on NSs. The input image was filtered using a Gaussian filter to remove noisy pixels. Each pixel of histopathology image A was adapted to NS $A\{(T^R, T^G, T^B), (F^R, F^G, F^B), (I^R, I^G, I^B)\}$. Afterward, the T image from each channel was converted by using an adaptive threshold method using the local maximum to a binary image, as reported in Algorithm 5.

The experimental results were performed using five distinct breast pathology slides. A total of 300 mitosis cases were found in 50 breast microscopic images. Several evaluation metrics were measured to assess the overall classification system accuracy to prove the robustness of the system. The Moth-flame swarm optimization was also used to select optimized morphological features. A comparative study was conducted between the NS-based system versus state-of-the-art studies. The system achieved high performance related to the previous ones with precision, recall, and F-score values of 65.42%, 66.03%, and 65.73%, respectively.

Algorithm 5 Neutrosophic sets for mitosis detection

Read RGB microscopic image

Apply Gaussian filter for the input image

For z:=1:3 **do** For each channel in filtered image

Calculate T, I, F subsets for each pixel

End

Enhance True subset by applying an adaptive threshold method based on local mean intensity value to get T

Obtain the final segmented image

3.4 NSs for glomerular basement membrane segmentation

The NSs and shearlet transform were combined to segment rats' microscopic pathology images by Guo et al. (2017). Initially, the shearlet transform was utilized to extract shearlet features. Afterward, the image was transformed to the neutrosophic domain, where the α-mean operator was applied to remove the indeterminacy from the image. Finally, the k-mean clustering was used, as reported in Algorithm 6.

The experiments were performed using the microscopic kidney images of 10 rats. The total number of images was 1371 WBCs, which contained healthy and nonhealthy WBCs. Three metrics were measured to evaluate the detection process, namely SPM as well as the distances between a segmented boundary point and a reference standard point (Hdist, and AvgDist). The achieved results were 0.68, 4.59, and 1.99 average values of SPM, HDist, and AvgDist, respectively.

3.5 NSs for dermoscopy image analysis

Another category of microscopic images is dermoscopy. To capture dermoscopic images, a skin surfacing microscopy device called a dermoscopy device is used (Jalil & Marzani, 2008). In Ashour, Guo, et al. (2018), Ashour, Hawas, et al. (2018), and Guo et al. (2018), the authors proposed three different segmentation algorithms to segment skin lesions from dermoscopic images.

In Algorithm 7, the authors optimized the α-mean value for NS, which was introduced in Algorithm 6 using default values without optimization. The dataset was divided into a training set to train the genetic algorithm (GA) to obtain the optimal α-mean value.

Algorithm 6 Shearlet transform and NS-based GBM *K*-means segmentation

    Apply shearlet transform to extract the features from the microscopic image

    Map the resultant features in the NS domain

    Use the α-mean operator on T

    Measure the entropy of T

    Repeat the previous steps iteratively until reach fixed entropy value

    Use the K-means clustering with T

    Segment the clustered

Algorithm 7 Neutrosophic optimized *K*-means segmentation

Split the microscopic dermoscopic images into training and testing

For the trained set:

Produce random α-mean using GA

Read dermoscopic images

Map dermoscopic images of the trained set on the NS

Cluster the dermoscopic images using k-mean clustering algorithm

Obtain the optimized α-mean value based on Jaccard index objective function

after number of iterations using GA.

For the test dataset:

Read dermoscopic image

Map dermoscopic images of the test set on the NS using optimized α-mean

Apply the K-means clustering

Then, the test set was processed without running GA again. After mapping the dermoscopic input image on the NS domain, the *K*-mean clustering algorithm was utilized to segment the images.

The experiments were performed on the International Skin Imaging Collaboration (ISIC) public dataset. In this study, 50 images were used for training the GA to obtain the optimized α-mean value, although 850 images were used during the test process. A comparative study was investigated showing the robustness of the optimization-based system. The optimized α-mean neutrosophic *k*-mean clustering algorithm was compared with γ–*k*-means ($\alpha = 0.85$), γ–*k*-means ($\alpha = 0.01$), and the *k*-means algorithm. The optimized α-mean neutrosophic *k*-mean clustering achieved the highest accuracy, dice, sensitivity and specificity values of 99.3%, 91.3%, 87.1%, and 99%, respectively.

Algorithm 8 reports the mapping process of the original images on the NS domain, where the histogram-based clustering estimation was applied to obtain the number of clusters and their optimal centers. Finally, the neutrosophic C-means clustering procedure was applied to the NS image to segment the input image.

In the experiments, 900 images were used for training while 379 images were used for testing. The C-means neutrosophic clustering algorithm achieved higher performance compared to Algorithm 7 with accuracy, dice, sensitivity, and specificity values of 96.281%, 93.696%, 98.354%, and 92.845%, respectively.

In Algorithm 9, the input images were transformed into the shearlet domain. Then, the input images were mapped on the

---

Algorithm 8 Neutrosophic *c*-means (NCM) Segmentation

> *Read* dermoscopic images
> *Map* dermoscopic images of the trained set on the NS
> **Obtain** the optimal number of clusters and their centroids using HBCE algorithm
> *Cluster* the dermoscopic images using C-means clustering algorithm
> *Obtain* the segmented image

Algorithm 9 Shearlet neutrosophic *c*-means and region growing segmentation

> *Read* dermoscopic images and **extract** the red channel
> *Apply* shearlet transform to extract the features from the microscopic image
> *Map* the resultant features in the NS domain
> *Cluster* the dermoscopic images using c-means clustering algorithm
> **Apply** adaptive region growing algorithm
> *Obtain* the segmented image

NS domain for further use of the NCM algorithm to cluster the image. Finally, the adaptive region growing procedure was used for lesion boundary detection.

In the experiments, the shearlet neutrosophic c-means and region growing segmentation algorithm realized superior performance compared to the methods reported in Algorithms 7 and 8 with accuracy, dice, sensitivity, and specificity values of 95.3%, 90.4%, 97.5%, and 88.8%, respectively.

4 Conclusions

Microscopic images making decision problems involve impreciseness, uncertainty, vagueness, inconsistency, incompleteness, and indeterminacy. Such limitations are due to the existence of multiobjects, object orientation, multiappearance colors, and different staining degrees. Thus, NSs are playing a significant role in solving such problems.

NSs contributed in increasing the performance of several MIA systems on different tissues from the human body, including enhancement of blood smear images, segmentation of WBCs inside blood smear microscopic images, segmentation of the glomerular basement membrane from kidney tissue, and finally mitosis detection from breast tissue. Consequently, this chapter highlighted the importance of NSs in different microscopic applications in the MIA domain to help researchers with NS applications. The preceding studies established the imperative role of NS in the MIA applications. Furthermore, the NSs similarity measurement provides more information about NS. The similarity measurement algorithm under multicriteria has been used with fixed weights coefficients and adaptive-weights coefficients. On medical image processing, such as CT, MRI, and ultrasound, the processed image is usually a grayscale intensity image. On the microscopic images case, these images are present in the RGB color format. The NSs have processed different color space components, which can be very helpful with other microscopic tissue images.

Furthermore, it is perceived that the k-means clustering method can be cohesive with NS to diminish the uncertainty in the microscopic images. Consequently, it is suggested to incorporate NS with other clustering procedures, such as F-means clustering. Also, thresholding can be applied on the neutrosophic T subset before the segmentation algorithm to strengthen the output image intensity. This technique can be useful with other subsets. Such an NS algorithm combination can be applied in different medical diagnosis applications as a future trend. Researchers need to employ NS in image compression, image registration, and image restoration. Additionally, it is recommended to optimize the NSs similarity score, as previously done by Ashour, Hawas, et al. (2018), for optimizing NS.

References

Aggarwal, S., Biswas, R., & Ansari, A. Q. (2010). Neutrosophic modeling and control. In *International conference on computer and communication technology (ICCCT), 2010* (pp. 718–723): IEEE.

Amin, K. M., Shahin, A. I., & Guo, Y. (2016). A novel breast tumor classification algorithm using neutrosophic score features. *Measurement, 81*, 210–220.

Ansari, A. Q., Biswas, R., & Aggarwal, S. (2013). Extension to fuzzy logic representation: Moving towards neutrosophic logic-A new laboratory rat. In *IEEE international conference on fuzzy systems (FUZZ), 2013* (pp. 1–8): IEEE.

Ashour, A. S., Beagum, S., Dey, N., Ashour, A. S., Pistolla, D. S., Nguyen, G. N., et al. (2018). Light microscopy image de-noising using optimized LPA-ICI filter. *Neural Computing and Applications, 29*(12), 1517–1533.

Ashour, A. S., Guo, Y., Kucukkulahli, E., Erdogmus, P., & Polat, K. (2018). A hybrid dermoscopy images segmentation approach based on neutrosophic clustering and histogram estimation. *Applied Soft Computing, 69*, 426–434.

Ashour, A. S., Hawas, A. R., Guo, Y., & Wahba, M. A. (2018). A novel optimized neutrosophic k-means using genetic algorithm for skin lesion detection in dermoscopy images. *Signal, Image and Video Processing,* 1–8.

Bhattacharyya, S., Dutta, P., & Chakraborty, S. (2015). *Hybrid soft computing approaches: Research and applications. Vol. 611*. Springer.

Biswas, P., Pramanik, S., & Giri, B. C. (2014). A new methodology for neutrosophic multi-attribute decision making with unknown weight information. *Neutrosophic Sets and Systems, 3*, 42–52.

Broumi, S., & Deli, I. (2015). *Correlation measure for neutrosophic refined sets and its application in medical diagnosis*. Infinite Study.

Broumi, S., & Smarandache, F. (2013). Correlation coefficient of interval neutrosophic set. In *Vol. 436. Applied mechanics and materials* (pp. 511–517): Trans Tech Publications.

Byun, J., Verardo, M. R., Sumengen, B., Lewis, G. P., Manjunath, B. S., & Fisher, S. K. (2006). Automated tool for the detection of cell nuclei in digital microscopic images: Application to retinal images. *Molecular Vision, 12*(105–107), 949–960.

Chakraborty, S., Chatterjee, S., Dey, N., Ashour, A. S., Ashour, A. S., Shi, F., et al. (2017). Modified cuckoo search algorithm in microscopic image segmentation of hippocampus. *Microscopy Research and Technique, 80*(10), 1051–1072.

Chang, C. W., Sud, D., & Mycek, M. A. (2007). Fluorescence lifetime imaging microscopy. *Methods in Cell Biology, 81*, 495–524.

Chi, P., & Liu, P. (2013). An extended TOPSIS method for the multiple attribute decision making problems based on interval neutrosophic set. *Neutrosophic Sets and Systems, 1*(1), 63–70.

Dey, N., Ashour, A. S., Ashour, A. S., & Singh, A. (2015). Digital analysis of microscopic images in medicine. *Journal of Advanced Microscopy Research, 10*(1), 1–13.

Dey, N., Ashour, A. S., Chakraborty, S., Samanta, S., Sifaki-Pistolla, D., Ashour, A. S., et al. (2016). Healthy and unhealthy rat hippocampus cells classification: A neural based automated system for Alzheimer disease classification. *Journal of Advanced Microscopy Research, 11*(1), 1–10.

Eisa, M. (2014). A new approach for enhancing image retrieval using neutrosophic sets. *International Journal of Computer Applications, 95*(8).

Elnazer, S., Morsy, M., & Abo-Elsoud, M. E. A. (2014). *Brain tumor segmentation using hybrid of both netrosopic modified nonlocal fuzzy C-mean and modified level sets*. Infinite Study.

Ghosh, A., Sarkar, A., Ashour, A. S., Balas-Timar, D., Dey, N., & Balas, V. E. (2015). Grid color moment features in glaucoma classification. *International Journal of Advanced Computer Science and Applications, 6*(9), 1–14.

Guo, Y., Ashour, A. S., & Smarandache, F. (2018). A novel skin lesion detection approach using neutrosophic clustering and adaptive region growing in Dermoscopy images. *Symmetry, 10*(4), 119.

Guo, Y., Ashour, A. S., & Sun, B. (2017). A novel glomerular basement membrane segmentation using neutrsophic set and shearlet transform on microscopic images. *Health Information Science and Systems, 5*(1), 15.

Guo, K., & Labate, D. (2009). Characterization and analysis of edges using the continuous shearlet transform. *SIAM Journal on Imaging Sciences, 2*(3), 959–986.

Guo, Y., & Şengür, A. (2014). A novel image edge detection algorithm based on neutrosophic set. *Computers & Electrical Engineering, 40*(8), 3–25.

Guo, Y., Şengür, A., & Tian, J. W. (2016). A novel breast ultrasound image segmentation algorithm based on neutrosophic similarity score and level set. *Computer Methods and Programs in Biomedicine, 123*, 43–53.

Guo, Y., Şengür, A., & Ye, J. (2014). A novel image thresholding algorithm based on neutrosophic similarity score. *Measurement, 58*, 175–186.

Guo, Y., Zhou, C., Chan, H. P., Chughtai, A., Wei, J., Hadjiiski, L. M., et al. (2013). Automated iterative neutrosophic lung segmentation for image analysis in thoracic computed tomography. *Medical Physics, 40*(8), 081912.

Hanafy, I. M., Salama, A. A., Khaled, O. M., & Mahfouz, K. M. (2014). Correlation of neutrosophic sets in probability spaces. *Journal of Applied Mathematics, Statistics and Informatics, 10*(1), 45–52.

Hanafy, I. M., Salama, A. A., & Mahfouz, K. (2012). Correlation of neutrosophic data. *International Refereed Journal of Engineering and Science (IRJES), 1*(2), 39–43.

Hore, S., Chakroborty, S., Ashour, A. S., Dey, N., Ashour, A. S., Sifaki-Pistolla, D., et al. (2015). Finding contours of hippocampus brain cell using microscopic image analysis. *Journal of Advanced Microscopy Research, 10*(2), 93–103.

Jalil, B., & Marzani, F. (2008). *Multispectral image processing applied to dermatology.* Le2i Laboratory Universite de Bourgogne.

Jayanthi, M. (2016, March). Comparative study of different techniques used for medical image segmentation of liver from abdominal CT scan. In *International conference on wireless communications, signal processing and networking (WiSPNET)* (pp. 1462–1465). IEEE.

Kotyk, T., Dey, N., Ashour, A. S., Balas-Timar, D., Chakraborty, S., Ashour, A. S., et al. (2016). Measurement of glomerulus diameter and Bowman's space width of renal albino rats. *Computer Methods and Programs in Biomedicine, 126,* 143–153.

Leng, W. Y., & Shamsuddin, S. M. (2010). Writer identification for Chinese handwriting. *International Journal of Advances in Soft Computing and Its Applications, 2*(2), 142–173.

Mohan, J., Krishnaveni, V., & Guo, Y. (2014). A survey on the magnetic resonance image denoising methods. *Biomedical Signal Processing and Control, 9,* 56–69.

Mukhopadhyay, S., Feldman, M. D., Abels, E., Ashfaq, R., Beltaifa, S., Cacciabeve, N. G.,et al.Gill, R. M. , (2018). Whole slide imaging versus microscopy for primary diagnosis in surgical pathology: A multicenter blinded randomized noninferiority study of 1992 cases (pivotal study). *The American Journal of Surgical Pathology, 42*(1), 39.

Nguyen, G. N., Son, L., Ashour, A. S., & Dey, N. (2017). A survey of the state-of-the-arts on neutrosophic sets in biomedical diagnoses. *International Journal of Machine Learning and Cybernetics,* 1–13.

Pantanowitz, L., Valenstein, P. N., Evans, A. J., Kaplan, K. J., Pfeifer, J. D., Wilbur, D. C.,et al.Colgan, T. J. , (2011). Review of the current state of whole slide imaging in pathology. *Journal of Pathology Informatics, 2.*

Peng, J. J., Wang, J. Q., & Yang, W. E. (2017). A multi-valued neutrosophic qualitative flexible approach based on likelihood for multi-criteria decision-making problems. *International Journal of Systems Science, 48*(2), 425–435.

Peng, J. J., Wang, J. Q., Zhang, H. Y., & Chen, X. H. (2014). An outranking approach for multi-criteria decision-making problems with simplified neutrosophic sets. *Applied Soft Computing, 25,* 336–346.

Sadeghian, F., Seman, Z., Ramli, A. R., Kahar, B. H. A., & Saripan, M. I. (2009). A framework for white blood cell segmentation in microscopic blood images using digital image processing. *Biological Procedures Online, 11*(1), 196.

Sayed, G. I., Ali, M. A., Gaber, T., Hassanien, A. E., & Snasel, V. (2015). A hybrid segmentation approach based on neutrosophic sets and modified watershed: A case of abdominal CT liver parenchyma. In *11th international computer engineering conference (ICENCO), 2015* (pp. 144–149): IEEE.

Sayed, G. I., & Hassanien, A. E. (2017). Moth-flame swarm optimization with neutrosophic sets for automatic mitosis detection in breast cancer histology images. *Applied Intelligence, 47*(2), 397–408.

Selinummi, J., Seppälä, J., Yli-Harja, O., & Puhakka, J. A. (2005). Software for quantification of labeled bacteria from digital microscope images by automated image analysis. *Biotechniques, 39*(6), 859–863.

Sezgin, M., & Sankur, B. (2004). Survey over image thresholding techniques and quantitative performance evaluation. *Journal of Electronic Imaging, 13*(1), 146–166.

Shahin, A. I., Amin, K. M., Sharawi, A. A., & Guo, Y. (2018). A novel enhancement technique for pathological microscopic image using neutrosophic similarity score scaling. *Optik, 161*, 84–97.

Shahin, A. I., Guo, Y., Amin, K. M., & Sharawi, A. A. (2018). A novel white blood cells segmentation algorithm based on adaptive neutrosophic similarity score. *Health Information Science and Systems, 6*(1), 1.

Shahin, A. I., Guo, Y., Amin, K. M., & Sharawi, A. A. (2019). White blood cells identification system based on convolutional deep neural learning networks. *Computer Methods and Programs in Biomedicine, 168*, 69–80.

Shan, J., Cheng, H. D., & Wang, Y. (2012). A novel segmentation method for breast ultrasound images based on neutrosophic l-means clustering. *Medical Physics, 39*(9), 5669–5682.

Smarandache, F. (Ed.). (2003). A unifying field in logics: Neutrosophic logic. In *Neutrosophy, neutrosophic set, neutrosophic probability: Neutrosophic logic: Neutrosophy, neutrosophic set, neutrosophic probability*: Infinite Study.

Smarandache, F. (2010). Neutrosophic set—A generalization of the intuitionistic fuzzy set. *Journal of Defense Resources Management, 1*(1), 107.

Sodenkamp, M. (2013). Models, methods and applications of group multiple-criteria decision analysis. *Operations Research, 181*(1), 393–421.

Sonka, M., Hlavac, V., & Boyle, R. (2014). *Image processing, analysis, and machine vision*. Cengage Learning.

Sulaiman, S. N., & Isa, N. A. M. (2010). Adaptive fuzzy-K-means clustering algorithm for image segmentation. *IEEE Transactions on Consumer Electronics, 56*(4).

Tek, F. B., Dempster, A. G., & Kale, I. (2009). Computer vision for microscopy diagnosis of malaria. *Malaria Journal, 8*(1), 153.

Tian, Z. P., Zhang, H. Y., Wang, J., Wang, J. Q., & Chen, X. H. (2016). Multi-criteria decision-making method based on a cross-entropy with interval neutrosophic sets. *International Journal of Systems Science, 47*(15), 3598–3608.

Tu, A., Ye, J., & Wang, B. (2018). Symmetry measures of simplified neutrosophic sets for multiple attribute decision-making problems. *Symmetry, 10*(5), 144.

Vasiljevic, J., Reljin, B., Sopta, J., Mijucic, V., Tulic, G., & Reljin, I. (2012). Application of multifractal analysis on microscopic images in the classification of metastatic bone disease. *Biomedical Microdevices, 14*(3), 541–548.

Wilbur, D. C., Madi, K., Colvin, R. B., Duncan, L. M., Faquin, W. C., Ferry, J. A., et al. (2009). Whole-slide imaging digital pathology as a platform for teleconsultation: A pilot study using paired subspecialist correlations. *Archives of Pathology & Laboratory Medicine, 133*(12), 1949–1953.

Ye, J. (2013a). Another form of correlation coefficient between single valued neutrosophic sets and its multiple attribute decision-making method. *Neutrosophic Sets and Systems, 1*(1), 8–12.

Ye, J. (2013b). Multicriteria decision-making method using the correlation coefficient under single-valued neutrosophic environment. *International Journal of General Systems, 42*(4), 386–394.

Ye, J. (2014a). A multicriteria decision-making method using aggregation operators for simplified neutrosophic sets. *Journal of Intelligent & Fuzzy Systems, 26*(5), 2459–2466.

Ye, J. (2014b). Similarity measures between interval neutrosophic sets and their applications in multicriteria decision-making. *Journal of Intelligent & Fuzzy Systems, 26*(1), 165–172.

Yu, B., Niu, Z., & Wang, L. (2013). Mean shift based clustering of neutrosophic domain for unsupervised constructions detection. *Optik—International Journal for Light and Electron Optics, 124*(21), 4697–4706.

Zhang, H. Y., Ji, P., Wang, J. Q., & Chen, X. H. (2015). An improved weighted correlation coefficient based on integrated weight for interval neutrosophic sets and its application in multi-criteria decision-making problems. *International Journal of Computational Intelligence Systems, 8*(6), 1027–1043.

Zhang, H. Y., Wang, J. Q., & Chen, X. H. (2014). Interval neutrosophic sets and their application in multicriteria decision making problems. *The Scientific World Journal, 2014.*

Zhang, M., Zhang, L., & Cheng, H. D. (2010). A neutrosophic approach to image segmentation based on watershed method. *Signal Processing, 90*(5), 1510–1517.

Further reading

Bäck, T., & Jacobsson, L. (2010). The α-camera: A quantitative digital autoradiography technique using a charge-coupled device for ex vivo high-resolution bioimaging of α-particles. *Journal of Nuclear Medicine, 51*(10), 1616–1623.

Ye, J. (2014c). Single valued neutrosophic cross-entropy for multicriteria decision making problems. *Applied Mathematical Modelling, 38*(3), 1170–1175.

Ye, J. (2014d). *Vector similarity measures of simplified neutrosophic sets and their application in multicriteria decision making.* Infinite Study.

Zhang, H., Wang, J., & Chen, X. (2016). An outranking approach for multi-criteria decision-making problems with interval-valued neutrosophic sets. *Neural Computing and Applications, 27*(3), 615–627.

3

Advanced neutrosophic set-based ultrasound image analysis

Deepika Koundal, Bhisham Sharma

Department of Computer Science and Engineering, Chitkara University School of Engineering and Technology, Chitkara University, Himachal Pradesh, India

1   Introduction

Diagnostic Ultrasound (US) has become popular for its high quality, economy, safe nature, and portability. This modality is very attractive due to its noninvasive and nonionizing radiation for medical applications. It is very economical in comparison to other modalities of medical imaging, which makes it broadly accepted for follow-up, diagnosis, and medical monitoring. It is extensively employed for the diagnosis of various types of diseases found in the breast, liver, prostate, thyroid, and coronaries as well as carotid atherosclerosis, in addition to obstetrics and cardiology. However, ultrasound images are affected by a low signal-to-noise ratio, artifacts, and poor quality. An active field of research as well as a challenging task is to extract the valuable information from ultrasound images for diagnosis. Many problems are being overcome and several schemes have been introduced for abnormality detection, characterization, and diagnosis in various types of organs.

For diagnosis of diseases, ultrasound is the most commonly used imaging modality as it is very safe, accessible, portable, user-friendly, and does not use any ionizing radiation (Bosch & Tuinman, 2018; Koundal, Gupta, & Singh, 2012a, 2012b). Ultrasound provides an apparent image of soft tissues such as the thyroid, liver, and kidney that cannot be displayed well on X-ray images (Wells & Liang, 2011). A standard ultrasound system consists of the transducer for scanning, a signal processing device,

Neutrosophic Set in Medical Image Analysis. https://doi.org/10.1016/B978-0-12-818148-5.00003-5

and a display device. The basic idea is to emanate signals and to gather reflected echoes on the video display screen (Wells, 1999). The transducer is a hand-held gadget about the size of a microphone connected via cord to the scanner. The transducer utilizes a collection of piezoelectric components to transmit high-frequency echoing waves and to receive the sound waves from the scattering structures (McDicken, 1976). When the transducer is compressed against the skin, it produces small inaudible sound waves into the body (Szabo, 2004). As the sound waves reflect from tissues, internal organs, and fluids, the microphone in the transducer accounts for small variations in the direction and pitch of sound waves. When a sound pulse hits an object, it echoes or bounces back. By these echoes, it is possible to find the distance, shape, size, and consistency (solid or filled with fluid) of an object. In the imaging system, the amplitude of each reflected wave is denoted by a dot. The brightness of the dot signifies the power of the returned echo. The location of the dot denotes the depth from which the returning echo was received. These dots are combined to produce a whole image. It gives real-time imaging for directing invasive procedures such as FNA and biopsies. In medicine, ultrasound is used to find variations in the growth of tissues and vessels and to locate abnormal tissues such as nodules as well as their size and contours. The thyroid, breast, liver, kidney, etc., are appropriate for ultrasound study due to their superficial location, vascularity, size, and echogenicity. The majority of nodules are benign and pose no health hazard, so their identification is of great significance to evade needless biopsies. If the nodules are malignant, they will require further diagnosis or prognosis. Thus, the sonographic appearance of a nodule-based on size or the presence of multiple nodules may aid in making decisions for performing biopsies.

The granular appearance, known as a speckle, is a significant feature of the ultrasound image. Speckle noise is an interference pattern that is fully deterministic if the transducer settings and the location of all scatterers in the medium is known (Gupta, Chauhan, & Sexana, 2004). It is also known as multiplicative noise and is difficult to remove as compared to traditional additive Gaussian noise (Huang & Yang, 2013; Lee, Yen, & Ueng, 2012). Artifacts are the result of physical properties of the ultrasound itself, which occur commonly in the ultrasound display. The removal of artifacts is necessary for accurate ultrasound analysis, as artifacts may lead to unnecessary concern or clinical intervention. Artifacts in ultrasound imaging may be categorized into four main types: falsely perceived objects, missing structures, structures with a misregistered location, and degraded images. These artifacts occur from noise or incorrect anatomical imaging. An incorrect display of anatomy during imaging can cause reverberation, speed displacement, and shadowing artifacts (Feldman, Katyal, & Blackwood, 2009; Hindi, Peterson, & Barr, 2013).

Ultrasound images have fuzziness due to speckle noise, vague nodule boundaries, and low contrast between suspicious and surrounding tissues. The nodule boundaries in ultrasound are indistinct and difficult to differentiate because of artifacts. These artifacts cause images of poor quality and low contrast with blurred, indeterminate, and ambiguous edges. Therefore, segmentation of a nodule is a challenging chore due to the low contrast and uncertainty caused by one of the artifacts that is known as speckle noise in ultrasound images. Thus, the main concern is speckle noise. Speckle can be considered as noise as it causes fuzzy, ambiguous, and vague structures in tissues under observation. It is also known as a multiplicative noise that degrades the quality of US images by appearing as arbitrary bright and dark spots.

A number of techniques have been proposed using neutrosophic sets (NSs). NSs are widely used in various types of medical image-processing applications. Several authors have introduced several neutrosophic based techniques for denoising, segmentation, classification, etc.. It has been observed from the literature that numerous denoising methods on the basis of NSs have been given for removing salt and pepper noise as well as Rician, Gaussian, and speckle noise (Guo, Cheng, & Zhang, 2009; Koundal, Gupta, & Singh, 2013, 2016b; Mohan, Chandra, Krishnaveni, & Guo, 2012, 2013; Mohan, Krishnaveni, & Guo, 2011, 2012, 2013b, 2013c; Qi, Liu, & Xu, 2016). For denoising, a neutrosophic based γ-median has been presented for removing Gaussian noise (Mohan, Krishnaveni, & Guo, 2012).

Further, Guo et al. (2009) have presented a denoising scheme-based on NS for removing Gaussian and salt and pepper noise using several variances. Qi et al. (2016) have also introduced a neutrosophic based pixel-wise adaptive method for removing salt and pepper noise. Mohan et al. have given a neutrosophic based wiener filter for removing Rician noise (Mohan, Chandra, et al., 2012, 2013; Mohan, Krishnaveni, et al., 2011, 2012, 2013b; Mohan, Krishnaveni, & Huo, 2015). Furthermore, the neutrosophic based KUAN (NKUAN) method and the neutrosophic LEE (NLEE) method have been presented for speckle noise removal (Koundal et al., 2012a). Another neutrosophic based speckle removal method on the basis of Gamma and Nakagami noise distribution has also been presented (Koundal et al., 2016b). Bajger, Ma, and Bottema (2009) utilized neutrosophic based denoising methods for the denoising of mammograms. For facial recognition problems, another neutrosophic based preprocessing method has been introduced.

In the literature, a number of authors have reported different types of NS-based image segmentation methods. Zhang, Zhang, and Cheng (2010a) reported a neutrosophy-based watershed segmentation approach. Cheng and Guo (2008) presented the NS-based thresholding method for segmenting natural and artificial images. Later, Anter, Hassanien, ElSoud, and Tolba (2014) improved the segmentation algorithm by integrating neutrosophic and fuzzy c-means for CT images. Guo and Sengur (2015a) presented a neutrosophic c-means clustering (NCM) method for data partitioning, particularly indistinct and fuzzy data. Its efficiency was tested on both image segmentation and data clustering applications.

Further, a neutrosophic evidential C-means clustering scheme was introduced with the incorporation of the Dezert–Smarandache theory for the segmentation of images (Guo & Sengur, 2015b). Another NS-based improved fuzzy C-means (IFCM) scheme has been presented for the segmentation of images (Guo & Sengur, 2015b). Akhtar, Agarwal, and Burjwal (2014) introduced a neutrosophic k-means clustering for image segmentation. Karabatak, Sengur, and Guo (2013) have given another neutrosophic based segmentation algorithm for color images with improved parameters and entropy-based criteria. Another method called iterative neutrosophic lung segmentation for lung and rib segmentation has been introduced on the basis of expectation maximization analysis and morphological operations (EMM). Zhang et al. (2010a) presented a region merge method to segment natural images for resolving oversegmentation. Sengur and Guo (2011) have presented another automatic method that combined the color with texture information in the wavelet and neutrosophic domains for segmentation of images (Mathew & Simon, 2014). A neutrosophic similarity clustering (NSC) was presented for segmenting images (Guo, Şengür, & Ye, 2014). A NS-based on an improved artificial bee colony approach was introduced for segmenting synthetic aperture radar (SAR) images (Hanbay & Talu, 2014). A neutrosophy-based unsupervised algorithm for color image segmentation has been reported. An unsupervised segmentation method was introduced that synthesized the neutrosophic set and mean shift (NS-MS) (Yu, Niu, & Wang, 2013).

An automatic segmentation approach was introduced for segmenting jaw lesions in X-ray images. It involved noise removal and a NS-based hybrid fuzzy c-means approach (NFCM)

(Alsmadi, 2018). Another segmentation scheme was presented that can correctly and automatically segment the coronary arteries from computed tomography angiography images (Chen et al., 2015). A fully automatic segmentation method based on neutrosophic logic and the watershed method was introduced for the extraction of the liver using CT images, which helped in the diagnosis of liver disease and treatment planning (Sayed, Ali, Gaber, Hassanien, & Snasel, 2015; Siri & Latte, 2017). Furthermore, an unsupervised texture-color image segmentation method with an effective indeterminacy reduction operation has been presented that integrated the nonsubsampled contourlet transform (NSCT) with NS (Heshmati, Gholami, & Rashno, 2016).

A texture-based image segmentation method was introduced with the integration of Gabor filters and a neutrosophic graph cut (NGC). It has been revealed from results that the method has achieved better performance for texture segmentation. The NGC-based image segmentation method was introduced to find qualified rendering images for a thyroid ultrasound. In this, an energy function using neutrosophic values is introduced and segmentation of different anatomic regions is achieved by a maximum flow algorithm (Guo et al., 2017). An indeterminacy filtering and neutrosophic c-means clustering was introduced (Guo, Xia, Şengür, & Polat, 2017). Neutrosophic based segmentation was carried out for tumor detection in an MRI image (Kaur & Kaur, 2016). Further, an image segmentation-based on neutrosophy with the integration of quantum behaved particle swarm optimization (QPSO) was presented (Jianhu, Xiao, Hongmei, Jun, & Xiaomin, 2016; Zhao, Wang, Zhang, Hu, & Jian, 2016). Furthermore, texture features are incorporated with neutrosophic theory for medical image segmentation (Akbulut, Sengür, & Guo, 2016; Koundal, 2017).

Singala and Agrawal (2014) presented a neutrosophic assessment schema for SAR imagery segmentation using swarm optimization techniques. The method provided better results in comparison to swarm optimization algorithms. A neutrosophic cloud detection and localization with wavelet transform was introduced for satellite remote sensing images. This method is efficient for the detection of thin and thick clouds using Landsat images (Mathew, Surya, & Simon, 2013). A computer-assisted diagnosis (CAD) system has been introduced for the classification of breast cancer using thermograms. Further, for the classification of breast parenchyma, different kernel functions were used in a support vector machine (Gaber et al., 2015).

A neutrosophic based image retrieval system has been presented (Eisa, 2014; Rashno & Sadri, 2017). Another neutrosophic segmentation method has been introduced with QPSO (Sayed & Hassanien, 2017). Rashno et al. introduced a fully automatic segmentation method for the segmentation of cysts and fluid-related regions of diabetic macular edema subjects in two-dimensional (2D) optical coherence tomography (OCT). The OCT images are segmented using the NS-based graph shortest path (Rashno et al., 2016; Rashno & Sadri, 2017).

This chapter discusses some of the current neutrosophic based advanced techniques using ultrasound images involving various types of organs. The focus of the chapter is in the techniques, methodologies, and systems introduced by multidisciplinary research teams for CAD.

2 Neutrosophic based CAD system for ultrasound image analysis

2.1 CAD system

Computer-aided diagnosis (CADx) is becoming a popular research area in diagnostic ultrasound imaging. The analysis of ultrasound images suffers from a high interobserver variation rate, as it requires well-trained experienced radiologists and is operator-dependent. Therefore, to reduce the operator-dependent nature and to make the diagnosis practice reproducible, CADx systems are becoming widespread (Chang et al., 2000). There are many advantages of a CADx system, one of which is that it can attain statistical and computational features that cannot be computed intuitively and visually by medical practitioners. Generally, CADx systems for nodule diagnosis in ultrasound images involve various stages such as preprocessing, segmentation, feature extraction, and classification, as shown in Fig. 1.

2.1.1 Preprocessing

Preprocessing of the image is the very first step for improving the quality of ultrasound images. It is used to suppress possible variations that arise during image acquisition or to remove noise or unwanted information from ultrasound images without evading vital information. These variations hinder further image analysis steps.

2.1.2 Image segmentation

Segmentation of images plays a very significant role in the detection of significant regions that are used for the analysis of tissue types, pathological regions, and anatomical structures. The

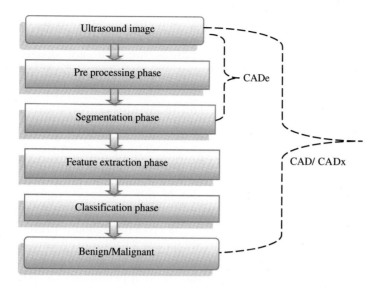

Fig. 1 General framework for a computer-aided diagnosis (CADx) system for ultrasound images.

first task is to define a region of interest (ROI) within the organ for eliminating unnecessary regions from processing. After ROI generation, the next task is to segment the disease within the ROI. A correct boundary estimation of a disease helps in further classification and categorization of diseases. Thus, good image segmentation is necessary to maintain the accuracy and sensitivity of the lesion detection and classification system (Guo & Şengür, 2013). After the segmentation of the disease, features can be computed from it to eliminate the false detection rate for accurate and better diagnosis.

2.1.3 Classification

After segmentation, the suspicious areas can be categorized as malignant or benign on the basis of selected features using various classification techniques. The malignant nodules with vague boundaries and distinct histopathological components are often fused with adjoining tissues, making the delineation of tissue a difficult task. To address these issues, the CADx system has crucial importance in segmentation, classification of benign or malignant tissue, and estimation of the volume in ultrasound images (Ju & Cheng, 2013). For this, a fully computerized system is required for improving the accuracy and for decreasing the misdiagnosis rate for earlier detection and diagnosis of diseases.

Presently, researchers are focusing much attention toward neutrosophy-based methods to solve various image-processing problems due to its capability of handling indeterminate information. In the literature, a number of authors have reported different types of NS-based image-processing methods (Bajger et al., 2009; Faraji & Qi, 2013; Salama & Elagamy, 2013). The neutrosophic based denoising and segmentation methods are discussed (Nguyen, Ashour, & Dey, 2019).

2.2 Breast ultrasound image analysis

Shan et al. have presented a segmentation method named the neutrosophic *L*-means (NLM) clustering method for breast ultrasound (BUS) images (Shan, Cheng, & Wang, 2012). NLM has obtained improved accuracy with fair computational speed. The major constraints of NLM are that it cannot segment more than one lesion and it failed under a severe shadowing effect. Furthermore, a Neutrosophic similarity score (NSS) method is presented with the integration of a level set for breast tumor segmentation on ultrasound images (Guo & Şengür, 2013; Guo, Şengür, & Tian, 2016). The ultrasound image was mapped to the NS domain through membership subsets. Afterward, NSS was utilized to quantify the membership degree of the true region. Eventually, a level set was applied for segmenting the breast tumor in ultrasound images. The experiments showed that NSS can segment the breast tumor accurately and effectively.

Further, a fully automatic, robust, and effective NS-based segmentation method was introduced for BUS images. In this, the ultrasound image is mapped to a binary image, and then the watershed method has been employed for segmenting mapped images to locate the tumor in the segmented area (Zhang, Zhang, & Cheng, 2010b). Further, an approach is presented for the classification of breast nodule characteristics into circumscribed and noncircumscribed classes. The nodule is segmented automatically by integrating the NS and watershed methods along with relevant features extracted from the nodule. The results indicated that the approach had successfully carried out the classification of margin characteristics of the nodule using BUS images. Nugroho, Rahmawaty, Triyani, and Ardiyanto (2017) presented a normalization algorithm using fuzzy *c*-means with neutrosophic clustering to enhance and segment the image. The method has achieved better performance in segmenting the nodule from BUS images than that without normalization.

Lotfollahi, Gity, Ye, and Far (2018) introduced a neutrosophic based semiautomatic segmentation method. It used the region-based active contour that segmented the BUS images more precisely, even with intensity and inhomogeneity. A nonlocal means filter has been used for removing speckle noise and a fuzzy logic technique has been used for enhancing contrast. This method can be modified for different organs using ultrasound images and is not limited only to BUS images. Classification of lesions into benign and malignant has not been done.

Furthermore, a technique called information gain-based neutrosophic *c*-means (IGNLM) clustering has been presented (Lal, Kaur, & Gupta, 2018). The technique incorporates the information gain calculated from the local neighborhood for updating the membership values in the NLM clustering process. For clustering decisions about a pixel, the existing NLM method takes into account only its membership value and distance from the cluster center, but pays no attention to the significant characteristics that exist in an image in that the neighboring pixels have similar features and their probability of belongingness to the same cluster is high. This neighborhood information has been exploited in the technique by using a concept of entropy called information gain. It has been subsequently used to improve the segmentation capability of the NLM clustering process. From the results, the technique is fully automatic and robust as it produced homogeneous clustering, even in the presence of shadow regions (Lal et al.). Zhang et al. (2010b) ultrasound image is transformed to the NS domain and then watershed algorithm is employed for segmenting the mapped image. Finally, the tumor is located in the segmented area. Segmentation of the tumor is an essential step for CAD systems of BUS images. As ultrasound images suffer from poor quality, the fuzzy connectedness method failed to segment the objects with weak boundaries. Therefore, neutrosophic connectedness (neutro-connectedness) and neutrosophic subsets have been defined to generalize the fuzzy connectedness and fuzzy subsets. The neutro-connectedness modeled the inherent uncertainty and indeterminacy of the spatial topological features of the image. The method has been evaluated by the average Hausdroff error, the false-positive ratio, and the similarity ratio, as compared to the fuzzy connectedness method. The method is robust and more accurate for the segmentation of tumors in BUS images (Xian, Cheng, & Zhang, 2014).

Experiments have been performed on BUS images to show the applicability of neutrosophic based methods in image denoising and segmentation. One of the visual results on breast cancer using an ultrasound image of the neutrosophic based denoising and segmentation method is shown in Fig. 2. Fig. 2A shows an original image, Fig. 2B illustrates a denoised image, Fig. 2C shows an image of segmented cancer from BUS images, and Fig. 2D illustrates the delineated boundary of cancer using BUS images.

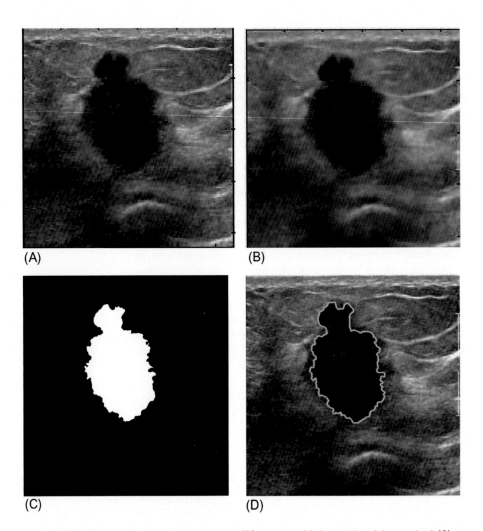

Fig. 2 Case-22-U1: (A) malignant solid mass breast cancer, (B) neutrosophic based denoising method, (C) neutrosophic based segmentation method, and (D) delineated cancer in breast ultrasound. Source: http://www.onlinemedicalimages. com/index.php/en/index.php?option=com_record&view=images&id=22

2.3 Thyroid ultrasound image analysis

Furthermore, the NKUAN and the NLEE methods have been presented for speckle noise reduction (Koundal et al., 2012a). The experiments have demonstrated that NS methods performed well as compared to KUAN and LEE on simulated artificial images that are corrupted by speckle with various noise levels. The visual results also revealed that NKUAN and NLEE removed the speckle and preserved the edges. Another method known as the neutrosophic based Nakagami-based total variation (NNTV) method has been presented. The NNTV method transformed the image into the NS domain and employed filtering for removing noise. The method was analyzed qualitatively and quantitatively by evaluation measures and calculating the mean opinion score from three experts on real ultrasound images (Koundal, Gupta, & Singh, 2018). Further, a neutrosophic based nonconvex speckle reduction method based on gamma noise statistics has been introduced to maintain a good balance between texture preservation and speckle suppression (Koundal, Gupta, & Singh, 2016a).

Another automated segmentation method was introduced that combined the spatial neutrosophic clustering with level sets for segmenting thyroid nodules using ultrasound images. The results have shown that it can delineate more than one nodule effectively and accurately (Koundal et al., 2016b). Koundal et al. (2017a) introduced a texture information-based image segmentation method. The cluster center and objective function are updated by integrating texture information in the NS domain. The results verified that the method is able to segment the object more accurately and efficiently. The results are superior to other methods, even in case of images having low contrast and vague boundaries (Koundal, 2017).

The neutrosophic based denoising and segmentation method using a thyroid ultrasound image is illustrated in Fig. 3, where Fig. 3A illustrated the original image, Fig. 3B showed the denoised image, Fig. 3C illustrated the segmented nodule in the thyroid ultrasound image, and Fig. 3D exhibited the marked periphery of the thyroid nodule in the ultrasound image.

2.4 Other ultrasound image analysis

Kaur and Singh (2016) presented the segmentation approach by deploying a NS with fuzzy c-means for a blood vessel. The image is analyzed to check if it is diseased. Diseases are detected with the use of region growing and are classified as cotton exudates, lesions, and wool spots using the neural network classification method. The method is compared with other methods and is tested on the Standard Diabetic Retinopathy Database (DIARETDB1) and the DRIVE database. Koundal et al. (2017b) made a comparison of the NCM clustering and the IFCM clustering, integrating spatial information for segmenting medical images.

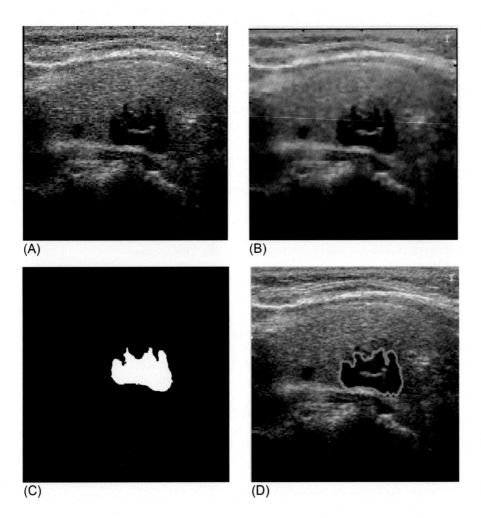

(A)

(B)

(C)

(D)

Fig. 3 (A) DDTI case 635 (thyroid malignant nodule), (B) neutrosophic based denoising method, (C) neutrosophic based segmentation method, and (D) delineated nodule. Source: http://cimalab.intec.co/applications/thyroid/thyroid.php?caso=51

3 Ultrasound image in neutrosophic domain

3.1 Image transformation in neutrosophic domain

The three membership functions called true (TM), indeterminate (IM), and false (FM) are the components of a NS that are used for representing $\langle A \rangle$, $\langle$Neut-$A\rangle$ and $\langle$Anti-$A\rangle$, respectively. Each pixel in the NS domain has been denoted as $P_{NI} = \{TM, IM, FM\}$, where TM, IM, and FM are the likelihoods of pixels that are associated with the set of white, indeterminate, and black pixels, respectively (Guo & Cheng, 2009). The image in the NS domain is illustrated in Fig. 4. The *TM* membership function can be determined as given below:

$$TM = \frac{\hat{f}_{ij} - \hat{f}_{\min}}{\hat{f}_{\max}} \qquad (1)$$

where *j* ranges from 0 to $(m-1, i$ ranges from 0 to $n-1, \hat{f}_{\min}$ is the minimum gray level value, $\hat{f}_{ij}$ is the local mean achieved, and $\hat{f}_{\max}$ is the maximum pixel value.

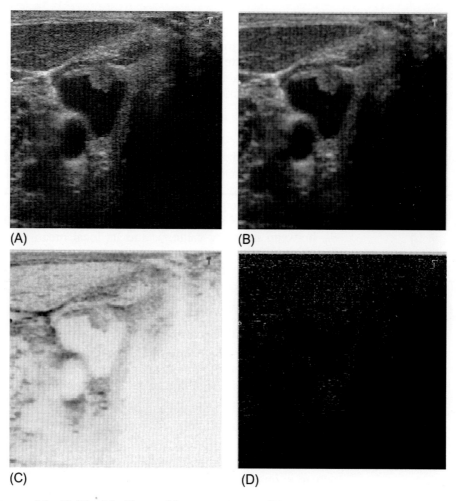

(A)

(B)

(C)

(D)

Fig. 4 Ultrasound (img7): (A) original image, (B) true membership, (C) false membership, and (D) indeterminate membership. Source: http://cimalab.intec.co/applications/thyroid/thyroid.php?caso=10

$$\hat{f}_{ij} = \frac{1}{wi \times wi} \sum_{m=i-\frac{wi}{2}}^{i+\frac{wi}{2}} \sum_{n=j-\frac{wi}{2}}^{j+\frac{wi}{2}} f_{mn} \qquad (2)$$

where wi represents the size of the window, f_{mn} signifies the noisy image, and $\hat{f}_{ij}$ denotes the local mean of pixels on a window. The membership function IM can be calculated as:

$$IM = \frac{\delta_{ij} - \delta_{\min}}{\delta_{\max}} \qquad (3)$$

$$\delta_{ij} = \text{abs}\left(f_{ij} - \hat{f}_{ij}\right) \qquad (4)$$

where $\delta_{\min}$ is the minimum absolute difference value, $\delta_{\max}$ is the maximum absolute difference value, δ_{ij} is the absolute difference value between pixel values f_{ij} and local mean values $\hat{f}_{ij}$. The false membership function FM is determined as

$$FM = 1 - TM \qquad (5)$$

The true membership TM in the neutrosophic domain is processed by normalization of the gray levels in $[0, 1]$, as represented in Eq. (1). The pixels in ultrasound images may represent the texture information or speckle noise; therefore, it is hard to differentiate. Thus, the neighborhood mean, $\hat{f}_{ij}$, is used for determining the local mean of pixels on a window. The absolute difference, δ_{ij}, between intensity value, f_{ij}, and its local mean value, $\hat{f}_{ij}$, is for computing the indeterminate component of the image. The false membership function, FM, can be calculated as the complement of TM (Guo et al., 2009).

3.2 Neutrosophic entropy

The entropy in the NS domain, "En", is employed to measure the indeterminacy degree of images that captured the uncertainities. The En of IM is defined as

$$En_{IM}(k) = -\sum_{k=\min\{IM\}}^{\max\{IM\}} p_{IM}(k)\ln p_{IM}(k) \qquad (6)$$

The entropy is used to remove the fuzziness and uncertainty presented in images. It evaluated the distribution of gray levels in an image. If the entropy value is less, then the intensities have unequal probability. If the intensities have equal probability, then it is a uniform image. The IM values d measure the indeterminate degree of pixels. The variations in *TM* influenced the element distribution in *IM* to make the set *IM* correlate with *TM* and vary the entropy of *IM*.

3.3 Transforming neutrosophic domain to gray level domain

In general, after applying various image-processing operations such as segmentation and denoising, the neutrosophic image is transformed back to the gray level domain by Eq. (7).

$$\hat{\hat{f}} = \hat{f}_{\min} + \left(\hat{f}_{\max} + \hat{f}_{\min} \right) \cdot \widehat{TM} \tag{7}$$

where $\hat{f}_{\min}$ is the minimum intensity value, $\hat{f}_{\max}$ is the maximum gray level value, and the $\widehat{TM}$ component is based on *IM* after the neutrosophic filtering operation.

4 Discussion

Currently, the analysis of ultrasound images has gone through a new era of research aided by advances in neutrosophic theory. The rising commercial and clinical interest is in utilizing portable as well as inexpensive ultrasound devices outside the conventional clinic based settings. This paper highlights some challenges ahead while presenting a perception on this transformation and the probable opportunities in the analysis of ultrasound images that may have high influence on healthcare in the future. Various authors have implemented neutrosophic based techniques on generic images such as the integration of neutrosophic with the Chan–Vese algorithm, principal component analysis, and shearlet transform (Ali, Khan, & Tung, 2018; Amin, Elfattah, Hassanien, & Schaefer, 2014; Ashour, Hawas, Guo, & Wahba, 2018; Cheng, Guo, & Zhang, 2011; Dhar & Kundu, 2017; Guo et al., 2014; Guo, Jiang, et al., 2017; Guo & Şengür, 2014a, 2014b; Guo, Xia, et al., 2017; Hu et al., 2017; Ju & Cheng, 2013; Ponnusamy & Babu, 2016; Qureshi & Ahamad, 2018; Salafian, Kafieh, Rashno, Pourazizi, & Sadri, 2018; Sert & Alkan, 2019; Thanh & Ali, 2017a, 2017b; Zhang, 2010; Zhang & Wang, 2014; Zhang & Zhang, 2015). Most of the work is also carried out on color images using neutrosophy (Guo, Şengür, Akbulut, & Shipley, 2018; Zhang, Zhang, & Cheng, 2012). All this work is required to be implemented using ultrasound images in the future.

Augmented reality- (AR) and virtual reality-based ultrasound will revolutionize medical imaging. AR technologies intermingle the data obtained from different image modalities with real-world aspects. An AR system has been introduced that aids doctors to see real-time data from an ultrasound probe directly into a patient's body through an AR headset rather than on a screen. The system displays from an ultrasound directly. This provides a single unified view instead of splitting the attention of physicians between screen and patient. Physicians generally used a hand-held scanner to determine the blood vessels surrounding the wound. But the AR system helps them in locating those vessels directly by emphasizing them in a 3D image shown in an AR headset.

Another open area in ultrasound image analysis is neutrosophic based image registration and fusion. Image registration and fusion are of great significance in recognizing medical images. A novel method can be drawn to fuse two or more images by using some operations in the neutrosophic domain. The real-time ultrasound image fusion with other imaging modalities will provide priors (statistics on motion or likely shape) that would commence further potential to modify ultrasound images for real-time diagnosis. This will be helpful where large datasets are available and CT/MR images have already attained a component of patient management as it manage the storage capacity, there may be main benefits in taking account of automated fusion of images that are yet to be recognized. Another domain in ultrasound image analysis is Neutrosophic based image classification. In this area, more research is required to be carried out on natural images or disease detection in leafs. Another emerging area is neutrosophic based image retrieval in ultrasound images. This area also requires more work to be done to develop a neutrosophic based retrieval system for ultrasound images. Hybrid methods can be designed by integrating neutrosophic domain methods with other methods such as wavelets to show their effectiveness over other domains. Table 1 lists the advantages and disadvantages of various neutrosophic based methods for different types of tissues using ultrasound images.

5 Conclusion

Neutrosophy is employed as a vital tool for removing uncertainty from ultrasound images, which are widely used for various applications in image processing. The ultrasound images are inherently fuzzy and contain uncertain information. The neutrosophic based methods can handle the uncertain information of the images effectively to achieve better results. The image is

Table 1 Ultrasound image analysis-based on various NS-based image-processing methods

References	Methods	Tissue	Advantages	Disadvantages
Shan et al. (2012)	NLM	Breast	Better accuracy with fair computational speed	Cannot segment more than one lesion as well as failed under severe shadowing effect
Guo et al. (2016)	Neutrosophic similarity score	Breast	Segment the tumor accurately and effectively	Semiautomatic Fewer images used
Zhang et al. (2010b)	NS watershed	Breast	Fully automatic, effective, and robust Segment low-contrast US images with high accuracy	Oversegmentation
Nugroho et al. (2017)	Normalization method	Breast	Enhance contrast	—
Lotfollahi et al. (2018)	NS-based active contour	Breast	Accurate Efficient	Semiautomatic
Xian et al. (2014)	Neutrosophic connectedness (neutro-connectedness)	Breast	Handle weak boundary leakage problem	Not fully automatic
Lal et al. (2018)	(IGNLM) clustering	Breast	Fully automatic, robust Produced homogeneous clustering even in the presence of shadow regions	Cannot segment multiple nodules
Koundal et al. (2012a)	NKUAN, NLEE	Thyroid	Effective in speckle removal	Edges and details are not preserved
Koundal et al. (2018)	NNTV	Thyroid	Speckle suppressed and edges preserved	Other organs yet to be explored
Koundal et al. (2016a)	Neutrosophic based nonconvex speckle reduction	Thyroid	Speckle noise suppressed	Edges and details are not preserved
Koundal et al. (2016b)	SNDRLS	Thyroid	Delineate more than one nodule effectively and accurately	Failed to delineate iso-echoic nodules
Koundal (2017)	Texture-based NS	Thyroid	Segment nodules of different tissues	Experiments are performed on fewer images
Kaur and Singh (2016)	NS-based FCM and neural network	Retinal images	Detected and classified various disease with 97.6% accuracy	Need to improve accuracy

defined as an NS using three membership sets: true, indeterminate, and false. The NS-based methods can handle the indeterminacy and uncertainty of the images effectively. We will continue to study it in the foreseeable future. This work would help researchers in successfully solving CAD problems by thoroughly introducing various methods that can improve the ultrasound image quality and assist doctors in making decisions. Additionally, there are many characteristics still needed to be considered in the future to obtain better accuracy and performance. The present study recommends some challenges and directions for further exploring the area of ultrasound image analysis in detail. The classification techniques can be integrated with texture features to develop a CADx system that can be more helpful for diagnostic purposes. Moreover, research involving bigger real-time image datasets with feedback information is needed to validate the benefits of neutrosophic based methods on other tissues. The future research US images as most of the work is only done in B-mode US images.

References

Akbulut, Y., Sengür, A., & Guo, Y. (2016, September). Texture segmentation based on Gabor filters and neutrosophic graph cut. In: *International conference on advanced technology & sciences (ICAT'16), Konya, Turkey* (pp. 1–3).

Akhtar, N., Agarwal, N., & Burjwal, A. (2014, September). K-mean algorithm for image segmentation using neutrosophy. In: *2014 international conference on advances in computing, communications and informatics (ICACCI)* (pp. 2417–2421): IEEE.

Ali, M., Khan, M., & Tung, N. T. (2018). Segmentation of dental X-ray images in medical imaging using neutrosophic orthogonal matrices. *Expert Systems With Applications, 91*, 434–441.

Alsmadi, M. K. (2018). A hybrid fuzzy C-means and neutrosophic for jaw lesions segmentation. *Ain Shams Engineering Journal, 9*(4), 697–706.

Amin, K. M., Elfattah, M. A., Hassanien, A. E., & Schaefer, G. (2014, December). A binarization algorithm for historical arabic manuscript images using a neutrosophic approach. In: *2014 9th international conference on computer engineering & systems (ICCES)* (pp. 266–270): IEEE.

Anter, A. M., Hassanien, A. E., ElSoud, M. A. A., & Tolba, M. F. (2014). Neutrosophic sets and fuzzy c-means clustering for improving ct liver image segmentation. In: *Proceedings of the fifth international conference on innovations in bio-inspired computing and applications (IBICA) 2014* (pp. 193–203): Cham: Springer.

Ashour, A. S., Hawas, A. R., Guo, Y., & Wahba, M. A. (2018). A novel optimized neutrosophic k-means using genetic algorithm for skin lesion detection in dermoscopy images. *Signal, Image and Video Processing, 12*(7), 1311–1318.

Bajger, M., Ma, F., & Bottema, M. J. (2009, December). Automatic tuning of MST segmentation of mammograms for registration and mass detection algorithms. In: *2009 digital image computing: Techniques and applications* (pp. 400–407): IEEE.

Bosch, F. H., & Tuinman, P. R. (2018). The golden age of ultrasound is only just beginning. *Netherlands Journal of Critical Care, 26*(2), 56–57.

Chang, R. F., Kuo, W. J., Chen, D. R., Huang, Y. L., Lee, J. H., & Chou, Y. H. (2000). Computer-aided diagnosis for surgical office-based breast ultrasound. *Archives of Surgery, 135*(6), 696–699.

Chen, S. T., Wang, T. D., Lee, W. J., Huang, T. W., Hung, P. K., Wei, C. Y., et al. (2015). Coronary arteries segmentation based on the 3D discrete wavelet transform and 3D neutrosophic transform. *BioMed Research International, 2015*, 1–9 Article ID 798303.

Cheng, H. D., & Guo, Y. (2008). A new neutrosophic approach to image thresholding. *New Mathematics and Natural Computation, 4*(03), 291–308.

Cheng, H. D., Guo, Y., & Zhang, Y. (2011). A novel image segmentation approach based on neutrosophic set and improved fuzzy c-means algorithm. *New Mathematics and Natural Computation, 7*(1), 155–171.

Dhar, S., & Kundu, M. K. (2017). Accurate segmentation of complex document image using digital shearlet transform with neutrosophic set as uncertainty handling tool. *Applied Soft Computing, 61*, 412–426.

Eisa, M. (2014). A new approach for enhancing image retrieval using neutrosophic sets. *International Journal of Computer Applications, 95*(8), 12–20.

Faraji, M.R. and Qi, X., 2013, July. An effective neutrosophic set-based preprocessing method for face recognition. In 2013 IEEE international conference on multimedia and expo workshops (ICMEW) (pp. 1-4). IEEE.

Feldman, M. K., Katyal, S., & Blackwood, M. S. (2009). US artifacts. *Radiographics, 29*(4), 1179–1189.

Gaber, T., Ismail, G., Anter, A., Soliman, M., Ali, M., Semary, N., Hassanien, A.E. and Snasel, V., 2015, August. Thermogram breast cancer prediction approach based on Neutrosophic sets and fuzzy c-means algorithm. In 2015 37th annual international conference of the IEEE engineering in medicine and biology society (EMBC) (pp. 4254-4257). IEEE.

Guo, Y., & Cheng, H. D. (2009). New neutrosophic approach to image segmentation. *Pattern Recognition, 42*(5), 587–595.

Guo, Y., Cheng, H. D., & Zhang, Y. (2009). A new neutrosophic approach to image denoising. *New Mathematics and Natural Computation, 5*(03), 653–662.

Guo, Y., Jiang, S. Q., Sun, B., Siuly, S., Şengür, A., & Tian, J. W. (2017). Using neutrosophic graph cut segmentation algorithm for qualified rendering image selection in thyroid elastography video. *Health Information Science and Systems, 5*(1), 8.

Guo, Y., & Şengür, A. (2013). A novel image segmentation algorithm based on neutrosophic filtering and level set. *Neutrosophic Sets and Systems, 1*, 46–49.

Guo, Y., & Şengür, A. (2014a). A novel image edge detection algorithm based on neutrosophic set. *Computers & Electrical Engineering, 40*(8), 3–25.

Guo, Y., & Şengür, A. (2014b). A novel image segmentation algorithm based on neutrosophic similarity clustering. *Applied Soft Computing, 25*, 391–398.

Guo, Y., & Sengur, A. (2015a). NCM: Neutrosophic c-means clustering algorithm. *Pattern Recognition, 48*(8), 2710–2724.

Guo, Y., & Sengur, A. (2015b). NECM: Neutrosophic evidential c-means clustering algorithm. *Neural Computing and Applications, 26*(3), 561–571.

Guo, Y., Şengür, A., Akbulut, Y., & Shipley, A. (2018). An effective color image segmentation approach using neutrosophic adaptive mean shift clustering. *Measurement, 119*, 28–40.

Guo, Y., Şengür, A., & Tian, J. W. (2016). A novel breast ultrasound image segmentation algorithm based on neutrosophic similarity score and level set. *Computer Methods and Programs in Biomedicine, 123*, 43–53.

Guo, Y., Şengür, A., & Ye, J. (2014). A novel image thresholding algorithm based on neutrosophic similarity score. *Measurement, 58*, 175–186.

Guo, Y., Xia, R., Şengür, A., & Polat, K. (2017). A novel image segmentation approach based on neutrosophic c-means clustering and indeterminacy filtering. *Neural Computing and Applications, 28*(10), 3009–3019.

Gupta, S., Chauhan, R. C., & Sexana, S. C. (2004). Wavelet-based statistical approach for speckle reduction in medical ultrasound images. *Medical and Biological Engineering and Computing, 42*(2), 189–192.

Hanbay, K., & Talu, M. F. (2014). Segmentation of SAR images using improved artificial bee colony algorithm and neutrosophic set. *Applied Soft Computing, 21*, 433–443.

Heshmati, A., Gholami, M., & Rashno, A. (2016). Scheme for unsupervised colour–texture image segmentation using neutrosophic set and non-subsampled contourlet transform. *IET Image Processing, 10*(6), 464–473.

Hindi, A., Peterson, C., & Barr, R. G. (2013). Artifacts in diagnostic ultrasound. *Reports in Medical Imaging, 6*, 29–48.

Hu, K., Ye, J., Fan, E., Shen, S., Huang, L., & Pi, J. (2017). A novel object tracking algorithm by fusing color and depth information based on single valued neutrosophic cross-entropy. *Journal of Intelligent & Fuzzy Systems, 32*(3), 1775–1786.

Huang, J., & Yang, X. (2013). Fast reduction of speckle noise in real ultrasound images. *Signal Processing, 93*(4), 684–694.

Jianhu, Z., Xiao, W., Hongmei, Z., Jun, H. U., & Xiaomin, J. (2016). The neutrosophic set and quantum-behaved particle swarm optimization algorithm of side scan sonar image segmentation. *Acta Geodaetica et Cartographica Sinica, 45*(8), 935–942.

Ju, W., & Cheng, H. D. (2013). A novel neutrosophic logic SVM (N-SVM) and its application to image categorization. *New Mathematics and Natural Computation, 9*(01), 27–42.

Karabatak, E., Sengur, A., & Guo, Y. (2013). Modified neutrosophic approach to color image segmentation. *Journal of Electronic Imaging, 22*(1), 013005.

Kaur, G. and Kaur, H., 2016, March. An automated method of segmentation for tumor detection by neutrosophic sets and morphological operations using MR images. In 2016 conference on emerging devices and smart systems (ICEDSS) (pp. 163-168). IEEE.

Kaur, I., & Singh, L. M. (2016). *A method of disease detection and segmentation of retinal blood vessels using fuzzy c-means and neutrosophic approach.* Infinite Study.

Koundal, D. (2017). Texture-based image segmentation using neutrosophic clustering. *IET Image Processing, 11*(8), 640–645.

Koundal, D., Anand, V., & Bhat, S. (2017, December). Comparative analysis of neutrosophic and intuitionistic fuzzy set with spatial information on image segmentation. In: *2017 fourth international conference on image information processing (ICIIP)* (pp. 1–5): IEEE.

Koundal, D., Gupta, S., & Singh, S. (2012a). Speckle reduction filter in neutrosophic domain. In: *International conference of biomedical engineering and assisted technologies* (pp. 786–790).

Koundal, D., Gupta, S., & Singh, S. (2012b). Computer-aided diagnosis of thyroid nodule: a review. *International Journal of Computer Science and Engineering Survey, 3*(4), 67.

Koundal, D., Gupta, S., & Singh, S. (2013). Survey of computer-aided diagnosis of thyroid nodules in medical ultrasound images. In: *Advances in computing and information technology* (pp. 459–467): Berlin, Heidelberg: Springer.

Koundal, D., Gupta, S., & Singh, S. (2016a). Automated delineation of thyroid nodules in ultrasound images using spatial neutrosophic clustering and level set. *Applied Soft Computing, 40*, 86–97.

Koundal, D., Gupta, S., & Singh, S. (2016b). Speckle reduction method for thyroid ultrasound images in neutrosophic domain. *IET Image Processing, 10*(2), 167–175.

Koundal, D., Gupta, S., & Singh, S. (2018). Neutrosophic based Nakagami total variation method for speckle suppression in thyroid ultrasound images. *IRBM, 39* (1), 43–53.

Lal, M., Kaur, L., & Gupta, S. (2018). Automatic segmentation of tumors in B-mode breast ultrasound images using information gain based neutrosophic clustering. *Journal of X-Ray Science and Technology,* Preprint, 1–17.

Lee, M. S., Yen, C. L., & Ueng, S. K. (2012). Speckle reduction with edges preservation for ultrasound images: Using function spaces approach. *IET image processing, 6*(7), 813–821.

Lotfollahi, M., Gity, M., Ye, J. Y., & Far, A. M. (2018). Segmentation of breast ultrasound images based on active contours using neutrosophic theory. *Journal of Medical Ultrasonics, 45*(2), 205–212.

Mathew, J. M., & Simon, P. (2014, January). Color texture image segmentation based on neutrosophic set and nonsubsampled contourlet transformation. In: *International conference on applied algorithms* (pp. 164–173): Cham: Springer.

Mathew, J. M., Surya, S. R., & Simon, P. (2013, December). Automatic cloud detection based on neutrosophic set in satellite images. In: *2013 international conference on control communication and computing (ICCC)* (pp. 210–215): IEEE.

McDicken, W. N. (1976). *Diagnostic ultrasonics.* Crosby Lockwood Staples.

Mohan, J., Chandra, A. T. S., Krishnaveni, V., & Guo, Y. (2012). Evaluation of neutrosophic set approach filtering technique for image denoising. *The International Journal of Multimedia & Its Applications, 4*(4), 73.

Mohan, J., Chandra, A. T. S., Krishnaveni, V., & Guo, Y. (2013). Image denoising based on neutrosophic wiener filtering. In *Advances in computing and information technology* (pp. 861–869). Berlin, Heidelberg: Springer.

Mohan, J., Krishnaveni, V., & Guo, Y. (2011, November). A neutrosophic approach of MRI denoising. In: *2011 international conference on image information processing* (pp. 58–66): IEEE.

Mohan, J., Krishnaveni, V., & Guo, Y. (2012). Performance analysis of neutrosophic set approach of median filtering for MRI denoising. *International Journal of Electronics and Communication Engineering & Technology, 3,* 148–163.

Mohan, J., Krishnaveni, V., & Guo, Y. (2013b). MRI denoising using nonlocal neutrosophic set approach of Wiener filtering. *Biomedical Signal Processing and Control, 8*(6), 779–791.

Mohan, J., Krishnaveni, V., & Guo, Y. (2013c). A new neutrosophic approach of Wiener filtering for MRI denoising. *Measurement Science Review, 13*(4), 177–186.

Mohan, J., Krishnaveni, V., & Huo, Y. (2015, February). Automated brain tumor segmentation on MR images based on neutrosophic set approach. In: *2015 2nd international conference on electronics and communication systems (ICECS)* (pp. 1078–1083): IEEE.

Nguyen, G. N., Ashour, A. S., & Dey, N. (2019). A survey of the state-of-the-arts on neutrosophic sets in biomedical diagnoses. *International Journal of Machine Learning and Cybernetics, 10*(1), 1–13.

Nugroho, H. A., Rahmawaty, M., Triyani, Y., & Ardiyanto, I. (2017, October). Neutrosophic and fuzzy C-means clustering for breast ultrasound image segmentation. In: *2017 9th international conference on information technology and electrical engineering (ICITEE)* (pp. 1–5): IEEE.

Ponnusamy, J. A. R., & Babu, C. N. K. (2016). Breast lesion segmentation using generalised simulated annealing and neutrosophic region growing algorithm in breast MRI. *Academic Journal of Cancer Research, 9*(4), 75–81.

Qi, X., Liu, B., & Xu, J. (2016). A neutrosophic filter for high-density salt and pepper noise based on pixel-wise adaptive smoothing parameter. *Journal of Visual Communication and Image Representation, 36*, 1–10.

Qureshi, M. N., & Ahamad, M. V. (2018). *An improved method for image segmentation using K-means clustering with neutrosophic logic.* Infinite Study.

Rashno, A., Koozekanani, D. D., Drayna, P. M., Nazari, B., Sadri, S., Rabbani, H., et al. (2016). Neutrosophic C-means clustering in kernel space and its application in image segmentation. *Journal of Image and Graphics, 21*(10), 1316–1327.

Rashno, A., & Sadri, S. (2017). Content-based image retrieval with color and texture features in neutrosophic domain. *In 2017 3rd international conference on pattern recognition and image analysis (IPRIA),* (pp. 50–55).

Salafian, B., Kafieh, R., Rashno, A., Pourazizi, M. and Sadri, S., 2018. Automatic segmentation of choroid layer in edi oct images using graph theory in neutrosophic space. arXiv preprint arXiv: 1812.01989.

Salama, A. A., & Elagamy, H. (2013). Neutrosophic filters. *International Journal of Computer Science Engineering and Information Technology Research (IJCSEITR), 3*(1), 2013.

Sayed, G. I., Ali, M. A., Gaber, T., Hassanien, A. E., & Snasel, V. (2015, December). A hybrid segmentation approach based on neutrosophic sets and modified watershed: A case of abdominal CT Liver parenchyma. In: *2015 11th international computer engineering conference (ICENCO)* (pp. 144–149): IEEE.

Sayed, G. I., & Hassanien, A. E. (2017). Moth-flame swarm optimization with neutrosophic sets for automatic mitosis detection in breast cancer histology images. *Applied Intelligence, 47*(2), 397–408.

Sengur, A., & Guo, Y. (2011). Color texture image segmentation based on neutrosophic set and wavelet transformation. *Computer Vision and Image Understanding, 115*(8), 1134–1144.

Sert, E., & Alkan, A. (2019). Image edge detection based on neutrosophic set approach combined with Chan–Vese algorithm. *International Journal of Pattern Recognition and Artificial Intelligence, 33*(3), 1954008.

Shan, J., Cheng, H. D., & Wang, Y. (2012). A novel segmentation method for breast ultrasound images based on neutrosophic l-means clustering. *Medical Physics, 39*(9), 5669–5682.

Singala, R., & Agrawal, A. (2014, December). Evaluation schema for SAR image segmentation based on swarm optimization in neutrosophic domain. In: *2014 IEEE international symposium on signal processing and information technology (ISSPIT)* (pp. 343–348): IEEE.

Siri, S. K., & Latte, M. V. (2017). A novel approach to extract exact liver image boundary from abdominal CT scan using neutrosophic set and fast marching method. *Journal of Intelligent Systems.*

Szabo, T. L. (2004). *Diagnostic ultrasound imaging: inside out.* Academic Press.

Thanh, N.D. and Ali, M., 2017a, July. Neutrosophic recommender system for medical diagnosis based on algebraic similarity measure and clustering. In 2017 IEEE international conference on fuzzy systems (FUZZ-IEEE) (pp. 1-6). IEEE.

Thanh, N. D., & Ali, M. (2017b). A novel clustering algorithm in a neutrosophic recommender system for medical diagnosis. *Cognitive Computation, 9*(4), 526–544.

Wells, P. N. (1999). Ultrasonic imaging of the human body. *Reports on Progress in Physics, 62*(5), 671.

Wells, P. N., & Liang, H. D. (2011). Medical ultrasound: imaging of soft tissue strain and elasticity. *Journal of the Royal Society Interface, 8*(64), 1521–1549.

Xian, M., Cheng, H. D., & Zhang, Y. (2014, August). A fully automatic breast ultrasound image segmentation approach based on neutro-connectedness. In *2014 22nd international conference on pattern recognition* (pp. 2495–2500): IEEE.

Yu, B., Niu, Z., & Wang, L. (2013). Mean shift based clustering of neutrosophic domain for unsupervised constructions detection. *Optik, 124*(21), 4697–4706.

Zhang, M. (2010). *Novel approaches to image segmentation based on neutrosophic logic,* (pp. 29–38). Logan, UT: Utah State University.

Zhang, G., & Wang, D. (2014). Neutrosophic image segmentation approach integrated LPG & PCA. *Journal of Image & Graphics, 19*(5), 693–700.

Zhang, L., & Zhang, M. (2015). Segmentation of blurry images based on interval neutrosophic set. *Journal of Information & Computational Science, 12*(7), 2769–2777.

Zhang, M., Zhang, L., & Cheng, H. D. (2010a). Segmentation of ultrasound breast images based on a neutrosophic method. *Optical Engineering, 49*(11), 117001.

Zhang, M., Zhang, L., & Cheng, H. D. (2010b). A neutrosophic approach to image segmentation based on watershed method. *Signal Processing, 90*(5), 1510–1517.

Zhang, L., Zhang, M., & Cheng, H. D. (2012). Color image segmentation based on neutrosophy. *Optical Engineering, 51*(3), 037009.

Zhao, J., Wang, X., Zhang, H., Hu, J., & Jian, X. (2016). Side scan sonar image segmentation based on neutrosophic set and quantum-behaved particle swarm optimization algorithm. *Marine Geophysical Research, 37*(3), 229–241.

Neutrosophic set in medical image denoising

4

Neutrosophic set in medical image denoising

Mohan Jayaraman*, Krishnaveni Vellingiri†, Yanhui Guo‡
*Department of ECE, SRM Valliammai Engineering College, Kattankulathur,
India. †Department of ECE, PSG College of Technology, Coimbatore, India.
‡Department of Computer Science, University of Illinois at Springfield,
Springfield, IL, United States*

1 Introduction

In modern medicine, due to the technological advancements in medical imaging, most clinicians make a diagnosis and provide treatment for a variety of medical conditions based on useful information provided by medical images. The medical conditions include abnormalities in the brain and spinal cord; diseases in the heart, liver, pancreas, and other abdominal organs; injuries or abnormalities in the joints; and abnormalities in various parts of the body. These could be the appearance of features such as tumors or lesions that are abnormally observed, changes in shape such as the shrinkage or enlargement of particular structures, or changes in image intensity compared to normal tissue. In order to achieve the best diagnosis, medical images should be free of noise and artifacts that occur during the acquisition process. Therefore, image denoising is a significant step in medical image analysis to enhance the quality of the images to guarantee precise diagnosis.

Among different medical imaging modalities, MRI is a notable medical imaging technique for comprehensively visualizing the human body's internal structure, where the nuclei in a magnetic field absorbs and reemits electromagnetic radiation. MRI has numerous applications in medicine, material science, and engineering. In clinical practices, MRI is used primarily to determine pathological/physiological changes of human tissues (Wright, 1997). In MRI, the image is formed by measuring the signal coming from certain protons/nuclei in a subject using the interaction between the nuclear spin and the electromagnetic field

Neutrosophic Set in Medical Image Analysis. https://doi.org/10.1016/B978-0-12-818148-5.00004-7

(Wright, 1997). Nuclear spin is a fundamental property of protons and neutrons. Each unpaired proton and neutron possesses the value of nuclear spin $= 1/2$, which is commonly used for NMR. Only incompletely paired nuclei, which possess an odd number of protons and/or neutrons, have net spins that induce magnetic moments. Hydrogen is one such element with an uncancelled (unpaired) spin. The hydrogen nuclei spin around their axes as small magnets. Mainly, the human body includes water molecules and fat. Usually, the hydrogen protons in the water molecules are imaged to show the human tissues' pathological/physiological changes (Rummeny, Reimer, & Heindel, 2009).

MRI scanners produce a strong stationary magnetic field. In current clinical practice, the field strength varies from 0.5 to 3 T. For research purposes, magnets with the strength of 7 T or 11 T and above are also used. When an individual is placed in the static magnetic field, the hydrogen atoms with a spin will tend to align themselves along the direction of the magnetic field, a process called magnetization. These protons process around the direction of the magnetic field with a frequency proportional to the static magnetic field, called the Larmor frequency. For hydrogen nuclei in a typical 1.5 T field, the Larmor frequency is approximately 64 MHz (Rummeny et al., 2009). The average magnetization of the protons along the magnetic field direction is known as the longitudinal net magnetization. At the Larmor frequency, a brief radio-frequency (RF) pulse is applied to make the protons absorb energy, brought out of equilibrium and the longitudinal magnetization flipped into the transverse plane to produce transverse magnetization, which is called excitation. When the RF pulse ends, the protons will return to equilibrium by reemitting the energy absorbed, which is called relaxation. This reemitting energy by the protons is observed as MR signals. The MRI system detects this signal for further image reconstruction, where the phase and frequency of the signal data are gathered in the k-space, which is the abstract platform used to position the acquired data (Rodriguez, 2004). Then, for this k-space, a two-dimensional (2D) inverse Fourier transform is calculated to create a gray-scale image.

During the acquisition process, random noise affects the MR, which degrades the diagnosis using the acquired MRI images and affects the performance of any further image analysis procedures. The typical noise type that affects the magnitude of MR images follows Rician distribution, which is signal-dependent (Gudbjartsson & Patz, 1995). Particularly, Rician noise introduces random fluctuations/bias, the removal of which is a challenging task. Therefore, denoising is used as a preprocessing stage prior to several image-processing procedures to enhance the MR image quality for precise diagnosis. Accordingly, several researchers were interested to implement different denoising approaches to reduce the Rician noise on MR images by different assumptions, merits, and demerits (Anand & Sahambi, 2010; Coupe et al., 2008; He & Greenshields, 2009; Manjon et al., 2008; Nowak, 1999; Rajan, Jeurissen, Verhoye, Audekerke, & Sijbers, 2011). Generally, efficient denoising techniques have to remove noise while preserving the image anatomical structures. However, this is considered a challenging problem in MR image denoising, owing to the trade-off problem between noise removal and preserving the significant features. To resolve this challenging task, the neutrosophic theory can be used, where neutrosophy is the root of neutrosophic logic that generalizes the classical/fuzzy set. In addition, it is considered the base of the neutrosophic probability that generalizes the classical probability.

Neutrosophy defines knowledge fuzziness and inaccuracy in the data, such as the images (Smarandache, 2003). For images, noise is considered a type of indeterminant information. Thus, the NS can be efficiently applied to noisy images during the denoising process to achieve superior performance. Therefore, in this chapter, new methodologies for denoising MR images based on the NS theory to realize a balance between noise reduction and structure conservation are discussed.

2 Noise in MR images

In MR image acquisition, the noise still pretentious the images' visual quality even if the MR scanners has endured remarkable developments in speed of acquisition, spatial resolution, and signal to noise ratio (SNR). Typically, an MRI contains varying noise amounts from different sources, such as the noise from the eddy currents, physiological processes, stochastic variation, and rigid/nonrigid body motion (Redpath, 1998; Zhu et al., 2009). The thermal noise is considered the major noise source in the MR images, and it is produced from the MR scanners that affects the scanned objects. Generally, the thermal noise's variance is considered the sum of the variance from stochastic processes that represent the electronics, coils in the MR scanners, and the patient's body (Macovski, 1996). These noise sources degrade the MR images' acquisition and the measurements from the acquired data. For example, tissue characteristics, the radio-frequency (RF) coil, pulse sequence, static field intensity, voxel size, and the receiver bandwidth all affect the SNR. As follows, the noise characteristics in MR images are introduced.

For a single coil acquisition during the MRI scanning process, the obtained raw data are complex numbers that denote the Fourier transform (FT) result on the magnetization scattering in a volumetric tissue at a specific time (Kuperman, 2000). These raw data are then converted into magnitude, phase, and frequency components using the inverse FT to characterize the morphological and physiological features of the region of interest in the scanned organ (Wright, 1997; Zhu et al., 2009). Consequently, in the k-space, the noise is presumed to have a Gaussian distribution with the same variance on real and imaginary components due to the FT linear and orthogonal properties (Edelstein, Bottomley, & Pfeifer, 1984; Gudbjartsson & Patz, 1995; Henkelman, 1985). Thus, the PDF (probability density function) changes for the acquired data. In the spatial domain, the data magnitude has a Rician model distribution, and the error between the intensity of the original and the measured data is called Rician noise (Gudbjartsson & Patz, 1995).

Typically, the complex Gaussian process is used to model the complex spatial MR data. Thus, this complex spatial signal can be formulated as:

$$C(X) = A(X) + n(\sigma_n^2) \tag{1}$$

where A represent the noiseless original signal and the complex uncorrelated Gaussian noise is $n(\sigma_n^2) = n_r(X; \sigma_n^2) + jn_i(X; \sigma_n^2)$ that has zero mean and σ_n^2 noise variance. Hence, the magnitude of the complex signal represents the Rician distributed envelope, which is given by (Aja-Fernandez, Tristan-Vega, & Alberola-Lopez, 2009; Gudbjartsson & Patz, 1995):

$$M(X) = \sqrt{\left| A(X) + n(\sigma_n^2) \right|^2} \tag{2}$$

Additionally, the PDF can be expressed as follows:

$$p_M(M|A, \sigma_n) = \frac{M}{\sigma_n^2} e^{-(M^2 + A^2)/2\sigma_n^2} I_0\left(\frac{AM}{\sigma_n^2}\right) u(M) \tag{3}$$

where $I_0(\cdot)$ represents the adapted zeroth-order Bessel function, $u(\cdot)$ the Heaviside step function, and M is a variable representing the MR magnitude. Typically, the Rician distribution in high SNR tends to be equivalent to a Gaussian distribution with $\sqrt{A^2 + \sigma_n^2}$ mean and σ_n^2 variance as follows:

$$p_M(M|A, \sigma_n) \approx \frac{1}{\sqrt{2\pi\sigma_n^2}} e^{-\left(M^2 - \sqrt{A^2 + \sigma_n^2}\right)/2\sigma_n^2} u(M) \tag{4}$$

However, with zero SNR in the image background, the Rician PDF can be represented as a Rayleigh distribution that has PDF that can be formulated as follows (Aja-Fernandez et al., 2009; Gudbjartsson & Patz, 1995):

$$p_M(M, \sigma_n) = \frac{M}{\sigma_n^2} e^{-\frac{M^2}{2\sigma_n^2}} u(M) \tag{5}$$

Generally, in the low SNR ranges, the Rician noise is problematic as it introduces a signal-dependent bias. During denoising the squared MR images, the bias remains as a constant term $2\sigma_n^2$, which can be removed easily (Manjon et al., 2008; Nowak, 1999) by subtracting the bias term from the noisy image as follows:

$$E(A^2) = E(M^2) - 2\sigma_n^2 \tag{6}$$

The postprocessing noise reduction techniques are applied to guarantee the high-quality MR image, which is of extreme importance in a more accurate diagnosis.

The noise-driven anisotropic diffusion filter for removing Rician noise from MR images was introduced by Krissian and Aja-Fernández (2009). In this filter, parameters are selected automatically from the estimated noise. The diffusion filter's convergence rate can be improved by combining the linear, planar, and volumetric components of the local image structure while conserving contours to guarantee an intuitive and robust filtering process. Zhang and Ma (2010) proposed the anisotropic coupled diffusion equation-based MR image denoising method. In the coupled partial diffusion equations, one equation consists of a diffusion direction controlling term (anisotropic diffusion term), the assurance of the correlation between the filtered image and the initial image (fidelity term), and controlling the diffusion speed of each pixel (diffusion gene). Therefore, this method offers acceptable noise reduction with detail protection ability in the denoised MR images.

Coupe, Yger, and Barillot (2006) proposed a three-dimensional (3D) MR image denoising method by using optimized (multithreading) implementation of the nonlocal mean (NLM) filter. The computational time of the filter is considerably decreased up to 50 times. They later extended this work with fully automated blockwise implementation of an NLM filter (Coupe et al., 2008) for denoising 3D MR images. This is achieved by tuning the smoothing parameter automatically; the NL means was computed by selecting the utmost significant voxels, blockwise implementation, and parallelized computation. By using this approach, the computational time is reduced up to 60 times compared to the original NLM filter. The dynamic nonlocal means (DNLM) denoising method was introduced by Gal et al. (2009) for denoising the dynamic contrast enhanced MR images. This method is implemented as a variation of the NLM algorithm by exploiting information redundancy in different volumes of images that are acquired at different time intervals. In 3D MR images, an improved NLM filter with preprocessing (PENLM) was proposed to remove the Rician noise by Liu, Udupa, Odhner, Hackney, and Moonis (2005). In this method, first, the squared magnitude image gets denoised by the NLM filter, and then bias deviation is removed by performing the unbiased correction. The weight of the NLM filter is considered based on the Gaussian-filtered image in order to decrease the noise disturbance. For 3D MR image denoising, Manjon, Coupe, Buades, Collins, and Robles (2012) introduced a denoising method that exploits the self-similarity and sparseness properties of the images. For denoising the same types of image, Coupe, Manjon, Robles, and Collins (2012) proposed an adaptive multiresolution of the blockwise nonlocal means filter. This filter uses the spatial and frequency information in the image to adapt the amount of denoising by using an adaptive soft wavelet coefficient mixing to enhance the NLM filter performance.

In all these MR image denoising methods, there are computational burdens due to the calculation complexity of the pixel/voxel weight. In this chapter, the NS-based MR image denoising method was used to achieve a balance between noise reduction and structure preservation with reduced computational complexity.

3 Neutrosophic set-based MR image denoising

For NS-based MR image denoising, the noisy MR image is transferred to the NS domain that is defined by true, indeterminacy, and false subsets, which are symbolized as $T, I,$ and $F,$ respectively. The entropy is used to measure its indeterminacy. In the present work, the filtering operator is performed on T and F to reduce the indeterminacy set and obtain the denoised image, as illustrated in Fig. 1.

In this chapter, three NS-based MR image denoising methods, including the NS of γ-median filtering (NS-median) (Mohan, Krishnaveni, & Guo, 2011), the NS of ω-Wiener filtering (NS-Wiener) (Mohan, Krishnaveni, & Guo, 2013a), and the nonlocal NS of ω-Wiener filtering (NLNS-Wiener) (Mohan, Krishnaveni, & Guo, 2013b), were introduced.

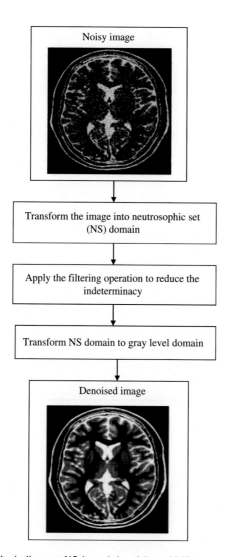

Fig. 1 General block diagram NS-based denoising of MR image.

3.1 Neutrosophic image

The noisy MR image is mapped into NS space, where the NS image H_{NS} is defined by T, I, and F. A pixel $H(a, b)$ in an image is mapped into the NS domain, $H_{NS}(a, b) = \{T(a, b), I(a, b), F(a, b)\}$, where $T(a, b)$, $I(a, b)$, and $F(a, b)$ are the true, indeterminate, and false sets, respectively (Guo, Cheng, & Zhang, 2009), which are represented for an image G as:

$$T(a, b) = \frac{\overline{G}(i, j) - \overline{G}_{\min}}{\overline{G}_{\max} - \overline{G}_{\min}} \qquad (7)$$

$$\overline{G}(a, b) = \frac{1}{w \times w} \sum_{x=a-w/2}^{a+w/2} \sum_{y=b-w/2}^{b+w/2} G(x, y) \qquad (8)$$

$$I(a, b) = \frac{\delta(a, b) - \delta_{\min}}{\delta_{\max} - \delta_{\min}} \qquad (9)$$

$$\delta(a, b) = abs\left(G(a, b) - \overline{G}(a, b)\right) \qquad (10)$$

$$F(a, b) = 1 - T(a, b) \qquad (11)$$

where the pixels in the window have $\overline{G}(a, b)$ local mean, and $\delta(a, b)$ denotes the absolute value of the difference between intensity $G(a, b)$ and its $\overline{G}(a, b)$.

For a gray-scale image, the entropy is calculated to assess the gray level distribution. Maximum entropy occurs when the intensities have equal probability with uniform distribution. Small entropy occurs with the intensities having different probabilities with nonuniform distribution. The entropy in the neutrosophic image is considered the totality of the T, I, and F entropies, which is used to measure the element distribution in the NS domain (Guo et al., 2009); that is expressed as:

$$En_{NS} = En_T + En_I + En_F \qquad (12)$$

$$En_T = -\sum_{k=\min\{T\}}^{\max\{T\}} p_T(k) \ln p_T(k) \qquad (13)$$

$$En_I = -\sum_{k=\min\{I\}}^{\max\{I\}} p_I(k) \ln p_I(k) \qquad (14)$$

$$En_F = -\sum_{k=\min\{T\}}^{\max\{F\}} p_F(k) \ln p_F(k) \qquad (15)$$

where the entropies are En_T, En_I, and En_F for T, I, and F respectively. Furthermore, the probabilities of the element k are $p_T(k)$, $p_I(k)$, and $p_F(k)$ in T, I, and F, respectively. The $I(a, b)$ value is engaged to calculate the indeterminacy of element $H_{NS}(a, b)$. To produce the correlated T and F with I, the changes in T and F effect the element distribution in I and the entropy of I. The general flowchart for NS-based denoising of MR images is shown in Fig. 2.

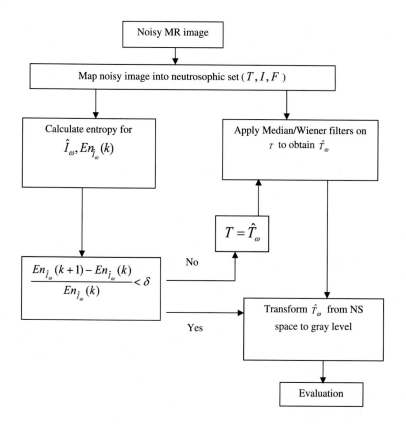

Noisy MR image

Map noisy image into neutrosophic set (T, I, F)

Calculate entropy for $\hat{I}_\omega, En_{\hat{I}_\omega}(k)$

Apply Median/Wiener filters on T to obtain $\hat{T}_\omega$

$T = \hat{T}_\omega$

$$\frac{En_{\hat{I}_\omega}(k+1) - En_{\hat{I}_\omega}(k)}{En_{\hat{I}_\omega}(k)} < \delta$$

No

Yes

Transform $\hat{T}_\omega$ from NS space to gray level

Evaluation

Fig. 2 General flowchart of NS approach for denoising MR images.

3.2   Neutrosophic set method of γ-median filtering

As discussed in the above section, the MR image is mapped into the T, I, and F sets. The $I(a, b)$ values are used to calculate the indeterminate of $H_{NS}(a, b)$. To generate the correlated set I with T and F, the variations in T and F effect the element spreading in I and change the entropy of I. A γ-median filter operator named $\hat{H}_{NS}(\gamma)$ is denoted as (Guo et al., 2009):

$$\hat{H}_{NS}(\gamma) = H\left(\hat{T}(\gamma), \hat{I}(\gamma), \hat{F}(\gamma)\right) \tag{16}$$

$$\hat{T}(\gamma) = \begin{cases} T & I < \gamma \\ \hat{T}_\gamma & I \geq \gamma \end{cases} \tag{17}$$

$$\hat{T}_\gamma(a, b) = \underset{(x, y) \in S_{a,b}}{\text{median}} \{T(x, y)\} \tag{18}$$

$$\hat{F}(\gamma) = \begin{cases} F & I < \gamma \\ \hat{F}_\gamma & I \geq \gamma \end{cases} \tag{19}$$

$$\hat{F}_\gamma(a, b) = \underset{(x, y) \in S_{a,b}}{\mathrm{median}} \{F(x, y)\} \tag{20}$$

$$\hat{I}_\gamma(a, b) = \frac{\delta_{\hat{T}}(a, b) - \delta_{\hat{T}_{\min}}}{\delta_{\hat{T}_{\max}} - \delta_{\hat{T}_{\min}}} \tag{21}$$

$$\delta_{\hat{T}}(a, b) = abs\left(\hat{T}(a, b) - \overline{\hat{T}}(a, b)\right) \tag{22}$$

$$\overline{\hat{T}}(a, b) = \frac{1}{w \times w} \sum_{x=a-w/2}^{a+w/2} \sum_{y=b-w/2}^{b+w/2} \hat{T}(x, y) \tag{23}$$

where at the location (a, b), the absolute value $\delta_{\hat{T}}(a, b)$ of the difference between the intensity $\hat{T}(a, b)$ and its local mean $\overline{\hat{T}}(a, b)$ after the γ-median filter operator is used.

For MR image denoising, the NS-based median filtering is listed as follows:

1. Map the MR image in the NS domain.
2. Apply the γ-median filter operator on T to obtain $\hat{T}_\gamma$.
3. Calculate the entropy of $\hat{I}_\gamma, En_{\hat{I}_\gamma}(k)$.
4. Go to step 5, if $\frac{En_{\hat{I}_\gamma}(k+1) - En_{\hat{I}_\gamma}(k)}{En_{\hat{I}_\gamma}(k)} < \delta$; Else $T = \hat{T}_\gamma$, go to 2.
5. Transform $\hat{T}_\gamma$ from the NS domain to the gray level.

There are two methods to improve the NS median MR image denoising method's performance (Mohan et al., 2011). One method is to apply the new filtering method instead of the median filter on T and F to reduce the indeterminacy. Hence, the NS Wiener technique is proposed for MR image denoising of uniformly distributed Rician noise (Mohan et al., 2013a). On the other side, in the second technique, the noisy MR image is prefiltered by using the NLM algorithm to reduce the noise before transforming the noisy image to the NS domain, and then the filtered image is used for further noise reduction in the NS domain. Hence, the NLNS Wiener technique is proposed for MR image denoising of uniformly distributed Rician noise (Mohan et al., 2013b).

3.3 Neutrosophic set method of ω-Wiener filter

Similar to the preceding methods, the MR image is converted first to the NS space as T, I, and F subsets. $I(a, b)$ is used to calculate the indeterminate degree of element $H_{NS}(a, b)$. A ω-Wiener filter operator for H_{NS}, $\hat{H}_{NS}(\omega)$ is expressed as:

$$\hat{H}_{NS}(\omega) = H\left(\hat{T}(\omega), \hat{I}(\omega), \hat{F}(\omega)\right) \tag{24}$$

$$\hat{T}(\omega) = \begin{cases} T & I < \omega \\ \hat{T}_\omega & I \geq \omega \end{cases} \tag{25}$$

$$\hat{T}_\omega(a, b) = \underset{(x, y) \in S_{a,b}}{\text{Wiener}} \{T(x, y)\} \tag{26}$$

$$\hat{F}(\omega) = \begin{cases} F & I < \omega \\ \hat{F}_\omega & I \geq \omega \end{cases} \tag{27}$$

$$\hat{F}_\omega(a, b) = \underset{(x, y) \in S_{a,b}}{\text{Wiener}} \{F(x, y)\} \tag{28}$$

$$\hat{I}_\omega(a, b) = \frac{\delta_{\hat{T}}(a, b) - \delta_{\hat{T}_{\min}}}{\delta_{\hat{T}_{\max}} - \delta_{\hat{T}_{\min}}} \tag{29}$$

$$\delta_{\hat{T}}(a, b) = abs\left(\hat{T}(a, b) - \overline{\hat{T}}(a, b)\right) \tag{30}$$

$$\overline{\hat{T}}(a, b) = \frac{1}{w \times w} \sum_{x=a-w/2}^{a+w/2} \sum_{y=b-w/2}^{b+w/2} \hat{T}(x, y) \tag{31}$$

where $\delta_{\hat{T}}(a, b)$ is the absolute number of the difference between the intensity $\hat{T}(a, b)$ and its local mean value $\overline{\hat{T}}(a, b)$ at (a, b) after the ω-Wiener filter operator.

The MR image NS-based denoising technique using the Wiener filter is given as:

1. Map the image in the NS domain.
2. Apply the ω-Wiener filter operator on T to obtain $\hat{T}_\omega$.
3. Calculate the entropy of $\hat{I}_\omega, En_{\hat{I}_\omega}(k)$.
4. Go to step 5, if $\frac{En_{\hat{I}_\omega}(k+1) - En_{\hat{I}_\omega}(k)}{En_{\hat{I}_\omega}(k)} < \delta$, else $T = \hat{T}_\omega$, go to Step 2.
5. Convert $\hat{T}_\omega$ from the NS back to the image domain.

3.4 Nonlocal neutrosophic set method of ω-Wiener filter

The noisy MR image is filtered by using the NLM algorithm to improve the denoising method performance. In this procedure, a nonlocal means (NLM) operation is applied. The NLM technique is used on the noisy MR images to produce a reference image. In the image, assume a noisy image $u = \{u(a) | a \in I\}$, thus by applying the nonlocal mean (Buades, Coll, & Morel, 2005), the estimated value $NL[u](a)$ for a pixel a can be calculated as a weighted average as follows:

$$NL[u](a) = \sum_{b \in I} w(a, b) u(b) \tag{32}$$

where the weights set $\{w(a, b)\}_b$ depends on the likeness between the pixels a and b, and fulfills the constraints $0 \le w(a, b) \le 1$ and $\sum_b w(a, b) = 1$. This similarity is related to the likeness of the intensity vectors $u(N_a)$ and $u(N_b)$, where N_c is the neighborhood centered at a pixel c. This similarity is calculated as a reducing function of the weighted Euclidean distance, $\|u(N_a) - u(N_b)\|_{2,\sigma}^2$, where $\sigma > 0$ is the Gaussian kernel's standard deviation. Using the Euclidean distance to the noisy neighborhoods increases the succeeding equality:

$$E\|u(N_a) - u(N_b)\|_{2,\sigma}^2 = \|u(N_a) - u(N_b)\|_{2,\sigma}^2 + 2\sigma^2 \tag{33}$$

After calculating the Euclidean distance between the vectors, the weight of the pixel is assigned as follows:

$$w(a, b) = \frac{1}{Z(a)} e^{-\frac{\|u(N_a) - u(N_b)\|_{2,\sigma}^2}{h^2}} \tag{34}$$

where $Z(a)$ is the normalization constant as:

$$Z(a) = \sum_b e^{-\frac{\|u(N_a) - u(N_b)\|_{2,\sigma}^2}{h^2}} \tag{35}$$

In addition, h is considered a filtering degree that controls the exponential function decay, and hence the weights decay is related to the Euclidean distances.

After prefiltering on the noisy MR image, the NLM prefiltered image is mapped to the NS domain, the entropy is computed, and a ω-Wiener filtering operation is performed on T and F in order to reduce the indeterminacy; hence, the noise is removed from the image. The Rician noise characteristics are adopted by estimating the σ of the noise from the noisy MR image using the local skewness estimation of the magnitude data distribution (Rajan, Poot, Juntu, & Sijbers, 2010). The bias is reduced by subtracting $2\sigma^2$ from the squared denoised image, as discussed by Nowak (Nowak, 1999). The summary of the NLNS-based Wiener filter MR image denoising is given by:

1. Apply the NLM algorithm to the noisy MR image.
2. Map the NLM filtered image in the NS domain.
3. Apply the ω-Wiener filter on the T to obtain T_ω.
4. Calculate the entropy of $\hat{I}_\omega, En_{\hat{I}_\omega}(k)$.
5. Go to step 6, if $\frac{En_{\hat{I}_\omega}(k+1) - En_{\hat{I}_\omega}(k)}{En_{\hat{I}_\omega}(k)} < \delta$, else $T = \hat{T}_\omega$, go to Step 3.
6. Convert $\hat{T}_\omega$ from the NS domain to the gray-level domain.

4 Performance evaluation metrics of NS-based denoising of MR image

The effectiveness of the denoising procedures can be evaluated using metrics used for assessing the MR image denoising method performance. For quantitative assessment, the PSNR, the mean absolute difference (MAD), the structural similarity (SSIM) index (Wang, Bovik, Sheikh, & Simoncell, 2004), and the Bhattacharyya coefficient (BC) (Bhattacharyya, 1943) are evaluated. Generally, PSNR is used as the quality measure because it can be simply calculated. But, according to Wang et al. (2004), another objective quality measure is the SSIM, which depends on the structural content of the image. The BC values depend on the image histogram that shows the similarity between the original and denoised images. MAD is used for measuring the dispersion of the data. Along with PSNR, SSIM, BC, and MAD are also adopted as quantitative metrics. According to Rajan et al. (2011), an MRI denoising method is effective and good when it gives a higher value of PSNR, SSIM, and BC and a lower value of MAD.

4.1 Peak signal-to-noise ratio

The PSNR is an independent quality that measures the estimated value deviation from the true value in decibels (dB). It can be measured as follows:

$$ \text{PSNR} = -10 \log \left[\frac{\sum_{a=0}^{H-1} \sum_{b=0}^{W-1} (S(a,b) - S_d(a,b))^2}{H \times W \times 255^2} \right] \qquad (36) $$

where $H \times W$ is the image's size, and $S(a,b)$, and $S_d(a,b)$ are the pixel (a,b) intensities in the original and denoised images, respectively.

4.2 Structural similarity index

The PSNR cannot be considered as optimal in terms of the perceived quality (Wang et al., 2004). However, the SSIM is considered an efficient alternative to improve the error measures, which is reliable to the visual perception. It measures the similarity in structure between the original and denoised images and is in [0, 1]. Let x and y be two nonnegative images, where one of them has perfect quality. Thus, the SSIM can be used to measure the similarity of the second image using the following formula:

$$\text{SSIM}(x, y) = \frac{\left(2\mu_x\mu_y + C_1\right)\left(2\sigma_{xy} + C_2\right)}{\left(\mu_x^2 + \mu_y^2 + C_1\right)\left(\sigma_x^2 + \sigma_y^2 + C_2\right)} \tag{37}$$

where C_1 and C_2 are constants, which can be given by $C_1 = (K_1 L)^2$, and $C_2 = (K_2 L)^2$ as K_1, $K_2 << 1$ is a small constant and L is the dynamic range of the pixel values. In addition, μ_x and μ_y are the estimated mean intensity, and σ_x and σ_y are the standard deviations, respectively, where σ_{xy} is given by:

$$\sigma_{xy} = \frac{1}{N-1} \sum_{i=1}^{N} (x_i - \mu_x)\left(y_i - \mu_y\right) \tag{38}$$

4.3 Bhattacharyya coefficient

The BC is a correlation metric that determines the statistical similarity between two images. It measures the closeness between two image histograms. The distances between the histogram of the denoised image and that of the original image are estimated by BC, which is given by (Bhattacharyya, 1943):

$$\text{BC}(m, n) = \sum_{x=0}^{255} \sqrt{m(x)n(x)} \tag{39}$$

where m and n are the two histograms. The range of BC is 0 to 1, where a closer BC value to 1 specifies similar histograms of m and n.

4.4 Mean absolute difference

The MAD is the absolute deviation mean value of a set of data about the data's mean. It is a better choice for measuring the dispersion of the data. The MAD for a dataset $\{x_i\}$ is calculated using the following expression:

$$\text{MAD}(\{x_i\}) = \text{mean}(|x_i - \text{mean}(\{x_i\})|) \tag{40}$$

4.5 Residual image

The residual image is obtained by deducting the denoised image from the noisy one (Manjon et al., 2008). It is calculated to prove the traces of anatomical information that are detached in the denoising process. Henceforth, it discloses the extreme smoothening and blurring of small details that exist in an image.

5 MRI dataset

The experiments are applied on two MRI datasets, namely a simulated MR Brainweb database (Kwan, Evans, & Pike, 1999) and a clinical dataset. The simulated MR image dataset consists of a T1/T2 weighted axial, a PD weighted axial, a T1/T2 weighted axial with a multiple sclerosis (MS) lesion, and a PD weighted axial with MS lesion volumes of $181 \times 217 \times 181$ voxels and a voxel resolution of $1\,\text{mm}^3$. They are degraded by different degrees of Rician noise (1%–15% of maximum intensity) (Manjon, Coupe, Marti-Bonmati, Collins, & Robles, 2010). The MS is a neurological disease that may be observed as small plates in the brain MR images. In the complex domain, the Rician noise is created from white Gaussian noise. First, the real and imaginary images are calculated as:

$$S_r(x_i) = S_0(x_i) + \eta_1(x_i), \eta_1(x_i) \sim N(0, \sigma) \tag{41}$$

$$S_i(x_i) = \eta_2(x_i), \eta_2(x_i) \sim N(0, \sigma) \tag{42}$$

where S_0 is the original image and σ is the standard deviation of the added white Gaussian noise. Thus, the noisy image can be considered as:

$$S_N(x_i) = \sqrt{S_r(x_i)^2 + S_i(x_i)^2} \tag{43}$$

The squared magnitude image has a signal independent noise bias that can be easily removed (Rajan et al., 2010). Another dataset includes a clinical MRI from the PSG Institute of Medical Sciences and Research (PSG IMS & R), Coimbatore, Tamilnadu, India. This dataset consists of more than 70 patients with different age groups; both male and female images were acquired using a Siemens Magnetom Avanto 1.5T Scanner. It contains T1 weighted and T2 weighted axials as well as coronal and sagittal images with 5 mm thickness and 512×512 pixels.

6 Results and discussion

The performance of the NS median, the NS Wiener, and the NLNS Wiener methods was compared with different standard procedures, such as the nonlocal maximum likelihood (NLML) method (He & Greenshields, 2009), the restricted local maximum likelihood (RLML) method (Rajan et al., 2011), the nonlocal mean

(NLM) filter (Buades et al., 2005), the total variation (TV) minimization scheme (Rudin, Osher, & Fatemi, 1992), the Wiener filter, and anisotropic diffusion (AD) (Perona & Malik, 1990). In the present chapter, the setting of the parameters of the NLML method is as follows: the window size $m=11$ and neighborhood size $n=3$ and $k=25$ (He & Greenshields, 2009). For the RLML filter, the neighborhood window size for denoising is assumed to be $7 \times 7 \times 3$ and the neighborhood size for local computation range $3 \times 3 \times 3$ (Rajan et al., 2011). For the NLM filter, there are three main parameters, namely the search window (w) size, the neighborhood window (f) size, and the filtering (h) degree. In this chapter, these parameter settings are chosen as $w=5$ and $f=2$ while h is proportional to the noise level of the image (Gal et al., 2009). For TV minimization, a range from 0.01 to 1 is used for the parameter λ with a step of 0.01, and the number of iterations varies from 1 to 10 (Coupe et al., 2008). In the AD filter, the used parameter K ranges from 0.05 to 1 with a step of 0.05 and the number of iterations from 1 to 15.

The PSNR, SSIM, BC, and MAD obtained for the T1 weighted MR images with different noise degrees (1%–15%) using the Wiener, TV, ADF, NLM, NLML, RLML, NS median, NS Wiener, and the NLNS Wiener denoising techniques are depicted in Fig. 3. From the PSNR value presented in Fig. 3A, it is clear that the NLNS Wiener filter produces good PSNR values compared with the Wiener, TV, ADF, NLM, NLML, RLML, NS median, and NS Wiener methods for all noise levels. The NLNS Wiener filter gives an average PSNR gain of 7.81, 7.01, 8.66, 6.15, 5.59, 5.06, 5.52, and 1.86 dB compared to Wiener, TV, ADF, NLM, NLML, RLML, NS median, and NS Wiener methods, respectively. In Fig. 3B, the SSIM value gives the similarity measures between the original image and the denoised image. Compared to the Wiener, TV, ADF, NLM, NLML, RLML, NS median, and NS Wiener methods, the SSIM value of the NLNS Wiener filter is measured an average of 5.12%, 4.48%, 3.57%, 3.42%, 3.06%, 2.02%, 1.36%, and 0.15% higher values, respectively, for all noise levels. This higher value of SSIM shows that the NLNS Wiener filter outperforms the other techniques.

The statistical similarity measure BC value is plotted in Fig. 3C. Compared to the Wiener, TV, ADF, NLM, NLML, RLML, NS median, and NS Wiener methods, the NLNS Wiener filter has produced an average of 6.97%, 6.6%, 7.3%, 5.8%, 3.8%, 3.22%, 3.1%, and 1.82% higher BC values, respectively. This higher value of BC ensures that the denoised image produced by the NLNS Wiener filter has strong correlation with the original image.

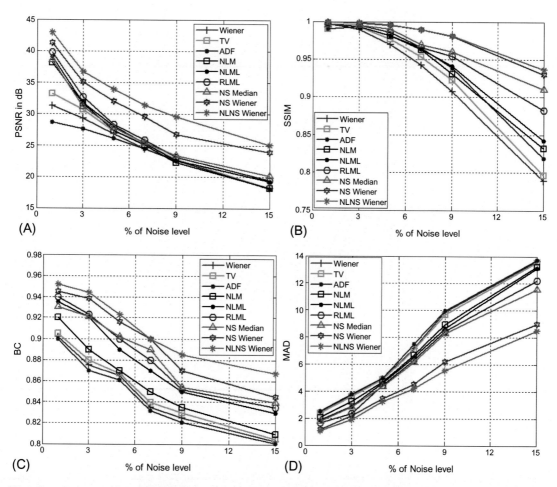

Fig. 3 Quantitative analysis of NLNS Wiener filter for T1 weighted Brainweb simulated MR images in terms of (A) PSNR, (B) SSIM, (C) BC, and (D) MAD for different levels of noise levels (1%–15%).

In Fig. 3D, the MAD value for different levels of noise is plotted. The MAD value for the NLNS Wiener filter is measured an average of 2.89, 2.81, 3, 2.4, 2.19, 1.82, 1.75, and 0.34 lower values, respectively, compared to the Wiener, TV, ADF, NLM, NLML, RLML, NS median, and NS Wiener methods. The lower value of MAD shows that the NLNS Wiener filter outperforms the other techniques.

The qualitative comparison of the NS median, NS Wiener, and NLNS Wiener methods on a pathological case is shown in Fig. 4. To enable visual analysis, the magnification of the part of the image is shown in Fig. 4. In this analysis, three continuous slices

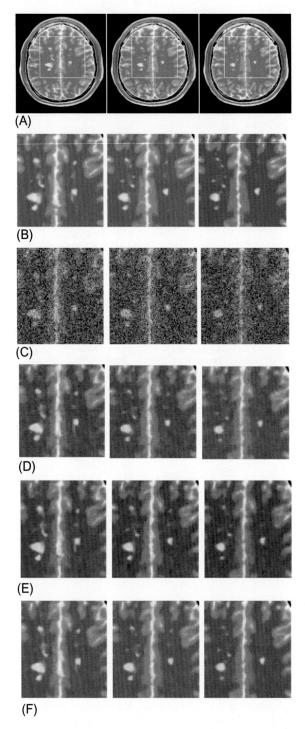

Fig. 4 Qualitative comparison of the denoising methods on simulated T2 weighted with MS lesion of slice numbers 104, 105, and 106: (A) Original images. To enable the visual analysis, the images are shown with magnification of the white rectangle region. (B) Part of the original image. (C) part of the noisy image with 15% of Rician noise. (D) denoised with NS Median method. (E) denoised with NS Wiener method. (F) denoised with NLNS Wiener method.

of T2 weighted MR images with MS lesions (slice numbers 104, 105, and 106) from the Brainweb database with 15% Rician noise are used. In Fig. 4A, the original images of the T2 weighted slices 104, 105, and 106 are shown. The magnified version of the original and noisy images with 15% Rician noise for the white rectangle marked region is shown in Fig. 4B and C. The denoised result of the NS median, NS Wiener, and NLNS Wiener methods are shown in Fig. 4D–F. From these images, it can be perceived that the NLNS Wiener method maintains visually better MS lesions compared to the NS median and NS Wiener methods.

Table 1 reports the comparison results using the different denoising techniques based on the quantitative parameters. Generally, the higher the values of PSNR, SSIM, and BC, the lower the value of MAD, showing the superiority of NS-based MR image denoising methods compared to the other denoising approaches.

In the clinical data, denoising results obtained for the T2 weighted Sagittal MR image of a normal brain with $TR = 4460$ ms, $TE = 85$ ms, 5 mm thickness, and 512×512 resolution are illustrated in Fig. 5. In Fig. 5A, the original image is shown. The denoised images of the Wiener, TV, ADF, and NLM methods are demonstrated in Fig. 5B–F, respectively. Moreover, the residual images are shown in Fig. 5C–J, respectively. From these images, it is clear that there are more traces of anatomical structures in the residual images. Even though the NLML and RLML methods produce good denoised images as shown in Fig. 5G and L, there are fewer traces of anatomical structures present in the residual images (Fig. 5K and P). The NS median, NS Wiener, and NLNS Wiener methods give detailed information and the edges in the denoised images are kept, as shown in Fig. 5M–O. While comparing the residual images as shown in Fig. 5Q–S, it is seen that the NLNS Wiener approach is superior to the NS median and NLNS Wiener methods.

In the Wiener, TV, ADF, NLM, NLML, and RLML methods for denoising MR images, the filtering operation is performed directly in the noisy MR image. In the NS-based MR image denoising methods, the noisy MR image is characterized by T, I, and F membership sets in the NS domain. The entropy of the NS evaluates the indeterminacy. The filtering operation has been performed on T and F to reduce the indeterminacy and the denoised image is obtained. Therefore, from the quantitative and qualitative evaluation of the MR image denoising methods on the Brainweb database and the clinical MRI dataset, it is clear that the NS-based MR image denoising methods such as NS median, NS Wiener, and NLNS Wiener outperform the other state-of-the-art studies, such as the Wiener, TV, ADF, NLM, NLML, and RLML methods.

Table 1 Performance of the NLNS Wiener filter compared to other denoising techniques on simulated MR images dataset.

MR image	Methods	PSNR (dB)	Metrics SSIM	BC	MAD
PD-weighted brain MRI with	Wiener	24.42	0.9427	0.835	7.2
MS lesions corrupted by 7% Rician noise	TV	24.54	0.9545	0.84	7.5
	ADF	25.37	0.9642	0.832	7.12
	NLM	25.36	0.9647	0.85	6.52
	NLML	26.52	0.9694	0.876	6.45
	RLML	26.62	0.9734	0.883	6.4
	NS Median	27.19	0.9787	0.89	6.18
	NS Wiener	29.5	0.9889	0.9	4.52
	NLNS Wiener	31.37	0.9895	0.902	4.18
T2 weighted brain MRI with MS	Wiener	22.12	0.8337	0.82	10.06
lesions corrupted by 9% Rician noise	TV	22.59	0.9345	0.809	9.92
	ADF	22.67	0.9466	0.816	10.09
	NLM	23.39	0.9495	0.823	8.86
	NLML	23.75	0.9512	0.835	8.73
	RLML	23.96	0.9594	0.843	8.36
	NS Median	24.4	0.9696	0.85	8.28
	NS Wiener	26.19	0.9887	0.86	6.39
	NLNS Wiener	27.24	0.9816	0.88	5.65
T1 weighted brain MRI with	Wiener	16.78	0.7870	0.808	13.71
MS lesions corrupted by 15% Rician noise	TV	16.82	0.7901	0.809	13.69
	ADF	16.84	0.8127	0.806	13.74
	NLM	16.88	0.8370	0.83	13.241
	NLML	18.96	0.8426	0.836	12.87
	RLML	19.22	0.8842	0.841	12.21
	NS Median	20.51	0.9062	0.846	11.657
	NS Wiener	23.53	0.9263	0.855	9.17
	NLNS Wiener	25.23	0.9284	0.867	8.65

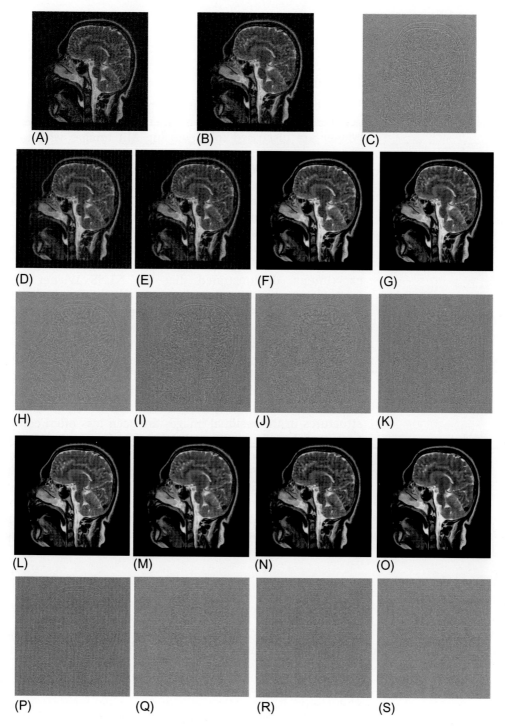

Fig. 5 Denoising results of clinical T2 weighted sagittal MRI: (A) Original image, (B) denoised with Wiener filter, (D) denoised with TV technique, (E) denoised with ADF technique, (F) denoised with NLM technique, (G) denoised with NLML technique, (L) denoised with RLML technique, (M) denoised with NS Median technique, (N) denoised with the NS Wiener technique, (O) denoised with the NLNS Wiener technique, (C), (H), (I), (J), (K), (P), (Q), (R), and (S) are the corresponding residual images.

7 Conclusions

In this chapter, the neutrosophic approach of MR image denoising methods such as NS median, NS Wiener, and NLNS Wiener are discussed for denoising MR images with uniform Rician noise. Numerous validations were performed with both synthetic and clinical MR images. The performances are analyzed based on the noise removal and structure preservation and compared with Wiener, TV, ADF, NLM, NLML, and RLML. For noise removal, the quantitative metrics such as PSNR, SSIM, BC, and MAD are used. As for the Wiener, TV, ADF, NLM, NLML, and RLML, the NS-based filters (NS median, NS Wiener, and NLNS Wiener) are able to restore images degraded by Rician noise. Also, experiments demonstrated that the NLNS Wiener filtering method can remove noise efficiently with different degrees of noise compared to the NS median filter and the NS Wiener filter.

Validation on the structure-preservation ability of the NS-based denoising methods is done by comparing the denoised image with its original noise-free image and by visual inspection of the residual image. It is found that the denoised image of the NLNS Wiener method has high correlation with the original image. And also, for high noise level, the traces of anatomical structures in the residual images are seen less often compared to that of the Wiener, TV, ADF, NLM, NLML, RLML, NS median, and NS Wiener methods. The preservation of the fine structural details such as pathological signatures is explained with the experimental results of T2 weighted MR images with MS lesions of three continuous slices (slices 104, 105, and 106). From the results, the NLNS Wiener technique displayed better performance over the NS median and NS Wiener methods in preserving the given pathology and removing the noise.

References

Aja-Fernandez, S., Tristan-Vega, A., & Alberola-Lopez, C. (2009). Noise estimation in single and multiple coil MR data based on statistical models. *Magnetic Resonance Imaging, 27*(10), 1397–1409.

Anand, C. S., & Sahambi, J. S. (2010). Wavelet domain non-linear filtering for MRI denoising. *Magnetic Resonance Imaging, 28*(6), 842–861.

Bhattacharyya, A. (1943). On a measure of divergence between two statistical populations defined by their probability distributions. *Bulletin of the Calcutta Mathematical Society, 35*, 99–109.

Buades, A., Coll, B., & Morel, J. M. (2005). A review of image denoising algorithms, with a new one. *Multiscale Modeling Simulation, 4*(2), 490–530.

Coupe, P., Manjon, J. V., Robles, M., & Collins, D. L. (2012). Adaptive multiresolution nonlocal means filter for 3D MR image denoising. *IET Image Processing, 6*, 558–568.

Coupe, P., Yger, P., Barillot, C., Larsen, R., Nielsen, M., & Sporring, J. (2006). Fast nonlocal means denoising for MR images. In: *Proceedings of the ninth international conference on medical image computing and computer-assisted intervention (MICCAI)* (pp. 33–40). Denmark: MICCAI.

Coupe, P., Yger, P., Prima, S., Hellier, P., Kervrann, C., & Barillot, C. (2008). An optimized blockwise nonlocal means denoising filter for 3-D magnetic resonance images. *IEEE Transactions on Medical Imaging, 27*(4), 425–441.

Edelstein, W. A., Bottomley, P. A., & Pfeifer, L. M. (1984). A signal-to-noise calibration procedure for NMR imaging systems. *Medical Physics, 11*(2), 180–185.

Gal, Y., Mehnert, A. J. H., Bradley, A. P., McMahon, K., Kennedy, D., & Crozier, S. (2009). Denoising of dynamic contrast-enhanced MR images using dynamic nonlocal means. *IEEE Transactions on Medical Imaging, 29*, 302–310.

Gudbjartsson, H., & Patz, S. (1995). The Rician distribution of noisy MRI data. *Magnetic Resonance in Medicine, 34*(6), 910–914.

Guo, Y., Cheng, H. D., & Zhang, Y. (2009). A new neutrosophic approach to image denoising. *New Mathemetics and Natural Computation, 5*(3), 653–662.

He, L., & Greenshields, I. R. (2009). A nonlocal maximum likelihood estimation method for Rician noise reduction in MR images. *IEEE Transactions on Medical Imaging, 28*(2), 165–172.

Henkelman, R. M. (1985). Measurement of signal intensities in the presence of noise in MR images. *Medical Physics, 12*(2), 232–233.

Krissian, K., & Aja-Fernández, S. (2009). Noise driven anisotropic diffusion filtering of MRI. *IEEE Transactions on Image Processing, 18*, 2265–2274.

Kuperman, V. (2000). *Magnetic resonance imaging physical principles and applications.* San Diego, USA: Academic Press.

Kwan, R. K., Evans, A. C., & Pike, G. B. (1999). MRI simulation based evaluation of image processing and classification methods. *IEEE Transactions on Medical Imaging, 18*(11), 1085–1097.

Liu, J., Udupa, J. K., Odhner, D., Hackney, D., & Moonis, G. (2005). A system for brain tumor volume estimation via MR imaging and fuzzy connectedness. *Computerized Medical Imaging and Graphics, 29*, 21–34.

Macovski, A. (1996). Noise in MRI. *Magnetic Resonance in Medicine, 36*(3), 494–497.

Manjon, J. V., Carbonell-Caballer, J., Lull, J. J., Garcia-Marti, G., Marti-Bonmati, L., & Robles, M. (2008). MRI denoising using non-local means. *Medical Image Analysis, 12*, 514–523.

Manjon, J. V., Coupe, P., Buades, A., Collins, D. L., & Robles, M. (2012). New methods for MRI denoising based on sparseness and self-similarity. *Medical Image Analysis, 16*, 18–27.

Manjon, J. V., Coupe, P., Marti-Bonmati, L., Collins, D. L., & Robles, M. (2010). Adaptive non-local means denoising of MR images with spatially varying noise levels. *Magnetic Resonance Imaging, 31*(1), 192–203.

Mohan, J., Krishnaveni, V., & Guo, Y. (2011). A neutrosophic approach of MRI denoising. In *Proceedings of the IEEE international conference on image information processing, Simla, India* (pp. 1–6).

Mohan, J., Krishnaveni, V., & Guo, Y. (2013a). A new neutrosophic approach of Wiener filtering for MRI denoising. *Measurement Science Review, 13*(4), 177–186.

Mohan, J., Krishnaveni, V., & Guo, Y. (2013b). MRI denoising using non local neutrosophic set approach of wiener filtering. *Biomedical Signal Processing and Control, 8*(6), 779–791.

Nowak, R. D. (1999). Wavelet-based Rician noise removal for magnetic resonance imaging. *IEEE Transaction on Image Processing, 8*(10), 1408–1419.

Perona, P., & Malik, J. (1990). Scale-space and edge detection using anisotropic diffusion. *IEEE Transactions on Pattern Analysis and Machine Intelligence, 12*(7), 629–639.

Rajan, J., Jeurissen, B., Verhoye, M., Audekerke, J. V., & Sijbers, J. (2011). Maximum likelihood estimation-based denoising of magnetic resonance images using restriced local neighborhoods. *Physics in Medicine and Biology, 56*(16), 5221–5234.

Rajan, J., Poot, D., Juntu, J., & Sijbers, J. (2010). Noise measurement from magnitude MRI using local estimates of variance and skewness. *Physics in Medicine and Biology, 55*(16), 441–449.

Redpath, T. W. (1998). Signal-to-noise ratio in MRI. *British Journal of Radiology, 71* (847), 704–707.

Rodriguez, A. O. (2004). Principles of magnetic resonance imaging. *Revista Mexicana De Fisica, 50*(3), 272–286.

Rudin, L. I., Osher, S., & Fatemi, E. (1992). Nonlinear total variation based noise removal algorithms. *Physica D: Nonlinear Phenomena, 60*(1-4), 259–268.

Rummeny, E. J., Reimer, P., & Heindel, W. (2009). *MR imaging of the body* (2nd ed.). Stuttgart, Germany: Thieme Publications.

Smarandache, F. (2003). A unifying field in logics neutrosophic logic. In *Neutrosophy. Neutrosophic set, neutrosophic probability.* (3rd ed.). Rehoboth: American Research Press.

Wang, Z., Bovik, A. C., Sheikh, H. R., & Simoncell, E. P. (2004). Image quality assessment: From error visibility to structural similarity. *IEEE Transactions on Image Processing, 13*(4), 600–612.

Wright, G. A. (1997). Magnetic resonance imaging. *IEEE Signal Processing Magazine, 14*(1), 56–66.

Zhang, F., & Ma, L. (2010). MRI denoising using the anisotropic coupled diffusion equations. In *Proceedings of the third international conference on Biomedical Engineering and Informatics* (pp. 397–401).

Zhu, H., Li, Y., Ibrahim, J. G., Shi, X., An, H., Chen, Y., Gao, W., Lin, W., Rowe, D. B., & Peterson, B. S. (2009). Regression models for identifying noise sources in magnetic resonance imaging. *Journal of the American Statistical Association, 104* (486), 623–637.

5

Advanced optimization-based neutrosophic sets for medical image denoising

Amira S. Ashour*, Yanhui Guo†

*Department of Electronics and Electrical Communications Engineering, Faculty of Engineering, Tanta University, Tanta, Egypt. †Department of Computer Science, University of Illinois at Springfield, Springfield, IL, United States

1   Introduction

Medical images are essential for the diagnosis of different diseases, such as skin lesions, brain tumors, bone fractures, abdominal diseases, and diabetic retinopathy. For each disease type, different modalities for medical imaging are used. Digital medical images have a vital role in healthcare, monitoring systems, technology, and several other applications, including microscopic imaging (Gaietta et al., 2002), dermoscopic imaging (Argenziano et al., 2008; Ashour, Guo, Kucukkulahli, Erdogmus, & Polat, 2018; Ashour, Hawas, Guo, & Wahba, 2018; Guo, Ashour, & Smarandache, 2018; Jaworek-Korjakowska & Kleczek, 2018; Kittler et al., 2006; Menzies et al., 2009; Menzies, Stevenson, Altamura, & Byth, 2011; Vesal, Patil, Ravikumar, & Maier, 2018; Wahba, Ashour, Napoleon, Elnaby, & Guo, 2017), X-ray imaging (Koyama et al., 2007), computed tomography (CT) (Hsieh, 2009), magnetic resonance imaging (MRI) (Rajinikanth, Dey, Satapathy, & Ashour, 2018; Tian, Dey, Ashour, McCauley, & Shi, 2017), ultrasound imaging (Cheng, Shan, Ju, Guo, & Zhang, 2010; Guo et al., 2002, 2006; Saba et al., 2016; Zeng, Wang, Yu, & Guo, 2013), video monitoring systems (Gowen, O'Donnell, Cullen, & Bell, 2008; Gowen, O'Donnell, Cullen, Downey, & Frias, 2007; Wang, Rose, & Chang, 2004), and geographical information systems (Jones, 2014). Each medical modality includes specific capturing procedures that introduce noise in the captured medical images. Thus, during the acquisition and processing of the images,

Neutrosophic Set in Medical Image Analysis. https://doi.org/10.1016/B978-0-12-818148-5.00005-9

different types of degradations occur such as blurring, noise, and low contrast, which affect the image quality due to the photometric and electronic sources in the image acquisition devices as well as during the acquisition procedure (Bovik, 2010; Davros, 2010; Dougherty, 2009; Gravel, Beaudoin, & De Guise, 2004; Krupinski et al., 2007; Nakroshis, Amoroso, Legere, & Smith, 2003; Patil & Jadhav, 2013; Russ, 2016). Typically, blurring occurs due to the optical capturing system or the relative motion between the object and camera, leading to imperfect image formation (Ji & Liu, 2008; Liang, Doermann, & Li, 2005; Park, Park, & Kang, 2003; Zilly, Kluger, & Kauff, 2011). Additionally, different noise types may corrupt the original image, causing a decrease in the visual quality of the digital image due to such random unwanted signals (Bankman, 2008; Lehmann, Gonner, & Spitzer, 1999; Vaseghi, 2008).

In the imaging process, the major noise sources include improper acquisition, imperfect instruments, interference, and transmission channel/medium effect. Also, misaligned lenses, scattering, cameras, and weak focal length in the image-capturing devices are considered noise sources. Image acquirement tools are application-specific, where they are different for different applications. Thus, the image acquisition process hosts different noise types that may destroy vital information in the image. For example, in telemedicine and telecommunication applications, medical images and the visual information are transmitted in digital image forms, respectively, through which the transmitted images are corrupted with noise. The presence of noise disturbs the original information within the image. Therefore, the received image requires preprocessing before any further use in applications. Noisy images have undesirable contrast and quality. Hereafter, noise removal is vital in the different image/medical image applications for enhancing the contrast and quality of the image for accurate diagnosis. This directed researchers to state noise models for different noise types, where it is challenging to remove noise from images without the preceding information of the noise model. Additionally, several studies were conducted to design efficient image denoising and restoration techniques (Akar, 2016; AksamIftikhar, Jalil, Rathore, & Hussain, 2014; Ashour et al., 2015; 2018; Dey et al., 2015; Dey, Ashour, Shi, & Balas, 2018; Gravel et al., 2004; Jakhete & Ingole, 2018; Jena, Patel, & Sinha, 2018; Nandi et al., 2015).

Image denoising techniques are essential in the preprocessing phase and further image-processing phases, including identification, segmentation, fusion, classification, and compression. Image denoising is a complex problem-based task, where different image types inherit different noise types such as Gaussian noise, impulse noise, Poisson noise, multiplicative noise, speckle noise, and salt and pepper noise (Mythili & Kavitha, 2011;

Rodríguez, 2013; Rodríguez, Rojas, & Wohlberg, 2012; Verma & Ali, 2013). Generally, denoising procedures range from low constancy methods, such as location invariant mean filtering (Motwani, Gadiya, Motwani, & Harris, 2004), to complex high-quality methods, including vector median filtering (Lukac, Smolka, Martin, Plataniotis, & Venetsanopoulos, 2005; Ng & Ma, 2006), nonlocal means filtering (Buades, Coll, & Morel, 2005; Coupé, Hellier, Kervrann, & Barillot, 2009; Manjón, Coupé, Martí-Bonmatí, Collins, & Robles, 2010), and wavelet-based filtering (Nowak, 1999; Portilla, Strela, Wainwright, & Simoncelli, 2003). For an instant, a nonlinear-median filter is efficient for impulse noise reduction (Hamza & Krim, 2001) while a statistics-based median filter (SBMF) removes salt and pepper noise (Chan, Ho, & Nikolova, 2005; Malviya & Ahmia, 2014). A vector median filter (VMF) and a median filter (MF) can be used for impulse noise reduction (Lukac et al., 2005). A Wiener filter, an averaging filter, and a sliding double window filter (SDWF) can be used efficiently for additive white Gaussian noise (AWGN) reduction (Dabov, Foi, Katkovnik, & Egiazarian, 2006; Ercelebi & Koc, 2006).

Recently, neutrosophic set theory has had a great impact on deducing the vagueness, ambiguity, fuzziness, and uncertainty (Broumi, Deli, & Smarandache, 2014; Broumi & Smarandache, 2013; Broumi, Smarandache, Talea, & Bakali, 2016; Nguyen, Ashour, & Dey, 2017; Smarandache, 2014; Ye, 2014). This attracts researchers to apply the neutrosophic set (NS) for image/medical image denoising as well as other image-processing phases (Cheng, Guo, & Zhang, 2011; Guo, Ashour, & Sun, 2017; Guo, Cheng, Tian, & Zhang, 2009; Guo, Cheng, & Zhang, 2009; Koundal, Gupta, & Singh, 2012; Mohan, Chandra, Krishnaveni, & Guo, 2012, 2013; Mohan, Krishnaveni, & Guo, 2012, 2013a, 2013b; Qi, Liu, & Xu, 2016; Sengur & Guo, 2011). Typically, an NS consists of three neutrosophic subsets: truth degree T, indeterminacy degree I, and false degree F. For image denoising using NS, the image is converted into the NS domain and a specific operator based on one of the traditional denoising filters is then used to decrease the image indeterminacy. Consequently, an indeterminacy filter can be employed to reduce the noise (Guo, Budak, Şengür, & Smarandache, 2017; Guo, Xia, Şengür, & Polat, 2017). However, such an NS and the indeterminacy filter include different key parameters that affect their performance. Hence, optimization procedures are widely used in several applications (Qasem & Shamsuddin, 2011; Samanta, Choudhury, Dey, Ashour, & Balas, 2017). Accordingly, in 2018, researchers proposed a procedure to optimize the main parameters in the NS during medical image processing (Ashour, Hawas, et al., 2018).

Because the denoising procedure is problem-based, it depends on the noise type that depends sequentially on the imaging device.

The current work plans to propose a novel denoising technique in dermoscopic images using an optimized indeterminacy filter (OIF). Gaussian noise and impulse noise are the most dominate noise types in dermoscopic images due to the existence of lesion regions of different contrasts, the presence of air bubbles, and hair. Furthermore, dermoscopy devices mainly either have an attached digital camera or a built-in camera. The captured images using such digital cameras endure quantization noise, thermal sensor noise, AWGN, and impulse noise due to the camera sensors. Accordingly, the most dominant noise type that corrupts dermoscopy images is the Gaussian noise, which corrupts images during the acquisition process. The AWGN is signal-independent, statistical noise that follows the Gaussian probability density (Foi, Trimeche, Katkovnik, & Egiazarian, 2008). Accordingly, in the present work, for denoising the dermoscopic images, the effect of electronic fluctuations and intrinsic thermal are resolved.

Consequently, in the proposed work, an OIF is used where the GA-based optimization is applied to define the optimal value of the filter size h. This optimized filter is used to reduce the previously added AWGN on the dermoscopy images to model the generated noise due to the dermoscopic digital camera. A comparative study is conducted to show the impact of the proposed denoising method in comparison to using traditional denoising methods such as the Wiener filter and median filter as well as the default IF without optimization.

The structure of the remaining sections includes the related studies in Section 2 and the methods of the proposed method in Section 3. In Section 4, the experimental results including the visualization of the NS steps as well as the comparative results of the proposed filter with a Wiener filter, a median filter, and the traditional IF without optimization are introduced with extensive discussion. Last, Section 5 reports the presented work's conclusion with suggested future work.

2   Related work

Medical images have a significant role for diagnosis and treatment plans. Each modality has its own procedure and protocol to acquire the image of a specific organ under investigation. Accordingly, based on the used modality (medical instrument), some artifacts and noise types may affect the acquired medical image. Typically, noise corrupts the acquired image during the acquisition process due to the imperfect instruments and/or the thermal effects and the sensors/electronic equipment in the medical device. It leads to variation in the signal as well as distortion in the acquired image, which affects the image quality. Noise corrupts the image because of light, the CCD camera, and sensors/detectors.

In medical applications, the degraded medical images caused by noise can be improved using filters to reduce/remove such noise. With the impact of neutrosophic theory, especially the NS to reduce uncertainty, recently researchers initiated the deployment of NS for medical image denoising. Guo, Cheng, and Zhang (2009) applied the NS into the image domain by defining the γ-median filtering operator for image denoising and decreasing the indeterminacy of T and F. The authors evaluated this new denoising filter on different types of noisy images of different noise types and noise levels.

In MR images, Mohan, Guo, Krishnaveni, and Jeganathan (2012) applied the NS approach of the Wiener filter to remove the Rician noise. The MRI image was transformed to the NS domain using T, I, and F. Then, in the neutrosophic image domain, the entropy was calculated to measure the indeterminacy. Finally, a ω-Wiener filter was used to reduce the indeterminacy in T and F for removing the Rician noise from the MR image. Mohan et al. (2013a) designed another filtering scheme for Rician noise removal from MR images using the nonlocal NS (NLNS) method of Wiener filtering. The NS was applied into the MR image domain with defining some operators for denoising using the nonlocal mean. Then, the produced image was mapped into the NS domain by defining the entropy of the NS to quantify the indeterminacy. The ω-Wiener filtering operation was used on T and F to reduce the indeterminacy and remove the noise.

However, no preceding work has employed the NS for dermoscopy image denoising. Because the dermoscopy device consists of a digital camera (attached or built-in), a nonpolarized light source, a magnifier, and a transparent plate along with gel (liquid medium) between the skin and instrument to reduce the skin surface reflections. The advanced dermoscopy device uses polarized light instead of gel (Silveira et al., 2009). These components of dermoscopy induce noise into the captured image, which can be modeled as Gaussian noise. In addition, several other artifacts negatively affect the image quality, such as the existence of hair, air bubbles, and illumination. Therefore, the NS is recommended in this work with the optimized IF for denoising the dermoscopic images.

3   Methodology of the proposed method

The AWGN is a basic noise model that mimics the random processes effect. It has the following characteristics: additive, as it can be added to any intrinsic noise; white, due to its uniform power distribution through the information frequency band; and normal distribution in the time domain with zero average value in the time domain value. Typically, the AWGN has probability density function with Gaussian distribution (Wio & Toral, 2004). Generally, denoising methods can be categorized into spatial and transform domain filtering (He, Sun, & Tang, 2013; Katkovnik, Foi, Egiazarian, & Astola, 2010; Motwani, Gadiya, Motwani, & Harris, 2004). In the current work, the indeterminacy filter (IF) is applied to the neutrosophic image.

3.1 Neutrosophic image

Recently, the neutrosophic set has had a significant role in delineating the uncertainty and indeterminacy in any information. In the NS, every event is defined using three components that express truth (T), indeterminacy (I), and falsity (F) degrees. These three subsets are used to produce the neutrosophic image O_{MNS} by mapping the input image into the NS domain. Hence, in the NS domain, a pixel $o(x,y)$ in the image is defined as, $O_{MNS}(x,y) = O(t,i,f) = \{T(x,y), I(x,y), F(x,y)\}$, which represents the memberships as true, indeterminate, and false subsets. Assume $K(x,y)$ and $\overline{K}(x,y)$ denote the intensity value of the pixel (x,y) and its corresponding local mean value. Therefore, the T and F neutrosophic subsets are stated as (Guo & Cheng, 2009):

$$T(x,y) = \frac{\overline{K}(x,y) - \overline{K}_{min}}{\overline{K}_{max} - \overline{K}_{min}} \tag{1}$$

$$F(x,y) = 1 - T(x,y) \tag{2}$$

Let $\xi(x,y)$ denote the absolute value of the difference between $K(x,y)$ and $\overline{K}(x,y)$, which can be expressed as follows:

$$\xi(x,y) = abs(K(x,y) - \overline{K}(x,y)) \tag{3}$$

Thus, the indeterminacy membership can be calculated using the following expression:

$$I(x,y) = \frac{\xi(x,y) - \xi_{min}}{\xi_{max} - \xi_{min}} \tag{4}$$

This membership measures the indeterminacy of O_{MNS}. Moreover, in the NS domain, the element distribution is expressed using the entropy of the NS image, which is the summation of the three subsets' entropies, namely E_T, E_I, and E_F as follows:

$$E_{NS} = E_T + E_I + E_F \tag{5}$$

$$E_T = - \sum_{i=\min\{T\}}^{\max\{T\}} p_T(i) \ln(p_T(i)), \tag{6}$$

$$E_I = - \sum_{i=\min\{I\}}^{\max\{I\}} p_I(i) \ln(p_I(i)), \tag{7}$$

$$E_F = - \sum_{i=\min\{F\}}^{\max\{F\}} p_F(i) \ln(p_F(i)) \tag{8}$$

where $p_T(i)$, $p_I(i)$, and $p_F(i)$ are the elements' probabilities in the three subsets T, F, and I, respectively. Afterward, the NS images are filtered using the optimized IF to diminish the indeterminacy information.

3.2 Optimized neutrosophic indeterminacy filtering

After mapping the dermoscopic noisy image into the NS domain, an IF is applied to reduce the uncertain noisy information on the NS. The IF is defined using the I subset to reduce the indeterminacy in the noisy images. This IF has a kernel function that can be defined as follows (Guo, Budak, et al., 2017):

$$W_I(a, b) = \frac{1}{2\pi\sigma_I^2} e^{-\frac{a^2 + b^2}{2\sigma_I^2(x, y)}} \tag{9}$$

In this kernel function, the local neighborhood has coordinate values a and b, where this kernel has window size h. Additionally, σ_I is the kernel function's standard deviation (SD), which is a linear function $f(.)$ related to the indeterminate degree $I(x, y)$ that is given by:

$$\sigma_I(x, y) = f(I(x, y)) = rI(x, y) + q \tag{10}$$

In the present work, the Gaussian distribution is defined, which is equivalent to $f(I(x,y))$. Also, r and q are controlling coefficients of the SD value in the linear function consistent with the indeterminacy value. These coefficients are used where, with a high indeterminate degree, the σ_I becomes large. Thus, the IF generates a smoothing process on the current pixel using its neighbors, whereas with a low indeterminate degree, the σ_I value is small and the IF generates less smoothing on the current pixel with its neighbors.

Subsequently, the filtered denoising result of the IF can be expressed as:

$$T'(x, y) = T(x, y) \oplus W_I(a, b) = \sum_{b=y-\frac{m}{2}}^{b+\frac{m}{2}} \sum_{a=x-\frac{m}{2}}^{a+\frac{m}{2}} T(x - a, y - b) W_I(a, b)$$

$$\tag{11}$$

In the present work, to improve the performance of the IF, the kernel (window) size h is optimized using the genetic algorithm.

3.3 Optimization using GA

The optimal value of the IF size is obtained using an efficient optimization algorithm, namely the GA (Maulik & Bandyopadhyay, 2000; Pal & Wang, 2017). Typically, the three main operations in the GA are selection, crossover, and mutation. The GA is originated based on the concept of the chromosomes, which are called populations in the optimization problem. These populations represent a set of solutions that are nominated to produce offspring (new solutions) based on their fitness. The new population is generated from solutions of one population. The new populations are then processed to find the best population that achieved the best fitness function (FF), where each time the superior population continues in the next evolution level. The main process of the optimization using GA is as follows in Algorithm 1.

3.4 Proposed denoising filter

In the present work, the preceding GA process is applied to find the optimal kernel size of the IF during the training step of the proposed OIF denoising filter. A fitness function (FF) is minimized to specify the optimal kernel size:

Algorithm 1 Genetic algorithm

Start
  Produce a random *number of* populations (solutions)
  Compute the FF of these solutions
  Generate a new solution by using the following operations:
      Select two parent chromosomes from the population based on their fitness
      Crossover the parents to generate new offspring
      Mutate new offspring
      Allocate new offspring
  Use the newly generated population for another iteration
      If the end limit (sopping criteria) achieved
  Stop and *specify* the pre-eminent solution
      End if
  Repeat the previous steps
End

$$FF = \frac{1}{Avr(PSNR)} \qquad (12)$$

where *PSNR* is the peak signal-to-noise ratio between the original and filtered images after using the OIF during the training phase, which is the most important metric to evaluate the denoising filter performance, and *Avr(.)* is an average operator to calculate the average value of the PSNR values on the dermoscopic images in the training dataset. Thus, Eq. (12) can be rewritten as:

$$FF = \frac{J}{\displaystyle\sum_{imgae=1}^{J} PSNR} \qquad (13)$$

where *J* is the number of images in the training dataset where the PSNR in dB is given by (Chen & Wu, 2001; Zhang & Karim, 2000):

$$PSNR = 10 \log_{10} \left(\frac{\displaystyle\sum_x \sum_y 255^2}{\displaystyle\sum_x \sum_y \left(g(x,y) - \widehat{g}(x,y) \right)^2} \right) \qquad (14)$$

where $g(x,y)$ and $\widehat{g}(x,y)$ represent the original image and filtered image using the OIF, respectively. By finding the optimal kernel size after achieving the best FF, the proposed OIF kernel function in Eq. (9) can be expressed as:

$$W_{I-optimized}(a_o, b_o) = \frac{1}{2\pi\sigma_I^2} e^{-\frac{a_o^2 + b_o^2}{2\sigma_I^2(x,y)}} \qquad (15)$$

where a_o and b_o are the optimal values of the local neighborhood coordinate values a and b, which are based on the optimal kernel size h_o. Accordingly, the OIF filtered results can be expressed as a modified version of Eq. (11) as follows:

$$
\begin{aligned}
T'_{Optimized}(x,y) &= T(x,y) \oplus W_{I-optimized}(a_o, b_o) \\
&= \sum_{b_o=y-\frac{m}{2}}^{b_o+\frac{m}{2}} \sum_{a_o=x-\frac{m}{2}}^{a_o+\frac{m}{2}} T(x-a_o, y-b_o) W_{I-optimized}(a_o, b_o)
\end{aligned}
$$

$$(16)$$

Thus, the steps of the proposed OIF for denoising are demonstrated in Algorithm 2 as follows.

Algorithm 2 Proposed optimized indeterminacy filter (OIF)-based denoising filter

Read original colored dermoscopy images

Convert the colored image to gray-scale

Add Gaussian noise to model the effect of the dermoscopy device during the acquisition process

Enhance/Restore the image the IF by using the following procedure:

<u>*Start 1*</u>: To find h_o

Training phase:

    Define the default IF parameters initially during the optimization as: $h_{default} = 5$, which is equivalent to $a = 5$ and $b = 5$
        as well as $\sigma_l = 1$ of the Gaussian filter within the IF

    Define the fitness function

    Map the dermoscopy noisy image on the NS domain by calculating the NS subsets T, I, and F

    Modify the image using the I subset to create the updated T using $h_{default}$

    Repeat the preceding three steps with applying the GA to find h_o using the predefined FF

    Save h_o

<u>*Stop 1*</u>

<u>*Start 2*</u>

Testing phase:

    Map the testing image on the NS set

    Filter the mapped image using OIF with its optimal kernel size h_o without further use of the GA

<u>*Stop 2*</u>

  End

---

4   Experimental results and discussion

In the present chapter, the ISIC (International Skin Imaging Collaboration) 2016 dermoscopy image dataset (https://challenge.kitware.com/) was used for evaluating the proposed OIF method. From this dataset, 20 randomly selected images are used to optimize the kernel size h in the IF for further use in the denoising process while 900 dermoscopic images were used for testing the proposed method using h_o. In the ISIC 2016 (https://challenge.kitware.com/#phase/5667455bcad3a56fac786791), to ensure totally noise-free dermoscopic images, we used these dermoscopic images after preprocessing as noise-free images, and then added synthetic/artificial Gaussian noise to simulate real-world dermoscopic images for evaluation.

4.1   Genetic algorithm for designing the OIF

The used parameters in the GA for optimizing h are as follows: 20 generations of five stall generation limit, 10 population size, and a fitness limit of $1e^{-4}$, where the average PSNR was used to calculate the FF. Fig. 1 shows that the GA converged to the best fitness after the six generations only.

On the 20 dermoscopic skin training images, Fig. 1 illustrated the best and mean fitness value where the mean fitness designates the average value of all FF output over one generation. Additionally, the best fitness was obtained by executing the GA over the 20 images in the training dataset. The results established that the GA converged at the sixth generation specifying h_o, where there was no further improvement in the FF value after the sixth generation. The experimental results showed that, before optimization, the default value of h was 5 as used in (Guo, Budak, et al., 2017; Guo, Xia, et al., 2017); however, the obtained optimal value is $h_o = 7$. Therefore, in the test phase, the optimal $h_o = 7$ of the IF was used in the design of the OIF for further use in the denoising process.

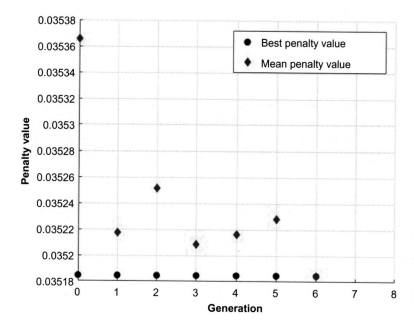

Fig. 1 Penalty value (i.e., fitness function value) versus the number of generations using 20 training images to find the optimal kernel size.

4.2 Optimized indeterminacy filter-based neutrosophic set

In the present work, the noisy dermoscopic images were mapped on the NS domain for further filtering using the optimized IF. Fig. 2 demonstrates an example of the dermoscopy images, namely the ISIC_0000395 image showing the original colored image, its gray-scale version, and the same image after adding the Gaussian noise to model the noise effect in the dermoscopy images.

Moreover, Fig. 3 illustrates the NS stages for the same ISIC_0000395 dermoscopic image, where the NS procedure is an iterative process.

Fig. 3 shows that the restored image after applying the iterative NS process and filtering with the proposed OIF was obtained after the fifth NS iteration, which visually has the same visualization of the original image without noise in Fig. 2B. These steps show that each time, the result of the T subset is updated using the I and F subsets. Finally, the best-filtered image is obtained after the fifth iteration.

4.3 Comparative study with other denoising filters

To evaluate the efficiency of the proposed OIF-based NS method for denoising the noisy dermoscopy images after adding Gaussian noise of zero mean value and 0.01 variance, other denoising filters are used, namely the median filter, the Wiener filter, and the NS-based IF with kernel size $h=5$. Fig. 4 shows the visual comparison of the output of using each of the involved filters in this comparative study.

Fig. 4 shows the visual superiority of the filtered images using the proposed method compared to the corresponding filtered images using the other filtering techniques, even with different

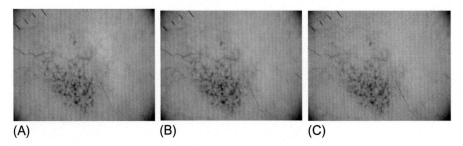

(A)　　　　　　　　(B)　　　　　　　　(C)

Fig. 2 ISIC_0000395 dermoscopic image: (A) original image, (B) gray-scale image, and (C) gray-scale image with AWGN noise.

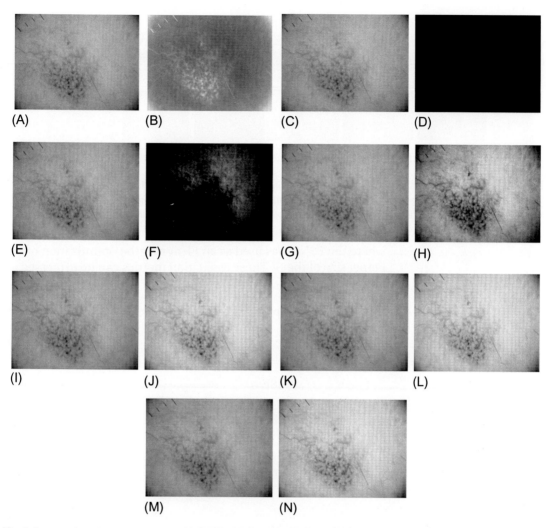

Fig. 3 Proposed method iterative steps: (A) initial T1, (B) initial F_1, (C) new image after applying filter of level 0, (D) new image after update by I and F on iteration 0, (E) new image after applying filter of level 1, (F) new image after update by I and F on iteration 1, (G) new image after applying filter of level 2, (H) new image after update by I and F on iteration 2, (I) new image after applying filter of level 3, (J) new image after update by I and F on iteration 3, (K) new image after applying filter of level 4, (L) new image after update by I and F on iteration 4, (M) new image after applying filter of level 5, and (N) new image after update by I and F on iteration 5 (final filtered image).

lesion color and/or size. Along with the visual comparative study of the proposed filter to other filters, different metrics were measured. These metrics are the mean absolute error (MAE), the mean squared error (MSE), the maximum absolute difference (MAX), the root of MSE (RMSE), and the signal-to-noise ratio (SNR),

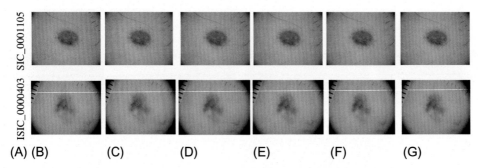

Fig. 4 (A) Image number in the ISIC2016 dataset, (B) original image, (C) noisy image after adding Gaussian noise, (D) filtered image using median filter, (E) filtered image using Wiener filter, (F) filtered image using IF-based NS with default kernel size of 5, and (G) filtered image using the proposed OIF-based NS filter of optimized kernel size of 7.

where the PSNR was used as an FF during the optimization of the kernel size of the IF. These evaluation metrics can be expressed as follows:

$$\text{MAE} = \frac{1}{X \times Y} \sum_x \sum_y \left| g(x,y) - \widehat{g}(x,y) \right| \qquad (17)$$

$$\text{MSE} = \frac{\sum_x \sum_y \left(g(x,y) - \widehat{g}(x,y) \right)^2}{X \times Y} \qquad (18)$$

$$\text{MAX} = \max \left(\left| g(x,y) - \widehat{g}(x,y) \right| \right) \qquad (19)$$

$$\text{SNR} = 10 \times \log_{10} \times \frac{\sum_x \sum_y \widehat{g}(x,y)^2}{\sum_x \sum_y \left(g(x,y) - \widehat{g}(x,y) \right)^2} \qquad (20)$$

In the present work, these metrics are calculated after using the OIF in the test images. The average values of the measured metrics are included in comparative studies using the IF without optimization, median filter, and Wiener filter. Table 1 reports the average of the evaluation metrics over the 900 images that were used as a test dataset in the present chapter, where the PSNR was used as the fitness function during the GA optimization of the kernel size on the training dataset.

The same results in Table 1 were illustrated in Fig. 5 as follows.

Table 1 along with Fig. 5 proved the superiority of the proposed denoising filter using the OIF-based NS. The proposed filter achieved the best maximum SNR and PSNR of values of 27.75

Table 1 Comparative study of the performance evaluation metrics.

Filter type	ISNR	SNR	PSNR	MSE	RMSE	MAE	MAX
Median	7.18	23.62	27.35	124.12	11.03	8.46	161.816
Wiener	7.43	23.87	27.59	113.43	10.65	8.12	97.40
IF-based NS using $h=5$ (default)	10.26	26.71	30.43	66.85	7.90	4.94	121.61
Proposed OIF-based NS $h_o=7$	7.79	27.75	31.47	57.86	7.18	3.52	128.27

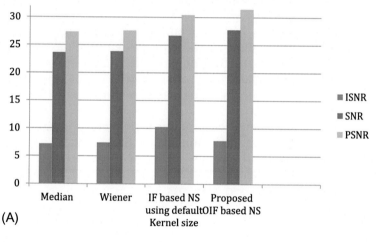

(A)

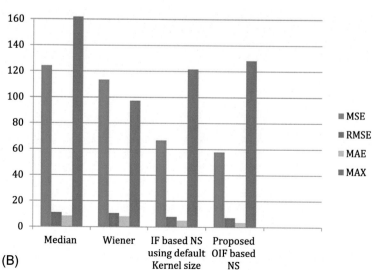

(B)

Fig. 5 Comparative study of the performance evaluation metrics.

and 31.47, respectively. Furthermore, it achieved the best minimum MSE and RMSE of values of 57.86 and 7.18, respectively.

5 Conclusions

In medical imaging, accurate disease analysis of medical images such as X-ray, CT, MRI, PET, dermoscopy, and microscopy is crucial, where the loss and/or distortion in the medical image may cause immense diagnostic errors. In medical image analysis, image denoising is a significant preprocessing stage to reconstruct accurately the original medical image from its noisy observation with the preservation of the imperative detailed features, including textures and edges. Because skin lesions are a dangerous disease that may lead to death, this chapter was interested to model the noise of the dermoscopy device from the captured dermoscopic image, and then enhance the quality of the dermoscopy images that suffer from Gaussian noise. Thus, the proposed optimized indeterminacy filter-based neutrosophic set was applied for denoising.

Consequently, in the current study, the noisy images were mapped on the NS domain for further filtering using the OIF. The optimal value of the kernel size in the IF was obtained using the GA. The results established the outstanding performance of the proposed OIF-based NS filter of $h_o = 7$ compared to the median, Wiener, and IF-based NS with $h = 5$ filters. The experimental results established the superiority of the OIF filter compared to the median, Wiener, and traditional IF without optimization. It realized the SNR, PSNR, MSE, and RMSE of values 27.75, 31.47, 57.86, and 7.18, respectively.

References

Akar, S. A. (2016). Determination of optimal parameters for bilateral filter in brain MR image denoising. *Applied Soft Computing, 43*, 87–96.

AksamIftikhar, M., Jalil, A., Rathore, S., & Hussain, M. (2014). Robust brain MRI denoising and segmentation using enhanced non-local means algorithm. *International Journal of Imaging Systems and Technology, 24*(1), 52–66.

Argenziano, G., Mordente, I., Ferrara, G., Sgambato, A., Annese, P., & Zalaudek, I. (2008). Dermoscopic monitoring of melanocytic skin lesions: Clinical outcome and patient compliance vary according to follow-up protocols. *British Journal of Dermatology, 159*(2), 331–336.

Ashour, A. S., Beagum, S., Dey, N., Ashour, A. S., Pistolla, D. S., Nguyen, G. N., & Shi, F. (2018). Light microscopy image de-noising using optimized LPA-ICI filter. *Neural Computing and Applications, 29*(12), 1517–1533.

Ashour, A. S., Guo, Y., Kucukkulahli, E., Erdogmus, P., & Polat, K. (2018). A hybrid dermoscopy images segmentation approach based on neutrosophic clustering and histogram estimation. *Applied Soft Computing, 69*, 426–434.

Ashour, A. S., Hawas, A. R., Guo, Y., & Wahba, M. A. (2018). A novel optimized neutrosophic k-means using genetic algorithm for skin lesion detection in dermoscopy images. *Signal, Image and Video Processing*, 1–8.

Ashour, A. S., Samanta, S., Dey, N., Kausar, N., Abdessalemkaraa, W. B., & Hassanien, A. E. (2015). Computed tomography image enhancement using cuckoo search: A log transform based approach. *Journal of Signal and Information Processing, 6*(03), 244.

Bankman, I. (Ed.), (2008). *Handbook of medical image processing and analysis*: Elsevier.

Bovik, A. C. (2010). *Handbook of image and video processing.* Academic Press.

Broumi, S., Deli, I., & Smarandache, F. (2014). Interval valued neutrosophic parameterized soft set theory and its decision making. *Neutrosophic Theory and Its Applications*, 410.

Broumi, S., & Smarandache, F. (2013). Correlation coefficient of interval neutrosophic set. In *Vol. 436. Applied mechanics and materials* (pp. 511–517): Trans Tech Publications.

Broumi, S., Smarandache, F., Talea, M., & Bakali, A. (2016). An introduction to bipolar single valued neutrosophic graph theory. In *Vol. 841. Applied mechanics and materials* (pp. 184–191): Trans Tech Publications.

Buades, A., Coll, B., & Morel, J. M. (2005). A non-local algorithm for image denoising. In *Vol. 2. IEEE computer society conference on computer vision and pattern recognition, 2005. CVPR 2005, 2*(pp. 60–65): IEEE.

Chan, R. H., Ho, C. W., & Nikolova, M. (2005). Salt-and-pepper noise removal by median-type noise detectors and detail-preserving regularization. *IEEE Transactions on Image Processing, 14*(10), 1479–1485.

Chen, T., & Wu, H. R. (2001). Space variant median filters for the restoration of impulse noise corrupted images. *IEEE Transactions on Circuits and Systems II: Analog and Digital Signal Processing, 48*(8), 784–789.

Cheng, H. D., Guo, Y., & Zhang, Y. (2011). A novel image segmentation approach based on neutrosophic set and improved fuzzy c-means algorithm. *New Mathematics and Natural Computation, 7*(01), 155–171.

Cheng, H. D., Shan, J., Ju, W., Guo, Y., & Zhang, L. (2010). Automated breast cancer detection and classification using ultrasound images: A survey. *Pattern recognition, 43*(1), 299–317.

Coupé, P., Hellier, P., Kervrann, C., & Barillot, C. (2009). Nonlocal means-based speckle filtering for ultrasound images. *IEEE Transactions on Image Processing, 18*(10), 2221–2229.

Dabov, K., Foi, A., Katkovnik, V., & Egiazarian, K. (2006). Image denoising with block-matching and 3D filtering. In *Vol. 6064.* In *Image processing: Algorithms and systems, neural networks, and machine learning*: International Society for Optics and Photonics.

Davros, W. (2010). Digital image processing for medical applications. *Medical Physics, 37*(2), 948–949.

Dey, N., Ashour, A. S., Beagum, S., Pistola, D. S., Gospodinov, M., Gospodinova, E. P., & Tavares, J. M. R. (2015). Parameter optimization for local polynomial approximation based intersection confidence interval filter using genetic algorithm: An application for brain MRI image de-noising. *Journal of Imaging, 1*(1), 60–84.

Dey, N., Ashour, A. S., Shi, F., & Balas, V. E. (2018). *Soft computing based medical image analysis.* Academic Press.

Dougherty, G. (2009). *Digital image processing for medical applications.* Cambridge University Press.

Ercelebi, E., & Koc, S. (2006). Lifting-based wavelet domain adaptive Wiener filter for image enhancement. *IEE Proceedings-Vision, Image and Signal Processing, 153*(1), 31–36.

Foi, A., Trimeche, M., Katkovnik, V., & Egiazarian, K. (2008). Practical Poissonian-Gaussian noise modeling and fitting for single-image raw-data. *IEE Transactions on Image Processing, 17*(10), 1737–1754.

Gaietta, G., Deerinck, T. J., Adams, S. R., Bouwer, J., Tour, O., Laird, D. W., … Ellisman, M. H. (2002). Multicolor and electron microscopic imaging of connexin trafficking. *Science, 296*(5567), 503–507.

Gowen, A. A., O'Donnell, C. P., Cullen, P. J., & Bell, S. E. J. (2008). Recent applications of chemical imaging to pharmaceutical process monitoring and quality control. *European Journal of Pharmaceutics and Biopharmaceutics, 69*(1), 10–22.

Gowen, A. A., O'Donnell, C., Cullen, P. J., Downey, G., & Frias, J. M. (2007). Hyperspectral imaging—An emerging process analytical tool for food quality and safety control. *Trends in Food Science & Technology, 18*(12), 590–598.

Gravel, P., Beaudoin, G., & De Guise, J. A. (2004). A method for modeling noise in medical images. *IEEE Transactions on Medical Imaging, 23*(10), 1221–1232.

Guo, Y., Ashour, A. S., & Smarandache, F. (2018). A novel skin lesion detection approach using neutrosophic clustering and adaptive region growing in dermoscopy images. *Symmetry, 10*(4), 119.

Guo, Y., Ashour, A. S., & Sun, B. (2017). A novel glomerular basement membrane segmentation using neutrsophic set and shearlet transform on microscopic images. *Health Information Science and Systems, 5*(1), 15.

Guo, Y., Budak, Ü., Şengür, A., & Smarandache, F. (2017). A retinal vessel detection approach based on shearlet transform and indeterminacy filtering on fundus images. *Symmetry, 9*(10), 235.

Guo, Y., Cai, Y. Q., Cai, Z. L., Gao, Y. G., An, N. Y., Ma, L., … Gao, J. H. (2002). Differentiation of clinically benign and malignant breast lesions using diffusion-weighted imaging. *Journal of Magnetic Resonance Imaging, 16*(2), 172–178.

Guo, Y., & Cheng, H. D. (2009). New neutrosophic approach to image segmentation. *Pattern Recognition, 42*(5), 587–595.

Guo, Y., Cheng, H. D., Huang, J., Tian, J., Zhao, W., Sun, L., & Su, Y. (2006). Breast ultrasound image enhancement using fuzzy logic. *Ultrasound in Medicine & Biology, 32*(2), 237–247.

Guo, Y., Cheng, H. D., Tian, J., & Zhang, Y. (2009). A novel approach to speckle reduction in ultrasound imaging. *Ultrasound in Medicine & Biology, 35*(4), 628–640.

Guo, Y., Cheng, H. D., & Zhang, Y. (2009). A new neutrosophic approach to image denoising. *New Mathematics and Natural Computation, 5*(03), 653–662.

Guo, Y., Xia, R., Şengür, A., & Polat, K. (2017). A novel image segmentation approach based on neutrosophic c-means clustering and indeterminacy filtering. *Neural Computing and Applications, 28*(10), 3009–3019.

Hamza, A. B., & Krim, H. (2001). Image denoising: A nonlinear robust statistical approach. *IEEE Transactions on Signal Processing, 49*(12), 3045–3054.

He, K., Sun, J., & Tang, X. (2013). Guided image filtering. *IEEE Transactions on Pattern Analysis & Machine Intelligence,* (6), 1397–1409.

Hsieh, J. (2009). *Computed tomography: Principles, design, artifacts, and recent advances.* Bellingham, WA: SPIE.

Jakhete, M. D., & Ingole, P. V. (2018). Survey of image de-noising on square structure and hexagonal structure. In *2018 International conference on advances in communication and computing technology (ICACCT)* (pp. 102–108): IEEE.

Jaworek-Korjakowska, J., & Kleczek, P. (2018). Region adjacency graph approach for acral melanocytic lesion segmentation. *Applied Sciences, 8*(9), 1430.

Jena, B., Patel, P., & Sinha, G. R. (2018). An efficient random valued impulse noise suppression technique using artificial neural network and non-local mean filter. *International Journal of Rough Sets and Data Analysis (IJRSDA), 5*(2), 148–163.

Ji, H., & Liu, C. (2008). Motion blur identification from image gradients. In *IEEE conference on computer vision and pattern recognition, 2008. CVPR 2008* (pp. 1–8): IEEE.

Jones, C. B. (2014). *Geographical information systems and computer cartography.* Routledge.

Katkovnik, V., Foi, A., Egiazarian, K., & Astola, J. (2010). From local kernel to non-local multiple-model image denoising. *International Journal of Computer Vision, 86*(1), 1.

Kittler, H., Guitera, P., Riedl, E., Avramidis, M., Teban, L., Fiebiger, M., ... Menzies, S. (2006). Identification of clinically featureless incipient melanoma using sequential dermoscopy imaging. *Archives of Dermatology, 142*(9), 1113–1119.

Koundal, D., Gupta, S., & Singh, S. (2012). Speckle reduction filter in neutrosophic domain. In *International conference of biomedical engineering and assisted technologies* (pp. 786–790).

Koyama, K., Tsunemi, H., Dotani, T., Bautz, M. W., Hayashida, K., Tsuru, T. G., ... Kissel, S. E. (2007). X-ray imaging spectrometer (XIS) on board Suzaku. *Publications of the Astronomical Society of Japan, 59*(Suppl. 1), S23–S33.

Krupinski, E. A., Williams, M. B., Andriole, K., Strauss, K. J., Applegate, K., Wyatt, M., ... Seibert, J. A. (2007). Digital radiography image quality: Image processing and display. *Journal of the American College of Radiology, 4*(6), 389–400.

Lehmann, T. M., Gonner, C., & Spitzer, K. (1999). Survey: Interpolation methods in medical image processing. *IEEE Transactions on Medical Imaging, 18*(11), 1049–1075.

Liang, J., Doermann, D., & Li, H. (2005). Camera-based analysis of text and documents: A survey. *International Journal of Document Analysis and Recognition (IJDAR), 7*(2–3), 84–104.

Lukac, R., Smolka, B., Martin, K., Plataniotis, K. N., & Venetsanopoulos, A. N. (2005). Vector filtering for color imaging. *IEEE Signal Processing Magazine, 22* (1), 74–86.

Malviya, S., & Ahmia, H. (2014). Image enhancement using improved mean filter at low and high noise density. *International Journal of Emerging Engineering Research and Technology, 2*(3), 45–52.

Manjón, J. V., Coupé, P., Martí-Bonmatí, L., Collins, D. L., & Robles, M. (2010). Adaptive non-local means denoising of MR images with spatially varying noise levels. *Journal of Magnetic Resonance Imaging, 31*(1), 192–203.

Maulik, U., & Bandyopadhyay, S. (2000). Genetic algorithm-based clustering technique. *Pattern Recognition, 33*(9), 1455–1465.

Menzies, S. W., Emery, J., Staples, M., Davies, S., McAvoy, B., Fletcher, J., ... Burton, R. C. (2009). Impact of dermoscopy and short-term sequential digital dermoscopy imaging for the management of pigmented lesions in primary care: A sequential intervention trial. *British Journal of Dermatology, 161*(6), 1270–1277.

Menzies, S. W., Stevenson, M. L., Altamura, D., & Byth, K. (2011). Variables predicting change in benign melanocytic nevi undergoing short-term dermoscopic imaging. *Archives of Dermatology, 147*(6), 655–659.

Mohan, J., Chandra, A. T. S., Krishnaveni, V., & Guo, Y. (2012). Evaluation of neutrosophic set approach filtering technique for image denoising. *The International Journal of Multimedia & Its Applications, 4*(4), 73.

Mohan, J., Chandra, A. T. S., Krishnaveni, V., & Guo, Y. (2013). Image denoising based on neutrosophic wiener filtering. In *Advances in computing and information technology* (pp. 861–869). Berlin, Heidelberg: Springer.

Mohan, J., Guo, Y., Krishnaveni, V., & Jeganathan, K. (2012). MRI denoising based on neutrosophic wiener filtering. In *IEEE international conference on imaging systems and techniques (IST), 2012* (pp. 327–331): IEEE.

Mohan, J., Krishnaveni, V., & Guo, Y. (2012). Performance analysis of neutrosophic set approach of median filtering for MRI denoising. *International Journal of Electrical & Communication Engineering & Technology, 3*, 148–163.

Mohan, J., Krishnaveni, V., & Guo, Y. (2013a). MRI denoising using nonlocal neutrosophic set approach of Wiener filtering. *Biomedical Signal Processing and Control, 8*(6), 779–791.

Mohan, J., Krishnaveni, V., & Guo, Y. (2013b). A new neutrosophic approach of Wiener filtering for MRI denoising. *Measurement Science Review, 13*(4), 177–186.

Motwani, M. C., Gadiya, M. C., Motwani, R. C., & Harris, F. C. (2004). Survey of image denoising techniques. In *Proceedings of GSPX* (pp. 27–30).

Mythili, C., & Kavitha, V. (2011). Efficient technique for color image noise reduction. *The Research Bulletin of Jordan, ACM, 1*(11), 41–44.

Nakroshis, P., Amoroso, M., Legere, J., & Smith, C. (2003). Measuring Boltzmann's constant using video microscopy of Brownian motion. *American Journal of Physics, 71*(6), 568–573.

Nandi, D., Ashour, A. S., Samanta, S., Chakraborty, S., Salem, M. A., & Dey, N. (2015). Principal component analysis in medical image processing: A study. *International Journal of Image Mining, 1*(1), 65–86.

Ng, P. E., & Ma, K. K. (2006). A switching median filter with boundary discriminative noise detection for extremely corrupted images. *IEEE Transactions on Image Processing, 15*(6), 1506–1516.

Nguyen, G. N., Ashour, A. S., & Dey, N. (2017). A survey of the state-of-the-arts on neutrosophic sets in biomedical diagnoses. *International Journal of Machine Learning and Cybernetics*, 1–13.

Nowak, R. D. (1999). Wavelet-based Rician noise removal for magnetic resonance imaging. *IEEE Transactions on Image Processing, 8*(10), 1408–1419.

Pal, S. K., & Wang, P. P. (2017). *Genetic algorithms for pattern recognition.* CRC Press.

Park, S. C., Park, M. K., & Kang, M. G. (2003). Super-resolution image reconstruction: A technical overview. *IEEE Signal Processing Magazine, 20*(3), 21–36.

Patil, J., & Jadhav, S. (2013). A comparative study of image denoising techniques. *International Journal of Innovative Research in Science, Engineering and Technology, 2*(3), 787–794.

Portilla, J., Strela, V., Wainwright, M. J., & Simoncelli, E. P. (2003). Image denoising using scale mixtures of Gaussians in the wavelet domain. *IEEE Transactions on Image Processing, 12*(11), 1338–1351.

Qasem, S. N., & Shamsuddin, S. M. (2011). Radial basis function network based on time variant multi-objective particle swarm optimization for medical diseases diagnosis. *Applied Soft Computing, 11*(1), 1427–1438.

Qi, X., Liu, B., & Xu, J. (2016). A neutrosophic filter for high-density salt and pepper noise based on pixel-wise adaptive smoothing parameter. *Journal of Visual Communication and Image Representation, 36*, 1–10.

Rajinikanth, V., Dey, N., Satapathy, S. C., & Ashour, A. S. (2018). An approach to examine magnetic resonance angiography based on Tsallis entropy and deformable snake model. *Future Generation Computer Systems, 85*, 160–172.

Rodríguez, P. (2013). Total variation regularization algorithms for images corrupted with different noise models: A review. *Journal of Electrical and Computer Engineering, 2013*, 10.

Rodríguez, P., Rojas, R., & Wohlberg, B. (2012). Mixed Gaussian-impulse noise image restoration via total variation. In *IEEE international conference on acoustics, speech and signal processing (ICASSP), 2012* (pp. 1077–1080): IEEE.

Russ, J. C. (2016). *The image processing handbook*. CRC Press.

Saba, L., Dey, N., Ashour, A. S., Samanta, S., Nath, S. S., Chakraborty, S., … Suri, J. S. (2016). Automated stratification of liver disease in ultrasound: An online accurate feature classification paradigm. *Computer Methods and Programs in Biomedicine, 130*, 118–134.

Samanta, S., Choudhury, A., Dey, N., Ashour, A. S., & Balas, V. E. (2017). Quantum-inspired evolutionary algorithm for scaling factor optimization during manifold medical information embedding. In *Quantum inspired computational intelligence* (pp. 285–326).

Sengur, A., & Guo, Y. (2011). Color texture image segmentation based on neutrosophic set and wavelet transformation. *Computer Vision and Image Understanding, 115*(8), 1134–1144.

Silveira, M., Nascimento, J. C., Marques, J. S., Marçal, A. R., Mendonça, T., Yamauchi, S., … Rozeira, J. (2009). Comparison of segmentation methods for melanoma diagnosis in dermoscopy images. *IEEE Journal of Selected Topics in Signal Processing, 3*(1), 35–45.

Smarandache, F. (2014). *Neutrosophic theory and its applications*. Vol. I. Collected Papers. Infinite Study.

Tian, Z., Dey, N., Ashour, A. S., McCauley, P., & Shi, F. (2017). Morphological segmenting and neighborhood pixel-based locality preserving projection on brain fMRI dataset for semantic feature extraction: An affective computing study. *Neural Computing and Applications*, 1–16.

Vaseghi, S. V. (2008). *Advanced digital signal processing and noise reduction*. John Wiley & Sons.

Verma, R., & Ali, J. (2013). A comparative study of various types of image noise and efficient noise removal techniques. *International Journal of Advanced Research in Computer Science and Software Engineering*, (10), 3.

Vesal, S., Patil, S. M., Ravikumar, N., & Maier, A. K. (2018). A multi-task framework for skin lesion detection and segmentation. In *OR 2.0 context-aware operating theaters, computer assisted robotic endoscopy, clinical image-based procedures, and skin image analysis* (pp. 285–293). Cham: Springer.

Wahba, M. A., Ashour, A. S., Napoleon, S. A., Elnaby, M. M. A., & Guo, Y. (2017). Combined empirical mode decomposition and texture features for skin lesion classification using quadratic support vector machine. *Health Information Science and Systems, 5*(1), 10.

Wang, C. H., Rose, J. T., & Chang, F. K. (2004). A synthetic time-reversal imaging method for structural health monitoring. *Smart Materials and Structures, 13*(2), 415.

Wio, H. S., & Toral, R. (2004). Effect of non-Gaussian noise sources in a noise-induced transition. *Physica D: Nonlinear Phenomena, 193*(1–4), 161–168.

Ye, J. (2014). Similarity measures between interval neutrosophic sets and their applications in multicriteria decision-making. *Journal of Intelligent & Fuzzy Systems, 26*(1), 165–172.

Zeng, X., Wang, Y., Yu, J., & Guo, Y. (2013). Correspondence-beam-domain eigenspace-based minimum variance beamformer for medical ultrasound imaging. *IEEE Transactions on Ultrasonics, Ferroelectrics, and Frequency Control, 60*(12), 2670–2676.

Zhang, S., & Karim, M. A. (2000). Restoration of impulse noise corrupted images based on gradients. In *4115. Applications of digital image processing XXIII* (pp. 727–734): International Society for Optics and Photonics.

Zilly, F., Kluger, J., & Kauff, P. (2011). Production rules for stereo acquisition. *Proceedings of the IEEE, 99*(4), 590–606.

6

Neutrosophic set-based denoising of optical coherence tomography images

A.I. Shahin*, Yanhui Guo†, Amira S. Ashour‡

*Department of Biomedical Engineering, Higher Technological Institute, 10th of Ramadan City, Egypt. †Department of Computer Science, University of Illinois at Springfield, Springfield, IL, United States. ‡Department of Electronics and Electrical Communications Engineering, Faculty of Engineering, Tanta University, Tanta, Egypt

1 Introduction

OCT imaging has a significant role to play in the diagnosis of different diseases inside the retina (Walter, Klein, Massin, & Erginay, 2002). The advancement in medical imaging technology has led to the development of different medical devices, including optical coherence tomography (OCT), for imaging the different parts of the human body. Computer-assisted tools help the physician in the diagnosis while saving time and increasing accuracy (Drexler & Fujimoto, 2008). Such medical devices are equipped with electronic components, light sources, and power sources, which are considered noise sources that affect the acquired medical image. The noise type depends on the medical modality used to capture the medical image. Accordingly, medical image denoising can have a large impact in suppressing the noise and enhancing the quality and contrast of the image for accurate diagnosis. However, the automated OCT analysis imaging methods suffer from the inherent noise (Fang et al., 2012). Typically, OCT images are usually interference with speckle noise that poses fluent challenges during the segmentation of the retinal segmentation (Chen et al., 2013). The existing blood vessels in the retina make retinal layer boundaries appear discontinuous inside the OCT images. In addition, the intensity variation and motion artifacts decrease

Neutrosophic Set in Medical Image Analysis. https://doi.org/10.1016/B978-0-12-818148-5.00006-0

OCT image quality. Thus, preprocessing plays a crucial role in OCT image analysis, which helps to overcome all previous drawbacks.

Typically, the dominant noise type that affects OCT images is speckle noise, which has different reduction techniques (Schmitt, Xiang, & Yung, 1999). The first speckle noise denoising method used hardware physical techniques. Nevertheless, such a method is complicated and expensive while requiring significant modifications in the design of the OCT system. The second speckle noise denoising method relied on a software framework based on filter design and diffusion-based approaches. Each denoising technique has its assumptions, advantages, and limitations. Recently, for algorithmic speckle noise compensation, denoising methods were designed, including linear filtering, nonlinear filtering, statistical model, wavelet-based strategies, and diffusion-based methods (Vijay, Saranya Devi, Shankaravadivu, & Santhanamari, 2012). Moreover, other artificial intelligent, fuzzy methods, neutrosophic based methods (Adabi et al., 2016; Aravindan, Seshasayanan, & Vishvaksenan, 2018) can be employed for speckle noise reduction. Because neutrosophic sets (NSs) have proven to be an excellent procedure for different image-processing tasks (Guo & Sengur, 2015; Guo, Xia, Şengür, & Polat, 2017), the present chapter employs NS for speckle noise reduction.

A novel neutrosophic based denoising method was proposed to eliminate speckle noise from OCT images. The proposed method was evaluated on a huge new dataset for OCT image denoising. This OCT dataset employed in the experiments contained healthy normal OCT images beside ones with three different diseases. We validate the proposed algorithm with several image quality parameters.

In the following sections, Section 2 reports the different literature studies on NSs with their applications in medical image analysis, and then Section 3 includes the proposed OCT image denoising technique. Finally, the results are followed by the conclusions of the proposed method as reported in Sections 4 and 5, respectively.

2 Related work

The visual quality of the OCT images is often corrupted by speckle noise during the acquisition process. Such noise is due to the natural sequence of limited light bandwidth due to the multiple scatters within the coherence length. Several studies were conducted for denoising the speckle noise in the OCT images (Aggarwal, Biswas, & Ansari, 2010; Aum, Kim, & Jeong, 2015; Cameron et al., 2013; Duan et al., 2016; Duan, Tench, Gottlob, Proudlock, & Bai, 2015; Li, Idoughi, Choudhury, & Heidrich, 2017; Puvanathasan & Bizheva, 2007; Salinas & Fernández, 2007; Smarandache, 2003; Wong, Mishra, Bizheva, & Clausi, 2010). Duan implemented a variational image decomposition procedure to concurrently denoise and segment the OCT images (Duan et al., 2015). Then, the same authors in Duan et al. (2016) designed a second-order total generalized variation decomposition model for noise removal from the OCT images. To validate their procedure, simulated OCT images were evaluated. Salinas and Fernández (2007) conducted a comparative study between two different speckle noise reduction techniques based on nonlinear diffusion filtering on the OCT of normal patients with a limited number of experiment samples. Wong et al. (2010) denoised OCT images using the Bayesian estimation approach; however, only two images were utilized to validate the algorithm. Cameron et al. (2013) implemented a denoising procedure for OCT images based on the stochastic speckle noise compensation method. However, only three images were used for validation through three kinds of OCT images, namely a healthy normal retina, a healthy human corneo-scleral limbus, and a human limbus with pinguecula. Aum et al. employed a nonlocal means (NLM) denoising method for OCT images, which accomplished the highest contrast-to-noise ratio (CNR) and peak signal-to-noise ratio (PSNR) compared to the median, bilateral, and Wiener (Aum et al., 2015). The NLM algorithm was examined only through limited healthy normal OCT images. Puvanathasan and Bizheva (2007) realized a fuzzy interval method for OCT image denoising. The fuzzy method was compared with Wiener filtering and it achieved the best PSNR values. The performance was evaluated though healthy limited OCT images. Li et al. (2017) proposed a local statistics of empirical spectral (LSES) denoising method for OCT images. The PSNR and CNR were measured to compare the LSES with other denoising methods in Duan et al. (2016), Salinas and Fernández (2007), and Wong et al. (2010).

NSs have recently been utilized to process uncertainty, inconsistency, and incompleteness in a single framework (Aggarwal et al., 2010; Smarandache, 2003; Sodenkamp, 2013). Smarandache introduced neutrosophy as one of the most interesting philosophy theories (Smarandache, 2010), which includes the nature and origin of neutralities (Tu, Ye, & Wang, 2018). In real-world applications, the nonstandard interval method has several applications

(Eisa, 2014; Leng & Shamsuddin, 2010; Ye, 2014a, 2014b; Yu, Niu, & Wang, 2013; Zhang, Wang, & Chen, 2014). Ye presented a simplified NS that is widely applied in different engineering applications (Ye, 2014a). The NS plays an important role in numerous medical image analysis systems and applications (Ye, 2014a). Typically, neutrosophy theory is considered the basis of neutrosophic logic, which identifies the indeterminacy to solve practical problems using a specific model called ⟨Neut-A⟩ (Zhang, Zhang, & Cheng, 2010). Intuitionistic fuzzy logic and neutrosophic logic commonly represent the indeterminacy percentage compared to all other logics (Ansari, Biswas, & Aggarwal, 2013; Smarandache, 2010). Recently, NS has been applied in decision-making problems under certain criteria (Biswas, Pramanik, & Giri, 2014; Broumi & Deli, 2015; Broumi & Smarandache, 2013; Chi & Liu, 2013; Hanafy, Salama, Khaled, & Mahfouz, 2014; Hanafy, Salama, & Mahfouz, 2012; Peng, Wang, & Yang, 2017; Peng, Wang, Zhang, & Chen, 2014; Tian, Zhang, Wang, Wang, & Chen, 2016; Ye, 2013a, 2013b; Zhang, Ji, Wang, & Chen, 2015; Zhang, Wang, & Chen, 2016). A similarity measurement between different NSs leads to more valuable information about these set intervals and their similarity degree through such sets (Ye, 2014c). Moreover, the neutrosophic similarity score (NSS) is a novel measurement defined in Guo and Şengür (2014), which was used in several applications such as image thresholding (Guo, Şengür, & Ye, 2014), edge detection (Guo et al., 2014), image segmentation (Guo, Şengür, & Tian, 2016), and image classification (Amin, Shahin, & Guo, 2016). Consequently, the neutrosophic systems outperform their fuzzy counterparts in several applications (Bhattacharyya, Dutta, & Chakraborty, 2015; Mohan, Krishnaveni, & Guo, 2014).

Generally, neutrosophic methods are considered indiscriminate sets, which can retain all the compulsory characteristics to encode the medical information. The NS independently described by three subsets, namely the truth, indeterminate, and false components, is suitable to reduce the effect of the artifacts and noise in the microscopic images. Several artifacts can affect the captured microscopic images due to the staining procedure, the imaging procedure including the effect of the charge-coupled device camera, and other noise sources (Bäck & Jacobsson, 2010; Chang, Sud, & Mycek, 2007; Tek, Dempster, & Kale, 2009).

In this chapter, we propose a novel denoising technique for OCT images based on NS combined with a Wiener filter. The proposed algorithm is validated through a large number of OCT images, which include normal and abnormal cases.

3 Proposed methodology

3.1 Neutrosophic process

In the NS, $J=\{J_1,J_2,\ldots,J_m\}$ is an alternatives set, where J_i is denoted by $\{T(J_i),I(J_i),F(J_i)\}/J_i$, as $T(J_i)$, $I(J_i)$, and $F(J_i)$, which are the true, indeterminate, and false subsets, respectively. An image is interpreted in the NS domain (Aggarwal et al., 2010) using these three subsets T, I, and F, where a pixel in I_{NS} is signified as $P_{NS}(T, I, F)$, where T represents the true subset in the bright pixel set, I the indeterminate subset, and F the false subset. Thus, a pixel $P(x,y)$ can be represented in the NS domain as $P_{NS}(x,y)=\{T(x,y),I(x,y),F(x,y)\}$, where $T(x,y)$, $I(x,y)$, and $F(x,y)$ represent the three membership subsets. At the intensity criterion, the three subsets on the gray scale image are defined as (Guo et al., 2014):

$$T_s(x,y)=\frac{g(x,y)-g_{\min}}{g_{\max}-g_{\min}} \tag{1}$$

$$I_s(x,y)=1-\frac{Gd(x,y)-Gd_{\min}}{Gd_{\max}-Gd_{\min}} \tag{2}$$

$$F_s(x,y)=1-T_s(x,y) \tag{3}$$

where at the position of (x, y), $g(x,y)$, and $Gd(x,y)$ represent the intensity and the gradient magnitude values, respectively. Also, G_d is the gradient value derived from the Sobel filter, $Gd_{\min}$ and $Gd_{\max}$ are the minimum/maximum of the gradient values in the image, and G_d is defined as:

$$G_d=\sqrt[2]{G_X^2+G_Y^2} \tag{4}$$

where G_X and G_Y are defined as:

$$G_x=\begin{bmatrix}-1&0&1\\-2&0&2\\-1&0&1\end{bmatrix}, \quad G_y=\begin{bmatrix}1&0&1\\0&0&0\\-1&-2&-1\end{bmatrix} \tag{5}$$

3.2 Neutrosophic c-means (NCM)

Moreover, the neutrosophic memberships can be calculated based on the global intensity distribution in images. Neutrosophic c-means clustering (NCM) is a novel clustering procedure on defining and handling indeterminacy on the images (Guo & Sengur, 2015). In the NCM procedure, an objective function and membership can be represented as (Guo et al., 2017):

$$J(T, I, F, C) = \sum_{i=1}^{N} \sum_{j=1}^{C} (\varpi_1 T_{ij})^m \|x_i - a_j\|^2 + \sum_{i=1}^{N} (\varpi_2 I_i)^m \|x_i - \overline{a}_{i\max}\|^2$$

(6)

$$\overline{a}_{i\max} = \frac{a_{p_i} + a_{q_i}}{2}$$
$$p_i = \arg\max_{j=1,2,\ldots,A} (T_{ij})$$
$$q_i = \arg\max_{j \neq p_i \cap j=1,2,\ldots,A} (T_{ij})$$

(7)

where m is a constant. $\overline{a}_{i\max}$ is calculated, when p_i and q_i are the cluster numbers C with the top and second top value of T, respectively. Also, δ is a controlling parameter and ϖ_i is a weight factor.

For minimizing the objective function, a Lagrange method is employed. According to the optimization result, membership functions are updated iteratively as:

$$T_{ij} = \frac{K}{\varpi_1} (x_i - a_j)^{-\frac{2}{m-1}}$$
$$I_i = \frac{K}{\varpi_2} (x_i - \overline{a}_i \max)^{-\frac{2}{m-1}}$$
$$K = \left[\frac{1}{\varpi_1} \sum_{j=1}^{A} (x_i - a_j)^{-\frac{2}{m-1}} + \frac{1}{\varpi_2} (x_i - \overline{a}_i \max)^{-\frac{2}{m-1}} \right]^{-1}$$

(8)

where $\overline{a}_i \max$ depends on the indexes of the largest and second largest values of T_{ij}. The iteration will not stop until $|T_{ij}^{(k+1)} - T_{ij}^{(k)}| < \varepsilon$, where ε is a termination criterion and k is the iteration step.

3.3 Indeterminacy filter

A filter is designed based on the indeterminate value to eliminate the indeterminacy's effect in the information. An indeterminacy filter based on the Wiener filter is represented by:

$$\hat{\text{Im}}(x, y) = \mu + \frac{\sigma^2 - \upsilon(x, y)^2}{\sigma^2} (\text{Im}(x, y) - \mu)$$

(9)

$$\mu = \frac{1}{N \times M} \sum_{(m, n) \in \eta} \text{Im}(m, n)$$

$$\sigma^2 = \frac{1}{N \times M} \sum_{(m, n) \in \eta} \left(\text{Im}^2(x, y) - \mu^2 \right)$$

$$\upsilon(x, y) = f(I(x, y)) = aI(x, y) + b$$

(10)

where μ is the N-by-M local neighborhood of each pixel in the image Im, and v is a linear function $f(\cdot)$ related to the indeterminate degree. Also, a and b are the parameters in the linear function to map the indeterminate degree to the filter's parameter value.

3.4 Proposed denoising method

In the current technique, the original image is filtered using indeterminacy filtering based on neutrosophic values that are input into the NCM procedure. Also, the indeterminacy filtering is taken again using the neutrosophic values from the NCM results. All steps can be summarized in Algorithm 1.

The block diagram of the offered procedure is illustrated in Fig. 1.

4 Experimental results and discussions

The experiments are conducted using a platform with an Intel core i7-4510 @2.50 GHZ with 4 GB RAM. The proposed method is implemented using MATLAB 2018a software. A rich dataset for deep learning training with a large number of OCT images was provided in Kermany et al. (2018) and used in the present work. The dataset contains 207,130 OCT images for four different classes, as follows: 108,312 images (37,206 with choroidal neovascularization (CNV), 11,349 with diabetic macular edema (DME), 8617 with Drusen, and 51,140 normal) from 4686 patients.

Algorithm 1 Proposed NS-based speckle noise reduction method

Start
    Compute the local neutrosophic value T_s and I_s
    Apply the indeterminate filter to filter T_s using based on I_s
    Employ the NCM on the filtered T_s subset to calculate T_n and I_n
    Apply the indeterminate filter to filter T_n based on I_n
    Map the T_n back to image domain
    Obtain the denoised OCT image
End

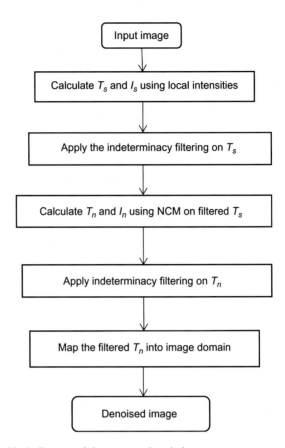

Fig. 1 The block diagram of the proposed technique.

The image quality assessment (IQA) metrics were developed to measure the image quality after enhancement procedures, such as color correction, deblurring, and denoising, which vary in the representation of the human visual system (HVS). Some of these IQAs that ignore the HVS are PSNR, CNR, mean square error (MSE), and absolute mean brightness error (Aum et al., 2015; Cameron et al., 2013; Li et al., 2017; Puvanathasan & Bizheva, 2007). On the other hand, other methods considered the HVS, including the information fidelity (VIF), the structural similarity index visual (SSIM), and the multiscale structural similarity index (Smarandache, 2003, 2010; Sodenkamp, 2013). In this work, both qualitative and quantitative measurements were considered. The quantitative metrics are based on PSNR, CNR, SSIM, MSE, and processing time.

4.1 Peak signal-to-noise ratio

The PSNR is one of the basic denoising metrics to validate the proposed algorithm. The higher the PSNR, the better the denoising technique is. PSNR can be given as:

$$\text{PSNR} = 10 \times \log \left(\frac{\sum (D^h - D^u)^2}{255^2} \right) \tag{11}$$

where D^h and D^u are ground truth and up sampled depth maps, respectively.

4.2 Contrast-to-noise ratio

The CNE is a useful metric that distinguishes between a region of background noise (reference) and an image feature (target), and can be expressed as:

$$\text{CNR} = 10 \times \log \left| \left(\frac{(\mu_t - \mu_r)}{\sqrt{(\sigma_t^2 + \sigma_r^2)}} \right) \right| \tag{12}$$

where μ_r and σ_r are the mean and standard deviation (SD) of the ground-truth area of an image, respectively, and μ_t and σ_t are the mean and SD of the target area of an image, respectively.

4.3 Mean square error

MSE depends on the image intensity scaling, so the enhancement algorithm should keep the output image near the original image. The lowest MSE value represents the best image quality.

$$\text{MSE} = \frac{1}{MN} \sum_{m=1}^{M} \sum_{n=1}^{N} \left[\hat{R}(m, n) - R(m, n) \right]^2 \tag{13}$$

where M and N are the height and width of an image, respectively, $\hat{R}$ is the processed image, and f is the ground-truth image. The lowest MSE value indicates the best denoising technique.

4.4 Structural similarity index

The SSI gives a similarity measurement between two different images. It is considered one of the most referenced quality metrics, and is related to the single-scale measurement that realizes its best performance when applied at an appropriate scale.

The highest SSIM indicates the best denoising technique. SSIM can be given as:

$$\text{SSIM} = \frac{\left(2\mu_x\mu_y + C1\right)\left(2\sigma_{xy} + C2\right)}{\left(\mu_x^2 + \mu_y^2 + C1\right)\left(\sigma_x^2 + \sigma_y^2 + C2\right)} \tag{14}$$

where μ_x and μ_y represent the estimated mean intensity of x and y, respectively. Also, the constants $C1$ and $C2$ have values of $C1 = (K_1 L)^2$ and $C2 = (K_2 L)^2$, where L is the pixels' dynamic range. Finally, σ_{xy} can be estimated as:

$$\sigma_{xy} = \frac{1}{N-1} \sum_{i=2}^{N} (x_i - \mu_x)\left(y_i - \mu_y\right). \tag{15}$$

4.5 Processing time

The required processing time to assess the proposed algorithm is very important to evaluate its performance. The OCT dataset has different image resolutions, which is important to be considered during measuring the algorithm efficiency. So, we investigate our proposed algorithm at different scales. We should keep the processing time reasonable compared with other previous denoising techniques.

In this chapter, the proposed algorithm is compared with previous denoising filtering techniques, such as total variation (TV), anisotropic diffusion filtering (ADF), NLM, and Wiener filtering. The parameter settings in each method are as follows: for ADF denoising, K ranging from 0.05 to 1, step $= 0.05$, and number of iterations $= 1–15$; for TV minimization, K ranging from 0.01 to 1, step $= 0.01$, and number of iterations $= 1–10$; for the NLM denoising technique, the size of the search window size ($w = 5$), the neighborhood window size ($f = 2$), and the degree the filtering (h), and for Wiener filtering, a filter window size $= 5$.

For each class in the given dataset, the proposed method performance was displayed compared to the previous denoising techniques. Fig. 2 illustrates a sample of the DME–OCT image before and after the denoising effect. Fig. 3 shows a sample of the CNV–OCT image before and after the denoising effect. Fig. 4 demonstrates a sample of the Drusen–OCT image before and after the denoising effect. Fig. 5 illustrates a sample of the normal OCT image before and after the denoising effect. The proposed algorithm reflects its superior performance compared with previous denoising techniques.

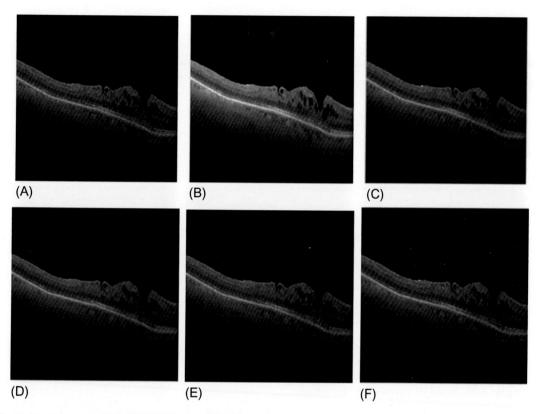

Fig. 2 Denoising results of DME–OCT image (A) original image, (B) TV method, (C) ADF method, (D) NLM method, (E) Wiener method, and (F) the proposed technique.

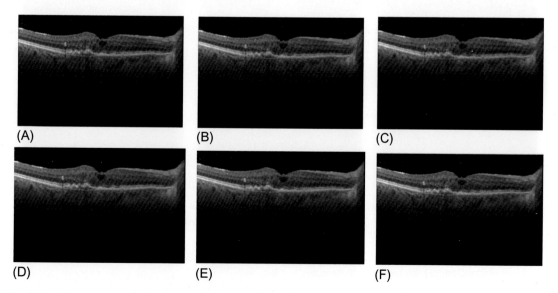

Fig. 3 Denoising results of CNV–OCT image (A) original image, (B) TV method, (C) ADF method, (D) NLM method, (E) Wiener method, and (F) the proposed technique.

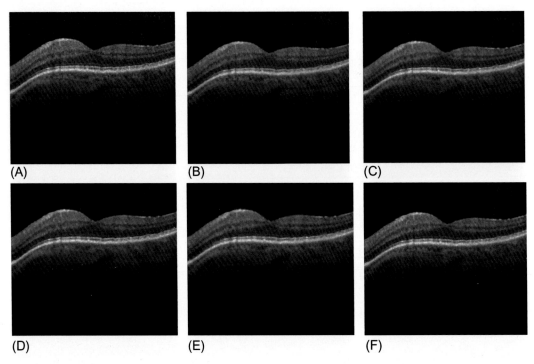

Fig. 4 Denoising results of Drusen–OCT image (A) original image, (B) TV method, (C) ADF method, (D) NLM method, (E) Wiener method, and (F) the proposed technique.

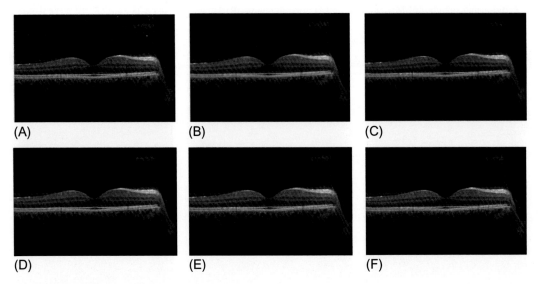

Fig. 5 Denoising results of normal OCT image (A) original image, (B) TV method, (C) ADF method, (D) NLM method, (E) Wiener method, and (F) the proposed technique.

The preceding visual images validate the superiority of the proposed algorithm. In addition, four quantitative metrics were measured: the PSNR, CNR, MSE, and SSIM. In addition, the proposed algorithm was evaluated using processing time compared with others in the literature. Fig. 6 reports the PSNR values of each class in the dataset separately.

Fig. 6 revealed that the proposed approach achieves the highest PSNR values for each class. On the other hand, the TV denoising method achieves the lowest PSNR values. The PSNR values of the NLM, Wiener, and ADF denoising techniques are intermediary, varying through different classes in the dataset. In Fig. 7, the CNR values of each dataset class are shown separately.

Fig. 7 shows that the proposed approach achieves the highest CNR values for each class. On the other hand, the CNR values of the TV, NLM, Wiener, and ADF denoising techniques vary through different classes in the dataset. Fig. 8 reports the MSE of the denoising techniques over the four classes.

Fig. 8 revealed that the TV method achieves the highest error with the different classes in the dataset. On the other hand, the proposed approach achieved the lowest error values with the different classes in the dataset. Fig. 9 shows the SSIM values of each dataset class separately.

Fig. 9 establishes the dominance of the proposed method to achieve the highest SSIM values for each class. On the other hand, the TV denoising method achieves the lowest SSIM values. The SSIM values of the NLM, Wiener, and ADF denoising techniques are intermediary, varying through different classes in the dataset. It is also noted that the variation of image quality parameters which utilized for proposed system evaluation between the

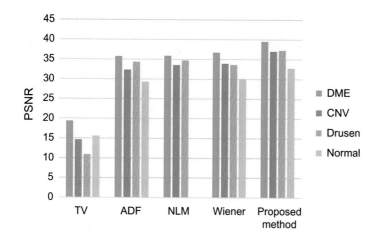

Fig. 6 Comparative evaluation based on PSNR values of the proposed approach for four different classes in the dataset.

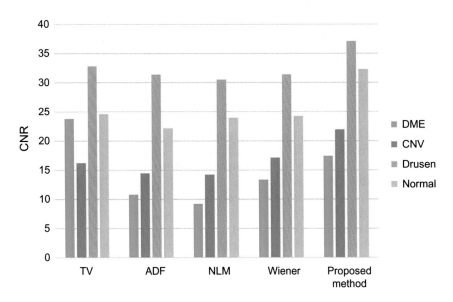

Fig. 7 Comparative evaluation based on CNR values of the proposed approach for four different classes in the dataset.

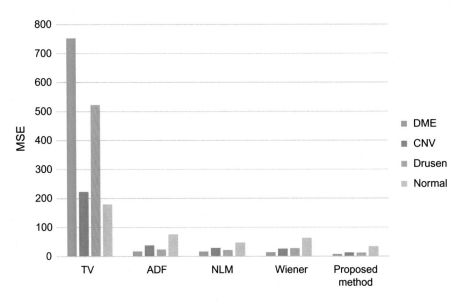

Fig. 8 Comparative evaluation based on MSE values of the proposed approach for four different classes in the dataset.

different OCT images classes. This means that it is important to validate OCT denoising algorithms through normal and abnormal OCT images. This relies on the change of OCT image structure and content due to the disease type. Moreover, Table 1 reports the

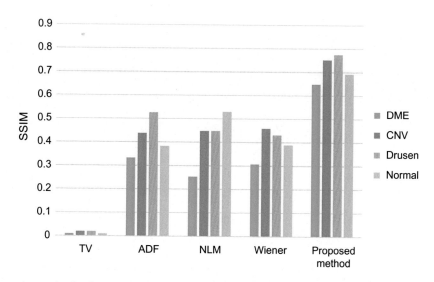

Fig. 9 Comparative evaluation based on SSIM values of the proposed approach for four different classes in the dataset.

mean and standard deviation (mean ± SD) values for all dataset images.

Table 1 shows that the proposed method has the capability to achieve the highest PSNR score (36.63615 ± 2.423). The NLM denoising technique achieved the second-highest PSNR score (34.7259 ± 0.963). The TV denoising technique achieves the lowest PSNR score (15.138025 ± 2.997). The proposed approach achieves the highest CNR score (27.19125 ± 7.851). The Wiener denoising

Table 1 The average mean ± SD of the evaluation metrics using the proposed technique compared to the others methods.

	TV	ADF	NLM	Wiener	Proposed method
PSNR	15.138025 ± 2.997	32.9337 ± 2.411	34.7259 ± 0.963	33.60465 ± 2.351	36.63615 ± 2.423
CNR	24.357075 ± 5.886	19.70788 ± 7.898	19.48093 ± 8.293	21.53228 ± 6.913	27.19125 ± 7.851
MSE	419.5 ± 233.659	38.80745 ± 22.713	28.73413 ± 11.708	32.9093 ± 18.519	16.682225 ± 10.383
SSIM	0.01 ± 0.0004	0.401475 ± 0.0714	0.47465 ± 0.1017	0.3928 ± 0.0571	0.7045375 ± 0.049

Table 2 Comparative results of the processing time in seconds.

| | Image size in pixels (width × height) | | | |
	208,896 pixels	253,952 pixels	262,144 pixels	380,928 pixels
TV	2.5109	3.1492	3.0055	4.8456
ADF	0.0133	0.0171	0.0194	0.028
NLM	61.7843	72.1451	76.442	116
Wiener	0.019	0.024	0.0264	0.0398
Proposed method	0.2498	0.219	0.245	0.358

technique achieves the second CNR score (34.7259 ± 0.963). The TV denoising technique achieves the second CNR score (24.357075 ± 5.886). It is also noticed converge of both (ADF and NLM) CNR scores, and they have also achieves the lowest CNR scores. The TV denoising technique achieves the highest error score (419.5 ± 233.659). In contrast, the proposed method realizes the lowest error scores (16.682225 ± 10.383). The proposed approach achieves the highest SSIM scores (0.7045375 ± 0.049). The NLM denoising technique achieved the second-highest SSIM score (0.47465 ± 0.1017). The TV denoising technique achieves the lowest SSIM scores (0.01 ± 0.0004).

Furthermore, Table 2 reports the comparison of the proposed method performance and other denoising approaches at different image resolutions in terms of the processing time.

Table 2 shows that the NLM method requires excessive processing time, which varies from 61.7843 to 116 s. On the other hand, the proposed approach requires a reasonable processing time that varies from 0.498 to 0.358 s. Sizes (from 300×500 to 500×1000) are used for testing the method efficiency. All approaches except TV denoising have computational time relative to the size of the image. The overall obtained results established the potential of the proposed technique.

5 Conclusion

For OCT image denoising, a comparative study of different techniques was conducted in the present work. The proposed method achieves an efficient performance for OCT image enhancement using the NSs. A novel OCT denoising technique based on the NS approach and Wiener filtering was proposed. The method is adapted to different OCT image classes with different resolutions. The OCT image is mapped in the NS using three membership sets: *T*, *I*, and *F*. In addition, the Wiener filter is applied to reduce the set's indetermination and to eliminate the noise from the OCT image.

The proposed algorithm was validated based on a comparison with the most common denoising techniques. The experimental results established that the OCT image denoising using the proposed method based on NS was enhanced efficiently. The proposed method achieved the highest PSNR, CNR, and SSIM scores with the lowest MSE scores. The processing time was more reasonable compared with other denoising methods. The proposed method is promising for other retinal image enhancements. In the future, it is decided to employ this process in the classification of OCT image classes.

References

Adabi, S., Conforto, S., Clayton, A., Podoleanu, A. G., Hojjat, A., & Avanaki, M. R. (2016, February). An intelligent speckle reduction algorithm for optical coherence tomography images. In: *4th international conference on photonics, optics and laser technology (PHOTOPTICS), 2016* (pp. 1–6): IEEE.

Aggarwal, S., Biswas, R., & Ansari, A. Q. (2010, September). Neutrosophic modeling and control. In: *International conference on computer and communication technology (ICCCT), 2010* (pp. 718–723): IEEE.

Amin, K. M., Shahin, A. I., & Guo, Y. (2016). A novel breast tumor classification algorithm using neutrosophic score features. *Measurement, 81*, 210–220.

Ansari, A. Q., Biswas, R., & Aggarwal, S. (2013, July). Extension to fuzzy logic representation: Moving towards neutrosophic logic-A new laboratory rat. In: *IEEE international conference on fuzzy systems (FUZZ), 2013* (pp. 1–8): IEEE.

Aravindan, T. E., Seshasayanan, R., & Vishvaksenan, K. S. (2018). Medical image denoising by using discrete wavelet transform: Neutrosophic theory new direction. *Cognitive Systems Research*.

Aum, J., Kim, J. H., & Jeong, J. (2015). Effective speckle noise suppression in optical coherence tomography images using nonlocal means denoising filter with double Gaussian anisotropic kernels. *Applied Optics, 54*(13), D43–D50.

Bäck, T., & Jacobsson, L. (2010). The α-camera: A quantitative digital autoradiography technique using a charge-coupled device for ex vivo high-resolution bioimaging of α-particles. *Journal of Nuclear Medicine, 51*(10), 1616–1623.

Bhattacharyya, S., Dutta, P., & Chakraborty, S. (Eds.), (2015). *Vol. 611. Hybrid soft computing approaches: Research and applications*: Springer.

Biswas, P., Pramanik, S., & Giri, B. C. (2014). A new methodology for neutrosophic multi-attribute decision making with unknown weight information. *Neutrosophic Sets and Systems, 3*, 42–52.

Broumi, S., & Deli, I. (2015). *Correlation measure for neutrosophic refined sets and its application in medical diagnosis*. Infinite Study.

Broumi, S., & Smarandache, F. (2013). Correlation coefficient of interval neutrosophic set. In *Vol. 436. Applied Mechanics and Materials* (pp. 511–517): Trans Tech Publications.

Cameron, A., Lui, D., Boroomand, A., Glaister, J., Wong, A., & Bizheva, K. (2013). Stochastic speckle noise compensation in optical coherence tomography using nonstationary spline-based speckle noise modelling. *Biomedical Optics Express, 4*(9), 1769–1785.

Chang, C. W., Sud, D., & Mycek, M. A. (2007). Fluorescence lifetime imaging microscopy. *Methods in Cell Biology, 81,* 495–524.

Chen, Q., Leng, T., Zheng, L., Kutzscher, L., Ma, J., de Sisternes, L.,et al. (2013). Automated Drusen segmentation and quantification in SD-OCT images. *Medical Image Analysis, 17*(8), 1058–1072.

Chi, P., & Liu, P. (2013). An extended TOPSIS method for the multiple attribute decision making problems based on interval neutrosophic set. *Neutrosophic Sets and Systems, 1*(1), 63–70.

Drexler, W., & Fujimoto, J. G. (2008). State-of-the-art retinal optical coherence tomography. *Progress in Retinal and Eye Research, 27*(1), 45–88.

Duan, J., Lu, W., Tench, C., Gottlob, I., Proudlock, F., Samani, N. N.,et al. (2016). Denoising optical coherence tomography using second order total generalized variation decomposition. *Biomedical Signal Processing and Control, 24,* 120–127.

Duan, J., Tench, C., Gottlob, I., Proudlock, F., & Bai, L. (2015). New variational image decomposition model for simultaneously denoising and segmenting optical coherence tomography images. *Physics in Medicine & Biology, 60*(22), 8901.

Eisa, M. (2014, June). A New Approach for Enhancing Image Retrieval using Neutrosophic Sets. *International Journal of Computer Applications, 95*(8), 12–20.

Fang, L., Li, S., Nie, Q., Izatt, J. A., Toth, C. A., & Farsiu, S. (2012). Sparsity based denoising of spectral domain optical coherence tomography images. *Biomedical Optics Express, 3*(5), 927–942.

Guo, Y., & Şengür, A. (2014). A novel image edge detection algorithm based on neutrosophic set. *Computers & Electrical Engineering, 40*(8), 3–25.

Guo, Y., & Sengur, A. (2015). NCM: Neutrosophic c-means clustering algorithm. *Pattern Recognition, 48*(8), 2710–2724.

Guo, Y., Şengür, A., & Tian, J. W. (2016). A novel breast ultrasound image segmentation algorithm based on neutrosophic similarity score and level set. *Computer Methods and Programs in Biomedicine, 123,* 43–53.

Guo, Y., Şengür, A., & Ye, J. (2014). A novel image thresholding algorithm based on neutrosophic similarity score. *Measurement, 58,* 175–186.

Guo, Y., Xia, R., Şengür, A., & Polat, K. (2017). A novel image segmentation approach based on neutrosophic c-means clustering and indeterminacy filtering. *Neural Computing and Applications, 28*(10), 3009–3019.

Hanafy, I. M., Salama, A. A., Khaled, O. M., & Mahfouz, K. M. (2014). Correlation of neutrosophic sets in probability spaces. *Journal of Applied Mathematics, Statistics and Informatics, 10*(1), 45–52.

Hanafy, I. M., Salama, A. A., & Mahfouz, K. (2012). Correlation of neutrosophic data. *International Refereed Journal of Engineering and Science (IRJES), 1*(2), 39–43.

Kermany, D. S., Goldbaum, M., Cai, W., Valentim, C. C. S., Liang, H., Baxter, S. L., et al. (2018). Identifying medical diagnoses and treatable diseases by image-based deep learning. *Cell, 172,* 1122–1131.

Leng, W. Y., & Shamsuddin, S. M. (2010). Writer identification for Chinese handwriting. *International Journal of Advances in Soft Computing and Its Applications, 2*(2), 142–173.

Li, M., Idoughi, R., Choudhury, B., & Heidrich, W. (2017). Statistical model for OCT image denoising. *Biomedical Optics Express, 8*(9), 3903–3917.

Mohan, J., Krishnaveni, V., & Guo, Y. (2014). A survey on the magnetic resonance image denoising methods. *Biomedical Signal Processing and Control, 9,* 56–69.

Peng, J. J., Wang, J. Q., & Yang, W. E. (2017). A multi-valued neutrosophic qualitative flexible approach based on likelihood for multi-criteria decision-making problems. *International Journal of Systems Science, 48*(2), 425–435.

Peng, J. J., Wang, J. Q., Zhang, H. Y., & Chen, X. H. (2014). An outranking approach for multi-criteria decision-making problems with simplified neutrosophic sets. *Applied Soft Computing, 25,* 336–346.

Puvanathasan, P., & Bizheva, K. (2007). Speckle noise reduction algorithm for optical coherence tomography based on interval type II fuzzy set. *Optics Express, 15*(24), 15747–15758.

Salinas, H. M., & Fernández, D. C. (2007). Comparison of PDE-based nonlinear diffusion approaches for image enhancement and denoising in optical coherence tomography. *IEEE Transactions on Medical Imaging, 26*(6), 761–771.

Schmitt, J. M., Xiang, S. H., & Yung, K. M. (1999). Speckle in optical coherence tomography. *Journal of Biomedical Optics, 4*(1), 95–105.

Smarandache, F. (Ed.), (2003). *A unifying field in logics: Neutrosophic logic. Neutrosophy, neutrosophic set, neutrosophic probability.* Infinite Study.

Smarandache, F. (2010). Neutrosophic set—A generalization of the intuitionistic fuzzy set. *Journal of Defense Resources Management, 1*(1), 107.

Sodenkamp, M. (2013). Models, methods and applications of group multiple-criteria decision analysis. *Operations Research, 181*(1), 393–421.

Tek, F. B., Dempster, A. G., & Kale, I. (2009). Computer vision for microscopy diagnosis of malaria. *Malaria Journal, 8*(1), 153.

Tian, Z. P., Zhang, H. Y., Wang, J., Wang, J. Q., & Chen, X. H. (2016). Multi-criteria decision-making method based on a cross-entropy with interval neutrosophic sets. *International Journal of Systems Science, 47*(15), 3598–3608.

Tu, A., Ye, J., & Wang, B. (2018). Symmetry measures of simplified neutrosophic sets for multiple attribute decision-making problems. *Symmetry, 10*(5), 144.

Vijay, M., Saranya Devi, L., Shankaravadivu, M., & Santhanamari, M. (2012). Image denoising based on adaptive spatial and wavelet thresholding methods. In *IEEE-international conference on advances in engineering, science and management (ICAESM-2012), March 30, 31, 2012* (p. 161).

Walter, T., Klein, J. C., Massin, P., & Erginay, A. (2002). A contribution of image processing to the diagnosis of diabetic retinopathy-detection of exudates in color fundus images of the human retina. *IEEE Transactions on Medical Imaging, 21*(10), 1236–1243.

Wong, A., Mishra, A., Bizheva, K., & Clausi, D. A. (2010). General Bayesian estimation for speckle noise reduction in optical coherence tomography retinal imagery. *Optics Express, 18*(8), 8338–8352.

Ye, J. (2013a). Another form of correlation coefficient between single valued neutrosophic sets and its multiple attribute decision-making method. *Neutrosophic Sets and Systems, 1*(1), 8–12.

Ye, J. (2013b). Multicriteria decision-making method using the correlation coefficient under single-valued neutrosophic environment. *International Journal of General Systems, 42*(4), 386–394.

Ye, J. (2014a). A multicriteria decision-making method using aggregation operators for simplified neutrosophic sets. *Journal of Intelligent & Fuzzy Systems, 26*(5), 2459–2466.

Ye, J. (2014b). Similarity measures between interval neutrosophic sets and their applications in multicriteria decision-making. *Journal of Intelligent & Fuzzy Systems, 26*(1), 165–172.

Ye, J. (2014c). Single valued neutrosophic cross-entropy for multicriteria decision making problems. *Applied Mathematical Modelling, 38*(3), 1170–1175.

Yu, B., Niu, Z., & Wang, L. (2013). Mean shift based clustering of neutrosophic domain for unsupervised constructions detection. *Optik—International Journal for Light and Electron Optics, 124*(21), 4697–4706.

Zhang, H. Y., Ji, P., Wang, J. Q., & Chen, X. H. (2015). An improved weighted correlation coefficient based on integrated weight for interval neutrosophic sets and its application in multi-criteria decision-making problems. *International Journal of Computational Intelligence Systems, 8*(6), 1027–1043.

Zhang, H. Y., Wang, J. Q., & Chen, X. H. (2014). Interval neutrosophic sets and their application in multicriteria decision making problems. *The Scientific World Journal, 2014.*

Zhang, H., Wang, J., & Chen, X. (2016). An outranking approach for multi-criteria decision-making problems with interval-valued neutrosophic sets. *Neural Computing and Applications, 27*(3), 615–627.

Zhang, M., Zhang, L., & Cheng, H. D. (2010). A neutrosophic approach to image segmentation based on watershed method. *Signal Processing, 90*(5), 1510–1517.

Further reading

Ye, J. (2014d). *Vector similarity measures of simplified neutrosophic sets and their application in multicriteria decision making.* Infinite Study.

Neutrosophic set in medical image clustering and segmentation

7

A survey on neutrosophic medical image segmentation

Abdulkadir Sengur*, Umit Budak[†], Yaman Akbulut[‡],
Murat Karabatak[§], Erkan Tanyildizi[§]

*Department of Electrical and Electronics Engineering, Technology Faculty, Firat University, Elazig, Turkey. [†]Electrical and Electronics Eng. Dept., Engineering Faculty, Bitlis Eren University, Bitlis, Turkey. [‡]Informatics Dept., Firat University, Elazig, Turkey. [§]Department of Software Engineering, Technology Faculty, Firat University, Elazig, Turkey

1 Introduction

Image segmentation, which is quite important for computer vision, is introduced as partitioning an image into its regions-based on some criteria where the regions are meaningful and disjoint (Cheng et al., 2001). Image segmentation is generally considered an intermediate step of some pattern-recognition applications (Comaniciu, Meer, & Member, 2002). Various image-segmentation approaches have been proposed (Akbulut et al., 2018; Chen et al., 2018; Das et al., 2019; Guo et al., 2018; Jain & Laxmi, 2018; Kumar et al., 2018; Turhan et al., 2018; Wang et al., 2018). These methods are broadly classified into three categories: threshold-, edge-, and region-based methods, respectively. The threshold-based image-segmentation approaches generally use the histogram of the input image to detect single or multiple thresholds (Naidu, Rajesh Kumar, & Chiranjeevi, 2018). Edge-based image segmentation techniques aim to detect the edges in an input image. Thus, segmentation is handled by determination of the region boundaries in the input image (Zhi & Shen, 2018). Region-based image segmentation techniques initially search for some seed points in the input image and proper region growing approaches are employed to reach the boundaries of the objects. Image segmentation is also important for some medical image applications (Yang et al., 2018). In medical image analysis, highly skilled physicians spend hours to determine some regions of medical images to indicate

Neutrosophic Set in Medical Image Analysis. https://doi.org/10.1016/B978-0-12-818148-5.00007-2

salient regions. This procedure can be handled in seconds with a proper image segmentation approach.

In the last decade, successful applications of neutrosophy in image segmentation have appeared in the medical environment. A neutrosophic set (NS) can be seen as the generalization of fuzzy sets (Smarandache, 2003). NS is different than fuzzy sets because it uses the indeterminacy set. More specifically, in NS theory, every event is symbolized with three membership degrees: truth, falsity, and indeterminacy. In another definition, in NS, an event A is represented by its neutrality Neut A and opposite Anti A.

In this chapter, we present a survey on neutrosophic medical image segmentation. A comprehensive literature review is presented on NS-based medical image segmentation approaches. The details of the approaches, the considered medical images, and the obtained performances are investigated in the literature review. We further detail the approaches and show some visual results. The limitations and prospective studies are also investigated. The literature review is presented in Section 2. NS-based medical image segmentation approaches are introduced and their results are presented in Section 3. In Section 4, the limitations and prospective studies are described. In Section 5, we give some conclusions.

2   Literature review

The NS theory was first introduced on image segmentation by the work of Guo and Cheng (2009). Guo et al. aimed to code the gray levels of an image in the context of NS theory. Each gray level was presented with NS triplets and the indeterminacy level was reduced by applying several operations such as alpha mean and beta enhancement. Actually, these operations aimed to reduce the noise level and enhance the contrast of the input image. Then, a modified k-means clustering algorithm was used for segmentation. In other words, the segmentation was achieved by pixel clustering. Authors used some gray-level images in their experiments and the results were evaluated visually. Later, Karabatak, Guo, and Sengur (2013) presented a modified version of the NS-based image segmentation approach and applied it on color image segmentation. As the proposal of Guo and Cheng (2009) suffers from oversegmentation and fixed α and β values, Karabatak et al. (2013) proposed a novel approach to alleviate such weaknesses. The authors used an entropy-based indeterminacy member calculation to fix the oversegmentation problem and an adaptive approach was performed on the α and β parameters. Then,

NS-based image segmentation attracted so many researchers from the image-processing domain, leading to dozens of studies about NS-based image segmentation being proposed so far (Akbulut et al., 2017; Gholami, Rashno, & Heshmati, 2016; Guo & Sengur, 2013; Guo & Sengur, 2015a; Guo & Sengur, 2015b; Guo & Sengur, 2015c; Guo & Şengür, 2013; Guo & Şengür, 2014; Guo, Şengür, & Tian, 2016; Jha et al., 2019; Otay & Kahraman, 2019; Sengur & Guo, 2011; Xu et al., 2018).

In the above paragraph, we briefly mentioned pioneering NS-based image segmentation studies and just cited other NS-based image segmentation approaches. So, NS-based medical image segmentation studies are reviewed in further paragraphs. Ali et al. (2018) proposed a neutrosophic orthogonal matrices-based clustering approach for image segmentation. The proposed approach initially transferred the input images into the NS domain and the inner products of the cutting matrix of the input image were calculated. Segmentation was then achieved by pixel clustering based on the orthogonal principle. The authors applied their method on a dental X-ray image dataset, which included 66 images. The authors obtained satisfactory results where the achievements were evaluated by cluster validity index values.

Ashour et al. (2018) proposed a novel image segmentation approach for dermoscopy images that was based on neutrosophic clustering and histogram estimation. The histogram estimation was used to obtain the exact number of clusters in the input image. The segmentation process was then carried out by the neutrosophic c-means clustering approach (Guo & Sengur, 2015b). The intensity and morphological features were considered in the clustering-based segmentation approach and the ISIC 2016 dermatology image dataset was used. The authors mentioned that the proposed method determined the lesion boundaries with 96.3% accuracy. Lee et al. (2018) used an NS-based approach for breast lesion segmentation in computed tomography (CT) images. The input CT images were initially converted to the neutrosophic domain and α-mean, β-enhancement, and γ-plateau operations were applied iteratively on the transferred image until the true membership value of the transferred image was no longer changed. Thus, the noises on CT images were eliminated. The RGI segmentation approach was then employed on noise-free CT images for lesion segmentation. A dataset that consisted of 122 breast lesions was used in the experiments and the average dice value was calculated for the performance evaluation metric. The presented dice value by the authors was 0.82.

Lotfollahi et al. (2018) proposed neutrosophy theory and an active contour model for breast ultrasound image segmentation.

The proposed approach considered the neutrosophy theory for reducing speckle noise and enhanced the tissue-related regions in the ultrasound images. The authors also improved the active contour models by integrating a weighted region-scalable Scheme. A total of 36 breast ultrasound images were used in the experiments and 95% true positives, 6% false positives, and 90% similarity scores were presented. Anter and Hassenian (2018b) proposed a CT liver tumor segmentation approach that was based on neutrosophic theory, the clustering approach, and watershed segmentation. The proposed approach initially applied various preprocessing methods to enhance the input CT images. The enhanced CT images were transformed into the NS domain and adaptive thresholding and morphological operators were employed for further enhancing the CT images in the NS domain. The watershed process with a connected component algorithm was used on the enhanced NS images for obtaining a postsegmentation. A fast fuzzy clustering approach was considered for final segmentation of the liver tumors. A total of 105 patients' CT slices were used in the experiments and six different indices were used to evaluate the segmentation results.

Lal, Kaur, and Gupta (2018a) proposed a neutrosophic clustering approach for tumor segmentation in B-mode breast ultrasound images. In the proposed scheme, initially the potential tumor regions were detected. Then, the desired tumor area was segmented based on the NS clustering approach that was based on the concept of information gain. The local neighborhood of each pixel was used for obtaining the information gain values. The membership values and the cluster centers were updated according to obtained values. Koundal, Gupta, and Singh (2018) proposed a fully automatic scheme for nodule segmentation in thyroid ultrasound images. The proposed approach employed an NS-based preprocessing stage for speckle reduction in thyroid ultrasound images. This process also preserved the important features that were used to determine the region of interest. The nodules were then segmented by the neutrosophic level-set method. Authors mentioned that their proposed segmentation method outperformed other methods by gaining a $95.92 \pm 3.70\%$ true positive (TP) rate. Lal, Kaur, and Gupta (2018b) developed a novel image segmentation technique that used the spatial neutrosophic clustering technique. The proposed technique extracted the boundary of tumors automatically in B-mode BUS images. The authors incorporated the spatial information into the neutrosophic ℓ-means (NLM) clustering and updated the membership values by using a type-2 membership function. A dataset that contained 60 BUS images was used in experiments and a boundary error metric was used as the performance evaluation criteria. The authors reported high performance compared with some existing methods.

Anter and Hassenian (2018a) developed an approach that was based on NS, optimization, and clustering theories. The authors used fast fuzzy *c*-means (FCM) and particle swarm optimization (PSO) for abdominal CT liver tumor detection. In the proposed approach, the NS was used to enhance the CT images by removing the speckle noise. Moreover, the CT images were further enhanced by removing both the high frequencies of the original images and the median filtering. The PSO was used to optimize the clustering and obtain the final segmentation of the tumors. The authors used the variance analysis, the Jaccard Index, and the dice coefficient to evaluate the segmentation results. The reported performance showed the efficiency of the proposed approach. Guo et al. (2017) proposed an efficient scheme for retinal vessel segmentation in color fundus images. The proposed method was based on the shearlet transform and NS-based indeterminacy filtering. Different from the other studies, in this work the shearlet transform was used to transfer the input fundus images into the NS domain. The indeterminacy filtering on the NS domain was used to enhance the input images. The authors used the neural network classifier for vessel pixel classification where the input features were obtained from neutrosophic images. Two publicly available datasets were used in the experimental studies and the receiver operating characteristic curve (ROC) and the area under the curve (AUC) were used for performance evaluation. The reported AUC values were 0.9476 and 0.9469 for each dataset, respectively.

Guo et al. (2013) improved a lung segmentation method with neutrosophic theory that was based on expectation maximization (EM) and binary morphological operations for pulmonary embolism detection in CT pulmonary angiography images. The developed scheme was based on an iterative NS approach. Anatomic features such as ribs and lungs were used in the initial segmentation and the segmentation was improved by using the iterative NS algorithm to obtain the final lung segmentation. In the experiments, five and 58 CT scans were used in training and test sets, respectively, and the obtained results were evaluated by various performance evaluation tests. The authors mentioned a clear improvement against the previous studies. Shan, Cheng, and Wang (2012) proposed a fully automatic breast tumor segmentation approach that was based on phase information and neutrosophic clustering. The authors initially employed preprocessing for denoising and contrast enhancement of the input CT images based on phase information, and then the region of interest was determined. After the quality of the input image was improved, the neutrosophic l-means clustering approach was used to determine tumor segmentation. The authors mentioned that the proposed neutrosophic l-means clustering approach was able to deal with uncertainty better than the other clustering approaches. Accuracy, efficiency, and sensitivity analysis were used for performance evaluation. According to the results, a true positive rate of 92.4% was presented by the authors.

Zhang (2010) proposed NS-based BUS image segmentation that was accurate, effective, and robust. The authors employed NS for developing a fully automatic algorithm. By integrating NS into their algorithm, the authors handled two conflicting opinions about speckles in ultrasound images. According to the authors, the proposed method highly improved the BUS segmentation where more accurate and robust segmentations were obtained. Xian, Cheng, and Zhang (2014) proposed an NS-based segmentation approach for BUS images. The authors developed the neutrosophic connectedness approach. The neutrosophic connectedness was used to characterize the uncertainty and indeterminacy of the spatial topological properties of the BUS images. A breast ultrasound database with 131 cases was used in experiments and the achievement was measured by similarity ratio, false positive ratio, and average Hausdroff error. The authors reported that the proposed method produced more accurate and robust segmentation than the compared methods. Gaber et al. (2015) proposed a two-phase approach for breast cancer segmentation and classification. The former phase was composed of NS-based image enhancement and fast fuzzy c-means-based clustering. The breast parenchyma regions in the thermogram images were segmented with a postsegmentation process. Support vector machines (SVM) were used for classification of breast parenchyma into normal or abnormal cases. Accuracy, precision, and recall were used for performance evaluation. The authors mentioned 100% accuracy in classification of the normal and abnormal cases.

Mohan, Krishnaveni, and Huo (2015) developed an approach for brain tumor segmentation that was based on neutrosophic c-means (NCM) clustering. The authors initially applied nonlocal NS-based Wiener filtering for image enhancement. A further fuzzy-based image enhancement was applied on the filtered images. The segmentation was achieved by the clustering enhanced image. Various evaluation metrics such as Jaccard similarity, dice coefficient, specificity, sensitivity, accuracy, false positive rate, and false negative rate were used and 100% segmentation was obtained for 20 test images. A hybrid approach was proposed by Sayed et al. (2016) for abdominal CT images. The developed approach was based on NS and the modified watershed algorithm. The authors initially used histogram equalization and median filtering to enhance the input CT images. After improving the CT images, neutrosophic memberships were calculated. The truth membership of the input CT image was used for further postprocessing. The liver region was segmented in the improved truth membership image by using the modified watershed algorithm. Performance evaluation was achieved by calculating the accuracy score and 95% overall accuracy was obtained. Alsmadi (2018) proposed an effective approach for jaw lesion segmentation in panoramic X-ray images. More specifically, a hybrid approach was considered by the author where fuzzy *c*-means and NS were used. The performance evaluation was carried out by calculating the area error metrics, specificity, sensitivity and similarity analyses. The author reported that the proposed method was successful in the detection of jaw lesions.

3 NS-based medical image segmentation methods

In this section, we explore several NS-based medical image segmentation approaches. Especially, the methodology and results are presented.

3.1 NSS and level set-based BUS image segmentation (Guo et al., 2016)

Factors such as speckle noise and poor quality of BUS images have greatly challenged researchers in medical image-processing applications. As a solution to this problem, NSS and level-set algorithms were used by Guo et al. (2016) for BUS image segmentation. The authors initially transferred the input images into the NS domain by using the equations that were introduced in Guo and Cheng (2009). The belongingness degree of the true tumor regions was determined by a similarity score. The segmentation of the tumor regions from the background was carried out by using the level-set method. The level-set method is a well-known image segmentation approach that is similar to the watershed algorithm.

Fig. 1 shows the flowchart of the BUS image segmentation method suggested by Cheng et al. (2001). As seen in Fig. 1, the input image goes through various stages to obtain the segmentation results. The input image is converted to the NS image by

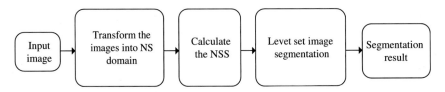

Fig. 1 The flowchart of the proposed method by Guo et al. (2016).

calculating the truth, falsity, and indeterminacy membership images. The NSS is calculated based on the truth, falsity, and indeterminacy memberships. The level-set method is considered to obtain the final segmentation of the NSS processed image. Their proposed method is detailed as below:

Let $A = \{A_1, A_2, \ldots, A_m\}$ and $C = \{C_1, C_2, \ldots, C_n\}$ be the set of alternatives and conditions in the NS domain, respectively, and the alternative A_i under the C_j condition denotes as $\{T_{C_j}(A_i), I_{C_j}(A_i), F_{C_j}(A_i)\}/A_i$, where the $T_{C_j}(A_i)$, $I_{C_j}(A_i)$ and $F_{C_j}(A_i)$ are true (T), indeterminate (I), and false (F) membership values, respectively.

The degree of similarity between the two alternatives is measured by a similarity score in the NS domain and is calculated by the following equation (Ye, 2013):

$$S_{C_j}(A_m, A_n) = \frac{T_{C_j}(A_m)T_{C_j}(A_n) + I_{C_j}(A_m)I_{C_j}(A_n) + F_{C_j}(A_m)F_{C_j}(A_n)}{\sqrt{T_{C_j}^2(A_m) + I_{C_j}^2(A_m) + F_{C_j}^2(A_m)} \times \sqrt{T_{C_j}^2(A_n) + I_{C_j}^2(A_n) + F_{C_j}^2(A_n)}} \quad (1)$$

If the NS is to be described on an image I_m, BP is a bright pixel set and I_{NS} is the image NS domain. When a pixel $P(x, y)$ is transformed in the neutrosophic set domain, $P_{NS}(x, y) = \{T(x, y), I(x, y), F(x, y)\}$, where $T(x, y)$, $I(x, y)$, and $F(x, y)$ are represented as memberships of bright, indeterminate, and dark pixels set, respectively.

Later, the authors applied the level-set algorithm to the NSS output. The level-set method is a well-known image segmentation approach and readers may refer to Osher and Sethian (1988) for detailed information about the method. Level-set approach-based image segmentation methods are usually used in two different ways such as edge- or region-based methods (Chan & Vese, 2001; Kimmel et al., 1997).

From the results that were given in Guo et al. (2016), the obtained segmentation results are quite similar to the ground-truth segmentations. The boundaries of the segmented regions are uniform and do not contain any irregular shapes. The authors also compared their achievements with a hybrid approach where NS and FCM algorithms were used. As a hybrid method's achievements are considered visually, it is seen that the boundaries of the segmented region are irregular when compared with ground-truth segmentation results. In other words, the achievements of NSS and level set-based methods are more sensitive to edge responses.

3.2 BUS image segmentation based on neutrosophic *l*-means clustering (Shan et al., 2012)

Shan et al. (2012) developed a fully automatic breast tumor detection method that was based on neutrosophic *l*-means (NLM) clustering. The authors opted to improve the image contrast by using a new phase feature and a new neutrosophic clustering method was used to determine the correct lesion border. Fig. 2 shows the flowchart of Shan et al.'s proposal.

As seen in Fig. 2, the proposed method consists of four main steps: ROI generation, speckle noise reduction, contrast improvement, and NLM clustering. The BUS images generally contain many different structures such as connective tissue, fat, and muscle. Furthermore, the lesion area is smaller than the whole image. That's why; the authors considered to use a region of interest (ROI) to increase the speed and accuracy of segmentation. The ROI defined as a rectangular region (Joo et al., 2004; Yap, Edirisinghe, & Bez, 2008) was applied in two steps: automatic seed point detection and region growing. Then, the ROI image was fed into the speckle reducing anisotropic diffusion (SRAD) method, which was previously proposed by Yu, Molloy, and Acton (2004). The SRAD approach is edge-sensitive diffusion for spotted images; likewise, conventional anisotropic diffusion is edge-sensitive diffusion for ruined images with additional noise. Then, the phase in max-energy orientation (PMO), which is a robust method for boundary detection from the image

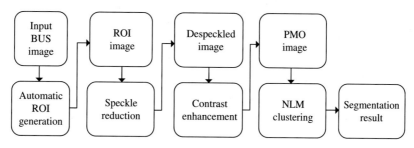

Fig. 2 The flowchart of the method proposed by Shan et al. (2012).

(Noble & Boukerroui, 2006), was applied to the smoothed ROI image. Finally, the authors applied the NLM algorithm for detection of tumor boundaries of the BUS image. The NLM is a new clustering method based on fuzzy c-tools and neutrosophic images and consists of six steps (Shan et al., 2012):

(1) Designate membership matrix as $U^{(k)} = [u_{xy}]$ and $k = 0$. Where x, y, and k are pixel index, cluster index, and iteration number, respectively.

(2) Increase iteration by k, calculate true ($T^{(k)}$), indeterminate ($I^{(k)}$), and false ($F^{(k)}$) for each k value and transform $T^{(k)}$ and $I^{(k)}$ into vectors VT and VI.

(3) Determine the center vectors $L^{(k)} = [l_q]$ as:

$$l_y = \frac{\sum_{x=1}^{N} u_{xy}^m (1 - VI_x) VT_x}{\sum_{x=1}^{N} u_{xy}^m (1 - VI_x)} \tag{2}$$

where m and N are the membership parameter and total pixel number in the given image, respectively.

(4) Update membership matrix as $U^{(k+1)} = [u_{xy}]$ by using:

$$u_{xy} = \frac{1}{\sum_{d=1}^{L} \left(\frac{\|VT_x - l_y\|}{\|VT_x - l_d\|} \right)^{2/m-1}} \tag{3}$$

where L shows the number of clusters.

(5) Update image,

$$G^{(k+1)} = \begin{cases} G^{(k)}, & \text{if } I^{(k)} < \lambda \\ G'^{(k)}, & \text{if } I^{(k)} \geq \lambda \end{cases} \tag{4}$$

$$G'^{(k)}(i,j) = \frac{\sum_{s=i-w/2}^{i+w/2} \sum_{t=j-w/2}^{j+w/2} G^{(k)}(s,t)}{w^2} \tag{5}$$

where w, (i, j), and λ are window size, pixel at the window center, and indeterminacy threshold, respectively.

$$\begin{cases} \text{stop}, & \|U^{(k+1)} - U^{(k)}\| < \varepsilon \\ \text{goto step2}, & \text{otherwise} \end{cases} \tag{6}$$

The authors also used the FCM algorithm to compare with their method. As reported in the paper, the tumor regions determined by the NLM method are quite similar to those of the radiologist. The borders of the segmentation are uniform and do not contain any holes in the background regions. The boundaries of the segmented regions do not contain any irregular shapes.

3.3 Iterative NS-based lung segmentation in thoracic CT images (Guo et al., 2013)

The detection of the lung in CT images is important for the detection of lung diseases and lung abnormalities. Besides, probable pathologies of different sizes in CT images make it difficult to accurately detect lung regions. For this reason, Guo et al. (2013) developed a novel approach that provides accurate lung segmentation. Because the authors could not accurately detect the lung limits in patients with lung diseases by the previously developed expectation-maximization (EM) analysis and morphological operations (EMM)-based method, they thought of using an iterative NS-based lung segmentation approach to improve the EMM segmentation method using anatomical features such as ribs and lungs. First, they extracted the lung regions with their developed EMM model by using the three-dimensional (3D) hierarchical EM segmentation method. Then, the initial EEM segmentation result was fed into INLS to determine the boundaries of the final lung regions.

In addition, the authors evaluated the segmentation results according to those segmented by a radiologist manually using percentage overlap area (*POA*), Hausdorff distance (*HD*), and average distance (*AD*) criteria. The reported mean and standard deviation of the POA, HD, and AD values were improved from $85.4 \pm 18.14\%$, $22.6 \pm 29.4\,\text{mm}$, and $3.5 \pm 5.4\,\text{mm}$ to $91.2 \pm 6.7\%$, $16.0 \pm 11.3\,\text{mm}$, and $2.5 \pm 1.0\,\text{mm}$ by using the combination of EMM and INLS, iteratively.

3.4 Spatial NS clustering and level set-based thyroid nodule segmentation in ultrasound images (Koundal, Gupta, & Singh, 2016)

One of the well-known imaging modalities for the detection of thyroid nodules is ultrasound (US) imaging (Koundal, 2012). After detection of the thyroid nodule, it must be delineated in the US images. Delineation of thyroid nodules accurately and effectively requires expert radiologists. As doing this delineation manually is a time-consuming operation due to speckle noise and low contrast of thyroid US images, automatic delineation of thyroid

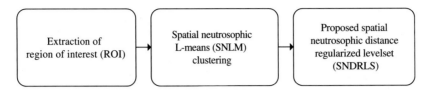

Fig. 3 Three steps of the Koundal et al.'s (2016) method.

nodules has become a significant case for radiologists. In this work, Koundal et al. (2016) used spatial neutrosophic clustering and the level-set method to determine the thyroid nodules in ultrasound images. The proposed method consists of three steps that are all automatically run. These steps are given in Fig. 3.

As Fig. 3 shows, the first step was the extraction of ROI. It is clear that the extraction of ROI saves time due to reducing computational costs (Savelonas et al., 2007). In the second step, US images are transformed into the NS domain. Eqs. (7)–(12) were used to calculate the NS domain image memberships. Thus, each of the pixels in the transformed image has three membership degrees: true T, false F, and indeterminacy I. Here, spatial neutrosophic L-means (SNLM) clustering combines spatial information such as blur, edge, and mean with neutrosophic L-means (NLM) clustering (Shan et al., 2012). In the NS domain, the T_{ij}, F_{ij}, and I_{ij} functions are defined as the following:

$$T_{ij} = 1 - \hat{g}_{ij} \tag{7}$$

$$\hat{g}_{ij} = \frac{1}{w_i \times w_i} \sum_{m=i-\frac{w_i}{2}}^{i+\frac{w_i}{2}} \sum_{n=j-\frac{w_i}{2}}^{j+\frac{w_i}{2}} g_{ij} \tag{8}$$

$$F_{ij} = 1 - T_{ij} \tag{9}$$

$$I_{ij} = B_{ij} * (1 - E_{ij}) \tag{10}$$

$$B_{ij} = \begin{cases} 2(1 - T_{ij}) & T_{ij} \geq 0.5 \\ 2T_{ij} & T_{ij} < 0.5 \end{cases} \tag{11}$$

$$E_{ij} = \begin{cases} 1 \text{ if } p \text{ is an edge} \\ 0 \text{ if } p \text{ is not an edge} \end{cases} \tag{12}$$

where T_{ij}, F_{ij}, and I_{ij} are the truth, falsity, and indeterminacy memberships in NS space, respectively. $\hat{g}_{ij}$ is the pixel's local mean on the window, B_{ij} is the blur matrix, and E_{ij} is the edge matrix. Level-set function requires the result of SNLM clustering to initialize itself. In the third step, the proposed SNDRLS method for thyroid US image segmentation is successfully completed. The proposed method is fully automatic without any human intervention.

In this work, 42 subjects were contributed to collect B-mode thyroid US images as a dataset. Six metrics were considered to evaluate the achievement of the proposed method on thyroid US images: TP, false positive (FP), overlap metric (OM), dice coefficient (DC), the HD, and mean absolute distance (MAD).

The comparison of the proposed SNDRLS method was carried out with other methods such as neutrosophic watershed (Zhang, Zhang, & Cheng, 2010), active contour without edges (ACWE) (Chan, Yezrielev Sandberg, & Vese, 2000), fuzzy level-set method (FLSM) (Li et al., 2011), and distance regularizer level-set evolution (DRLSE) (Li et al., 2010) using seven evaluation metrics: TP, FP, OM, DC, MAD, HD and execution time on the entire dataset.

3.5 NS and modified watershed algorithm-based segmentation approach for abdominal CT Liver Parenchyma (Sayed et al., 2016)

Liver cancer is one of the most common diseases worldwide, and it is often fatal. It is important to detect the disease in the early stages and to accurately determine the stage of the cancer. Computed tomography (CT) images are generally used to diagnose liver cancer because the CT offers more detail than general X-ray equipment. The segmentation of CT images by the radiologist or other experts is very time consuming and tedious. On the other hand, automatic segmentation of CT images is a crucial and difficult task for liver segmentation. Therefore, Sayed et al. (2016) proposed a fully automated liver segmentation approach based on NS and a modified watershed algorithm. The proposed approach has three stages: (1) preprocessing, (2) transformation, and (3) postprocessing. Fig. 4 shows the architecture of the proposed NS segmentation approach.

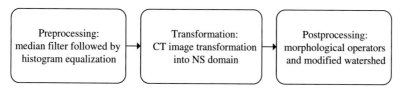

Fig. 4 The proposed NS segmentation approach.

Each stage is detailed as follows by researchers:

Preprocessing stage: Preprocessing is one of the indispensable steps of image segmentation to eliminate noise, enhance contrast, and resize images. When you remove noise from the image, at the same time, preserving the edges of the image is critical for the success of image segmentation. All images in the dataset (Mostafa et al., 2012) are JPEG format with 630×630. First, CT images were converted to grayscale and resized to 256×256. Then, the median filter was applied to remove the noise. Finally, the output of the median filter was fed into a histogram equalization filter to adjust the dynamic range and contrast of the image.

Transformation stage: The output grayscale image of the preprocessing stage was transformed into the NS domain. Thus, each pixel has three neutrosophic subsets: truth *T*, false *F*, and indeterminate *I*. *T* represents the objects, *F* represents the background of the image, and *I* represents the edges of the image. An NS image is defined as follows:

$$P_{NS}(i,j) = \{T(i,j), I(i,j), F(i,j)\} \tag{13}$$

$$\overline{g(i,j))} = \frac{1}{w \times w} \sum_{m=1-\frac{w}{2}}^{1+\frac{w}{2}} \sum_{n=1-\frac{w}{2}}^{1+\frac{w}{2}} g(m,n) \tag{14}$$

$$T(i,j) = \frac{\overline{g(i,j)} - \overline{g}_{min}}{\overline{g}_{max} - \overline{g}_{min}} g(m,n) \tag{15}$$

$$F(i,j) = 1 - T(i,j) \tag{16}$$

$$Ho(i,j) = abs\left(g(i,j) - \overline{g(i,j)}\right) \tag{17}$$

where $P_{NS}(i,j)$ is the pixel in NS, $\overline{g(i,j)}$ is the local mean of the image, and $Ho(i,j)$ is the homogeneity value of *T* at (i,j) (the absolute value of difference between intensity $g(i,j)$ and its local mean value $\overline{g(i,j)}$).

First, researchers assigned a gradient image $G(i,j)$ to the NS indeterminate image $I(i,j)$. The gradient image $G(i,j)$ was normalized according to Eq. (18).

$$G(i,j) = \frac{G(i,j) - G_{min}}{G_{max} - G_{min}} \tag{18}$$

where G_{max} is the maximum and G_{min} is the minimum intensity value of $G(i,j)$.

Postprocessing stage: In the postprocessing stage, morphological operators were applied on the NS truth image $T(i,j)$, which was obtained from the NS domain. A traditional watershed algorithm is sensitive to noise and it has an oversegmentation issue (Grau et al., 2004). Therefore, a developed watershed algorithm is employed to segment the liver parenchyma in the CT image. The developed watershed algorithm was compared with traditional watershed algorithms that use various distance types such as Euclidean distance, city block distance, chessboard distance, and quasi-Euclidean distance. In addition, several metrics were used to evaluate the performance between the developed approach and the other methods. These metrics are the dice coefficient (DC), the Jaccard index (JI), correlation, and true positive (TP). From the presented results, it was seen that the proposed approach achieved the highest accuracy rates in all metrics except TP. The adaptive thresholding method obtained a 97.62% TP value, that is, 2.19% better than the proposed approach. In addition, the worst evaluation scores were produced by the active contour method, where a 72.60% correlation value, a 75.32% DC value, a 61.46% JI value, and a 75.90% TP value were obtained. Except for the TP score, the adaptive threshold method produced the second-worst results when compared with the other. The adaptive threshold method produced an 84.87% correlation value, an 85.84% DC value, and a 76.95% JI value. On the other hand, as mentioned, the best TP value of 97.62% was produced by the adaptive threshold method. The region growing method also produced similar scores as the adaptive threshold method, where an 83.30% correlation value, an 84.06% DC value, a 74.35% JI value, and a 92.54TP value were obtained. Region growing produces the second-best scores where an 87.17% correlation value, an 88.66% DC value, an 80.52% JI value, and an 87.64% TP value were obtained.

The performance evaluation of the proposed method was carried out on CT images from 30 different patients by using some measurements such as true positive ratio, correlation, Jaccard index, and dice coefficient. The segmentation results show that the proposed method yields better results than the most common methods.

4   Limitations of NS-based medical image segmentation approaches

As the literature review shows, it is seen that NS has attracted much attention in medical image analysis. Especially, researchers used NS-based approaches in the detection of various lesions in medical images. As successful, robust, and efficient applications of NS in medical image segmentation have been proposed, there have been some limitations of NS-based approaches, including the following:

(1) In almost all NS-based medical image segmentation approaches, mapping the images from the intensity domain into the neutrosophic set domain has been carried out by using the equations of Guo and Cheng (2009). In Guo and Cheng (2009), the truth membership (T) was defined as the normalized local mean image and the falsity membership (F) was defined as $1 - T$. The indeterminacy membership (I) was defined as the normalized absolute value of the local difference. These membership expressions were used for all medical image types. This situation can be seen as a conflict because different medical images have different structures and necessitate different membership definitions.

(2) In almost all studies, the authors used α-mean and β-enhancement operations for making the input images more convenient for subsequent clustering procedures. These procedures were not convenient for all medical image types and need to be adjusted for different medical images. In addition, for other NS-based methods such as Neutrosophic Similarity Score and neutrosophic c-means, many parameters need to be tuned on the training set. The segmentation algorithm depends on the specific images.

(3) As the NS is generally applied for image enhancement in an iterative manner, this procedure may blur the input image that causes a loss of detail of the input image. So, a cost function should be incorporated into the NS-based segmentation approaches for preventing the blur problem.

(4) In almost all NS-based medical image segmentation approaches, NS has been combined with another scheme such as clustering, graph cut, level set, active contour, and mean shift. No new segmentation framework has been proposed where NS is only used for image segmentation. In other words, in all studies, the NS part is similar but the combined part is different.

5 Conclusions

In this survey, neutrosophy theory-based medical image segmentation approaches are investigated. Neutrosophy, which comes from neutrality, expresses the attributes with truth, falsity, and indeterminacy memberships. It is deduced as the extension of the fuzzy sets. Generally, neutrosophy deals with uncertainty.

Uncertainty, which can be considered as noise in image processing, is challenging in medical image segmentation. This situation makes the NS strong and robust in image-processing applications.

NS-based image segmentation approaches have achieved impressive performances in medical image segmentation applications. Especially, NS is powerful in image denoising and clustering, which can be seen in the building blocks of image segmentation. The general trend in NS-based medical image segmentation is transforming the input image into the NS domain and applying some operators for making the image more convenient for segmentation. Moreover, NS-based clustering algorithms have been developed for gray level clustering for image segmentation.

The above-mentioned situation should be adjusted for different type of medical images. In other words, the NS-based methodology that is applied to ultrasound images should not be applied to CT images. Convenient methods should be developed. The fuzzy membership functions can be considered to construct truth, falsity, and indeterminacy memberships. Some rule-based approaches can be developed to construct supervised medical image segmentation approaches.

In future studies, the NS-based deep-learning methods should be developed by the researchers. Recently, some attempts can be seen where deep learning and NS have been combined in some applications. However, that works only using NS as a preprocessing tool. So, more comprehensive studies should be developed. Similar to fuzzy neural networks, deep neutrosophic neural networks can be developed. Especially, NS and deep learning-based medical image segmentation may achieve better segmentation in the next few years.

References

Akbulut, Y., et al. (2017). KNCM: Kernel neutrosophic c-means clustering. *Applied Soft Computing Journal, 52*, 714–724.

Akbulut, Y., et al. (2018). An effective color texture image segmentation algorithm based on hermite transform. *Applied Soft Computing Journal, 67*, 494–504.

Ali, M., et al. (2018). Segmentation of dental X-ray images in medical imaging using neutrosophic orthogonal matrices. *Expert Systems with Applications, 91*, 434–441. Available at (2018). http://linkinghub.elsevier.com/retrieve/pii/S0957417417306322.

Alsmadi, M. K. (2018). A hybrid fuzzy C-means and neutrosophic for jaw lesions segmentation. *Ain Shams Engineering Journal, 9*(4), 697–706.

Anter, A. M., & Hassenian, A. E. (2018a). Computational intelligence optimization approach based on particle swarm optimizer and neutrosophic set for abdominal CT liver tumor segmentation. *Journal of Computational Science, 25*, 376–387.

Anter, A. M., & Hassenian, A. E. (2018b). CT liver tumor segmentation hybrid approach using neutrosophic sets, fast fuzzy c-means and adaptive watershed algorithm. *Artificial Intelligence in Medicine*.

Ashour, A. S., et al. (2018). A hybrid dermoscopy images segmentation approach based on neutrosophic clustering and histogram estimation. *Applied Soft Computing Journal, 69*, 426–434.

Chan, T. F., & Vese, L. A. (2001). Active contours without edges. *IEEE Transactions on Image Processing, 10*(2), 266–277.

Chan, T. F., Yezrielev Sandberg, B., & Vese, L. A. (2000). Active contours without edges for vector-valued images. *Journal of Visual Communication and Image Representation, 11*(2), 130–141.

Chen, L. C., et al. (2018). Deep lab: Semantic image segmentation with deep convolutional nets, atrous convolution, and fully connected CRFs. *IEEE Transactions on Pattern Analysis and Machine Intelligence, 40*(4), 834–848.

Cheng, H. D., et al. (2001). Color image segmentation: Advances and prospects. *Pattern Recognition, 34*(12), 2259–2281.

Comaniciu, D., Meer, P., & Member, S. (2002). Mean shift: A robust approach toward feature space analysis. *IEEE-PAMI, 24*(5), 603–619.

Das, S., et al. (2019). Color MRI image segmentation using quantum-inspired modified genetic algorithm-based FCM. In *Recent Trends in Signal and Image Processing* (pp. 151–164). Springer.

Gaber, T., et al. (2015). Thermogram breast cancer prediction approach based on neutrosophic sets and fuzzy c-means algorithm. *Proceedings of the annual international conference of the IEEE engineering in medicine and biology society, EMBS* (pp. 4254–4257).

Gholami, M., Rashno, A., & Heshmati, A. (2016). Scheme for unsupervised colour–texture image segmentation using neutrosophic set and non-subsampled contourlet transform. *IET Image Processing, 10*(6), 464–473. Available at:(2016). http://digital-library.theiet.org/content/journals/10.1049/iet-ipr.2015.0738.

Grau, V., et al. (2004). Improved watershed transform for medical image segmentation using prior information. *IEEE Transactions on Medical Imaging, 23*(4), 447–458.

Guo, Y., & Cheng, H. D. (2009). New neutrosophic approach to image segmentation. *Pattern Recognition, 42*(5), 587–595.

Guo, Y., & Sengur, A. (2013). A novel color image segmentation approach based on neutrosophic set and modified fuzzy c-means. *Circuits, Systems, and Signal Processing, 32*(4), 1699–1723.

Guo, Y., & Şengür, A. (2013). *A novel image segmentation algorithm based on neutrosophic filtering and level set. Vol. 1*(pp. 46–49). Neutrosophic Sets and Systems

Guo, Y., & Şengür, A. (2014). A novel image edge detection algorithm based on neutrosophic set. *Computers and Electrical Engineering, 40*(8), 3–25.

Guo, Y., & Sengur, A. (2015a). A novel 3D skeleton algorithm based on neutrosophic cost function. *Applied Soft Computing Journal, 36*, 210–217.

Guo, Y., & Sengur, A. (2015b). NCM: Neutrosophic c-means clustering algorithm. *Pattern Recognition, 48*(8), 2710–2724.

Guo, Y., & Sengur, A. (2015c). NECM: Neutrosophic evidential c-means clustering algorithm. *Neural Computing and Applications, 26*(3), 561–571.

Guo, Y., Şengür, A., & Tian, J. W. (2016). A novel breast ultrasound image segmentation algorithm based on neutrosophic similarity score and level set. *Computer Methods and Programs in Biomedicine, 123*, 43–53.

Guo, Y., et al. (2013). Automated iterative neutrosophic lung segmentation for image analysis in thoracic computed tomography. *Medical Physics, 40*(8).

Guo, Y., et al. (2017). A retinal vessel detection approach based on shearlet transform and indeterminacy filtering on fundus images. *Symmetry, 9*(10), 235. Available at: http://www.mdpi.com/2073-8994/9/10/235.

Guo, Y., et al. (2018). An effective color image segmentation approach using neutrosophic adaptive mean shift clustering. *Measurement: Journal of the International Measurement Confederation, 119,* 28–40.

Jain, S., & Laxmi, V. (2018). Color image segmentation techniques: A survey. *Proceedingsof the international conference on microelectronics, computing & communication systems* (pp. 189–197).

Jha, S., et al. (2019). Neutrosophic image segmentation with dice coefficients. *Measurement: Journal of the International Measurement Confederation, 134,* 762–772.

Joo, S., et al. (2004). Computer-aided diagnosis of solid breast nodules: Use of an artificial neural network based on multiple sonographic features. *IEEE Transactions on Medical Imaging, 23*(10), 1292–1300.

Karabatak, E., Guo, Y., & Sengur, A. (2013). Modified neutrosophic approach to color image segmentation. *Journal of Electronic Imaging, 22*(1) Available at: http://electronicimaging.spiedigitallibrary.org/article.aspx?doi=10.1117/1.JEI.22.1.013005.

Kimmel, R., et al. (1997). Geometric active contours. *International Journal of Computer Vision, 22*(1), 61–79. Available at: http://link.springer.com/article/10.1023/A:1007979827043.

Koundal, D. (2012). Computer-aided diagnosis of thyroid nodule: A review. *International Journal of Computer Science & Engineering Survey, 3*(4), 67–83.

Koundal, D., Gupta, S., & Singh, S. (2016). Automated delineation of thyroid nodules in ultrasound images using spatial neutrosophic clustering and level set. *Applied Soft Computing Journal, 40,* 86–97.

Koundal, D., Gupta, S., & Singh, S. (2018). Computer aided thyroid nodule detection system using medical ultrasound images. *Biomedical Signal Processing and Control, 40,* 117–130.

Kumar, S., et al. (2018). Colour image segmentation with histogram and homogeneity histogram difference using evolutionary algorithms. *International Journal of Machine Learning and Cybernetics, 9*(1), 163–183.

Lal, M., Kaur, L., & Gupta, S. (2018a). Automatic segmentation of tumors in B-Mode breast ultrasound images using information gain based neutrosophic clustering. *Journal of X-Ray Science and Technology, 26*(2), 209–225.

Lal, M., Kaur, L., & Gupta, S. (2018b). Modified spatial neutrosophic clustering technique for boundary extraction of tumours in B-mode BUS images. *IET Image Processing, 12*(8), 1338–1344.

Lee, J., et al. (2018). Neutrosophic segmentation of breast lesions for dedicated breast computed tomography. *Journal of Medical Imaging, 5*(1).

Li, C., et al. (2010). Distance regularized level set evolution and its application to image segmentation. *IEEE Transactions on Image Processing, 19*(12), 3243–3254.

Li, B. N., et al. (2011). Integrating spatial fuzzy clustering with level set methods for automated medical image segmentation. *Computers in Biology and Medicine, 41*(1), 1–10.

Lotfollahi, M., et al. (2018). Segmentation of breast ultrasound images based on active contours using neutrosophic theory. *Journal of Medical Ultrasonics, 45*(2), 205–212.

Mohan, J., Krishnaveni, V., & Huo, Y. (2015). Automated brain tumor segmentation on MR images based on neutrosophic set approach. In *2015 2nd international conference on electronics and communication systems (ICECS)* (pp. 1078–1083).

Mostafa, A., et al. (2012). Evaluating the effects of image filters in CT Liver CAD system. In *Proceedings—IEEE-EMBS international conference on biomedical and health informatics: Global grand challenge of health informatics, BHI 2012* (pp. 448–451).

Naidu, M. S. R., Rajesh Kumar, P., & Chiranjeevi, K. (2018). Shannon and Fuzzy entropy based evolutionary image thresholding for image segmentation. *Alexandria Engineering Journal, 57*(3), 1643–1655.

Noble, J. A., & Boukerroui, D. (2006). Ultrasound image segmentation: A survey. *IEEE Transactions on Medical Imaging, 25*(8), 987–1010.

Osher, S., & Sethian, J. A. (1988). Fronts propagating with curvature-dependent speed: Algorithms based on Hamilton-Jacobi formulations. *Journal of Computational Physics, 79*(1), 12–49.

Otay, I., & Kahraman, C. (2019). A state-of-the-art review of neutrosophic sets and theory. In *Fuzzy multi-criteria decision-making using neutrosophic sets* (pp. 3–24). Springer.

Savelonas, M. A., et al. (2007). Computational characterization of thyroid tissue in the radon domain. In *Proceedings—IEEE symposium on computer-based medical systems* (pp. 189–192).

Sayed, G. I., et al. (2016). A hybrid segmentation approach based on neutrosophic sets and modified watershed: A case of abdominal CT Liver parenchyma. In *2015 11th international computer engineering conference: Today information society what's next?* (pp. 144–149): ICENCO.

Sengur, A., & Guo, Y. (2011). Color texture image segmentation based on neutrosophic set and wavelet transformation. *Computer Vision and Image Understanding, 115*(8), 1134–1144.

Shan, J., Cheng, H. D., & Wang, Y. (2012). A novel segmentation method for breast ultrasound images based on neutrosophic l-means clustering. *Medical Physics, 39*(9), 5669–5682.

Smarandache, F. (2003). *A unifying field in logics: Neutrosophic logic. Neutrosophy, neutrosophic set, neutrosophic probability: Neutrosophic logic: Neutrosophy, neutrosophic set, neutrosophic probability, infinite study.*

Turhan, M., et al. (2018). Neutrosophic weighted support vector machines for the determination of school administrators who attended an action learning course based on their conflict-handling styles. *Symmetry, 10*(5).

Wang, C., et al. (2018). Superpixel-based color-depth restoration and dynamic environment modeling for kinect-assisted image-based rendering systems. *The Visual Computer, 34*(1), 67–81.

Xian, M., Cheng, H. D., & Zhang, Y. (2014). A fully automatic breast ultrasound image segmentation approach based on neutro-connectedness. In *Proceedings—International conference on pattern recognition* (pp. 2495–2500).

Xu, G., et al. (2018). A neutrosophic approach based on TOPSIS method to image segmentation. *International Journal of Computers, Communications & Control, 13*(6).

Yang, B., et al. (2018). Lung tumor segmentation based on the multi-scale template matching and region growing. In *Progress in biomedical optics and imaging—Proceedings of SPIE.*

Yap, M. H., Edirisinghe, E. A., & Bez, H. E. (2008). A novel algorithm for initial lesion detection in ultrasound breast images. *Journal of Applied Clinical Medical Physics, 9*(4), 181–199.

Ye, J. (2013). Multicriteria decision-making method using the correlation coefficient under single-valued neutrosophic environment. *International Journal of General Systems, 42*(4), 386–394.

Yu, Y., Molloy, J. A., & Acton, S. T. (2004). Three-dimensional speckle reducing anisotropic diffusion. *IEEE Transactions on Image Processing, 11*(11), 1987–1991.

Zhang, L. (2010). Segmentation of ultrasound breast images based on a neutrosophic method. *Optical Engineering, 49*(11).

Zhang, M., Zhang, L., & Cheng, H. D. (2010). A neutrosophic approach to image segmentation based on watershed method. *Signal Processing, 90*(5), 1510–1517.

Zhi, X. H., & Shen, H. B. (2018). Saliency driven region-edge-based top down level set evolution reveals the asynchronous focus in image segmentation. *Pattern Recognition, 80*, 241–255.

8

Neutrosophic set in medical image clustering

Ahmed Refaat Hawas*, Amira S. Ashour*, Yanhui Guo†

*Department of Electronics and Electrical Communications Engineering, Faculty of Engineering, Tanta University, Tanta, Egypt. †Department of Computer Science, University of Illinois at Springfield, Springfield, IL, United States

1   Introduction

Clustering is an unsupervised procedure to group the data. It groups the data instances without prior information by transforming the set of features to subsets, where similar features are labeled as being in the same subset. Data clustering finds the similarities in data to assign them into the same group. Clustering groups a dataset into several groups such that the similarity within a group is larger than that of clusters. The main aim of clustering is to construct boundaries among the different data clusters based on unlabeled data. It finds the grouping clusters in multidimensional feature space, which is a challenging process due to the different sizes and shapes of the clusters (Jain, Duin, & Mao, 2000). Clustering procedures can be considered partitioned and hierarchical, such as partition around medoids (PAM), K-means, and the EM (expectation-maximization) algorithm-based Gaussian mixture models (Revathi & Nalini, 2013). In the PAM clustering method, a sequence of centrally located medoids (objects located in a set of selected objects) is determined in the clusters. These medoids are obtained by minimizing the objects' average dissimilarity to their closest selected object (Van der Laan, Pollard, & Bryan, 2003). In K-means clustering, a data point is assigned to a specific cluster on convergence using the L2 norm to determine the optimal clusters and their corresponding centroids (El Agha & Ashour, 2012; Shmmala & Ashour, 2013; Steinley, 2006). However, for clustering using the EM algorithm, probabilistic assignments are preserved rather than deterministic ones, where multivariate

Neutrosophic Set in Medical Image Analysis. https://doi.org/10.1016/B978-0-12-818148-5.00008-4

Gaussian distributions are employed. It gives a probability of any data point belonging to any centroid using the expectation instead of the L2 norm (Basu, Banerjee, & Mooney, 2002; Frey & Jojic, 2003). Generally, the main clustering algorithm is the K-means (hard C-means), which is used for hard segmentation (Ghosh & Dubey, 2013).

In medical applications, images contain imprecise information and fuzziness, leading to more complicated clustering, segmentation, and classification procedures. Hence, fuzzy clustering can be considered in such applications for processing uncertainty and fuzziness to classify the data points that are inherent in several clusters with dissimilar degrees of membership (Bezdek, Hall, & Clarke, 1993). In hard clustering (nonfuzzy clustering), the data is separated into crisp clusters at which each data point fits one specific cluster. Data points in fuzzy clustering can be assigned to several clusters, where the membership levels specify the degree to which the data points fit to the dissimilar clusters (De, Biswas, & Roy, 2001). Different fuzzy-based clustering methods were developed, including fuzzy c-means (FCM) (Chen, Giger, & Bick, 2006; Chuang, Tzeng, Chen, Wu, & Chen, 2006), possibilistic fuzzy c-means (Pal, Pal, Keller, & Bezdek, 2005), and relational evidential c-means (RECM) (Masson & Denœux, 2009). Nevertheless, the main limitations of fuzzy clustering methods include the required stopping criterion, the problem of local minima that leads to nonoptimal solutions, and neglecting pixel spatial context due to noise and artifacts (Koundal, Gupta, & Singh, 2012). To overcome the limitations of the fuzzy-based methods, the neutrosophic set (NS), which is a general form of the fuzzy set, becomes more prevalent in several image-processing stages.

Numerous techniques were settled to diminish the indeterminacy based on the NS. Guo and Sengur (2015) implemented a neutrosophic c-means (NCM) procedure for uncertain data clustering by using the fuzzy c-means and the NS frameworks. The clustering process was expressed as a constrained minimization problem to minimize a predefined objective function. This objective function included ambiguity rejection and distance rejection, which handled the patterns near the cluster boundaries and those away from all the clusters, respectively. The NS provided the ability to cope with uncertainty from the incomplete description of the clusters. Sengur and Guo (2011) designed a c-k-means clustering scheme by transforming both the wavelet domain features and the texture information of an image to the NS domain, concurrently. The entropy was measured to estimate the image's indeterminacy in the NS domain; then, the proposed c-K-means clustering was applied. Furthermore, Mohan, Krishnaveni, and Guo (2015) implemented a nonlocal neutrosophic Wiener filter to increase the image quality in a proposed neutrosophic-based K-means clustering technique on magnetic resonance brain tumor images. Guo and Cheng (2009) applied NS-based K-means clustering for image segmentation by mapping the image to the NS domain using three membership sets, T, I, and F, representing the truth degree, indeterminacy, and falsity, respectively. Furthermore, two operators were used to decrease the indeterminacy in the NS procedure for effective clustering.

In the preceding NS-based studies for image processing, a high-pass filter, namely Sobel, of mask size 3×3 was employed to define the neutrosophic set membership function. Consequently, this chapter included a comparative study on the shape and size of the edge detection filter that was used during the calculations of the indeterminacy (uncertainty) neutrosophic subset I in the NS. Different filters, namely the Sobel filter, the Prewitt filter, and the unsharp filter, are involved in this study with different mask sizes. To study the effect of the filters on the clustering process, a neutrosophic set-based K-means clustering is employed in the current study, where the pixels are clustered according to their values of T and I. Furthermore, the proposed algorithm is applied to accurate lesion region segmentation in dermoscopic images from the International Skin Imaging Collaboration (ISIC) 2016 Challenge dataset (International Skin Imaging Collaboration, n.d.).

The remaining sections are structured as follows. Section 2 introduces the methodology of the proposed comparative study of the filter design in the calculations of the indeterminacy neutrosophic subset I in the NS. Section 3 includes the results, comparative study, and discussion. Finally, the conclusions are represented in Section 4.

2 Methodology

Skin lesion clustering and segmentation are challenging due to the inconsistent structures of the dermoscopic images, and the existence of noise/artifacts/air bubbles/dense hairs. Moreover, skin lesion dermoscopy images have a smooth color transition between the pigmented lesion regions and the background. For accurate diagnosis, researchers are interested in implementing efficient clustering, segmentation, and classification methods to overcome indeterminacy and uncertainty in dermoscopic images based on the NS (Aljanabi, Özok, Rahebi, & Abdullah, 2018;

Ashour, Guo, Kucukkulahli, Erdogmus, & Polat, 2018; Ashour, Hawas, Guo, & Wahba, 2018; Castillejos, Ponomaryov, Nino-de-Rivera, & Golikov, 2012; Celebi & Zornberg, 2014; Dalal et al., 2011; Emre Celebi et al., 2007; Gómez, Butakoff, Ersboll, & Stoecker, 2008; Guo, Ashour, & Smarandache, 2018; Kockara, Mete, Chen, & Aydin, 2010; Korotkov & Garcia, 2012; Melli, Grana, & Cucchiara, 2006; Oliveira et al., 2016; Sookpotharom, 2009; Wahba, Ashour, Guo, Napoleon, & Elnaby, 2018; Wahba, Ashour, Napoleon, Elnaby, & Guo, 2017; Wighton, Sadeghi, Lee, & Atkins, 2009; Yuan, Situ, & Zouridakis, 2009). Because skin lesions have a globular shape, the neutrosophic K-means clustering algorithm is employed in this chapter, as it has the ability to create tighter clusters compared to hierarchical clustering algorithms. Typically, k-means clustering has a superintended role in many applications, owing to its efficiency and simplicity. However, to reduce the indeterminacy in the dermoscopic images, it is essential to map the image in the NS domain prior to the clustering stage.

In the present chapter, different high-pass filters are used to calculate the indeterminacy neutrosophic subset I in the NS domain. Accordingly, it studies the effect of changing the filter (operator) design on the calculations of uncertainty subset I for further skin lesion segmentation using neutrosophic K-means (NKM) clustering. The optimized value of the α-mean operation of the NS is used to reduce the indeterminacy of the image. Accordingly, in the current study, $\alpha_{optimal} = 0.0014$ is used, which was obtained using the genetic algorithm (GA) on the same dermoscopic image dataset (Ashour, Hawas, et al., 2018). This $\alpha_{optimal}$ is used as a threshold value to determine the pixel points that will be taken for the average filtering operation. Finally, another threshold value in the I set is used to select the pixels for the clustering process with a low indeterminacy value. Afterward, the dermoscopic image is clustered using the K-means clustering scheme to segment the skin lesion regions.

2.1 Neutrosophic image

Neutrosophy is the base of the neutrosophic set, neutrosophic statistics, neutrosophic logic, and neutrosophic probability, which was established by Smarandache (1999, 2003). The neutrosophy theory is based on the relation between any entity $<B>$ and its opposite $<Anti\text{-}B>$ and $<Non\text{-}B>$, which is neither $<B>$ nor $<Anti\text{-}B>$ and can be expressed also as $<Neut\text{-}B>$. As a generalization to the classic set, fuzzy set, and the interval-valued fuzzy set, the neutrosophic set (NS) was introduced to delineate the uncertainty and indeterminacy in any information. For any event $<B>$ in the NS, three membership sets (neutrosophic components) are defined. These MFs are defined to estimate the degrees of truth, indeterminacy (neither true nor false), and falsity, which are expressed as T, I, and F, respectively. These neutrosophic subsets are used to map the image into the NS space to produce the NS image. Any image is transformed to its neutrosophic image, which is denoted as $<T, I, F>$, by computing the three subsets, namely T, I, and F as $\{T(j, k), I(j, k), F(j, k)\}$ for each pixel $R(j, k)$ in the neutrosophic image (Cheng, Shan, Ju, Guo, & Zhang, 2010).

In the present work, to identify the skin lesion in the NS domain, $<B>$ is considered the lesion in the dermoscopic image, $<Neut\text{-}B>$ is used to represent the lesion boundaries, and $<Anti\text{-}B>$ represents the background. Thus, the neutrosophic components T, I, and F are used to symbolize $<B>$, $<Neut\text{-}B>$, and $<Anti\text{-}B>$, respectively, where $<B>$ and $<Anti\text{-}B>$ include the region information and $<Neut\text{-}B>$ includes the boundary information.

In the neutrosophic image, a pixel can be implied as follows:

$$R(t, i, f) = \{T(j, k), I(j, k), F(j, k)\} \tag{1}$$

where $R(t, i, f)$ is the mapped form of the pixel $R(j, k)$ in the NS domain. The percentage of t represents the lesion (true subset), the percentage of i denotes the boundaries (indeterminate subset), and the percentage of f denotes the background (false subset), as $t \in T$, $i \in I$, and $f \in F$. For an image R, three subsets of the neutrosophic components ($T(j, k)$, $I(j, k)$, and $F(j, k)$) can be expressed in terms of the pixel intensity value $R(j, k)$ of the pixel (j, k) as follows:

$$T(j, k) = \frac{R(j, k) - R_{\min}}{R_{\max} - R_{\min}} \tag{2}$$

where $R_{\min}$ and $R_{\max}$ are the minimum and maximum intensity values, respectively. In addition, the neutrosophic subset F can be expressed as:

$$F(j, k) = 1 - T(j, k) \tag{3}$$

Finally, the third indeterminacy neutrosophic subset I, which represents the boundary information (edges between the objects in the image), can be given by:

$$I(j, k) = \frac{\zeta(j, k) - \zeta_{\min}}{\zeta_{\max} - \zeta_{\min}} \tag{4}$$

where $\zeta_{\min}$ and $\zeta_{\max}$ are the minimum and maximum absolute difference values, respectively. Moreover, $\zeta(j,k)$ is the local mean value of the original image's intensity values at the same pixel location, which can be given by:

$$\zeta(j,k) = \sum_{c=k-m/2}^{k+m/2} \sum_{l=j-m/2}^{j+m/2} R(c,l)*S(c,l) \tag{5}$$

where $S(c,l)$ is a high-pass filter to obtain difference values, m is the size of the filter (window/mask), and $R(c,l)$ is the local image during the masking process. This high-pass filter is used mainly to compute the indeterminacy of the neutrosophic image, $I(j,k)$, where its different types/sizes are studied in the present work. Because the entropy of the neutrosophic image indicates the element distribution in the NS space, the entropy of I is augmented due to the uniform distribution of the elements, where the entropy of I is calculated as follows:

$$Ent_I = - \sum_{i=\min\{I\}}^{\max\{I\}} pr_I(i) \ln(pr_I(i)) \tag{6}$$

where $pr_I(i)$ is the elements' probabilities in the I neutrosophic subset. Subsequently, the changes in T and F should influence the distribution of the elements and the entropy of I to correlate T and F with I, where I is used to calculate the indeterminacy of the neutrosophic image.

2.2 High-pass filter for gradient computing in I subset

The present work compares different types/sizes of the gradient filter (high-pass filter) $S(c,l)$, which is used in the calculations of the I subset in Eqs. (4) and (5). For accurate NS representation of the original skin lesion images in the NS space, it is essential to select the filter type and size, which are used in Eq. (5) for further efficient representation of the subset $I(j,k)$ that is used to measure the indeterminacy of the neutrosophic image $R(t,i,f)$. This inspired the novel contribution of the present chapter to study the effect of a different filter (type/size), which is mainly a high-pass operator (mask/filter), while calculating the neutrosophic I component in the NS. Afterward, a trial-and-error procedure is used to determine a threshold Th_I to modify the clustering process using the computed I subset. Only the pixel that satisfied $I < Th_I$

will be included in the clustering process using K-means, where the pixels that have $I > Th_I$ will be excluded from the clustering process, and their clustering results are obtained by their neighbor pixels. Accordingly, the clustering process will use T for only the points whose I values are less than the threshold. The I subset is defined for each pixel in the neutrosophic set domain.

A comparative study of using different high-pass filters to calculate the gradient for computing the I subset is evaluated by the results of the final neutrosophic K-means clustering of the dermoscopic image. Typically, the Sobel filter of size 3×3 was the default filter in the preceding NS studies in the different image-processing applications (Ashour, Hawas, et al., 2018). Accordingly, Sobel, Prewitt, or unsharp with different sizes (3×3, 5×5, 7×7, and 9×9) were included in the present study. A brief description of each filter is introduced as follows (Annadurai, 2007; Pitas, 2000; Prewitt, 1970; Solomon & Breckon, 2011).

2.2.1 Sobel operator

The Sobel filter (H_{Sobel}) with a different window (mask) size can be represented as follows. At size 3×3, $H_{sobel\ (3 \times 3)}$ is given by:

1	2	1
0	0	0
-1	-2	-1

At size 5×5, $H_{sobel\ (5 \times 5)}$ is given by:

1	4	6	4	1
2	8	12	8	2
0	0	0	0	0
-2	-8	-12	-8	-2
-1	-4	-6	-4	-1

2.2.2 Prewitt operator

The Prewitt operator is a discrete differentiation operator that computes the gradient estimate of the image intensity function, where its output is the equivalent gradient vector or the norm of the gradient vector. It applies convolution on the image with a separable, integer, and small-valued filter in the horizontal/vertical directions. The Prewitt filter (H $_{Prewitt}$) with a different window (mask) size can be represented as follows. At size 3×3, H $_{Prewitt\ (3 \times 3)}$ is given by:

1	1	1
0	0	0
−1	−1	−1

At size 5×5, $H_{\text{Prewitt } (5 \times 5)}$ is given by:

1	2	3	2	1
1	2	3	2	1
0	0	0	0	0
−1	−2	−3	−2	−1
−1	−2	−3	−2	−1

2.2.3 Unsharp operator

The unsharp filter is mainly a sharpening operator that enhances the high-frequency components and edges in an image by subtracting a smoothed/unsharp form of the image from its original version. Assume an original image $f(x,y)$ is input into the unsharp mask, thus the produced edge image $d(x,y)$, which includes the high-pass components, can be expressed as follows:

$$d(x, y) = f(x, y) - f_{lowpass}(x, y) \qquad (7)$$

Then, for sharpening, the edge image is added back to the original image using the following expression:

$$f_{sharp}(x, y) = f(x, y) + s^* d(x, y) \qquad (8)$$

where s is a scaling constant. The unsharp filter (H_{Unsharp}) with a different window (mask) size can be represented as follows. At size 3×3, $H_{\text{Unsharp } (3 \times 3)}$ is given by:

−1/16	−2/16	−1/16
−2/16	12/16	−2/16
−1/16	−2/16	−1/16

At size 5×5, $H_{\text{Unsharp } (5 \times 5)}$ is given by:

−1/32	0	−2/32	0	−1/32
0	−1/32	−2/32	−1/32	0
−2/32	−2/32	24/32	−2/32	−2/32
0	−1/32	−2/32	−1/32	0
−1/32	0	−2/32	0	−1/32

2.3 Average filter-based neutrosophic set for K-means clustering

During the NS process, the I subset is used to modify the true subset T in the next NS version by identifying the pixels that will be considered in the next NS version. Accordingly, a threshold value ($\alpha_{optimal}=0.0014$) is employed in the identification procedure, where the local mean is used to handle the pixels whose I values are higher than $\alpha_{optimal}=0.0014$. The local mean of $T(j,k)$ can be given by:

$$T_{local}(j,k) = \frac{1}{n \times n} \sum_{c=k-n/2}^{k+n/2} \sum_{l=j-n/2}^{j+n/2} R(c,l) \tag{9}$$

Then, the update of the used pixel intensity in T is performed using the following expression:

$$T_{updated}(j,k) = \begin{cases} T_{local}(j,k), & I(j,k) > \alpha_{optimal} \\ T(j,k), & I(j,k) \leq \alpha_{optimal} \end{cases} \tag{10}$$

This updated value is used to generate the iterative new version of the image as follows:

$$R_{modified}(j,k) = R_{min} + (R_{max} - R_{min}) \times T_{updated}(j,k) \tag{11}$$

Consequently, this entropy of I is then used as a stopping criterion of the NS iterative process, which can be defined as:

$$\frac{Ent_I(i) - Ent_I(i+1)}{Ent_I(i)} < delta \tag{12}$$

2.4 Proposed neutrosophic K-means clustering

Typically, K-means clustering is considered one of the most efficient unsupervised segmentation techniques. It clusters the objects/pixels/data points into K groups, where the distance between the data points in the same group is small (Dhanachandra, Manglem, & Chanu, 2015). The K-means approach is an iterative process to calculate the average value of each cluster and to compute the distance of each point from the matched cluster, which is the nearest cluster. This iterative process is repeated until no further reduction can be obtained in the sum of the square errors in each cluster.

In the modified neutrosophic image, another threshold Th_I is used to determine the pixel points for a further clustering process. This threshold value Th_I affects the clustering process of the skin lesion images, as it is used to identify the indeterminacy pixels whose I value is higher than its value. Only the pixels in I that achieve $I(j, k) < Th_I$ will be used in T for further clustering using the K-means method. Other pixels will not participate in the K-means clustering process, and their clustering results are determined using their neighborhood's clustering results.

Consequently, the stages of the proposed comparative study of the effect of using different edge detection-based NS on the K-means clustering are reported in the following algorithm.

Algorithm: Proposed comparative study procedure

Start1

>*Input* the dermoscopic color image
>*Convert* the colored dermoscopic image into gray-scale image
>*Start2* neutrosophic set mapping procedure
>>*Set* $\alpha_{optimal} = 0.0014$ and number of iterations $= 100$
>>*Select* high-pass filter (Sobel, Prewitt, or unsharp) for the gradient calculation during the I computing for the comparative study
>>*Try* different window (mask) size for each selected filter from the size set of 3×3, 5×5, 7×7 and 9×9
>>*Compute* the first NS three neutrosophic subsets T, I, and F on the gray scale image
>>*Compute* the entropy of the first I (1st iteration)
>>*Start* the iterative steps of the NS, which are:
>>>*Step 1: Calculate* T, I, and F
>>>*Step 2: Generate* the next T (T updated) using previous I and $\alpha_{optimal}$
>>>*Step 3: Generate* new image version $R_{modified}$
>>>*Step 4: Calculate* the entropy
>>>>*If* the stopping criteria achieved
>>>>>**Break**
>>>>*Else*
>>>>>*Go to* Step 1
>>>>*Endif*
>*Stop2* of the NS procedure
>*Cluster* the selected pixels of $I(j, k) < Th_I$ on T using K-means clustering procedure
>*Label* the pixels that $I(j, k) \geq Th_I$ using their neighbors' clustering results
>*Stop 1*

In this work, the pixels in the skin lesion images are clustered in different assemblies using the neutrosophic image components, where the cluster of the lowest T value is considered the lesion candidate pixel. In addition, the accurate computing of I leads to the accurate determination of the lesion boundaries, which depends mainly on the filter type and size, as illustrated in the present work.

2.5   Evaluation metrics

In the present chapter, several evaluation metrics (Rundo et al., 2017), namely JAC, the Dice coefficient (Dice), specificity, sensitivity, and accuracy, are measured to evaluate the performance of the NS-based K-means clustering procedure using different edge-detection filters during the calculations of the neutrosophic I component in the NS. These metrics include the JAC index, which is a statistical measurement that can be expressed as follows:

$$\text{JAC}(O, Q) = \frac{Ar_O \cap Ar_Q}{Ar_O \cup Ar_Q} \qquad (13)$$

where $\cup$ is the union operation, $\cap$ is the intersection operation of any two sets, Ar_O represents the clustered/segmented skin lesion region using the NS-based K-means clustering, and Ar_Q is the ground-truth skin lesion region. A high JAC value indicates superior results compared to small JAC values, where if JAC$=1$ indicates complete similarity, JAC$=0$ shows no similarity.

Furthermore, the Dice index (Dice) compares the correspondence between two sets G and Z using the following formula:

$$\text{Dice} = \frac{2|G \cap Z|}{|G| + |Z|} \qquad (14)$$

Other performance metrics related to the detected lesion regions are the accuracy, sensitivity, and specificity. The accuracy measures the ratio of the true positive/negative results for clarifying the reliability of the diagnosis degree. The sensitivity measures the prediction ability of the used clustering method to detect the skin lesion regions. However, the specificity shows how the proposed clustering method predicts the other regions in the dermoscopic image.

3   Results and discussion

In the present chapter, 50 randomly selected skin lesion images from the ISIC 2016 challenge are used to evaluate the different filters used in the I subset calculations in the NS compared to the corresponding ground truth of each image. The optimal value $\alpha_{optimal}=0.0014$ as concluded in Ashour, Hawas, et al. (2018) is used during the performance evaluation calculations.

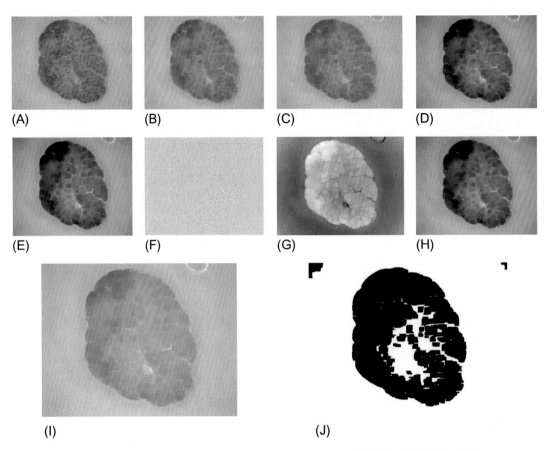

Fig. 1 The proposed approach steps using the unsharp filter of size 7×7: (A) Original ISIC_0010447 dermoscopic image, (B) preprocessed image after hair removal, (C) gray version of the preprocessed image, (D) first NS version after the first iteration, (E)–(H) last NS mapping operators after the last iteration as (E) last true image T; (F) last undetermined image I; (G) last false image F; (H) last NS version, (I) NS outputted image, (J) K-means clustered image (unsupervised segmented image).

Fig. 1 illustrates the consequential images of the different stages using an unsharp filter of size 7×7 of the NS mapping.

Fig. 1 shows that first the dermoscopic neutrosophic image of the three subsets T, F, and I is generated, as demonstrated in Fig. 1D after the first iteration, where the entropy value was computed before the next iteration. Afterward, the three subsets were created and the entropy was computed and compared with the preceding obtained entropy value. This procedure is recurrently occurring until the dissimilarity between the entropy value of the recent iteration and its preceding values divided by the preceding entropy is less than $\alpha_{optimal} = 0.0014$, that is, if $Ent_I(\text{iteration}_e + 1) - Ent_I(\text{iteration}_e) / Ent_I(\text{iteration}_e) < delta$ is achieved. Once this constraint is realized, the iterative procedure is terminated and the final T, F, and I operators of the NS image are obtained, as demonstrated in Figs. 1E–H.

3.1 Comparative study of different filters in designing the neutrosophic *I* subset in the NS domain

The K-means-based unsupervised segmentation for detecting and clustering of the selected dermoscopic images in the present study is displayed in Fig. 2 using different edge-detection filters with different sizes. The illustrated images have different lesion sizes, shapes, and skin surface roughnesses. Fig. 2C–E illustrated the clustered images using the Sobel filter, the Prewitt filter, and the unsharp filter, respectively. The red contours indicated the ground truth of the corresponding skin lesion as given in the ISIC 2016 dataset while the blue contours indicated the detected skin lesion regions using NS-based K-means clustering with different structures of the edge-detection filters.

Fig. 2 established that using an unsharp filter with a window size of 7×7 achieved superior results compared to the other window sizes of the same filter as well as compared to the other filter types, namely the Sobel and Prewitt operators. These results are because of the ability of the unsharp filter to sharpen and enhance the high-frequency components, which represent the edges in the dermoscopic images. However, all filters at different window sizes failed to identify the skin lesion contour in the ISIC_0010447 dermoscopic image caused by the presence of dissimilar color regions and/or dark regions in the same lesion part.

3.2 Performance evaluation

The evaluation metrics as well as the required computational time during the calculations of the NS mapping process, which are affected by the used edge-detection filter and its size, are measured in the present comparative study.

3.2.1 Evaluation metrics measurements

The average values of the measured evaluation metrics using the different edge-detection filters in the NS design are reported in Table 1.

Table 1 established the superiority of the unsharp filter of 7×7 window size in terms of the average accuracy of 95.25%, the JAC of

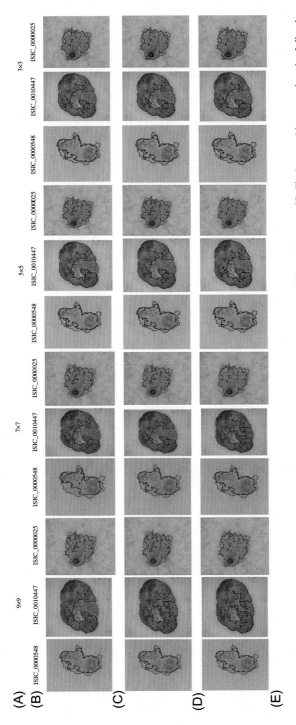

Fig. 2 Comparative clustering results: (A) size of each mask,(B) the image number in the ISIC 2016 dataset, (C–E) clustered image using the following edge-detector filter in NS-based K-means (blue contour): (C) using Sobel filter, (D) using Prewitt filter, and (E) using unsharp filter, where the red contour is the ground truth of the corresponding skin lesion.

Table 1 The average value of the different performance evaluation metrics using different edge-detection filters.

Filter type/size	JAC	Dice	Sensitivity (%)	Specificity (%)	Accuracy (%)
Sobel7x7	0.75	0.85	78.70	96.62	91.87
Prewitt5x5	0.76	0.85	79.14	96.62	91.96
Sobel9x9	0.76	0.85	79.16	96.62	91.96
Sobel5x5	0.76	0.85	79.18	96.62	91.96
Prewitt7x7	0.76	0.85	79.28	96.62	92.01
Prewitt9x9	0.76	0.85	79.49	96.62	92.12
Unsharp3x3	0.78	0.87	78.10	99.95	95.09
Sobel3x3	0.78	0.88	78.68	99.95	95.07
Prewitt3x3	0.78	0.88	78.69	99.95	95.07
Unsharp5x5	0.79	0.88	78.93	99.95	95.19
Unsharp9x9	0.79	0.88	78.95	99.95	95.19
Unsharp7x7	0.80	0.89	79.14	99.95	95.25

0.80, and the Dice of 0.89 values during the detection of the skin lesion regions compared to the use of the other filters of different sizes. However, in terms of the specificity, the best average value is 99.95%, which is obtained using the unsharp filter with window sizes of 3×3, 5×5, 7×7, and 9×9 as well as in the case of using the Sobel of size 3×3 and the Prewitt of size 3×3. Furthermore, the Prewitt with size 9×9 achieved the best average sensitivity of 79.49%. Figs. 3–5 illustrate the reported results in Table 1.

These experimental results proved the overall superiority of the unsharp filter of 7×7 to detect the boundaries of the skin lesion regions compared to the results of the other edge-detection filters at different window sizes.

3.2.2 Comparative study in terms of the computational time

Computational time is another metric to be considered in the computation of the I subset. Subsequently, the computational time of the NS process is measured to compare between the different filters of different sizes. Accordingly, Fig. 6 demonstrates a

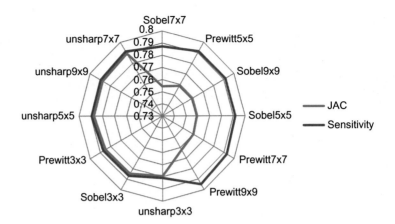

Fig. 3 Comparative average results of the JAC and sensitivity using the different edge-detection filters.

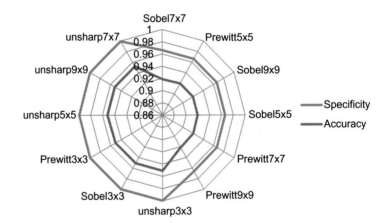

Fig. 4 Comparative average results of the specificity and accuracy using the different edge-detection filters.

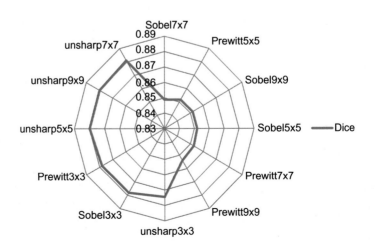

Fig. 5 Comparative average Dice using the different edge-detection filters.

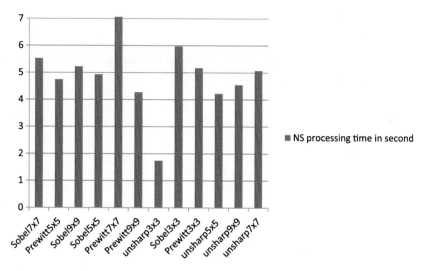

Fig. 6 Comparative average required processing time in seconds of the NS using the different edge-detection filters.

comparative study in terms of the NS average processing time in seconds (*Y*-axis).

Fig. 6 shows that the unsharp of window size 3×3 required the least computational time of 1.74 s while the Prewitt operator of size 7×7 took the maximum required computational time of 7.06 s. However, the unsharp filter of window size 7×7 took 5.07 s. Moreover, the other filter structures took computational times ranging from 4.2–6 s.

The preceding results established the importance of studying the edge-detection filter design used in the NS process to ensure the sharp detected boundaries. Hence, it is recommended to study the effect of changing the filter's type and size with different medical image types, such as magnetic resonance images, ultrasound images, and microscopic images, to ensure the most suitable filter structure to be used in the NS. Likewise, as illustrated in Fig. 2, all filter performances were deteriorated and failed to detect the skin lesion regions that included dissimilar color regions and/or dark regions. Therefore, it is recommended to implement a new filter to overcome such cases. In future works, it is also suggested to study the effect of different filter types/sizes during the calculation of the main three components of the NS (*T, I, F*), not only the filter in the *I* subset. Other clustering techniques such as NCM can be applied and compared to the K-means in such a comparative study.

4 Conclusions

Image clustering for unsupervised segmentation plays an imperative role in several applications, especially in medical image processing. During the clustering process, the pixels are categorized into the attribute regions based on the regions near the pixel locale. One of the urgent clustering medical applications is skin lesion detection and segmentation, which requires early and efficient diagnosis. Automated melanoma detection and segmentation are considered challenging processes, owing to the low contrast of skin lesions, the intraclass inconsistency of melanomas, and the existence of different artifacts in dermoscopic images such as air bubbles, hair, and noise.

Copious studies based on image processing were carried out to handle dermoscopic images for accurate diagnosis. Such studies recommended the use of neutrosophic theory to reduce/remove the uncertainty from dermoscopic images. The introduction section in this chapter referred to some of these studies that employed NS for skin lesion detection, clustering, segmentation, and classification. However, none of the studies studied the effect of the filter's type and size during the calculation of the main three components of NS (T, I, F). This inspired the recent work in this chapter to carry out such a comparative study compared to the widely used default filter, a Sobel of size 3×3. In addition, the effect of using different filter structures and sizes was evaluated by calculating the segmentation metrics, namely JAC, dice, specificity, sensitivity, and accuracy as well as the computation time per filter.

The proposed comparative study was conducted in the present work on randomly selected dermoscopic images from the public ISIC 2016 dataset. After converting the colored skin images into gray, a preprocessing step was applied before mapping the dermoscopic images into the neutrosophic set domain using the three neutrosophic subsets that represent the lesion region information, the lesion boundaries, and the background in the dermoscopic image. During this mapping process, different edge-detection filter structures of different types and sizes were examined as proposed. Finally, the mapped neutrosophic images were segmented using the K-means clustering procedure.

The comparative experimental results proved the outstanding performance using the unsharp filter of window size 7×7, which took 5.07s during the NS process and achieved the best average JAC of 0.80, dice of 0.89, and accuracy of 95.25% during detection of the skin lesion regions compared to the default Sobel filter of size 3×3 as well as the other filters of different sizes. Consequently, it is recommended to use other operators such as Roberts and Laplacian in future works.

References

Aljanabi, M., Özok, Y., Rahebi, J., & Abdullah, A. (2018). Skin lesion segmentation method for dermoscopy images using artificial bee colony algorithm. *Symmetry, 10*(8), 347.

Annadurai, S. (2007). *Fundamentals of digital image processing.* Pearson Education India.

Ashour, A. S., Guo, Y., Kucukkulahli, E., Erdogmus, P., & Polat, K. (2018). A hybrid dermoscopy images segmentation approach based on neutrosophic clustering and histogram estimation. *Applied Soft Computing, 69*, 426–434.

Ashour, A. S., Hawas, A. R., Guo, Y., & Wahba, M. A. (2018). A novel optimized neutrosophic k-means using genetic algorithm for skin lesion detection in dermoscopy images. *Signal, Image and Video Processing*, 1–8.

Basu, S., Banerjee, A., & Mooney, R. (2002). Semi-supervised clustering by seeding. In *Proceedings of 19th international conference on machine learning (ICML-2002.*

Bezdek, J. C., Hall, L. O., & Clarke, L. (1993). Review of MR image segmentation techniques using pattern recognition. *Medical Physics, 20*(4), 1033–1048.

Castillejos, H., Ponomaryov, V., Nino-de-Rivera, L., & Golikov, V. (2012). Wavelet transform fuzzy algorithms for dermoscopic image segmentation. *Computational and Mathematical Methods in Medicine, 2012.*

Celebi, M. E., & Zornberg, A. (2014). Automated quantification of clinically significant colors in dermoscopy images and its application to skin lesion classification. *IEEE Systems Journal, 8*(3), 980–984.

Chen, W., Giger, M. L., & Bick, U. (2006). A fuzzy c-means (FCM)-based approach for computerized segmentation of breast lesions in dynamic contrast-enhanced MR Images 1. *Academic Radiology, 13*(1), 63–72.

Cheng, H. D., Shan, J., Ju, W., Guo, Y., & Zhang, L. (2010). Automated breast cancer detection and classification using ultrasound images: A survey. *Pattern Recognition, 43*(1), 299–317.

Chuang, K. S., Tzeng, H. L., Chen, S., Wu, J., & Chen, T. J. (2006). Fuzzy c-means clustering with spatial information for image segmentation. *Computerized Medical Imaging and Graphics, 30*(1), 9–15.

Dalal, A., Moss, R. H., Stanley, R. J., Stoecker, W. V., Gupta, K., Calcara, D. A., ... Perry, L. A. (2011). Concentric decile segmentation of white and hypopigmented areas in dermoscopy images of skin lesions allows discrimination of malignant melanoma. *Computerized Medical Imaging and Graphics, 35*(2), 148–154.

De, S. K., Biswas, R., & Roy, A. R. (2001). An application of intuitionistic fuzzy sets in medical diagnosis. *Fuzzy Sets and Systems, 117*(2), 209–213.

Dhanachandra, N., Manglem, K., & Chanu, Y. J. (2015). Image segmentation using K-means clustering algorithm and subtractive clustering algorithm. *Procedia Computer Science, 54*, 764–771.

El Agha, M., & Ashour, W. M. (2012). Efficient and fast initialization algorithm for k-means clustering. *International Journal of Intelligent Systems and Applications, 4*(1), 21.

Emre Celebi, M., Alp Aslandogan, Y., Stoecker, W. V., Iyatomi, H., Oka, H., & Chen, X. (2007). Unsupervised border detection in dermoscopy images. *Skin Research and Technology, 13*(4), 454–462.

Frey, B. J., & Jojic, N. (2003). Transformation-invariant clustering using the EM algorithm. *IEEE Transactions on Pattern Analysis and Machine Intelligence, 25*(1), 1–17.

Ghosh, S., & Dubey, S. K. (2013). Comparative analysis of k-means and fuzzy c-means algorithms. *International Journal of Advanced Computer Science and Applications, 4*(4).

Gómez, D. D., Butakoff, C., Ersboll, B. K., & Stoecker, W. (2008). Independent histogram pursuit for segmentation of skin lesions. *IEEE Transactions on Biomedical Engineering, 55*(1), 157–161.

Guo, Y., Ashour, A. S., & Smarandache, F. (2018). A novel skin lesion detection approach using neutrosophic clustering and adaptive region growing in dermoscopy images. *Symmetry, 10*(4), 119.

Guo, Y., & Cheng, H. D. (2009). New neutrosophic approach to image segmentation. *Pattern Recognition, 42*(5), 587–595.

Guo, Y., & Sengur, A. (2015). NCM: Neutrosophic c-means clustering algorithm. *Pattern Recognition, 48*(8), 2710–2724.

International Skin Imaging Collaboration Website: http://www.isdis.net/index.php/isic-project.

Jain, A. K., Duin, R. P., & Mao, J. (2000). Statistical pattern recognition: A review. *IEEE Transactions on Pattern Analysis and Machine Intelligence, 22*(1), 4–37.

Kockara, S., Mete, M., Chen, B., & Aydin, K. (2010). Analysis of density based and fuzzy c-means clustering methods on lesion border extraction in dermoscopy images. In: *Vol. 11(6). BMC bioinformatics* (p. S26): BioMed Central.

Korotkov, K., & Garcia, R. (2012). Computerized analysis of pigmented skin lesions: A review. *Artificial Intelligence in Medicine, 56*(2), 69–90.

Koundal, D., Gupta, S., & Singh, S. (2012). Applications of neutrosophic and intuitionistic fuzzy set on Image processing. In *National conference on green technologies: Smart and efficient management (GTSEM-2012)* (pp. 1–4).

Masson, M. H., & Denœux, T. (2009). RECM: Relational evidential c-means algorithm. *Pattern Recognition Letters, 30*(11), 1015–1026.

Melli, R., Grana, C., & Cucchiara, R. (2006). Comparison of color clustering algorithms for segmentation of dermatological images. In *Vol. 6144. Medical imaging 2006: Image processing,* (p. 61443S). International Society for Optics and Photonics.

Mohan, J., Krishnaveni, V., & Guo, Y. (2015). Automated brain tumor segmentation on MR images based on neutrosophic set approach. In *2nd International conference on electronics and communication systems (ICECS), 2015* (pp. 1078–1083): IEEE.

Oliveira, R. B., Mercedes Filho, E., Ma, Z., Papa, J. P., Pereira, A. S., & Tavares, J. M. R. (2016). Computational methods for the image segmentation of pigmented skin lesions: A review. *Computer Methods and Programs in Biomedicine, 131,* 127–141.

Pal, N. R., Pal, K., Keller, J. M., & Bezdek, J. C. (2005). A possibilistic fuzzy c-means clustering algorithm. *IEEE Transactions on Fuzzy Systems, 13*(4), 517–530.

Pitas, I. (2000). *Digital image processing algorithms and applications.* John Wiley & Sons.

Prewitt, J. M. (1970). Object enhancement and extraction. *Picture Processing and Psychopictorics, 10*(1), 15–19.

Revathi, S., & Nalini, D. T. (2013). Performance comparison of various clustering algorithm. *International Journal of Advanced Research in Computer Science and Software Engineering, 3*(2).

Rundo, L., Militello, C., Russo, G., Garufi, A., Vitabile, S., Gilardi, M. C., & Mauri, G. (2017). Automated prostate gland segmentation based on an unsupervised fuzzy C-means clustering technique using multispectral T1w and T2w MR imaging. *Information, 8*(2), 49.

Sengur, A., & Guo, Y. (2011). Color texture image segmentation based on neutrosophic set and wavelet transformation. *Computer Vision and Image Understanding, 115*(8), 1134–1144.

Shmmala, F. A., & Ashour, W. (2013). Color based image segmentation using different versions of k-means in two spaces. *Global Advanced Research Journal of Engineering, Technology and Innovation, 1*(9), 30–41.

Smarandache, F. (1999). A unifying field in logics: Neutrosophic logic. In *Philosophy* (pp. 1–141): American Research Press.

Smarandache, F. (Ed.), (2003). *A unifying field in logics: Neutrosophic logic. Neutrosophy, neutrosophic set, neutrosophic probability: Neutrosophic logic: Neutrosophy, neutrosophic set, neutrosophic probability. Infinite study.*

Solomon, C., & Breckon, T. (2011). *Fundamentals of digital image processing: A practical approach with examples in Matlab.* John Wiley & Sons.

Sookpotharom, S. (2009). Border detection of skin lesion images based on fuzzy C-means thresholding. In *3rd International conference on genetic and evolutionary computing, 2009. WGEC'09* (pp. 777–780): IEEE.

Steinley, D. (2006). K-means clustering: A half-century synthesis. *British Journal of Mathematical and Statistical Psychology, 59*(1), 1–34.

Van der Laan, M., Pollard, K., & Bryan, J. (2003). A new partitioning around medoids algorithm. *Journal of Statistical Computation and Simulation, 73*(8), 575–584.

Wahba, M. A., Ashour, A. S., Guo, Y., Napoleon, S. A., & Elnaby, M. M. A. (2018). A novel cumulative level difference mean based GLDM and modified ABCD features ranked using eigenvector centrality approach for four skin lesion types classification. *Computer Methods and Programs in Biomedicine, 165,* 163–174.

Wahba, M. A., Ashour, A. S., Napoleon, S. A., Elnaby, M. M. A., & Guo, Y. (2017). Combined empirical mode decomposition and texture features for skin lesion classification using quadratic support vector machine. *Health Information Science and Systems, 5*(1), 10.

Wighton, P., Sadeghi, M., Lee, T. K., & Atkins, M. S. (2009). A fully automatic random walker segmentation for skin lesions in a supervised setting. In *International conference on medical image computing and computer-assisted intervention* (pp. 1108–1115). Berlin, Heidelberg: Springer.

Yuan, X., Situ, N., & Zouridakis, G. (2009). A narrow band graph partitioning method for skin lesion segmentation. *Pattern Recognition, 42*(6), 1017–1028.

9

Optimization-based neutrosophic set for medical image processing

Thilaga Shri Chandra Amma Palanisamy*, Mohan Jayaraman†, Krishnaveni Vellingiri‡, Yanhui Guo§

*Department of ECE, College of Engineering Guindy, Anna University, Chennai, India. †Department of ECE, SRM Valliammai Engineering College, Kattankulathur, India. ‡Department of ECE, PSG College of Technology, Coimbatore, India. §Department of Computer Science, University of Illinois at Springfield, Springfield, IL, United States

1 Introduction

In modern medicine, due to the technological advancements in digital medical imaging, most clinicians make a diagnosis and provide treatment for a variety of medical conditions based on useful information delivered by medical images. The medical conditions, including abnormalities in the brain and spinal cord; diseases in the heart, liver, pancreas, and other abdominal organs; injuries or abnormalities in the bone joints; and abnormalities in various parts of the body, can be visualized using the medical images (Rangayyan, 2005; Smith & Webb, 2011). These could be features such as tumors and lesions that are not normally seen; changes in shape, that is, shrinkage and enlargement of particular structures; and changes in image intensity within the image compared to normal tissue. The popular medical imaging modalities are X-ray imaging (Dorthe Wildenschild & Sheppard, 2013; Laval-Jeantet, D'Haenens, & Klausz, 1982), computed tomography (CT) (Homma, 2011; Hsieh, 2009), ultrasound imaging (Cheng, Shan, Ju, Guo, & Zhang, 2010; Saba et al., 2016; Zeng, Wang, Yu, & Guo, 2013), MRI (Kuperman, 2000; Rodriguez, 2004; Rummeny, Reimer, & Heindel, 2009; Wright, 1997), microscopic imaging (Gaietta et al., 2002; McNamara, Difilippantonio, Ried, & Bieber, 2017; Xing & Yang, 2016), optical coherence tomography (Abramoff, Garvin, & Sonka, 2010; Jordan, Menolotto, Bolster, Livingstone, & Giardini, 2017), dermoscopic imaging (Argenziano et al., 2008;

Neutrosophic Set in Medical Image Analysis. https://doi.org/10.1016/B978-0-12-818148-5.00009-6

Ashour, Guo, Kucukkulahli, Erdogmus, & Polat, 2018; Ashour, Hawas, Guo, & Wahba, 2018; Guo, Ashour, & Smarandache, 2018; Jaworek-Korjakowska & Kleczek, 2018; Kittler et al., 2006; Menzies et al., 2009; Menzies, Stevenson, Altamura, & Byth, 2011; Vesal, Patil, Ravikumar, & Maier, 2018; Wahba, Ashour, Napoleon, Elnaby, & Guo, 2017), and molecular imaging (Hirschmann, Wagner, Rasch, & Henckel, 2012; Lu, Wang, & Zhang, 2015; Segovia & Phillips, 2014; Yoder, 2013; Zheng et al., 2017).

A brain tumor is an abnormal mass of tissues that grows uncontrollably. A benign tumor has well-defined edges while a malignant one, that is, with irregular borders, invades the normal tissue (https://mayfieldclinic.com/pe-braintumor.htm). The metastasis tumors to the brain affect nearly 150,000 people a year. For example, the chance that people with lung cancer will develop metastatic brain tumors is 40% (https://www.aans.org/Patients/Neurosurgical-Conditions-and-Treatments/Brain-Tumors). More sophisticated diagnostic systems used for the early detection of tumors and innovative surgical and radiation approaches for treatment have helped to improve the quality of life for patients with brain tumors. MRI is the best medical imaging technique used in radiology to diagnose a brain tumor, as it visualizes brain structures and detects abnormalities in the brain with different contrast properties (Wright, 1997).

In order to detect the tumor in the brain MR images, image segmentation is used. Usually, segmentation is done in three methods: manual, semiautomatic, and automatic. In manual tumor segmentation, radiologists perform the tumor region extraction manually by going through multiple slices of MR images with their physiological and anatomical knowledge gained through practice and experience, which is a time-consuming process (Angulakshmi & Lakshmi Priya, 2017; Gordillo, Montseny, & Sobrevilla, 2013; Isin, Direkoglu, & Sah, 2016; Rajasekaran & Gounder, 2018; Tjahyaningtijas, 2018). In semiautomatic methods, both user interaction and software computing are used for segmentation. The user interaction is required for initialization, intervention, and evaluation of the software computing algorithms for segmenting the brain tumor. The efficiency and accuracy of this method will depend on the user/experts (Angulakshmi & Lakshmi Priya, 2017; Gordillo et al., 2013; Isin et al., 2016; Rajasekaran & Gounder, 2018; Tjahyaningtijas, 2018).

In the fully automatic method, the computer determines the brain tumor by segmenting the medical images without the interaction of the experts. This method requires artificial intelligence and machine-learning techniques with prior knowledge (Angulakshmi & Lakshmi Priya, 2017; Gordillo et al., 2013; Isin et al., 2016; Rajasekaran & Gounder, 2018; Tjahyaningtijas, 2018). The exploitation of optimized medical image analysis algorithms in a clinical context helps to provide more accuracy in the analysis. Optimization in medical image processing intends to find some solution that is the "best" according to some criterion. In addition, a powerful optimization method is considered for analyzing the medical images in terms of speed and optimal convergence. To realize a more accurate as well as the best diagnosis, medical image processing and analysis, such as image segmentation, classification, registration, and fusion, are used with improved performance using bio-inspired optimization procedures (Chithambaram & Perumal, 2017; Soleimani & Vincheh, 2013).

Optimization-based neutrosophic set approaches are used in medical image processing to enhance the performance metrics. In NS-based medical image-processing methods, optimization can be applied in either the medical image-processing algorithm or in the NS operations. In the first case, simple NS operations are used for medical image enhancement and optimized image processing techniques help to get accurate results. In breast cancer, Syed and Hassanein (2017) proposed an optimized detection method using NS and moth-flame optimization. The histopathological slide image is enhanced using a Gaussian filter. In order to focus on detecting mitosis cells, the morphological operations are performed to true subset images, which are obtained by mapping the enhanced image into the NS domain. An MFO algorithm is used for the best discriminating feature subset selection of mitosis cells from the total of 345 features by maximizing the f-score. To classify the mitosis and nonmitosis cells, this selected feature subset is fed to the classification and regression tree (CART). The MFO-based feature selection algorithm's robustness is compared to other metaheuristic algorithms, such as chicken swarm optimizer (CSO), grey wolf optimization (GWO), and ant bee colony (ABC) feature selection algorithms. From the obtained results, MFO offers good classification performance by selecting the minimum number of features as well as fast convergence. For automatic liver tumor segmentation, Anter and Hassenian (2018) integrated the NS, fast FCM, and PSO. The results proved the superiority and robustness of the used approach with accurate and fast convergence.

In the second case, optimization is used in NS operations for reducing the indeterminacy to increase the performance of medical image segmentation. Ashour, Hawas, Guo, and Wahba (2018) developed the skin lesion detection method from dermoscopy images using GA-optimized NS with k-means clustering. In this approach, the α-mean operation's α value of the NS domain is optimized by using GA optimization where the fitness function is the Jaccard index maximization. The dermoscopic images were mapped on the NS space by using this optimal α value and the skin lesion images in the NS domain were segmented using k-means clustering. The experimental results demonstrated that this approach achieved high average accuracies. In the present chapter, the optimization technique is used for guiding the image segmentation algorithm and NS is used to enhance the image quality. Here, automatic brain tumor segmentation from MR images is done by enhancing the MR images using a nonlocal mean operation and mapping to the NS domain followed by the modified PSO-guided fuzzy c-means (FCM) method for segmentation. The organization of the following sections is as follows: Section 2 introduces the methods employed in the methodology for automatic brain tumor segmentation in detail. Section 3 demonstrates the results, including the visualization of the NS steps and optimized tumor segmentation and localization with the evaluation metrics compared with the original FCM and NS-FCM. Finally, Section 4 includes the conclusions and suggested future work.

2 Methodology

The NS is applied into the MR image domain after enhancing the MR images using the nonlocal mean operation by defining the entropy of the NS to quantify the indeterminacy. Then, the FCM along with a modified PSO algorithm is used for segmenting the brain tumor from the MR images.

2.1 Nonlocal means

To enhance the brain tumor MR images, the nonlocal mean (NLM) operation is performed on the MR images. In the nonlocal means, a discrete noisy image is given as $u = \{u(a) \mid a \in I\}$ and the estimated value of a pixel a is $NL[u](a)$, which is computed by taking the weighted average of all the pixels in the image,

$$NL[u](a) = \sum_{b \in I} w(a, b) u(b) \tag{1}$$

where the family of weights $\{w(a,b)\}_b$ depends on the similarity between the pixels a and b, and satisfies the usual conditions $0 \leq w(a,b) \leq 1$ and $\sum_b w(a,b) = 1$ (Buades, Coll, & Morel, 2005).

The similarity between two pixels a and b depends on the similarity of the intensity gray level vectors $u(N_a)$ and $u(N_b)$, where N_a and N_b denote a square neighborhood of fixed size and centered at a pixel a and b, respectively. This similarity is measured as a decreasing function of the weighted Euclidean distance, $\|u(N_a) - u(N_b)\|_{2,\ \sigma}^2$, where $\sigma > 0$ is the standard deviation of the Gaussian kernel. Using the Euclidean distance to the noisy neighborhoods leads to the following equality:

$$E\|u(N_a) - u(N_b)\|_{2,\sigma}^2 = \|u(N_a) - u(N_b)\|_{2,\sigma}^2 + 2\sigma^2 \qquad (2)$$

These equality conditions illustrate the algorithm's robustness, where the Euclidean distance conserves the order of similarity between pixels, as expected. The pixels with a similar grey level neighborhood to $u(N_a)$ have larger weights in the average. These weights are given by:

$$w(a, b) = \frac{1}{Z(a)} e^{-\frac{\|u(N_a) - u(N_b)\|_{2,\sigma}^2}{h^2}} \qquad (3)$$

where $Z(a)$ is the normalizing constant using the following expression:

$$Z(a) = \sum_b e^{-\frac{\|u(N_a) - u(N_b)\|_{2,\sigma}^2}{h^2}} \qquad (4)$$

where the parameter h acts as a degree of filtering to control the decay of the exponential function leading to a decay of the weights as a function of the Euclidean distances. The three key parameters while using the NLM filter are the size of the search window (w), the size of the neighborhood window (f), and the degree of the filtering (h). The MR images are enhanced by choosing the parameters w and f as 6 and 3, respectively, and h is considered proportional to the intensity value of the image (Manjon et al., 2008; Mohan, Krishnaveni, & Guo, 2013a).

2.2 Neutrosophic image

The neutrosophic set is used to describe the uncertainty and indeterminacy in any information. In the NS, every event is defined by using the three components such as the true (T), indeterminate (I), and false (F) subsets (Smarandache, 2003). The nonlocal mean enhanced MR images are mapped into the neutrosophic image H_{NS}, which is described by three membership sets T, I, F. A pixel H in the image is described as $H(T, I, F)$ where $t, i,$ and f are the true, indeterminate, and false in the set, respectively, as t varies in T, i varies in I, and f varies in F. Afterward, the pixel $H(a, b)$ in the image space is transformed into the NS space $H_{NS}\ (a, b) = \{T(a, b), I(a, b), F(a, b)\}$. $T(a, b)$, $I(a, b)$ and $F(a, b)$ are the corresponding probabilities

(Cheng, Guo, & Zhang, 2011; Guo, Cheng, & Zhang, 2009; Mohan, Chandra, Krishnaveni, & Guo, 2012, 2013; Mohan, Krishnaveni, & Guo, 2012, 2013b), which are given by:

$$T(a, b) = \frac{\overline{G}(i, j) - \overline{G}_{\min}}{\overline{G}_{\max} - \overline{G}_{\min}} \tag{5}$$

$$\overline{G}(a, b) = \frac{1}{w \times w} \sum_{x=a-w/2}^{a+w/2} \sum_{y=b-w/2}^{b+w/2} G(x, y) \tag{6}$$

$$I(a, b) = \frac{\delta(a, b) - \delta_{\min}}{\delta_{\max} - \delta_{\min}} \tag{7}$$

$$\delta(a, b) = abs\big(G(a, b) - \overline{G}(a, b)\big) \tag{8}$$

$$F(a, b) = 1 - T(a, b) \tag{9}$$

where the pixels in the window have $\overline{G}(a, b)$ local mean, and $\delta(a, b)$ denotes the absolute value of difference between intensity $G(a, b)$ and its $\overline{G}(a, b)$.

For a gray-scale image, the entropy is calculated to assess the gray level distribution. Maximum entropy occurs when the intensities have equal probability with uniform distribution. Small entropy occurs with the intensities having different probabilities with nonuniform distribution. The entropy in the neutrosophic image is considered the totality of the T, I, and F entropies, which is used to measure the element distribution in the NS domain (Cheng et al., 2011; Guo et al., 2009; Mohan, Chandra, et al., 2012, 2013; Mohan, Krishnaveni, & Guo, 2012, 2013b), which is expressed as:

$$En_{NS} = En_T + En_I + En_F \tag{10}$$

$$En_T = -\sum_{k=\min\{T\}}^{\max\{T\}} p_T(k) \ln p_T(k) \tag{11}$$

$$En_I = -\sum_{k=\min\{I\}}^{\max\{I\}} p_I(k) \ln p_I(k) \tag{12}$$

$$En_F = -\sum_{k=\min\{T\}}^{\max\{F\}} p_F(k) \ln p_F(k) \tag{13}$$

where the entropies are En_T, En_I, and En_F for T, I, and F, respectively. Furthermore, the probabilities of the element k are $p_T(k)$, $p_I(k)$, and $p_F(k)$ in T, I, and F, respectively. The $I(a, b)$ value is engaged to calculate the indeterminacy of element $H_{NS}(a, b)$.

2.3 Fuzzy *c*-means clustering algorithm

Dunn (1973) developed the FCM algorithm, and later Bezdek, Coray, Gunderson, and Watson (1981) improved this one to assign each data point to one of the clusters. FCM is an unsupervised learning that is used for clustering, feature selection, image segmentation, and classifier design (Cannon, Dave, & Bezdek, 1986). Data points in FCM can belong to more than one cluster with different degrees of membership (Fukunaga, 2013). The fuzzification parameter (*m*) is used to determine the degree of fuzziness in the cluster. The FCM algorithm works its iterative manner, where the following objective function *J* is minimized:

$$J = \sum_{i=1}^{N} \sum_{j=1}^{C} (\delta_{ij})^m \|x_i - c_j\|^2 \tag{14}$$

where X is the set of N data elements, C is the required number of clusters, c_j is the center vector for the cluster, $1 \leq m \leq \infty$ is the fuzzifier, and $\delta_{ij} \in [0,1]$ is the degree of fuzzy membership for the *i*th data point x_i in cluster *j*. The norm, $\|x_i - c_j\|$ measures the closeness of the data point x_i to the center vector c_j of cluster *j*. The centroids and membership function can be simplified as follows:

$$c_j = \frac{\sum_{i=1}^{N} (\delta_{ij})^m x_i}{\sum_{i=1}^{N} (\delta_{ij})^m} \tag{15}$$

$$\delta_{ij} = \frac{1}{\sum_{k=1}^{C} \left(\frac{\|x_i - c_j\|}{\|x_i - c_k\|} \right)^{2/(m-1)}} \tag{16}$$

2.4 Modified particle swarm optimization

Kennedy and Eberhart (1995) hosted the PSO as a metaheuristic optimization procedure to find the global best solution. Like genetic algorithms (GAs), the state of the algorithm is represented by a population and it is iteratively modified until a termination condition gets satisfied. In PSO, the positions of the members of the population (i.e., particles) are updated iteratively by keeping the same population, whereas in GA, the population from generation to generation gets changed and uses crossover and mutation operations to pass down the genetic information of the best solution to the next generation. The PSO maintains a swarm of particles to find the solution to the considered optimization problem. To solve an M variable optimization problem, each particle holds an M-dimensional point in the search space. Each particle's fitness or quality is measured using a fitness function. The position, velocity, and fitness value of each particle are determined by the fitness function. For every iteration, each particle flies through the search space to obtain the best solution by having its own position and velocity. These parameters are updated based on their own previous iteration velocity, the distance from their own personal best position, and the distance from the position of the best particle in the swarm.

The optimization processes of PSO are initialized by random value for position and velocity of each particle and also initialize each particle's best position and the best position of the particle in the swarm. By using these values, the fitness value of each particle is determined. Based on the fitness value, each particle's best position and the best position of the particle in the swarm are updated as well as the velocity and position of each particle. These steps are iteratively done for each particle to find the superior solution until the optimal solution is established. Consider, the position of the particle a is $X_a = (x_{a1}, x_{a2}, \ldots, x_{aM})$ and velocity is $V_a = (v_{a1}, v_{a2}, \ldots, v_{aM})$ in M-dimensional space. In an iterative process, the current personal optimum position of particle a is $PB_a = (PB_{a1}, PB_{a2}, \ldots, PB_{aM})$ and the current swarm global optimum position is $GB = (GB_1, GB_2, \ldots, GB_M)$. The velocity of the particle a is updated by considering the inertia effect and the personal and social influence, which are calculated as follows:

$$v_{ab}(t+1) = \omega v_{ab}(t) + c_1 r_1 [PB_{ab} - x_{ab}(t)] + c_2 r_2 [GB_a - x_{ab}(t)] \quad (17)$$

The position of the particle is calculated as:

$$x_{ab}(t+1) = x_{ab}(t) + v_{ab}(t+1) \quad (18)$$

where ω is the inertia weight of PSO, which represents the inheritance of new velocity from the current one and has a range $0 < \omega < 1$; t is the iteration number. The parameters c_1 and c_2 are the learning factors of PSO that can help move each particle toward its personal best and global best positions; both are constants with the values between 0 and 4. The parameters r_1 and r_2 are uniformly distributed random numbers between 0 and 1.

In the modified PSO, to enhance the convergence of PSO and improve the optimization quality by using a linear decreasing way, the inertia weight ω has been calculated iteratively. Along with the PSO algorithm iteratively performed, its inertia weight ω to calculate the velocity will also be decreased linearly as given in Eq. (19) (Shi, Lai, & Qin, 2013).

$$\omega(t+1) = \omega_{\max} - t \times \frac{\omega_{\max} - \omega_{\min}}{t_{\max}} \qquad (19)$$

where $t_{\max}$ is the maximum number of iterations and $\omega_{\max}$ and $\omega_{\min}$ are the maximum and minimum of the inertia weights, respectively.

2.5 Proposed procedure

First, the MR images are enhanced using the nonlocal mean operation and the produced image is mapped into NS space by defining the entropy of the NS to quantify the indeterminacy. Then, the modified PSO algorithm guides the FCM to automatically segment the brain tumor from the MR images. The whole procedure can be summarized as below:

Algorithm 1

Apply NLM operation on MR images (*as discussed in* Section 2.1)

Convert enhanced MR images into the NS domain (*as discussed in* Section 2.2)

Modified PSO-FCM clustering approach for brain tumor segmentation

    - Initialize c_1, c_2, M, $t_{\max}$

    - Initialize no. of cluster c

    - Randomly initialize the position of the particles X (M dimension)

    - Initialize particle velocity V, cost of each particle to infinity.

    - Initialize each particle local best position PB and global best position GB and their cost

    Values

    - For each iteration t until t_{max} main loop

      - calculate inertia weight w

      - For each particle m

        - update velocity

        - update position

        - compute objective function J_m

      - end

      - If $J_m[t+1] < J_m^{best}$ update particle best cost value and position

      - If $J_m[t+1] < J^{best}$ update Global best cost value and position

      - end

Table 1 Configurations for modified PSO algorithm

Parameter	Value
Iteration t_{max}	150
Number of particles M	50
Individual weight factor c_1	2
Social weight factor c_2	2
Maximum inertia weight w_{max}	0.98
Minimum, inertia weight w_{min}	0.45

3 Results and discussion

3.1 Experimental results

A public brain tumor dataset (Cheng, 2017) is used for performance evaluation of the proposed system. To achieve the best performance, a modified PSO was employed to optimize the parameters in the proposed segmentation algorithm. The configuration of the modified PSO is listed in Table 1. To show the convergence of the modified PSO optimization, four MRI brain images with various tumors were used and their convergence was plotted in Fig. 1. From the plotting, it is clearly seen that the optimization procedure can become convergent in fewer than 100 iterations.

Figs. 2 and 3 illustrate the various steps of the proposed method undergone by MR images from the dataset (Hirschmann et al., 2012), image numbers 64 and 96, respectively. Fig. 2A is the original MR image number 64 and Fig. 3A is the original MR image number 96. Figs. 2B and 3B are the nonlocal mean enhanced MR images. The MR images in the NS domain such as the true subset, the false subset, the indeterminate subset, and the enhanced NS image are given in Figs. 2C–F and 3C–F respectively. The brain tumor segmented images using the proposed NS-modified PSO FCM method are shown in Figs. 2G and 3G. The final brain tumor traced MR images are depicted in Figs. 2H and 3H. From the results, we can see that the brain tumor can be segmented precisely due to the combination of NS and the optimization algorithm.

3.2 Evaluation results

The segmentation of the image is assessed by using several metrics, including the sensitivity, specificity, Jaccard similarity metric, and dice coefficient (Shattuck, Prasad, Mirza, Narr, & Toga, 2009).

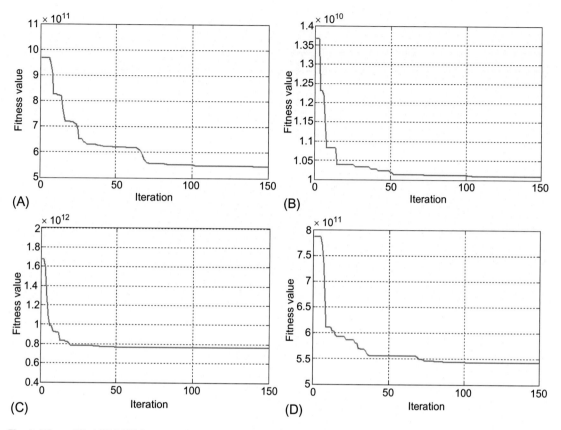

Fig. 1 NS-modified PSO FCM convergence curve for different MRI brain tumor images. (A) MR image number 64, (B) MR image number 96, (C) MR image number 138, and (D) MR image number 267.

Let U be the set of all voxels in the image, the set of voxels that is ground-truth labeled tumor, which is defined as $T \in U$. Similarly, $S \in U$ is the set of voxels that is labeled as tumor using the proposed method. The set of voxels common to T and S is called the true positive set, which is defined as $TP = T \cap S$. The set of voxels that is labeled as nontumor in both sets is called the true negative, which is defined as $TN = \overline{T} \cap \overline{S}$. The false positive set is the set of nontumor voxels labeled tumor voxels, which is defined as $FP = \overline{T} \cap S$. The false negative set is defined as $FN = T \cap \overline{S}$, where the tumor voxels are labeled as nontumor voxels. The success and error rates are then calculated using these sets as follows:

$$\text{Sensitivity} = \frac{|TP|}{|TP| + |FN|} \qquad (20)$$

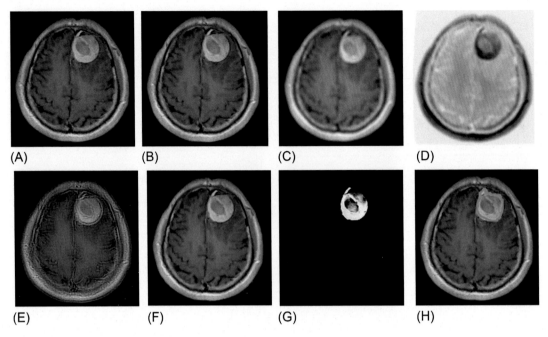

Fig 2 Results of image no. 64. (A) original image; (B) NLM filtered image; (C) NS true subset image; (D) NS false subset image; (E) NS indeterminate subset image; (F) enhance NS image; (G) NS-modified PSO FCM segmented image; (H) final result of tumor segmented image.

$$\text{Specificity} = \frac{|TN|}{|TN| + |FP|} = 1 - \text{Specificity} \tag{21}$$

In addition, the Jaccard similarity and the dice coefficient metrics are given, respectively, as follows:

$$J(T, S) = \frac{|TP|}{|TP| + |FP| + |FN|} \tag{22}$$

$$D(T, S) = \frac{|TP|}{\frac{1}{2}(|TP| + |FN| + |TP| + |FP|)} \tag{23}$$

To test the proposed process performance, 100 MRI images were randomly selected and four metrics—sensitivity, specificity, Jaccard, and dice—were calculated and compared with two other methods such as FCM and NS with FCM. The average results are reported in Table 2 and compared in Fig. 4.

The comparison results demonstrate the superiority of the proposed method with achieved best values of the four measured metrics compared to the other methods.

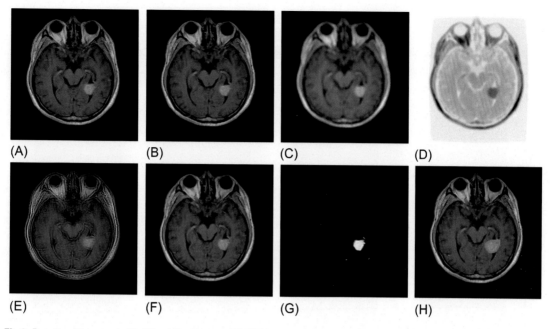

Fig 3 Results of image no. 96. (A) original image; (B) NLM filtered image; (C) NS true subset image; (D) NS false subset image; (E) NS indeterminate subset image; (F) enhance NS image; (G) NS-modified PSO FCM segmented image; (H) final result of tumor segmented image.

Table 2 Comparative study of the performance evaluation metrics

Method	Sensitivity	Specificity	Jaccard	Dice
FCM only	0.9214	0.9754	0.8132	0.8865
NS with FCM	0.9347	0.9805	0.8350	0.9201
Proposed NS-modified PSO FCM	0.9543	0.9858	0.8756	0.9432

4 Conclusions

MR imaging plays a vital role in the diagnosis of brain tumors because of its different imaging sequences and ability to visualize and differentiate different tissues in the brain. Automatic and

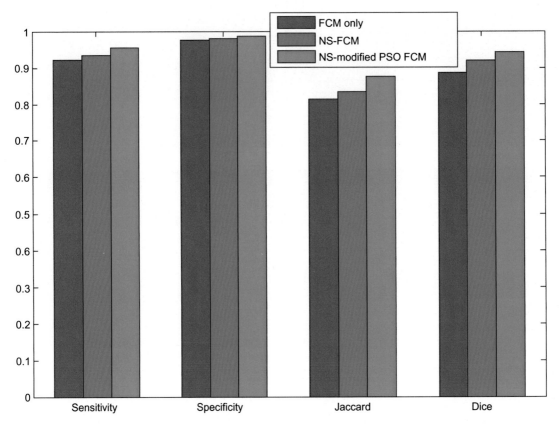

Fig. 4 Evaluation metrics comparative study using the proposed NS-modified PSO FCM method compared to the above-mentioned methods.

precise segmentation of the brain tumor is a significant task for early diagnosis and providing treatment to the patient for improving the survival rate. In this chapter, a fully automatic segmentation technique for brain tumor MR images based on neutrosophic and FCM clustering guided with a modified PSO algorithm was proposed. The performance of the proposed method was evaluated on 100 MR images and compared with the original FCM and NS-FCM by using several metrics. The results established the outstanding performance of the proposed technique with sensitivity, specificity, Jaccard, and dice coefficient values of 95.43%, 98.58%, 87.56%, and 94.32%, respectively. Therefore, the accuracy and efficiency of the medical image analysis are improved by applying the optimization-based NS. This method can also be extended for the segmentation of the skin lesion in dermoscopic images, tumor segmentation in abdomen CT images, and mitosis detection in breast cancer histopathology slide imaging.

References

Abramoff, M. D., Garvin, M. K., & Sonka, M. (2010). Retinal imaging and image analysis. *IEEE Reviews in Biomedical Engineering, 3*, 169–208.

Angulakshmi, M., & Lakshmi Priya, G. (2017). Automated brain tumour segmentation techniques—a review. *International Journal of Imaging Systems and Technology, 27*, 66–77.

Anter, A. M., & Hassenian, A. E. (2018). Computational intelligence optimization approach based on particle swarm optimizer and neutrosophic set for abdominal CT liver tumor segmentation. *Journal of Computer Science, 25*, 376–387.

Argenziano, G., Mordente, I., Ferrara, G., Sgambato, A., Annese, P., & Zalaudek, I. (2008). Dermoscopic monitoring of melanocytic skin lesions: clinical outcome and patient compliance vary according to follow-up protocols. *British Journal of Dermatology, 159*(2), 331–336.

Ashour, A. S., Guo, Y., Kucukkulahli, E., Erdogmus, P., & Polat, K. (2018). A hybrid dermoscopy images segmentation approach based on neutrosophic clustering and histogram estimation. *Applied Soft Computing, 69*, 426–434.

Ashour, A. S., Hawas, A. R., Guo, Y., & Wahba, M. A. (2018). A novel optimized neutrosophic k-means using genetic algorithm for skin lesion detection in dermoscopy images. *Signal, Image and Video Processing*, 1–8.

Bezdek, J. C., Coray, C., Gunderson, R., & Watson, J. (1981). Detection and characterization of cluster substructure. *SIAM Journal on Applied Mathematics, 40*, 339–372.

Buades, A., Coll, B., & Morel, J. M. (2005). A review of image denoising algorithms, with a new one. *Multiscale Modeling and Simulation, 4*(2), 490–530.

Cannon, R. L., Dave, J. V., & Bezdek, J. C. (1986). Efficient implementation of the Fuzzy c-means clustering algorithms. *IEEE Transactions on Pattern Analysis and Machine Intelligence, 8*, 248–255.

Cheng, J. (2017). *Brain tumor dataset. figshare. Dataset. (2017).* https://figshare.com/articles/brain_tumor_dataset/1512427.

Cheng, H. D., Guo, Y., & Zhang, Y. (2011). A novel image segmentation approach based on neutrosophic set and improved fuzzy c-means algorithm. *New Mathematics and Natural Computation, 7*(01), 155–171.

Cheng, H. D., Shan, J., Ju, W., Guo, Y., & Zhang, L. (2010). Automated breast cancer detection and classification using ultrasound images: a survey. *Pattern Recognition, 43*(1), 299–317.

Chithambaram, T., & Perumal, K. (2017). Brain tumor segmentation using genetic algorithm and ANN techniques. In *IEEE International Conference on Power, Control, Signals and Instrumentation Engineering (ICPCSI), Chennai* (pp. 970–982).

Dorthe Wildenschild, D., & Sheppard, A. P. (2013). X-ray imaging and analysis techniques for quantifying pore-scale structure and processes in subsurface porous medium systems. *Advances in Water Resources, 51*, 217–246.

Dunn, J. C. (1973). A fuzzy relative of the ISODATA process and its use in detecting compact, well-separated clusters. *Journal of Cybernetics, 3*, 32–57.

Fukunaga, K. (2013). *Introduction to statistical pattern recognition.* Academic press.

Gaietta, G., Deerinck, T. J., Adams, S. R., Bouwer, J., Tour, O., Laird, D. W., ... Ellisman, M. H. (2002). Multicolor and electron microscopic imaging of connexin trafficking. *Science, 296*(5567), 503–507.

Gordillo, N., Montseny, E., & Sobrevilla, P. (2013). State of the art survey on MRI brain tumor segmentation. *Magnetic Resonance Imaging, 31*(8), 1426–1438.

Guo, Y., Ashour, A. S., & Smarandache, F. (2018). A novel skin lesion detection approach using neutrosophic clustering and adaptive region growing in dermoscopy images. *Symmetry, 10*(4), 119.

Guo, Y., Cheng, H. D., & Zhang, Y. (2009). A new neutrosophic approach to image denoising. *New Mathematics and Natural Computation, 5*(03), 653–662.

Hirschmann, M. T., Wagner, C. R., Rasch, H., & Henckel, J. (2012). Standardized volumetric 3D-analysis of SPECT/CT imaging in orthopaedics: overcoming the limitations of qualitative 2D analysis. *BMC Medical Imaging, 12,* 5.

Homma, N. (2011). *CT image based computer-aided lung cancer diagnosis, theory and applications of CT imaging and analysis.* IntechOpen.

Hsieh, J. (2009). *Computed tomography: principles, design, artifacts, and recent advances.* Bellingham, WA: SPIE.

Isin, A., Direkoglu, C., & Sah, M. (2016). Review of MRI-based brain tumor image segmentation using deep learning methods. *Procedia Computer Science, 102,* 317–324.

Jaworek-Korjakowska, J., & Kleczek, P. (2018). Region adjacency graph approach for acral melanocytic lesion segmentation. *Applied Sciences, 8*(9), 1430.

Jordan, K. C., Menolotto, M., Bolster, N. M., Livingstone, I. A. T., & Giardini, M. E. (2017). A review of feature-based retinal image analysis. *Expert Review of Ophthalmology, 12*(3), 207–220.

Kennedy, J., & Eberhart, R. (1995). A new optimizer using particle swarm theory. In *Proceedings of the IEEE sixth international symposium on micro machine and human science, Nagoya, Japan* (pp. 39–43).

Kittler, H., Guitera, P., Riedl, E., Avramidis, M., Teban, L., Fiebiger, M., … Menzies, S. (2006). Identification of clinically featureless incipient melanoma using sequential dermoscopy imaging. *Archives of Dermatology, 142*(9), 1113–1119.

Kuperman, V. (2000). *Magnetic resonance imaging physical principles and applications.* San Diego, CA: Academic Press.

Laval-Jeantet, M., D'Haenens, M., & Klausz, J. (1982). Image analysis in X-ray radiography. In J. Sklansky, & J. C. Bisconte (Eds.), *Biomedical images and computers.* Berlin, Heidelberg: Springer. Lecture notes in medical informatics, 17.

Lu, W., Wang, J., & Zhang, H. H. (2015). Computerized PET/CT image analysis in the evaluation of tumour response to therapy. *The British Journal of Radiology, 88*(1048).

Manjon, J. V., Carbonell-Caballer, J., Lull, J. J., Garcia-Marti, G., Marti-Bonmati, L., & Robles, M. (2008). MRI denoising using non-local means. *Medical Image Analysis, 12,* 514–523.

McNamara, G., Difilippantonio, M., Ried, T., & Bieber, F. R. (2017). Microscopy and image analysis. *Current Protocols in Human Genetics, 94.* 4.4.1–4.4.89.

Menzies, S. W., Emery, J., Staples, M., Davies, S., McAvoy, B., Fletcher, J., … Burton, R. C. (2009). Impact of dermoscopy and short-term sequential digital dermoscopy imaging for the management of pigmented lesions in primary care: a sequential intervention trial. *British Journal of Dermatology, 161*(6), 1270–1277.

Menzies, S. W., Stevenson, M. L., Altamura, D., & Byth, K. (2011). Variables predicting change in benign melanocytic nevi undergoing short-term dermoscopic imaging. *Archives of Dermatology, 147*(6), 655–659.

Mohan, J., Chandra, A. T. S., Krishnaveni, V., & Guo, Y. (2012). Evaluation of neutrosophic set approach filtering technique for image denoising. *The International Journal of Multimedia & Its Applications, 4*(4), 73.

Mohan, J., Chandra, A. P. T. S., Krishnaveni, V., & Guo, Y. (2013). Image denoising based on neutrosophic wiener filtering. In *Advances in computing and information technology* (pp. 861–869). Berlin, Heidelberg: Springer.

Mohan, J., Krishnaveni, V., & Guo, Y. (2012). Performance analysis of neutrosophic set approach of median filtering for MRI denoising. *International Journal of Electronics and Communication Engineering & Technology, 3*, 148–163.

Mohan, J., Krishnaveni, V., & Guo, Y. (2013a). MRI denoising using non local neutrosophic set approach of wiener filtering. *Biomedical Signal Processing and Control, 8*(6), 779–791.

Mohan, J., Krishnaveni, V., & Guo, Y. (2013b). A new neutrosophic approach of Wiener filtering for MRI denoising. *Measurement Science Review, 13*(4), 177–186.

Rajasekaran, K. A., & Gounder, C. C. (2018). Advanced brain tumour segmentation from MRI images. In A. M. Halefoglu (Ed.), *High-resolution neuroimaging—Basic physical principles and clinical applications* (pp. 83–107): IntechOpen.

Rangayyan, R. M. (2005). *Biomedical image analysis.* Florida: CRC Press.

Rodriguez, A. O. (2004). Principles of magnetic resonance imaging. *Revista Mexicana de Fisica, 50*(3), 272–286.

Rummeny, E. J., Reimer, P., & Heindel, W. (Eds.), (2009). *MR imaging of the body.* (2nd ed.). Stuttgart: Georg Thieme Verlag.

Saba, L., Dey, N., Ashour, A. S., Samanta, S., Nath, S. S., Chakraborty, S., ... Suri, J. S. (2016). Automated stratification of liver disease in ultrasound: an online accurate feature classification paradigm. *Computer Methods and Programs in Biomedicine, 130*, 118–134.

Segovia, F., & Phillips, C. (2014). PET imaging analysis using a parcelation approach and multiple kernel classification. In *2014 International workshop on pattern recognition in neuroimaging, Tubingen* (pp. 1–4).

Shattuck, D. W., Prasad, G., Mirza, M., Narr, K. L., & Toga, A. W. (2009). Online resource for validation of brain segmentation methods. *NeuroImage, 45*, 431–439.

Shi, H., Lai, H. C., & Qin, X. Z. (2013). Image segmentation algorithm of cotton based on PSO and K-means hybrid clustering. *Computer Engineering and Applications, 49*, 226–229.

Smarandache, F. (2003). *A unifying field in logics neutrosophic logic, in neutrosophy. neutrosophic set, neutrosophic probability* (3rd ed.). Rehoboth, NM: American Research Press.

Smith, N. B., & Webb, A. (2011). *Introduction to medical imaging physics, engineering and clinical applications.* New York: Cambridge University press.

Soleimani, V., & Vincheh, F. H. (2013). Improving ant colony optimization for brain MRI image segmentation and brain tumor diagnosis. In: *First Iranian conference on pattern recognition and image analysis (PRIA), Birjand* (pp. 1–6).

Syed, G. I., & Hassanein, A. E. (2017). Moth-flame swarm optimization with neutrosophic sets for automatic mitosis detection in breast cancer histology images. *Applied Intelligence, 47*, 397–408.

Tjahyaningtijas, H. P. A. (2018). Brain tumor image segmentation in MRI image. *IOP Conference Series: Materials Science and Engineering, 336*, 1–4.

Vesal, S., Patil, S. M., Ravikumar, N., & Maier, A. K. (2018). A multi-task framework for skin lesion detection and segmentation. In *OR 2.0 context-aware operating theaters, computer assisted robotic endoscopy, clinical image-based procedures, and skin image analysis* (pp. 285–293). Cham: Springer.

Wahba, M. A., Ashour, A. S., Napoleon, S. A., Elnaby, M. M. A., & Guo, Y. (2017). Combined empirical mode decomposition and texture features for skin lesion classification using quadratic support vector machine. *Health Information Science and Systems, 5*(1), 10.

Wright, G. A. (1997). Magnetic resonance imaging. *IEEE Signal Processing Magazine, 14*(1), 56–66.

Xing, F., & Yang, L. (2016). Machine learning and its application in microscopic image analysis. In G. Wu, D. Shen, & M. R. Sabuncu (Eds.), *Machine learning and medical imaging* (pp. 97–127): Academic Press.

Yoder, K. K. (2013). Basic PET data analysis techniques. In S. Misciagna (Ed.), *Positron emission tomography—Recent developments in instrumentation, research and clinical oncological practice*: IntechOpen.

Zeng, X., Wang, Y., Yu, J., & Guo, Y. (2013). Correspondence-beam-domain eigenspace-based minimum variance beamformer for medical ultrasound imaging. *IEEE Transactions on Ultrasonics, Ferroelectrics, and Frequency Control, 60*(12), 2670–2676.

Zheng, X., Wei, W., Huang, Q., Song, S., Wan, J., & Huang, G. (2017). A computer-aided analysis method of SPECT brain images for quantitative treatment monitoring: performance evaluations and clinical applications. *BioMed Research International, 2017.*

Further reading

Chandra, S., Bhat, R., & Singh, H. (2009). A PSO based method for detection of brain tumors from MRI. In *World congress on nature & biologically inspired computing (NaBIC), Coimbatore* (pp. 666–671).

Chandra, G. R., & Rao, K. R. H. (2016). Tumor detection in brain using genetic algorithm. *Procedia Computer Science, 79*, 449–457.

Isa Jara, R., Buchelly, F. J., & Meschino, G. J. (2017). Improved particle swarm optimization algorithm applied to rigid registration in medical images. In I. Torres, J. Bustamante, & D. Sierra (Eds.), *VII Latin American congress on biomedical engineering CLAIB 2016, Bucaramanga, Santander, Colombia, October 26th–28th, 2016. IFMBE proceedings, Vol. 60.* Singapore: Springer.

Karnan, M., & Logheshwari, T. (2010). Improved implementation of brain MRI image segmentation using Ant colony system. In *IEEE international conference on computational intelligence and computing research, Coimbatore* (pp. 1–4).

Lin, C. L., Mimori, A., & Chen, Y. W. (2012). Hybrid particle swarm optimization and its application to multimodal 3D medical image registration. *Computational Intelligence and Neuroscience.*

Taherdangkoo, M., Bagheri, M. H., Yazdi, M., & Andriole, K. P. (2013). An effective method for segmentation of MR brain images using the ant colony optimization algorithm. *Journal of Digital Imaging, 26*(6), 1116–1123.

Zheng, L. T., Qian, G. P., & Lin, L. F. (2011). Medical image registration based on improved PSO algorithm. In J. Lee (Ed.), *Lecture notes in electrical engineering: Vol. 87. Advanced electrical and electronics engineering.* Berlin, Heidelberg: Springer.

10

Neutrosophic hough transform for blood cells nuclei detection

Amira S. Ashour*, Yanhui Guo[†], Ahmed Refaat Hawas*

*Department of Electronics and Electrical Communications Engineering, Faculty of Engineering, Tanta University, Tanta, Egypt. [†]Department of Computer Science, University of Illinois at Springfield, Springfield, IL, United States

1 Introduction

Microscopic images of the blood smear are regularly examined by hematologists for diagnosing blood disorders and diseases. These disorders indicate different diseases, which are mostly related to white blood cells (WBCs). Detection, recognition, and classification of blood cells and their diverse types have an excessive role in laboratory tests and the clinical diagnosis of blood diseases (Campo et al., 2011; Mohr & Liew, 2007; Ross et al., 2003; Yeoh et al., 2002). The main cell types include red cells, white cells (leukocyte), and blood platelets. The WBCs contain the cytoplasm and nucleus, where they include five categories: eosinophil, neutrophil, monocyte, lymphocyte, and basophil (Hiremath, Bannigidad, & Geeta, 2010). The nucleus is considered the core of WBCs and contain chromosomes, chromatin, and nucleolus. The cell's nucleus has significant features in the identification of the cell's type. Thus, to distinguish between the cytoplasm and nucleus of the WBC, the color, texture, morphology, and size are observed/measured. For diagnosing different blood diseases, blood tests are conducted by laboratory experts to investigate the blood samples under the microscope. These blood tests can be used for diagnosing different diseases as well as investigating the functionality of different body organs, such as the liver, thyroid, and kidney (Grimm, Neaton, & Ludwig, 1985; Hari, Prasad, & Rao, 2014; Hore et al., 2015; Neugebauer, Clement,

Neutrosophic Set in Medical Image Analysis. https://doi.org/10.1016/B978-0-12-818148-5.00010-2

Bocklitz, Krafft, & Popp, 2010; Padmanabhan et al., 2009; Piuri & Scotti, 2004; Shim et al., 2006; Yu et al., 2013). However, dissimilar kinds of blood smears may lead to inaccurate quantitative/qualitative information.

Traditional microscopic visual morphological inspection by the hematology experts is a tedious, inaccurate, expensive, and time-consuming task (Dey, Ashour, Ashour, & Singh, 2015; Mohapatra, Samanta, Patra, & Satpathi, 2011; Nazlibilek et al., 2014; Ongun et al., 2001a, 2001b; Poomcokrak & Neatpisarnvanit, 2008; Savkare & Narote, 2012; Suradkar, 2013; Terstappen & Loken, 1988; Theera-Umpon, 2005; Wu, Mei, & Lo, 2012). Moreover, the BCs have different types and subtypes that have a different shape and color, along with the different staining methods that also affect the appearance of the BC in the microscope sample. Consequently, several researchers have developed automated techniques for blood cell (BS) detection, counting, and classification (Allard et al., 2004; Angulo & Flandrin, 2003; Bacus & Weens, 1977; Bandekar, Wong, Clausi, & Gorbet, 2011; Di Ruberto, Dempster, Khan, & Jarra, 2002; Ghosh, Bhattacharjee, & Nasipuri, 2016; Guo, Zeng, & Wu, 2007; Habibzadeh, Krzyżak, & Fevens, 2013; Karunakar & Kuwadekar, 2011; Khan & Maruf, 2013; Nilsson & Heyden, 2005; Peltola, Toikka, Irjala, Mertsola, & Ruuskanen, 2007; Putzu & Di Ruberto, 2013; Rezatofighi & Soltanian-Zadeh, 2011; Riethdorf et al., 2007; Roy, Jin, Seo, Nam, & Seo, 2014; Savkare & Narote, 2011; Yang et al., 2004). Theera-Umpon (2005) proposed a fuzzy C-means procedure with morphological operations for segmenting the cytoplasm and nucleus of bone marrow WBC. Wang et al. (2007) identified the cell cycle stages in the images captured using time-lapse microscopy by detecting the cells using their shape and intensity information. Then, an online support vector machine (SVM) classifier was applied for cell staging identification.

Madhloom et al. (2010) implemented localization and segmentation of WBC nuclei. For separating the nucleus from the entire cell body, nucleus segmentation was applied using contrast stretching along with minimum filter, image arithmetic operation, and global threshold methods. This method achieved 85%–98% accuracy. Sinha and Ramakrishnan (2003) designed a blood cell counting method on the hue, saturation, and value (HSV) color space using a k-means clustering procedure for WBC segmentation for further cell categorization using the classification process. In this method, the texture, color, and shape features were extracted from the segmented nucleus and cytoplasm. In digital microscopic images, Hiremath et al. (2010) developed an automated method for identifying and classifying the WBCs, namely neutrophils, monocytes, and lymphocytes. A color-based segmentation scheme was applied with extracting geometric features from the segmented image to identify the different WBC types.

Markiewicz, Osowski, Marianska, and Moszczynski (2005) applied the SVM for automatic identification of the leukemia blast cells, where geometrical and texture features of the BCs were extracted. Othman and Ali (2014) isolated the leukocytes (WBCs) in the macroscopic images by segmentation and feature extraction using the shape feature moment. Prinyakupt and Pluempitiwiriyawej (2015) segmented the WBCs using thresholding, morphological properties, and ellipse curve fitting. Then, the feature extraction process was conducted on the segmented cytoplasm and nucleus regions followed by the sequential forward selection method using a greedy search algorithm to select the dominant features. Finally, naïve Bayes and linear classifiers were used in classification. Bergen, Steckhan, Wittenberg, and Zerfass (2008) localized erythrocytes in the BCs by combining pixel-wise classification with template matching, and then used the level-set method to extract the contours of the nucleus in the WBC regions. Mohamed, Far, and Guaily (2012) segmented BC images after enhancement using gray-scale contrast for automatic blood cell nuclei segmentation, where false objects were removed by determining the minimum size. Another method for WBC nucleus segmentation was proposed by Rezatofighi, Soltanian-Zadeh, Sharifian, and Zoroofi (2009) using the orthogonality theory and the Gram-Schmidt procedure.

Furthermore, Amin, Kermani, Talebi, and Oghli (2015) segmented cell nuclei from bone marrow and blood smears of normal individuals and acute lymphoblastic leukemia patients using a *k*-means algorithm. Afterward, from the segmented nuclei, statistical/geometric features were extracted for further classification to noncancerous or cancerous cells using a support vector machine. Ghosh, Das, Chakraborty, and Ray (2010) recognized the leukocyte using modified thresholding methods and fuzzy divergence. The nuclei were segmented using Cauchy, Gaussian, and Gamma distribution fuzzy membership functions for the image pixels. The results established the efficiency of using the Cauchy membership function for segmentation.

For malaria diagnosis, an automatic counting of infected RBCs was performed by Moallem et al. (2017) based on image segmentation and machine-learning methods. A preprocessing stage was employed to remove the WBCs using a WBC segmentation method based on the Chan-Vese level-set procedure for eliminating the boundaries of each WBC in the image. For each WBC, Dorini, Minetto, and Leite (2013) segmented the nucleus as well as the cytoplasm using the self-dual multiscale morphological toggle method for contour regularization. Then, a watershed transform was applied for boundary estimation of the nucleus. Afterward, cytoplasm region detection was performed using morphological transformations and granulometric analysis.

Moreover, for WBC segmentation, Li, Zhu, Mi, Cao, and Yao (2016) implemented a dual-threshold technique on a combination of HSV and RGB color spaces of the microscopic image. In the proposed dual-threshold procedure, the H component from the HSV color space image and the contrast stretch of the image's gray version were used to determine the optimal thresholds. Afterward, median filtering and morphological operations were employed for denoising. For the cytoplasm and nucleus of WBCs, a segmentation method was implemented by Zhang et al. (2014) by combining adjusted color space decomposition and k-means clustering.

Fatichah, Tangel, Widyanto, Dong, and Hirota (2012) proposed a self-supervised learning method based on initial unsupervised segmentation using a k-means approach to extract the foreground regions on the microscopic cell image followed by supervised segmentation refinement to train the SVM classifier for classifying each pixel of the image. Median color features were used to represent the topological structure. In addition, a weak edge enhancement operator was used to handle the fuzzy boundaries and to improve the segmentation accuracy. The Hough transform was employed by Cao, Zhong, Li, and Dong (2009) for detecting and localizing the red BCs (RBCs) in urine images. A Sobel operator was used for edge detection followed by the Hough transform for separating the RBC from the background. Then, the principal component analysis (PCA) was used to select the significant features for further classification using the linear discriminant analysis (LDA).

From the preceding extensive study, it is concluded that nucleus segmentation procedures were mainly based on morphological processes while pixel intensity threshold-based methods were employed for segmenting the cytoplasm (Sadeghian, Seman, Ramli, Kahar, & Saripan, 2009). Generally, for WBCs and nuclei segmentation, several approaches used color and feature extraction methods (Reta, Robles, Gonzalez, Diaz, & Guichard, 2010), active contours (Eom, Kim, Shin, & Ahn, 2006), and clustering techniques (Jiang, Liao, & Dai, 2003) while other methods used fuzzy morphological operations (Fatichah, Tangel, Widyanto, Dong, & Hirota, 2012).

Typically, in microscopic images of blood smears, there exist dissimilar shapes and sizes of the different WBC types as well as different texture characteristics of the cytoplasm and different morphological characteristic of the nucleus. Accordingly, in order to detect the nucleus from the microscopic image, a preextraction and detection of the WBC in the image is conducted. Thus, in the current chapter, the Hough transform (HT) was applied as it is considered an effective method for pattern recognition to extract unique features that describe the shapes, including lines, ellipses, and circles, as well as to detect the blood cells in the microscope images. However, the classic HT for circle detection suffers from several limitations, including the required large parameter space and low detection efficiency. In addition, the microscopic images may contain irregular illumination patterns that affect the microscopic image visualization and the detection performance. Moreover, a varied range of staining shades may be introduced during the staining process. All these artifacts lead to complicated segmenting of the WBC and their nuclei in the microscopic images.

Accordingly, the neutrosophic theory can be involved during the detection/segmentation processes to remove/reduce the effect of these artifacts and reduce the fuzziness from the microscopic images being segmented. In the present work, after detecting the WBCs from the background using HT detection of circular shapes, a neutrosophic set (NS) is then employed followed by k-means to detect the nucleus within the previously segmented WBC. Accordingly, the proposed method of HT-based NS with K-means nuclei segmentation is called HNK.

The structure of the remaining sections includes the methodology used in the proposed model in Section 2, followed by the experimental results and discussions in Section 3. Finally, the conclusions of the presented work are presented in Section 4.

2   Methodology

The microscopic image includes WBCs embedded in the blood smear, where the nuclei exist in the WBC. This study implemented a WBC detection procedure based on the circular Hough transform (CHT) with neutrosophic K-means (HNK) in blood cells images. Hence, the present method consists of two phases: the WBC detection phase using a Canny edge detector and the circular HT, and then the nucleus detection phase using the NS and K-means clustering for unsupervised segmentation.

The red channel is used instead of the gray-scale image to maintain image resolution. Also, this channel contains most of the information. The Canny edge operator is used to detect the circular shapes for further accurate circle shape detection using the Hough parameter space, which represents the interested WBC mask. The masked images are then mapped into the NS and that reduces the indeterminacy of the image. Subsequently, the image is segmented using the *K*-means method for final detection of the nucleus. Finally, the cell/nucleus detection is accomplished by the morphology operation.

2.1 White blood cell detection

Typically, a smooth transition in color exists in the microscopic images between the background and the region of interest. This identifies a low contrast between the WBC and the background. Because almost all the blood cells have elliptical shapes, which can be approximately considered a circular shape, this inspired the proposed method to apply the CHT (Atherton & Kerbyson, 1999; D'Orazio, Guaragnella, Leo, & Distante, 2004; Pedersen, 2007; Smereka & Dulęba, 2008) for detecting WBCs having an approximately circular shape. Additionally, in the present work, the amount of pixels to be processed by CHT was dramatically reduced by using Canny edge detection (Ding & Goshtasby, 2001).

2.1.1 Canny edge detection

The Canny edge detector is an edge detection operator that uses a multistage algorithm to detect a wide range of edges in images. It includes several steps, namely preprocessing for noise reduction using a 5×5 Gaussian filter, measuring the gradients to find the intensity gradient in the image, nonmaximum suppression, and thresholding with hysteresis. In the present work, the two key parameters of the Canny detector algorithm are the upper and lower threshold values. The lower threshold value is determined to find the faint pixels that are actually a part of an edge while the upper threshold value is used to determine the mark edges that are definite edges of the WBC.

2.1.2 Circular Hough transform

The CHT is a specialization of the Hough transform for feature extraction to detect circles. The main purpose of the CHT is to find circles in the image. The circle candidates are produced by voting in the Hough parameter space and then selecting the local maxima. In two-dimensional (2D) space, a circle can be described using the following expression:

$$(x - a)^2 + (y - b)^2 = r^2 \tag{1}$$

where a and b are the coordinates of the circle's center and r is the radius of the circle. If a 2D point (x,y) is fixed, then the CHT parameters can be obtained according to Eq. (1) as follows:

$$x = a + r\cos(\theta) \qquad (2)$$

$$y = b + r\sin(\theta) \qquad (3)$$

Thus, the parameter space is three-dimensional (3D), namely (a, b, r), where all the parameters that satisfy (x,y) would lie on the surface of an inverted right-angled cone whose apex is at $(x, y, 0)$. Typically, in the parameter space, to find the intersection point, an accumulator matrix is represented. Initially, the parameter space is divided into stacks using a grid. Then, an accumulator matrix is produced based on this grid, where the element in the accumulator matrix represents the number of circles in the parameter space. This number of circles is also called the voting number. Every element in the accumulator matrix is initially set to zero, then in the original space, each edge point can represent a circle in the parameter space and increase the voting number in this voting process. Afterward, in the accumulator matrix, the local maxima are found after voting. The local maxima positions are consistent with the circle centers in the original space. Hence, in the Hough space, a point can define a circle in the image domain; hereafter, an image Q in the image domain is mapped to the Hough space, represented by Q_{HT}.

2.2 Nuclei detection

In the preceding process, the CHT was used to detect the WBCs in the microscopic images. Afterward, in order to localize and detect the nucleus that exists inside the detected WBC, another detection process was employed on the Q_{HT} image for nucleus detection using NS followed by a clustering-based unsupervised segmentation procedure.

2.2.1 Neutrosophic CHT image

Neutrosophy theory has an outstanding impact for defining the indeterminacy in different information, including images, where the neutrosophic set (NS) is considered one of its methods. Typically, the NS is defined by three membership subsets to specify the truth, indeterminacy, and falsity degrees of T, I, and F, respectively, for every incident in the NS. These membership subsets are employed to map an input image to the NS domain producing the NS image. In the present work, the Q_{HT} is transformed into the NS domain to produce the CHT-NS-image Q_{HT}', which can be represented as follows (Guo, Ashour, & Smarandache, 2018; Guo, Ashour, & Sun, 2017):

$$Q'_{HT}(x, y) = Q_{HT}(t, i, f) = \{T_{HT}(x, y), I_{HT}(x, y), F_{HT}(x, y)\} \quad (4)$$

where T_{HT}, I_{HT} and F_{HT} represent the true, indeterminate, and false belonging to the bright pixel set in the Hough transformed image Q_{HT} when mapped to the NS domain. Assume $W(x, y)$ and $\overline{W}(x, y)$ denote the intensity and the local mean values of the pixel (x, y). Therefore, the three subsets can be given by (Ashour, Guo, Kucukkulahli, Erdogmus, & Polat, 2018):

$$T_{HT}(x, y) = \frac{\overline{W}(x, y) - \overline{W}_{\min}}{\overline{W}_{\max} - \overline{W}_{\min}} \quad (5)$$

$$I_{HT}(x, y) = \frac{\beta(x, y) - \beta_{\min}}{\beta_{\max} - \beta_{\min}} \quad (6)$$

$$F_{HT}(x, y) = 1 - T_{HT}(x, y) \quad (7)$$

where $\beta(x, y)$ is the absolute value $|W(x, y) - \overline{W}(x, y)|$. Accordingly, the value of $I_{HT}(x, y)$ is used to determine the indeterminacy of $Q_{HT}(x, y)$. In the NS domain, the element distribution is defined by the NS image entropy as a summation of the entropies of the three subset entropies, which is given by:

$$E_{NS} = E_{T_{HT}} + E_{I_{HT}} + E_{F_{HT}} \quad (8)$$

where the entropies of the three subsets are expressed as follows:

$$E_{T_{HT}} = - \sum_{i=\min\{T_{HT}\}}^{\max\{T_{HT}\}} p_{T_{HT}}(i) \ln(p_{T_{HT}}(i)) \quad (9)$$

$$E_{I_{HT}} = - \sum_{i=\min\{I_{HT}\}}^{\max\{I_{HT}\}} p_{I_{HT}}(i) \ln(p_{I_{HT}}(i)) \quad (10)$$

$$E_{F_{HT}} = - \sum_{i=\min\{F_{HT}\}}^{\max\{F_{HT}\}} p_{F_{HT}}(i) \ln(p_{F_{HT}}(i)) \quad (11)$$

where the three membership subsets, $p_{T_{HT}}(i)$, $p_{I_{HT}}(i)$, and $p_{F_{HT}}(i)$ denote the probabilities of the elements. The deviations in T_{HT} and F_{HT} are used to modify the element distribution in the image and the entropy of I_{HT} to modify T_{HT} and F_{HT} with I_{HT}. By applying this procedure to the detected WBC image, the nucleus can be detected accurately with the use of the K-means clustering procedure, where K-means clustering has a significant role in different applications.

2.2.2 K-means clustering

The K-means clustering procedure groups the data points into K clusters and defines the center positions of each cluster (Celebi, Kingravi, & Vela, 2013; Kodinariya & Makwana, 2013; Likas, Vlassis, & Verbeek, 2003; Magidson & Vermunt, 2002). It iterates over steps until the sum of the squared errors in each group cannot be decreased any more. These steps are: (i) for each cluster, compute the mean value, and (ii) assign each point to the nearest cluster by calculating the distance of each point from the corresponding cluster's mean value. Typically, the K-means satisfies the following condition (Ashour, Hawas, Guo, & Wahba, 2018):

$$D = \sum_{j=1}^{K} \sum_{i=1}^{d_j} \|G_i - Z_j\| \tag{12}$$

where d_j and Z_j are the number of pixels and the center of the jth cluster, respectively, as K is the total number of clusters. The K-means procedure aims to minimize D by satisfying the following condition:

$$Z_j = \frac{1}{d_j} \sum_{g_i \in C_j} G_i \tag{13}$$

In the dataset $G = \{g_i, i = 1, 2, ..., n\}$, g_i is a sample in the d-dimensional space and $C = \{C_1, C_2, ..., C_q\}$ is the segment that fulfilled $G = \cup_{i=1}^{q} C_i$.

2.3 Proposed method for WBCs and nuclei detection

In the present work, the following procedure is applied, as illustrated in Algorithm 1.

Algorithm 1: Proposed circle Hough transform neutrosophic *K*-means (HNK)

Start

Phase 1: WBC Detection

   Use only the red channel to keep image resolution and reserve all information of microscopic RGB image

   Apply Canny operator to detect the WBC edges of the red channel

   Transform the output of Canny operator to CHT using the following parameters set-up values: *Theta_sample_frequency* = 0.01,

$\theta = (0:$ *Theta_sample_frequency*: 2π), *Radius_sample_frequency* $=$ 1, $r_{max} = 60$, and $r_{min} = 14$

Determine a threshold for the selected circles using trial-and-error

Generate the mask by adding the selected circles

Extract the WBC by multiplying the generated binary mask with the original image

Phase 2: Nuclei Detection

Map the extracted WBC generated in phase 1 to the NS domain

Group the pixels using *K*-means

Obtain the detected nucleus

End

Fig. 1 demonstrates the steps of the proposed method.

In Fig. 1, the ROI refers to the region of interest, which is the detected WBC.

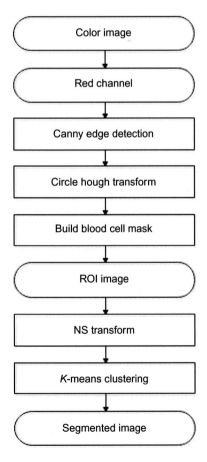

Fig. 1 Block diagram of the proposed method.

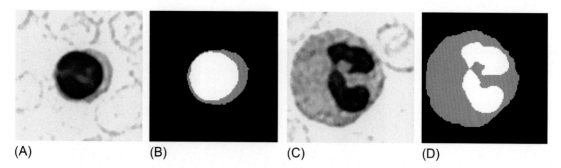

Fig. 2 Sample of the used dataset, where (A) and (C) original WBC images, and (B) and (D) their corresponding ground-truth images, respectively.

3   Results and discussions

In the present chapter, a 50 WBC images were selected randomly from the dataset in (Zheng, Wang, Wang, & Liu, 2018). The corresponding ground-truth segmented images are also included in the used dataset, where the cytoplasms, nuclei, and background were marked. Fig. 2 illustrates the sample original microscopic images (Fig. 2A) from the used dataset with the corresponding ground-truth image (Fig. 2B).

3.1   While blood cell detection results

According to the proposed method phases, the Canny detector was applied initially to identify all edges in the red channel of the original microscopic images, as illustrated in Fig. 3 for the image number 172 in the dataset.

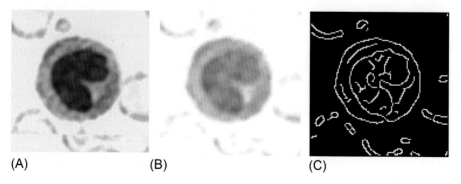

Fig. 3 Canny detector results, where (A) original image, (B) red channel, and (C) detected edges image using Canny operator.

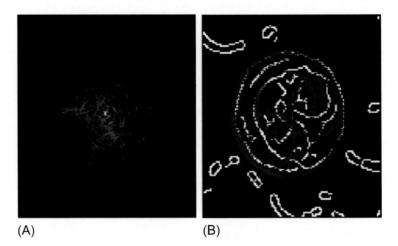

Fig. 4 Circular Hough transform results: (A) transformed red channel image into CHT domain and (B) CHT image on the canny output image.

(A)　　　　　　　　　　(B)

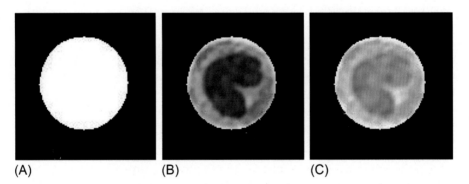

(A)　　　　　　(B)　　　　　　(C)

Fig. 5 Detected WBC for image 172 in the dataset: (A) computed binary mask from the CHT image, (B) extracted/detected ROI (WBC), and (C) *gray*-scale version of the detected WBC for further processes.

The edge-detected image is then input into the CHT, as reported in Fig. 4.

Then, the CHT image is used to generate a binary mask in order to detect the WBC by multiplying the original image with the generated binary mask, as shown in Fig. 5.

3.2 Nucleus detection results

The detected WBC is then input into phase 2 in order to detect the nucleus in the WBC by mapping the CHT image to the NS domain yielding to the following image display steps in Fig. 6, followed by *K*-means clustering.

Afterward, the *K*-means clustering is applied to the NS output image, resulting in the segmented nucleus as illustrated in Fig. 7.

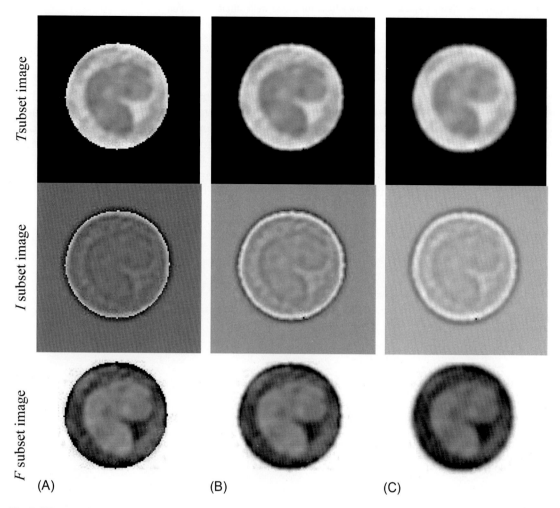

Fig. 6 NS steps for image 172 in the dataset: (A) initial inputted image to the NS in Phase 2, (B) the resultant subset image after the first modification/iteration, and (C) the last version after NS iterations.

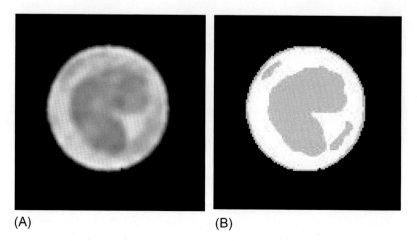

Fig. 7 Nucleus detection results: (A) NS output image and (B) *K*-means clustering output (detected nucleus).

3.3 Comparative study

In order to evaluate the performance of the proposed method visually, Fig. 8 demonstrates the nucleus detection of five images from the dataset using the proposed HNK method compared to using CHT with K-means without using the NS (HT-K-means) method, using the NS without CHT and without K-means (NS) method, and using the K-means only without CHT and without the NS (K-means) method.

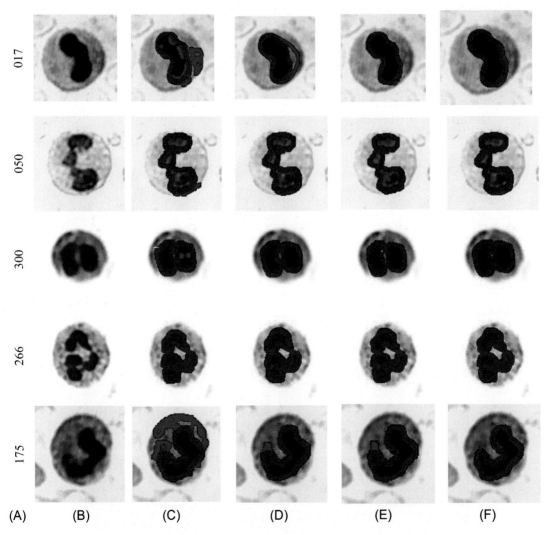

Fig. 8 Comparative study results: (A) image number (ID), (B) original image, and detected nucleus using (C) HT-K-means method, (D) only NS method, (E) only K-means method, and (F) proposed HNK method.

Table 1 Average values of the measured metrics over 50 selected images.

	JAC (%)	Dice (%)	Sensitivity (%)	Specificity (%)	Accuracy (%)
HT-*K*-means without NS	81.46	89.21	94.99	97.57	97.31
NS with *K*-means	83.71	91.04	96.31	98.05	97.85
K-means only	83.51	90.46	90.67	98.94	98.03
Proposed HNK	87.14	93.10	95.08	98.88	98.44

In Fig. 8, the red contour refers to the ground-truth image and the blue contour refers to the detected nucleus using the mentioned method. The results show that using NS improves the performance of the CHT by comparing Fig. 8C and F due to the ability of the NS to reduce the uncertainty. Additionally, Fig. 8 established the superiority of the proposed method compared to the other reported methods.

Finally, to evaluate the proposed HNK method for nuclei detection, the following evaluation metrics are measured, including the dice coefficient, JAC, specificity, sensitivity, and accuracy. These comparisons were conducted in terms of the performance evaluation metrics as reported in Table 1 and Fig. 9.

Fig. 9 along with Table 1 reported the evaluation metrics of the proposed method of values 87%, 93%, 95%, 99%, and 98%, of the JAC, Dice, sensitivity, specificity, and accuracy, respectively.

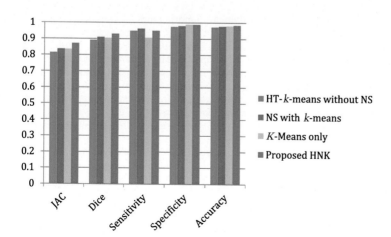

Fig. 9 Evaluation metrics comparative study using the proposed HNK method compared to the mentioned methods.

4   Conclusions

Microscopic images have a significant role in the diagnosis of blood diseases and disorders. However, the automated detection of WBCs is still considered a challenging task due to several limitations, where the WBC embedded in a cluttered and complicated smear along with the staining effect on the image quality, which inspired several researchers. Because the WBC can be estimated as an ellipsoid/circular shape, a circular Hough transform was proposed in this chapter to recognize the WBC after using the Canny detector.

The proposed method was divided into two phases, namely, the WBC detection phase based on the CHT, followed by the nucleus detection phase using the NS and the K-means clustering to segment the nucleus. The experimental results established the superiority of the proposed method for detecting the WBC as well as the nucleus in the used dataset of different WBC images with a varying complexity range that was used to validate the effectiveness of the proposed method in terms of different evaluation metrics compared to several reported methods.

References

Allard, W. J., Matera, J., Miller, M. C., Repollet, M., Connelly, M. C., Rao, C., Tibbe, A. G., Uhr, J. W., & Terstappen, L. W. (2004). Tumor cells circulate in the peripheral blood of all major carcinomas but not in healthy subjects or patients with nonmalignant diseases. *Clinical Cancer Research, 10*(20), 6897–6904.

Amin, M. M., Kermani, S., Talebi, A., & Oghli, M. G. (2015). Recognition of acute lymphoblastic leukemia cells in microscopic images using k-means clustering and support vector machine classifier. *Journal of Medical Signals and Sensors, 5*(1), 49.

Angulo, J., & Flandrin, G. (2003). Automated detection of working area of peripheral blood smears using mathematical morphology. *Analytical Cellular Pathology, 25*(1), 37–49.

Ashour, A. S., Guo, Y., Kucukkulahli, E., Erdogmus, P., & Polat, K. (2018). A hybrid dermoscopy images segmentation approach based on neutrosophic clustering and histogram estimation. *Applied Soft Computing, 69*, 426–434.

Ashour, A. S., Hawas, A. R., Guo, Y., & Wahba, M. A. (2018). A novel optimized neutrosophic k-means using genetic algorithm for skin lesion detection in dermoscopy images. *Signal, Image and Video Processing*, 1–8.

Atherton, T. J., & Kerbyson, D. J. (1999). Size invariant circle detection. *Image and Vision Computing, 17*(11), 795–803.

Bacus, J. W., & Weens, J. H. (1977). An automated method of differential red blood cell classification with application to the diagnosis of anemia. *Journal of Histochemistry and Cytochemistry, 25*(7), 614–632.

Bandekar, N., Wong, A., Clausi, D., & Gorbet, M. (2011). A novel approach to automated cell counting for studying human corneal epithelial cells. In *Engineering in Medicine and Biology Society, EMBC, 2011 annual international conference of the IEEE, August* (pp. 5997–6000): IEEE.

Bergen, T., Steckhan, D., Wittenberg, T., & Zerfass, T. (2008). Segmentation of leukocytes and erythrocytes in blood smear images. In: *Engineering in Medicine and Biology Society, 2008. EMBS 2008. 30th annual international conference of the IEEE, August* (pp. 3075–3078): IEEE.

Campo, E., Swerdlow, S. H., Harris, N. L., Pileri, S., Stein, H., & Jaffe, E. S. (2011). The 2008 WHO classification of lymphoid neoplasms and beyond: evolving concepts and practical applications. *Blood*, blood–2011.

Cao, G., Zhong, C., Li, L., & Dong, J. (2009). Detection of red blood cell in urine micrograph. In *Bioinformatics and biomedical engineering, 2009. ICBBE 2009. 3rd international conference on, June* (pp. 1–4): IEEE.

Celebi, M. E., Kingravi, H. A., & Vela, P. A. (2013). A comparative study of efficient initialization methods for the k-means clustering algorithm. *Expert Systems with Applications, 40*(1), 200–210.

Dey, N., Ashour, A. S., Ashour, A. S., & Singh, A. (2015). Digital analysis of microscopic images in medicine. *Journal of Advanced Microscopy Research, 10*(1), 1–13.

Di Ruberto, C., Dempster, A., Khan, S., & Jarra, B. (2002). Analysis of infected blood cell images using morphological operators. *Image and Vision Computing, 20*(2), 133–146.

Ding, L., & Goshtasby, A. (2001). On the Canny edge detector. *Pattern Recognition, 34*(3), 721–725.

D'Orazio, T., Guaragnella, C., Leo, M., & Distante, A. (2004). A new algorithm for ball recognition using circle Hough transform and neural classifier. *Pattern Recognition, 37*(3), 393–408.

Dorini, L. B., Minetto, R., & Leite, N. J. (2013). Semiautomatic white blood cell segmentation based on multiscale analysis. *IEEE Journal of Biomedical and Health Informatics, 17*(1), 250–256.

Eom, S., Kim, S., Shin, V., & Ahn, B. (2006). Leukocyte segmentation in blood smear images using region-based active contours. In *International Conference on Advanced Concepts for Intelligent Vision Systems, September* (pp. 867–876). Berlin, Heidelberg: Springer.

Fatichah, C., Tangel, M. L., Widyanto, M. R., Dong, F., & Hirota, K. (2012). Interest-based ordering for fuzzy morphology on white blood cell image segmentation. *Journal of Advanced Computational Intelligence and Intelligent Informatics, 16*(1), 76–86.

Ghosh, P., Bhattacharjee, D., & Nasipuri, M. (2016). Blood smear analyzer for white blood cell counting: a hybrid microscopic image analyzing technique. *Applied Soft Computing, 46*, 629–638.

Ghosh, M., Das, D., Chakraborty, C., & Ray, A. K. (2010). Automated leukocyte recognition using fuzzy divergence. *Micron, 41*(7), 840–846.

Grimm, R. H., Neaton, J. D., & Ludwig, W. (1985). Prognostic importance of the white blood cell count for coronary, cancer, and all-cause mortality. *JAMA, 254*(14), 1932–1937.

Guo, Y., Ashour, A. S., & Smarandache, F. (2018). A novel skin lesion detection approach using neutrosophic clustering and adaptive region growing in dermoscopy images. *Symmetry, 10*(4), 119.

Guo, Y., Ashour, A. S., & Sun, B. (2017). A novel glomerular basement membrane segmentation using neutrsophic set and shearlet transform on microscopic images. *Health Information Science and Systems, 5*(1), 15.

Guo, N., Zeng, L., & Wu, Q. (2007). A method based on multispectral imaging technique for white blood cell segmentation. *Computers in Biology and Medicine, 37*(1), 70–76.

Habibzadeh, M., Krzyżak, A., & Fevens, T. (2013). White blood cell differential counts using convolutional neural networks for low resolution images. In: *International Conference on Artificial Intelligence and Soft Computing, June* (pp. 263–274). Berlin, Heidelberg: Springer.

Hari, J., Prasad, A. S., & Rao, S. K. (2014). Separation and counting of blood cells using geometrical features and distance transformed watershed. In *Devices, Circuits and Systems (ICDCS), 2014 2nd International Conference on* (pp. 1–5): IEEE.

Hiremath, P. S., Bannigidad, P., & Geeta, S. (2010). *Automated identification and classification of white blood cells (leukocytes) in digital microscopic images.* IJCA special issue on "recent trends in image processing and pattern recognition" RTIPPR (pp.59–63).

Hore, S., Chakroborty, S., Ashour, A. S., Dey, N., Ashour, A. S., Sifaki-Pistolla, D., Bhattacharya, T., & Chaudhuri, S. R. (2015). Finding contours of hippocampus brain cell using microscopic image analysis. *Journal of Advanced Microscopy Research, 10*(2), 93–103.

Jiang, K., Liao, Q. M., & Dai, S. Y. (2003). A novel white blood cell segmentation scheme using scale-space filtering and watershed clustering. In *Vol. 5. Machine learning and cybernetics, 2003 international conference on, November* (pp. 2820–2825): IEEE.

Karunakar, Y., & Kuwadekar, A. (2011). An unparagoned application for red blood cell counting using marker controlled watershed algorithm for android mobile. In *Next generation mobile applications, services and technologies (NGMAST), 2011 5th international conference on, September* (pp. 100–104): IEEE.

Khan, H. A., & Maruf, G. M. (2013). Counting clustered cells using distance mapping. In *Informatics, electronics & vision (ICIEV), 2013 international conference on, May* (pp. 1–6): IEEE.

Kodinariya, T. M., & Makwana, P. R. (2013). Review on determining number of cluster in K-means clustering. *International Journal of Advance Research in Computer Science and Management Studies, 1*(6), 90–95.

Li, Y., Zhu, R., Mi, L., Cao, Y., & Yao, D. (2016). Segmentation of white blood cell from acute lymphoblastic leukemia images using dual-threshold method. *Computational and Mathematical Methods in Medicine 2016,* .

Likas, A., Vlassis, N., & Verbeek, J. J. (2003). The global k-means clustering algorithm. *Pattern Recognition, 36*(2), 451–461.

Madhloom, H. T., Kareem, S. A., Ariffin, H., Zaidan, A. A., Alanazi, H. O., & Zaidan, B. B. (2010). An automated white blood cell nucleus localization and segmentation using image arithmetic and automatic threshold. *Journal of Applied Sciences, 10*(11), 959–966.

Magidson, J., & Vermunt, J. (2002). Latent class models for clustering: a comparison with K-means. *Canadian Journal of Marketing Research, 20*(1), 36–43.

Markiewicz, T., Osowski, S., Marianska, B., & Moszczynski, L. (2005). Automatic recognition of the blood cells of myelogenous leukemia using SVM. In *Vol. 4. Neural networks, 2005. IJCNN'05. Proceedings. 2005 IEEE international joint conference on, July* (pp. 2496–2501): IEEE.

Moallem, G., Thoma, G., Poostchi, M., Yu, H., Silamut, K., Palaniappan, N., Antani, S., Hossain, M. A., Maude, R. J., & Jaeger, S. (2017). Detecting and segmenting white blood cells in microscopy images of thin blood smears. In *2017 IEEE Applied Imagery Pattern Recognition Workshop (AIPR), October* (pp. 220–225): IEEE.

Mohamed, M., Far, B., & Guaily, A. (2012). An efficient technique for white blood cells nuclei automatic segmentation. In: *Systems, Man, and Cybernetics (SMC), 2012 IEEE International Conference on, October* (pp. 220–225): IEEE.

Mohapatra, S., Samanta, S. S., Patra, D., & Satpathi, S. (2011). Fuzzy based blood image segmentation for automated leukemia detection. In *Devices and communications (ICDeCom), 2011 February, International conference on* (pp. 1–5): IEEE.

Mohr, S., & Liew, C. C. (2007). The peripheral-blood transcriptome: new insights into disease and risk assessment. *Trends in Molecular Medicine, 13*(10), 422–432.

Nazlibilek, S., Karacor, D., Ercan, T., Sazli, M. H., Kalender, O., & Ege, Y. (2014). Automatic segmentation, counting, size determination and classification of white blood cells. *Measurement, 55,* 58–65.

Neugebauer, U., Clement, J. H., Bocklitz, T., Krafft, C., & Popp, J. (2010). Identification and differentiation of single cells from peripheral blood by Raman spectroscopic imaging. *Journal of Biophotonics, 3*(8–9), 579–587.

Nilsson, B., & Heyden, A. (2005). Segmentation of complex cell clusters in microscopic images: application to bone marrow samples. *Cytometry Part A: The Journal of the International Society for Analytical Cytology, 66*(1), 24–31.

Ongun, G., Halici, U., Leblebicioglu, K., Atalay, V., Beksaç, M., & Beksaç, S. (2001a). Feature extraction and classification of blood cells for an automated differential blood count system. In *Vol. 4. Neural Networks, 2001. Proceedings. IJCNN'01. International Joint Conference on* (pp. 2461–2466): IEEE.

Ongun, G., Halici, U., Leblebicioglu, K., Atalay, V., Beksac, M., & Beksac, S. (2001b). An automated differential blood count system. In *Vol. 3. Engineering in Medicine and Biology Society, 2001. Proceedings of the 23rd Annual International Conference of the IEEE* (pp. 2583–2586): IEEE.

Othman, M. Z., & Ali, A. B. (2014). Segmentation and feature extraction of lymphocytes WBC using microscopic images. *International Journal of Engineering Research & Technology, 3*(12), 696–701.

Padmanabhan, A., Fritz, B. S., & Honeywell International Inc. (2009). *Miniaturized cytometer for detecting multiple species in a sample.* US Patent 7630063.

Pedersen, S. J. K. (2007). Circular hough transform. In *Aalborg University, vision, graphics, and interactive systems, 123* (p. 123).

Peltola, V., Toikka, P., Irjala, K., Mertsola, J., & Ruuskanen, O. (2007). Discrepancy between total white blood cell counts and serum C-reactive protein levels in febrile children. *Scandinavian Journal of Infectious Diseases, 39*(6–7), 560–565.

Piuri, V., & Scotti, F. (2004). Morphological classification of blood leucocytes by microscope images. In *Computational intelligence for measurement systems and applications* (pp. 103–108).

Poomcokrak, J., & Neatpisarnvanit, C. (2008). Red blood cells extraction and counting. In *The 3rd international symposium on biomedical engineering* (pp. 199–203).

Prinyakupt, J., & Pluempitiwiriyawej, C. (2015). Segmentation of white blood cells and comparison of cell morphology by linear and naïve Bayes classifiers. *Biomedical Engineering Online, 14*(1), 63.

Putzu, L., & Di Ruberto, C. (2013). White blood cells identification and counting from microscopic blood image. In *Proceedings of world academy of science, engineering and technology (no. 73, p. 363). World academy of science, engineering and technology (WASET), January.*

Reta, C., Robles, L. A., Gonzalez, J. A., Diaz, R., & Guichard, J. S. (2010). Segmentation of bone marrow cell images for morphological classification of acute leukemia. In *FLAIRS conference, May* (pp. 86–91).

Rezatofighi, S. H., & Soltanian-Zadeh, H. (2011). Automatic recognition of five types of white blood cells in peripheral blood. *Computerized Medical Imaging and Graphics, 35*(4), 333–343.

Rezatofighi, S. H., Soltanian-Zadeh, H., Sharifian, R., & Zoroofi, R. A. (2009). A new approach to white blood cell nucleus segmentation based on gram-schmidtorthogonalization. In *Digital Image Processing, 2009 International Conference on, March* (pp. 107–111): IEEE.

Riethdorf, S., Fritsche, H., Müller, V., Rau, T., Schindlbeck, C., Rack, B., Janni, W., Coith, C., Beck, K., Jänicke, F., & Jackson, S. (2007). Detection of circulating tumor cells in peripheral blood of patients with metastatic breast cancer: a validation study of the cell search system. *Clinical Cancer Research, 13*(3), 920–928.

Ross, M. E., Zhou, X., Song, G., Shurtleff, S. A., Girtman, K., Williams, W. K., Liu, H. C., Mahfouz, R., Raimondi, S. C., Lenny, N., & Patel, A. (2003). Classification of pediatric acute lymphoblastic leukemia by gene expression profiling. *Blood, 102*(8), 2951–2959.

Roy, M., Jin, G., Seo, D., Nam, M. H., & Seo, S. (2014). A simple and low-cost device performing blood cell counting based on lens-free shadow imaging technique. *Sensors and Actuators B: Chemical, 201*, 321–328.

Sadeghian, F., Seman, Z., Ramli, A. R., Kahar, B. H. A., & Saripan, M. I. (2009). A framework for white blood cell segmentation in microscopic blood images using digital image processing. *Biological Procedures Online, 11*(1), 196.

Savkare, S. S., & Narote, S. P. (2011). Automatic classification of normal and infected blood cells for parasitemia detection. *International Journal of Computer Science and Network Security, 11*, 94–97.

Savkare, S. S., & Narote, S. P. (2012). Automatic system for classification of erythrocytes infected with malaria and identification of parasite's life stage. *Procedia Technology, 6*, 405–410.

Shim, W. S., Kim, H. J., Kang, E. S., Ahn, C. W., Lim, S. K., Lee, H. C., & Cha, B. S. (2006). The association of total and differential white blood cell count with metabolic syndrome in type 2 diabetic patients. *Diabetes Research and Clinical Practice, 73*(3), 284–291.

Sinha, N., & Ramakrishnan, A. G. (2003). Automation of differential blood count. In *Vol. 2 TENCON 2003. Conference on Convergent Technologies for the Asia-Pacific Region, October* (pp. 547–551): IEEE.

Smereka, M., & Dulęba, I. (2008). Circular object detection using a modified Hough transform. *International Journal of Applied Mathematics and Computer Science, 18*(1), 85–91.

Suradkar, P. T. (2013). Detection of malarial parasite in blood using image processing. *International Journal of Engineering and Innovative Technology (IJEIT), (10)*, 2.

Terstappen, L. W., & Loken, M. R. (1988). Five-dimensional flow cytometry as a new approach for blood and bone marrow differentials. *Cytometry, 9*(6), 548–556.

Theera-Umpon, N. (2005). White blood cell segmentation and classification in microscopic bone marrow images. In *International conference on fuzzy systems and knowledge discovery, August* (pp. 787–796). Berlin, Heidelberg: Springer.

Wang, M., Zhou, X., Li, F., Huckins, J., King, R. W., & Wong, S. T. (2007). Novel cell segmentation and online learning algorithms for cell phase identification in automated time-lapse microscopy. In *Biomedical Imaging: From Nano to Macro, 2007. ISBI 2007. 4th IEEE International Symposium on, April* (pp. 65–68): IEEE.

Wu, T. F., Mei, Z., & Lo, Y. H. (2012). Optofluidic device for label-free cell classification from whole blood. *Lab on a Chip, 12*(19), 3791–3797.

Yang, Y., Zhang, Z., Yang, X., Yeo, J. H., Jiang, L., & Jiang, D. (2004). Blood cell counting and classification by nonflowing laser light scattering method. *Journal of Biomedical Optics, 9*(5), 995–1002.

Yeoh, E. J., Ross, M. E., Shurtleff, S. A., Williams, W. K., Patel, D., Mahfouz, R., Behm, F. G., Raimondi, S. C., Relling, M. V., Patel, A., & Cheng, C. (2002). Classification, subtype discovery, and prediction of outcome in pediatric acute lymphoblastic leukemia by gene expression profiling. *Cancer Cell, 1*(2), 133–143.

Yu, M., Bardia, A., Wittner, B. S., Stott, S. L., Smas, M. E., Ting, D. T., Isakoff, S. J., Ciciliano, J. C., Wells, M. N., Shah, A. M., & Concannon, K. F. (2013). Circulating breast tumor cells exhibit dynamic changes in epithelial and mesenchymal composition. *Science, 339*(6119), 580–584.

Zhang, C., Xiao, X., Li, X., Chen, Y. J., Zhen, W., Chang, J., Zheng, C., & Liu, Z. (2014). White blood cell segmentation by color-space-based k-means clustering. *Sensors, 14*(9), 16128–16147.

Zheng, X., Wang, Y., Wang, G., & Liu, J. (2018). Fast and robust segmentation of white blood cell images by self-supervised learning. *Micron, 107*, 55–71.

Neutrosophic sets in dermoscopic medical image segmentation

Yanhui Guo*, Amira S. Ashour†

*Department of Computer Science, University of Illinois at Springfield, Springfield, IL, United States. †Department of Electronics and Electrical Communications Engineering, Faculty of Engineering, Tanta University, Tanta, Egypt

1 Introduction

Medical image segmentation has an essential role in computer-aided diagnosis systems in different applications. The vast investment and development of medical imaging modalities such as microscopy, dermoscopy, X-ray, ultrasound, computed tomography (CT), magnetic resonance imaging (MRI), and positron emission tomography attract researchers to implement new medical image-processing algorithms. Image segmentation is considered the most essential medical imaging process as it extracts the region of interest (ROI) through a semiautomatic or automatic process. It divides an image into areas based on a specified description, such as segmenting body organs/tissues in the medical applications for border detection, tumor detection/segmentation, and mass detection.

Because segmentation partitions the image into coherent regions, clustering procedures can be applied for segmentation by extracting the global characteristics of the image to professionally separate the ROI from the background. Clustering has several techniques such as K-means clustering, hierarchical clustering, divisive clustering, and mean shift clustering. Moreover, due to the irregular and fuzzy borders in most of the medical images, fuzzy set and neutrosophic set theories become important in the segmentation process to handle uncertainty in the medical images. Accordingly, the fuzzy c-means algorithm (FCM) (Kang, Min, Luan, Li, & Liu, 2009) and neutrosophic c-means (NCM)

Neutrosophic Set in Medical Image Analysis. https://doi.org/10.1016/B978-0-12-818148-5.00011-4

clustering can be applied to improve different segmentation techniques. However, prior determination of the number of clusters and their centroids is essential in the clustering (Ashour, Guo, Kucukkulahli, Erdogmus, & Polat, 2018; Küçükkülahlı, Erdoğmuş, & Polat, 2016; Pei, Zhao, Dong, & Dong, 2017).

Additionally, for image segmentation, the gradient and intensity information is used. Various segmentation approaches can be used, including those based on boundaries such as the deformable model, while other approaches are region-based methods such as region merging, region growing, and active contour (Al-azawi, Abdulhameed, & Ahmed, 2017; Baldevbhai & Anand, 2012; Sharma & Aggarwal, 2010). However, most of the medical images have noise, intensity inhomogeneity, and weak boundaries, which require complex procedures (Li et al., 2011; Ma, Tavares, Jorge, & Mascarenhas, 2010; Pham, Xu, & Prince, 2000).

Developing intelligent/advanced methods for medical image segmentation has become a hotspot, leading to hybrid approaches for efficient segmentation based on the boundary and ROI by using the information of both boundaries and regions for image segmentation. Such approaches include graph-based methods such as graph cut segmentation, which is iterated to separate the object and background in the image using explicit segmentation's constraints by choosing seed points representing some pixels to belong to the object and other pixels from the background.

A graph-based method is mainly based on the concept of maximum flow/minimum cut between the source and sink nodes in the directed graphs to segment the objects in the image. Graph cut (GC) methods are effective in medical image segmentation due to their global energy advantages. Nevertheless, GC methods entail the interactive selection of the object/background seeds, which is time consuming. To tackle this disadvantage, a fully automated GC procedure based on mapping the image data into a high dimension using a kernel function, called kernel graph cuts (KGC), was developed (Salah, Mitiche, & Ayed, 2011).

One of the challenging medical image segmentation applications is skin lesion segmentation. Nevertheless, dermoscopic images have different lesion types of several artifacts, such as the fuzzy lesion borders and their irregularity characteristics, skin lines, hairs, air bubbles, multicolored areas within, and low contrast between the lesion and the nearby skin regions (Celebi, Iyatomi, Schaefer, & Stoecker, 2009; Korotkov & Garcia, 2012). Such artifacts raised the role of the neutrosophic set (NS) to remove the uncertainty during the segmentation process, which has an essential role to support accurate diagnosis and develop automated skin lesion computer-aided diagnosis systems (CADs).

Consequently, this chapter proposes a hybrid skin lesion segmentation system combining NS-based clustering and kernel graph cut segmentation using the NCM and KGC methods to realize an efficient and unsupervised skin lesion segmentation solution. In addition, a histogram-based clustering estimation (HBCE) procedure is applied to specify the required number of clusters for further use of the NCM technique.

The organization of the subsequent sections is as follows. Section 2 reports several related studies to the neutrosophic set, neutrosophic *c*-means, clustering-based unsupervised segmentation, graph cut, and the kernel graph cut in medical image segmentation and specifically for skin lesion segmentation. Section 3 introduces the framework of the different methods used in the proposed method. The experimental results with extensive discussion are included in Section 4. Finally, Section 5 provides the overall conclusion.

2 Related studies

Image segmentation is a challenging, complex task that is affected by numerous aspects, including noise, low contrast, illumination, and irregularity of the object boundaries. Moreover, skin cancer lesion segmentation in dermoscopic images has a significant role in developing automated clinical CADs to assist dermatologists. Nevertheless, skin cancer segmentation is complicated, owing to the dissimilarity of the lesion types, textures, sizes, colors, and shapes as well as the existence of hair and air bubbles.

Researchers developed different skin lesion segmentation procedures. Ghanta et al. (2017) implemented a unified probabilistic framework for automated human skin segmentation using an unsupervised model. Wang et al. (2011) implemented dermoscopy image segmentation using a watershed algorithm and neural network classifier, where a threshold procedure was used to exclude the large light blobs close to the lesion boundary. Rajab, Woolfson, and Morgan (2004) compared neural network edge detection and the region-based segmentation scheme using the optimal threshold for skin lesion detection/segmentation. Furthermore, Silveira et al. (2009) carried out a comparative study to evaluate different methods for dermoscopic image segmentation, including adaptive thresholding, adaptive snake, the level-set method, gradient vector flow, the fuzzy-based split/merge (FBSM) procedure, and the EM level set. This comparison concluded the superiority of the FBSM to develop a fully automated dermoscopic image segmentation process.

Clustering analysis has been used for dermoscopic image skin lesion segmentation. Zhou, Schaefer, Sadka, and Celebi (2009) employed an anisotropic mean shift scheme and a fuzzy c-means (FCM) method. Furthermore, Lee and Chen (2014) applied classical FCM clustering, which proved its impact compared to Otsu's thresholding method. Nevertheless, FCM suffers from its noise sensitivity and its dependency on the number of clusters and their centroids (Pham, 2001). Accordingly, the NS can be employed to resolve such disadvantages, where it is considered a dominant way to handle indeterminacy during the image-processing procedures. It inspired researchers to develop new image segmentation methods based on the NS. A nonlocal neutrosophic Wiener filter was applied to enhance the brain tumor images before using k-means clustering for segmentation by Mohan, Krishnaveni, and Huo (2015).

Sengur and Guo (2011) proposed an integrated NS and multiresolution wavelet transform for image segmentation. The c-k-means clustering method for segmentation was applied after mapping the texture/color features on the NS and wavelet domain. Afterward, Guo and Sengur (2015) improved the fuzzy c-means clustering procedure using NS to overcome the FCM inability to handle the data uncertainty by proposing neutrosophic c-means (NCM) clustering for image segmentation.

The neutrosophic set was combined with clustering analysis for skin lesion detection/segmentation. Guo, Ashour, and Smarandache (2018) applied the NCM clustering and adaptive region growing procedures. Additionally, Ashour, Hawas, Guo, and Wahba (2018) proposed an optimized NS method using a genetic algorithm to diminish the indeterminacy in the dermoscopic images followed by k-means clustering for segmenting the skin lesion regions. Because the initial setting of the number of clusters and their centroids is a critical issue in the clustering-based segmentation methods, a histogram-based clustering estimation (HBCE) procedure was proposed by Ashour, Guo, et al. (2018) to improve the NCM clustering method for dermoscopic image segmentation. Aside from these clustering-based segmentation methods, the graph-based image segmentation techniques have an accurate segmentation performance in several applications (Felzenszwalb & Huttenlocher, 2004; Tao, Jin, & Zhang, 2007).

Graph theory and algorithms have been applied in dermoscopic image segmentation. Sadeghi, Razmara, Lee, and Atkins (2011) detected the pigment network structures form cyclic graphs, where the image was converted to a graph and the features were extracted using the cyclic subgraphs matching the skin texture structures. Moreover, the normalized graph cuts method was used by Flores and Scharcanski (2014) to segment the skin image patches. To improve the segmentation performance, Salah et al. (2011) implemented a new parametric kernel graph cuts (KGC) method for multiregion image segmentation. The graph cut piecewise constant model becomes applicable by indirect mapping of the image data using a kernel function. This scheme gained the advantages of the kernel mapping process of the original image data along with the advantages of the graph cuts method. The evaluation performance on real medical motion maps and synthetic aperture radar images proved the effectiveness of this segmentation approach.

Another way to enhance the graph cut-based segmentation method, called a neutrosophic graph cut (NGC), was proposed by Guo, Akbulut, Şengür, Xia, and Smarandache (2017). In this segmentation procedure, images were mapped to the NS domain, and then an indeterminacy filter operation was used before applying the graph cuts for segmentation. From these related studies, the current chapter gathered the advantages of both the HBCE-based NCM clustering approach and the KGC in the proposed NKGC method for skin lesion segmentation.

3 Methodology

Image segmentation is considered a challenging image processing task, especially in medical applications. From the preceding studies, NS proved its valuable role to reduce the uncertainty and to handle the skin lesion images and other applications. Moreover, the NS clustering techniques, GC, and kernel GC have an effective role. Accordingly, this chapter offers a hybrid skin lesion segmentation system integrating the NCM clustering and the kernel graph cut segmentation procedure. To guarantee efficient utilization of the NCM clustering stage, the HBCE method was used to determine the required number of clusters and their centroids.

3.1 Neutrosophic image

The NS has an imperative role in medical image segmentation (Cheng, Guo, & Zhang, 2011; Guo et al., 2018; Guo, Ashour, & Sun, 2017; Guo & Cheng, 2009; Guo, Şengür, & Tian, 2016; Mohan, Krishnaveni, & Guo, 2013) to consider the indeterminacy/uncertainty information in an image. For an element $\langle A \rangle$ in NS, its opposite element $\langle Anti-A \rangle$ and its neutrality $\langle Neut-A \rangle$ are used to represent the indeterminacy in each event using three membership sets, namely truth (T), indeterminacy (I), and falsity (F). Consequently, a pixel $w(i,j)$ in an image can be mapped to the NS domain using the following expression (Guo, Ashour, & Sun, 2017):

$$w_{NS}(i,j) = \{T(i,j), I(i,j), F(i,j)\} \tag{1}$$

where $T(i,j)$, $I(i,j)$, and $F(i,j)$ are the membership functions (MFs) belonging to the foreground, indeterminate, and background, respectively. In the current work, the dermoscopy image is mapped to the NS domain using the following membership true and indeterminate functions:

$$T_{im}(i,j) = \frac{b(i,j) - b_{\min}}{b_{\max} - b_{\min}} \tag{2}$$

$$I_{im}(i,j) = \frac{s(i,j) - s_{\min}}{s_{\max} - s_{\min}} \tag{3}$$

where $b(i,j)$ is the intensity value of the pixel (i,j), and $s(i,j)$ represents the gradient magnitude at the same pixel in an image. Additionally, $b_{\max}$ and $b_{\min}$ are the maximum and minimum intensity values, respectively, in the whole image, while $s_{\max}$ and $s_{\min}$ are the maximum and minimum gradient magnitude, respectively, in the whole image. These MFs give the ability to the NS to measure the indeterminacy/uncertainty in the skin lesion dermoscopic image, including the fuzzy edges, noise, and artifacts. This neutrosophic image is considered the input to the clustering stage in the proposed system using HBCE-based NCM clustering for further segmentation by the kernel GC method.

3.2 Neutrosophic *c*-means clustering

For efficient NCM clustering, the number of clusters and their initial centroids in the NS image representation are determined before the clustering procedure using the histogram-based clustering estimation (HBCE) algorithm in Ashour, Guo, et al. (2018). Afterward the NCM is applied to measure the T and I membership functions of the outlier and uncertain cluster in the image, which represents the degrees of the determinacy and indeterminacy, respectively. These MFs are measured iteratively until a convergence to a saddle point is reached, where each pixel in the image is assigned to a specific cluster according to the membership value (Guo & Sengur, 2015). The MFs (T and I) of point a are defined as follows using the NCM procedure (Guo, Akbulut, et al., 2017):

$$T_{NCM-a} = \frac{Z}{f_1}(d_a - c_j)^{-\frac{2}{m-1}} \tag{4}$$

$$I_{NCM-a} = \frac{Z}{f_2}(d_a - \bar{c}_a\text{max})^{-\frac{2}{m-1}} \tag{5}$$

where d_a refer to a sample in a d-dimensional space at a point a, and c is the number of clusters with centroids c_j. Moreover, the objective function in the NCM depends on Z, which is given by:

$$Z = \left[\frac{1}{f_1}\sum_{j=1}^{C}(x_a - c_j)^{-\frac{2}{m-1}} + \frac{1}{f_2}(x_a - \bar{c}_a\text{max})^{-\frac{2}{m-1}} + \frac{1}{f_3}\lambda^{-\frac{2}{m-1}}\right]^{-1} \tag{6}$$

where f_1, f_2, and f_3 are weight factors, and λ is a control parameter (Guo, Akbulut, et al., 2017). Furthermore, $\bar{c}_a\text{max}$ is calculated using the largest and the second largest values of T, where these two values of the nearest determinate clusters are used to decrease the objective function in the NCM without dropping the clustering performance (Guo & Sengur, 2015). Because the NCM is an iterative procedure, the following constraint is applied during the updating of the NCM using ν as a stopping constant:

$$\left| T_{NCM-a}^{(k+1)} - T_{NCM-a}^{(k)} \right| < \nu \tag{7}$$

3.3 Kernel graph cuts

Graph cut is an efficient graph-based segmentation technique that has two main parts, namely the data part to measure the image data's conformity inside the segmentation areas, which includes the image's features, and the regularization part to smooth the boundaries of the segmented regions (ROI) by keeping the spatial information of the image (Felzenszwalb & Huttenlocher, 2004). Graph cut is considered an energy minimization process of the constructed graph G_{GC} for segmenting the ROI in an image using a set of seeds (ROI/background). For a set of vertices P, which represents the pixels/regions, and a set of edges H, which connects the neighboring vertices, thus, G_{GC} can be expressed as follows:

$$G_{GC} = (P, H) \tag{8}$$

The graph cut representation can be transformed into a maximum flow/minimal cut of the graph. Assume a map u, which allocates the pixels to different clusters. Thus, the two components of the energy function G_{func} in the graph cuts contain the data part O_{data} that calculates the difference between u and the allocated region and the regularization part O_{reg} that evaluates the boundaries' smoothness. Typically, a weight factor is given to these two parts; hence, the energy function can be given by (Luo et al., 2013):

$$G_{\text{func}}(u) = \Delta \cdot O_{\text{data}}(u) + (1 - \Delta) \cdot O_{\text{reg}}(u) \qquad (9)$$

where the weight has the range $0 \leq \Delta \leq 1$ to give a relative effect of the two parts. However, the data in the medical image is complex, leading to the insufficient use of piecewise Gaussian distribution to partition nonlinearly separated data. Thus, kernel functions can be used to map the image data to address the nonlinear problem. Subsequently, a KGC for automatic segmentation based on kernel functions was proposed in (Salah et al., 2011). The two parts in the energy function using the KGC are considered a modified version of the traditional GC parts. The modified KGC is the original kernel-induced data part that assesses the mapped image data deviation and the regularization term. The modified GC energy function using the kernel-induced energy function used in the KGC is given by (Luo et al., 2013; Salah et al., 2011):

$$G_{K\_\text{func}}(\{\eta_l\}, \beta) = \sum_{l \in L} \sum_{w \in R_l} R_K(C_w, \eta_l) + \alpha \sum_{\{w, q\} \in V} O_{\text{reg}}(\beta(w), \beta(q))$$

$$(10)$$

This energy function $G_{K\_\text{func}}(\{\eta_l\}, \beta)$ computes the kernel-induced distances between the region parameters η_l and the observations, where the indexing function β allocates each pixel w in the image to a specific region R_l by giving a label l to the pixel in a predetermined labels set.

Accordingly, the data part in the energy function in Eq. (9) is modified in Eq. (10) to include the kernel function $R_K(C_w, \eta_l)$. In this modified energy function formula, the kernel function is presented as a dot product in high-dimensional space (Malcolm, Rathi, & Tannenbaum, 2007), where C is the observation space and R is the higher-dimensional mapped space. The second part in Eq. (10) introduces the smooth regularization function $O_{\text{reg}}(\beta(w), \beta(q))$, where α is a positive factor and V is a neighborhood set enclosing all pairs of neighboring pixels $\{w, q\}$.

3.4 Proposed system

In the present work, the modified kernel-based energy function with the graph cut algorithm is applied for efficient dermoscopic image segmentation using the maximum flow procedure.

Algorithm 1: Proposed NKGC

Start

   Convert the original dermoscopic image to gray

   Calculate the histogram representation of the image

   Apply the HBCE procedure to determine the number of clusters and their centroids
         in the image

   Apply the NCM clustering method

   Segment the pixels using the KGC to segment the dermoscopic image

End

Moreover, the proposed method (NKGC) integrated both the HBCE-based NCM clustering technique and the KGC technique sequentially to guarantee efficient, unsupervised skin lesion segmentation, as summarized in the following Algorithm 1.

4 Experimental results and discussion

The proposed NKGC skin lesion segmentation method was trained and tested using selected dermoscopic images from the International Skin Imaging Collaboration dataset (ISIC 2016) for segmentation (International Skin Imaging Collaboration Website, n.d.). The corresponding binary ground-truth images are also included in the ISIC 2016 dataset for the performance evaluation stage of the proposed method. Different performance evaluation metrics of image segmentation were measured, such as accuracy, Jaccard index (JAC), dice similarity coefficient, sensitivity, and specificity (Ashour, Guo, et al., 2018).

4.1 Subjective comparison results of segmentation

The proposed NKGC method using HBCE-NCM-KGC for skin lesion segmentation was compared to the corresponding results using the GC, HBCE-NCM, and HBCE-NCM-GC methods, as demonstrated in Fig. 1. The detected boundaries of the skin lesion were outlined in blue, whereas the corresponding ground-truth images were in red.

Fig. 1B demonstrates the mismatching between the detected boundaries (contours) using GC only and the ground-truth detected ones with incorrect segmentation. The GC method detected false larger boundaries with nonuniform shapes compared to the correct ones due to required uncertainty reduction

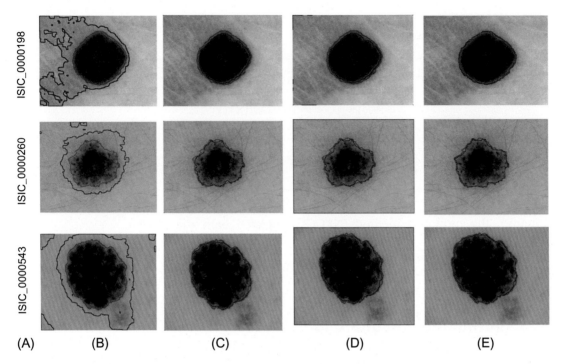

Fig. 1 The segmentation subjective comparative results of the proposed NKGC: (A) the number of the dermoscopic image in the test dataset from ISIC 2016, (B–E) the lesion region detection using: GC only, the HBCE-NCM only, the HBCE-NCM-GC, and the proposed HBCE-NCM-KGC (NKGC), respectively.

in the dermoscopic images, where generally in dermoscopic images there are different regions due to luminance, noise, and artifact parameters that require different models to represent the data. These parameters are represented in the data part of the GC in a way that does not preserve all the data forms and parameters.

However, using the HBCE-NCM procedure before using GC improved the boundary detection matching, as illustrated in Fig. 1C–D, due to removing the uncertainty in the dermoscopic images using the NCM method with the predetermined number of clusters and their centroids. Moreover, the proposed NKGC achieved the best match with the ground-truth results compared to the other reported methods, especially with dark skin lesions as in the image of ISIC_0000198.

The superiority of NKGC is because of the use of the kernel function that guides the contour to be more accurate, leading to accurate segmentation. However, the typical GC provided the worst results with the mismatching results of the segmented images and the corresponding ground-truth results.

4.2 Comparative study on performance evaluation

To evaluate the proposed NKGC method, different performance metrics are measured with reference to ground-truth boundaries with a comparative study using the other segmentation methods included in the present work. Table 1 reports the mean and standard deviation (Std) of the performance metric values in percentage average values over the selected images in the test dataset.

Table 1 proves the superiority of the proposed NKGC method compared to the other methods, which are illustrated also in Fig. 2. Furthermore, Fig. 3 shows the area under the curve (AUC) of the average values of the measured metrics using the different skin lesion segmentation methods.

Table 1 along with Figs. 2 and 3 establish the impact of the proposed NKGC method to segment the skin lesion regions with an accuracy of 97.41%. This proposed method accomplished the superior accuracy, JAC, dice, and sensitivity values while the traditional GC achieved the preeminent specificity value of 96.1%.

The proposed NKGC outperformed the traditional GC and the other methods, where the dermoscopic images include different artifacts that are reduced using NS. In addition, the traditional GC requires an interactive user interface to model the different regions within the image to represent the data. Such interactive graph cut methods applied general models by including a process to learn the region parameters as a part of the data during the segmentation process at each step. Nevertheless, the parameter learning based on each region in the image does not arise from the objective function in the GC method. This issue is resolved by using the kernel graph cuts that introduce kernel mapping in

Table 1 The performance metrics' mean ± Std using the proposed NKGC method compared to the other methods.

	Accuracy (%)	Dice (%)	JAC (%)	Sensitivity (%)	Specificity (%)
GC	83.66 ± 23.24	76.21 ± 25.43	67.53 ± 30.12	81.80 ± 28.09	96.1 ± 10.46
HBCE-NCM	95.03 ± 4.72	87.63 ± 9.31	79.02 ± 12.95	99.16 ± 0.57	82.3 ± 14.42
HBCE-NCM-GC	95.37 ± 4.78	88.6 ± 9.55	80.65 ± 13.46	99.17 ± 0.57	82.53 ± 14.32
Proposed NKGC	97.41 ± 2.04	93.27 ± 5.27	87.78 ± 8.31	99.21 ± 1.81	90.87 ± 5.54

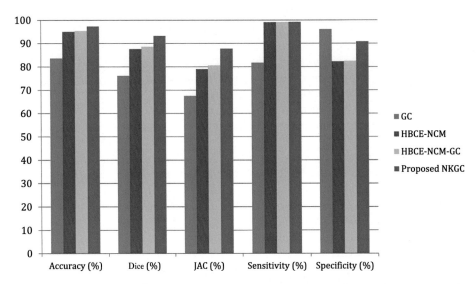

Fig. 2 The average values of the performance metrics using the proposed NKGC method compared to the other methods.

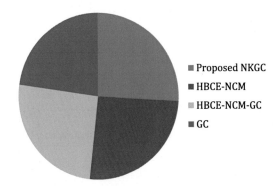

Fig. 3 The average values of the area under the curve using the proposed NKGC method compared to the other methods.

the unsupervised graph cut energy function to handle the multiregion segmentation of the dermoscopic images, instead of using only the Gaussian representation in the traditional GC.

Implicitly, the data of an image is mapped through a kernel function into higher-dimensionality data to guarantee an applicable model for the unsupervised graph cut formula. The proposed method combined the advantages of the NS as well as the KGC leading to effective and accurate skin lesion segmentation method.

5 Conclusions

Medical image segmentation is a challenging task suffering from the limitations and artifacts in the images, including weak boundaries, noise, similar intensities in the different regions, and the intensity inhomogeneity. This chapter proposed an integrated skin lesion segmentation method called NKGC for accurate diagnosis. The NKGC consisted of several stages, namely applying the HBCE procedure for predetermination of the required number of clusters and their centroids, using the NS in the NCM clustering algorithm to reduce the dermoscopic image uncertainty in the clustered images, and the kernel graph cut method was carried out for final segmentation of the input image. Selected images from the ISIC 2016 dermoscopic image dataset were used in the training and testing phases of the proposed approach.

Several performance metrics were measured in the comparative study between the proposed NKGC, the GC only, the HBCE-NCM, and the HBCE-NCM-GC. The experimental outcomes established the superiority of the NKGC method in segmenting the skin lesion with 97.41%, 87.78%, 93.27%, and 99.21% average values of accuracy, JAC, dice, and sensitivity, respectively, even with different lesion shape and size.

References

Al-azawi, R. J., Abdulhameed, A. A., & Ahmed, H. M. (2017). A robustness segmentation approach for skin cancer image detection based on an adaptive automatic thresholding technique. *American Journal of Intelligent Systems*, 7(4), 107–112.

Ashour, A. S., Guo, Y., Kucukkulahli, E., Erdogmus, P., & Polat, K. (2018). A hybrid dermoscopy images segmentation approach based on neutrosophic clustering and histogram estimation. *Applied Soft Computing*, 69, 426–434.

Ashour, A. S., Hawas, A. R., Guo, Y., & Wahba, M. A. (2018). A novel optimized neutrosophic k-means using genetic algorithm for skin lesion detection in dermoscopy images. *Signal, Image and Video Processing*, 1–8.

Baldevbhai, P. J., & Anand, R. S. (2012). Review of graph, medical and color image base segmentation techniques. *IOSR Journal of Electrical and Electronics Engineering*, 1(1), 1–19.

Celebi, M. E., Iyatomi, H., Schaefer, G., & Stoecker, W. V. (2009). Lesion border detection in dermoscopy images. *Computerized Medical Imaging and Graphics*, 33(2), 148–153.

Cheng, H. D., Guo, Y., & Zhang, Y. (2011). A novel image segmentation approach based on neutrosophic set and improved fuzzy c-means algorithm. *New Mathematics and Natural Computation*, 7(01), 155–171.

Felzenszwalb, P. F., & Huttenlocher, D. P. (2004). Efficient graph-based image segmentation. *International Journal of Computer Vision*, 59(2), 167–181.

Flores, E. S., & Scharcanski, J. (2014). Segmentation of pigmented melanocytic skin lesions based on learned dictionaries and normalized graph cuts. In *Graphics,* patterns and images (SIBGRAPI), 2014 27th SIBGRAPI conference on, August (pp. 33–40): IEEE.

Ghanta, S., Jordan, M. I., Kose, K., Brooks, D. H., Rajadhyaksha, M., & Dy, J. G. (2017). A marked poisson process driven latent shape model for 3D segmentation of reflectance confocal microscopy image stacks of human skin. *IEEE Transactions on Image Processing, 26*(1), 172–184.

Guo, Y., Akbulut, Y., Şengür, A., Xia, R., & Smarandache, F. (2017). An efficient image segmentation algorithm using neutrosophic graph cut. *Symmetry, 9*(9), 185.

Guo, Y., Ashour, A. S., & Smarandache, F. (2018). A novel skin lesion detection approach using neutrosophic clustering and adaptive region growing in dermoscopy images. *Symmetry, 10*(4), 119.

Guo, Y., Ashour, A. S., & Sun, B. (2017). A novel glomerular basement membrane segmentation using neutrsophic set and shearlet transform on microscopic images. *Health Information Science and Systems, 5*(1), 15.

Guo, Y., & Cheng, H. D. (2009). New neutrosophic approach to image segmentation. *Pattern Recognition, 42*(5), 587–595.

Guo, Y., & Sengur, A. (2015). NCM: neutrosophic c-means clustering algorithm. *Pattern Recognition, 48*(8), 2710–2724.

Guo, Y., Şengür, A., & Tian, J. W. (2016). A novel breast ultrasound image segmentation algorithm based on neutrosophic similarity score and level set. *Computer Methods and Programs in Biomedicine, 123*, 43–53.

International Skin Imaging Collaboration Website n.d. http://www.isdis.net/index.php/isic-project.

Kang, J., Min, L., Luan, Q., Li, X., & Liu, J. (2009). Novel modified fuzzy c-means algorithm with applications. *Digital Signal Processing, 19*(2), 309–319.

Korotkov, K., & Garcia, R. (2012). Computerized analysis of pigmented skin lesions: a review. *Artificial Intelligence in Medicine, 56*(2), 69–90.

Küçükkülahlı, E., Erdoğmuş, P., & Polat, K. (2016). Histogram-based automatic segmentation of images. *Neural Computing and Applications, 27*(5), 1445–1450.

Lee, H., & Chen, Y. P. P. (2014). Skin cancer extraction with optimum fuzzy thresholding technique. *Applied Intelligence, 40*(3), 415–426.

Li, C., Huang, R., Ding, Z., Gatenby, J., Metaxas, D. N., & Gore, J. C. (2011). A level set method for image segmentation in the presence of intensity inhomogeneities with application to MRI. *IEEE Transactions on Image Processing, 20*(7), 2007.

Luo, Q., Qin, W., Wen, T., Gu, J., Gaio, N., Chen, S., ... Xie, Y. (2013). Segmentation of abdomen MR images using kernel graph cuts with shape priors. *Biomedical Engineering Online, 12*(1), 124.

Ma, Z., Tavares, J. M. R., Jorge, R. N., & Mascarenhas, T. (2010). A review of algorithms for medical image segmentation and their applications to the female pelvic cavity. *Computer Methods in Biomechanics and Biomedical Engineering, 13*(2), 235–246.

Malcolm, J., Rathi, Y., & Tannenbaum, A. (2007). Graph cut segmentation with nonlinear shape priors. In *Vol. 4*, pp. IV–365. *Image processing, 2007. ICIP 2007. IEEE international conference on, September:* IEEE.

Mohan, J., Krishnaveni, V., & Guo, Y. (2013). MRI denoising using nonlocal neutrosophic set approach of Wiener filtering. *Biomedical Signal Processing and Control, 8*(6), 779–791.

Mohan, J., Krishnaveni, V., & Huo, Y. (2015). Automated brain tumor segmentation on MR images based on neutrosophic set approach. In *Electronics and Communication Systems (ICECS), 2015 2nd International Conference on, February* (pp. 1078–1083): IEEE.

Pei, J., Zhao, L., Dong, X., & Dong, X. (2017). Effective algorithm for determining the number of clusters and its application in image segmentation. *Cluster Computing, 20*(4), 2845–2854.

Pham, D. L. (2001). Spatial models for fuzzy clustering. *Computer Vision and Image Understanding, 84*(2), 285–297.

Pham, D. L., Xu, C., & Prince, J. L. (2000). Current methods in medical image segmentation. *Annual Review of Biomedical Engineering, 2*(1), 315–337.

Rajab, M. I., Woolfson, M. S., & Morgan, S. P. (2004). Application of region-based segmentation and neural network edge detection to skin lesions. *Computerized Medical Imaging and Graphics, 28*(1–2), 61–68.

Sadeghi, M., Razmara, M., Lee, T. K., & Atkins, M. S. (2011). A novel method for detection of pigment network in dermoscopic images using graphs. *Computerized Medical Imaging and Graphics, 35*(2), 137–143.

Salah, M. B., Mitiche, A., & Ayed, I. B. (2011). Multiregion image segmentation by parametric kernel graph cuts. *IEEE Transactions on Image Processing, 20*(2), 545–557.

Sengur, A., & Guo, Y. (2011). Color texture image segmentation based on neutrosophic set and wavelet transformation. *Computer Vision and Image Understanding, 115*(8), 1134–1144.

Sharma, N., & Aggarwal, L. M. (2010). Automated medical image segmentation techniques. *Journal of Medical Physics/Association of Medical Physicists of India, 35*(1), 3.

Silveira, M., Nascimento, J. C., Marques, J. S., Marçal, A. R., Mendonça, T., Yamauchi, S., … Rozeira, J. (2009). Comparison of segmentation methods for melanoma diagnosis in dermoscopy images. *IEEE Journal of Selected Topics in Signal Processing, 3*(1), 35–45.

Tao, W., Jin, H., & Zhang, Y. (2007). Color image segmentation based on mean shift and normalized cuts. *IEEE Transactions on Systems, Man, and Cybernetics, Part B (Cybernetics), 37*(5), 1382–1389.

Wang, H., Moss, R. H., Chen, X., Stanley, R. J., Stoecker, W. V., Celebi, M. E., … Menzies, S. W. (2011). Modified watershed technique and post-processing for segmentation of skin lesions in dermoscopy images. *Computerized Medical Imaging and Graphics, 35*(2), 116–120.

Zhou, H., Schaefer, G., Sadka, A. H., & Celebi, M. E. (2009). Anisotropic mean shift based fuzzy c-means segmentation of dermoscopy images. *IEEE Journal of Selected Topics in Signal Processing, 3*(1), 26–34.

IV

Neutrosophic set in medical image classification

12

Neutrosophic similarity score-based entropy measure for focal and nonfocal electroencephalogram signal classification

Abdulkadir Sengur*, Varun Bajaj[†], Murat Karabatak[‡], Erkan Tanyildizi[‡]

*Department of Electrical and Electronics Engineering, Technology Faculty, Firat University, Elazig, Turkey. †Department of Electronics and Communication, Indian Institute of Information Technology Design and Manufacturing, Jabalpur, India. ‡Department of Software Engineering, Technology Faculty, Firat University, Elazig, Turkey

1   Introduction

Epilepsy, a neurological disorder, is defined as sudden seizures. Generally, during a seizure period, muscle contractions, loss of consciousness, and tongue biting can be seen (Andrzejak, Schindler, & Rummel, 2012). According to the statistics, around 50 million people have epilepsy worldwide (Prilipko et al., 2005). The person with epilepsy needs to pay attention to himself during his daily activities to prevent getting into a dangerous situation. The EEG, which is an important measurement tool for monitoring the electrical activity level of the human brain, is generally used for clinical analysis of epilepsy (Bajaj & Pachori, 2012; Bajaj & Pachori, 2013; Pachori & Bajaj, 2011). More recently, various algorithms have been proposed for detection, identification, and classification of seizure signals. The convolutional neural networks (CNN) are explored to classify normal, preictal, and seizure classes (Acharya et al., 2018a; Truong et al., 2018). Discrete wavelet transform (DWT) and the SVM classifier are used for detection of seizure signals (Tzimourta et al., 2018). The multiscale radial basis

Neutrosophic Set in Medical Image Analysis. https://doi.org/10.1016/B978-0-12-818148-5.00012-6

functions (MRBF) have been explored to improve both time and frequency resolution simultaneously. The TF feature is extracted for MRBF-MPSO classification for epileptic EEG signals (Li et al., 2018). Gray level cooccurrence matrix (GLCM) features are extracted from time-frequency images used in SVM classifiers for seizure detection (Huang et al., 2018). Hurst exponents and autoregressive models are explored for classification of seizure EEG segments (Gupta, Singh, & Karlekar, 2018). Features extracted from the wavelet-based directed transfer function (WDTF) method have been fed into SVM for classification of seizures (Ren et al., 2018). Modified line length and Mahalanobis distance function are explored for seizure detection using EEG signals (Pathak et al., 2018). In Siuly et al. (2018), the detection of the seizure was accomplished by Hermite transform-based features and the least square (LS)-SVM classifier. The STFT-based rhythm has been explored for feature extraction for seizure detection (Tsiouris et al., 2017).

Epilepsy patients need either drugs or surgery for treatment. For efficient surgery, the exact location of the brain region that causes epilepsy needs to be determined. The determination of the exact location of the epileptic region is performed manually with a clinical procedure by the physician. This procedure is quite subjective and necessitates highly skilled physicians. This type of epilepsy is termed partial epilepsy and necessitates an F-EEG. An F-EEG is defined as an EEG that is recorded from a specific location of the brain where epilepsy chances are detected. Similarly, an NF-EEG is defined as an EEG that is recorded from the brain regions that do not contain any epilepsy chances.

Numerous methodologies were explored for identification of the F-EEG signals. Statistical measures such as mean and standard deviation of Euclidean distances (Gehlot et al., 2015) and area of analytic intrinsic mode functions (AIMFs) (Dwivedi et al., 2016) are used as features for analysis of F-EEG and NF-EEG signals. TF image-based features such as maximum count pixel intensity, entropy, inverse difference moment, power, and texture homogeneity are used for discrimination of F-EEG and NF-EEG signals (Walde et al., 2016). Zhu et al. (2013) used delay permutation entropy for localization of the focal epileptogenic region. The proposed work is evaluated on intracranial electroencephalography and experiments show that the delay permutation entropy index is an important measure for discrimination of the F-EEG and NF-EEG signals. Sharma, Pachori, and Rajendra Acharya (2015) used DWT for discrimination of the F-EEG and NF-EEG signals. The DWT coefficients are used to calculate the relative energy and entropy features. The ranked entropy and energy features are classified with k-NN, SVM, and probabilistic neural networks. Sharma, Pachori, and Acharya

(2015) proposed a method that uses EMD and entropy measures for discrimination of the F-EEG and NF-EEG signals. The intrinsic mode functions (IMFs) are obtained via EMD and various entropy measures such as the average entropy of Shannon, approximate, sample, phase, and Renyi are calculated. The LS-SVM approach is considered by the authors. In Sharma, Pachori, and Gautam (2014), the sample entropy and variance of the instantaneous frequency features extracted from IMFs obtained from EMD are used with LS-SVM.

Recently, in Rai, Bajaj, and Kumar (2015), bandwidth ratio features extracted from analytic intrinsic mode functions (IMFs) have been set as the input to unsupervised learning. Das and Bhuiyan (2016) presented a comprehensive analysis of the F-EEG and NF-EEG signals. Authors used EMD and DWT and various entropy-based spectral features were extracted for classification purposes. In Deivasigamani, Senthilpari, and Yong (2016), dual tree complex wavelet transform (DT-CWT)-based features and an adaptive neuro fuzzy inference system (ANFIS) were used for F-EEG and NF-EEG signal discrimination. In Gupta et al. (2017), various entropies such as log energy entropy, Stein's unbiased risk estimate entropy, and cross correntropy were extracted from flexible analytic wavelet transform (FAWT) methods for F-EEG signal classification. In Bhattacharyya, Pachori, and Acharya (2017), tunable Q wavelet transform (TQWT), multivariate fuzzy entropy features, and the LS-SVM classifier were used for classification of F-EEG and NF-EEG signals. In R. Sharma et al. (2017), TQWT, LS-SVM, and nonlinear features such as centered correntropy, permutation entropy, bispectral entropies, the largest Lyapunov exponent, fuzzy entropy, sample entropy, and fractal dimension features were considered for classification of F-EEG and NF-EEG signals. In M. Sharma et al. (2017), entropy-based features were extracted from the orthogonal wavelet filter banks, and the LS-SVM classifier was used for discrimination of F-EEG and NF-EEG signals. In Bajaj et al. (2017), rhythms and different kernel functions of LS-SVM were adopted for the discrimination of F-EEG and NF-EEG signals. In Fasil, Rajesh, and Thasleema (2018), the differential operation-based filtering for features energy and entropy with SVM classifier for classification of F-EEG and NF-EEG signals.

More recently, Bhattacharyya et al. (2016) used the empirical WT for F-EEG and NF-EEG signal classification. Specifically, empirical WT was used to transform the input EEG signals into rhythms. Area measure parameters were used as features that were classified with an LS-SVM classifier. In Sharma and Pachori (2018), the features obtained from deformation bandwidth, precession bandwidth, and amplitude bandwidth were used with the LS-SVM classifier for F-EEG and NF-EG signal discrimination. Acharya et al. (2018b) developed a computer-aided design (CAD) system for discrimination of F-EEG and NF-EEG signals. The authors investigated various features for F-EEG and NF-EEG signal classification and found that nonlinear features were more effective for discrimination of the F-EEG and NF-EEG signals. In Taran and Bajaj (2018), optimum allocation sampling was explored for homogeneous EEG clusters and spectral moment-based features were adopted for detection of F-EEG signals. The authors opted to use an extreme learning machine (ELM) classifier in their study. Raghu and Sriram (2018) introduced a tool called CADFES that enables detecting a focal epileptic seizure. The authors extracted 28 various features from time, frequency, and statistical measurements of the input EEG signals. SVM and k-NN classifiers were used in the classification stage of the developed tool.

In this chapter, the F-EEG and NF-EEG signal discrimination is carried out by a novel approach. The proposed approach initially converts the input EEG signals into color images by applying TF transformation (Şengür, Guo, & Akbulut, 2016). The STFT, which is an efficient method, is used. Each color channel of the obtained TF images is transferred into the neutrosophic domain independently and a Neutrosophic Similarity Score is calculated for each color channel of the TF images. Neutrosophy is a philosophy that brings together the knowledge of philosophy, logic, set theory, probability, and statistics (Smarandache, 2003). Neutrosophy is a generalization of fuzzy logic based on the assumption that t is true, i is indeterminate, and f is false. t, i, and f are in a range of T, I, and F. They are real values and there are no restrictions on them. After neutrosophic similarity image construction, an $n \times n$ sliding window is used to calculate the local entropy for each color channel. The local entropy values from each color channel are then concatenated for final feature vector construction. Various classifiers such as DT, k-NN, SVM, and EL are used for classification. The obtained results are evaluated based on accuracy and compared with some existing results.

2 Methodology

2.1 Neutrosophic domain image representation

In the neutrosophic domain, a pixel at (x,y) spatial location is represented with three memberships such as $T(x,y)$, $F(x,y)$, and $I(x,y)$. $T(x,y)$ shows the true membership, $F(x,y)$ represents the falsity membership, and $I(x, y)$ indicates the indeterminacy membership. The truth, falsity, and indeterminacy memberships are defined based on the gray-scale value and the local spatial information, as given in the following;

$$T_{C_g}(x, y) = \frac{g(x, y) - g_{min}}{g_{max} - g_{min}} \tag{1}$$

$$F_{C_g}(x, y) = 1 - T_{C_g}(x, y) \tag{2}$$

$$I_{C_g}(x, y) = \frac{Gd(x, y) - Gd_{min}}{Gd_{max} - Gd_{min}} \tag{3}$$

where $g(x, y)$ and $Gd(x, y)$ are the gray-scale and gradient magnitude at the pixel of (x, y) on the image while g_{min} and g_{max} show the minimum and maximum values of the g image and the Gd_{min} and Gd_{max} values of the gradient magnitude image, respectively.

2.2 Neutrosophic similarity score

Let $A = \{A_1, A_2, \ldots, A_m\}$ symbolize a set of alternatives and $C = \{C_1, C_2, \ldots, C_n\}$ denote a set of criteria accordingly. Thus, a neutrosophic set can be expressed in the context of A and C as the following;

$$A_i = \left\{ \left\langle C_j, T_{C_j}(A_i), I_{C_j}(A_i), F_{C_j}(A_i) \right\rangle \middle| C_j \in C \right\} i = 1, \ldots, m, j = 1, \ldots, n \tag{4}$$

where $T_{C_j}(A_i)$, $F_{C_j}(A_i)$, and $I_{C_j}(A_i)$ denote the membership values of the true, false, and indeterminacy at criterion C_j and $T_{C_j}(A_i)$, $F_{C_j}(A_i)$, $I_{C_j}(A_i)$ should be in the interval of $[0, 1]$. Thus a similarity measure between alternatives A_m and A_n in the multicriteria neutrosophic set is defined as (Guo, Şengür, & Ye, 2014);

$$S_{C_j}(A_m, A_n) = \frac{T_{C_j}(A_m)T_{C_j}(A_n) + F_{C_j}(A_m)F_{C_j}(A_n) + I_{C_j}(A_m)I_{C_j}(A_n)}{\sqrt{T_{C_j}^2(A_m) + F_{C_j}^2(A_m) + I_{C_j}^2(A_m)}\sqrt{T_{C_j}^2(A_n) + F_{C_j}^2(A_n) + I_{C_j}^2(A_n)}} \tag{5}$$

Let's consider the ideal alternative $A^* = \{\langle C_j, T_{C_j}(A^*), I_{C_j}(A^*), F_{C_j}(A^*)\rangle |$ $C_j \in C\} j = 1, \ldots, n$. Thus, the similarity measure between the alternative A_m and the ideal alternative A^* becomes;

$$S_{C_j}(A_m, A^*) = \frac{T_{C_j}(A_m)T_{C_j}(A_n) + F_{C_j}(A_m)F_{C_j}(A^*) + I_{C_j}(A^*)I_{C_j}(A^*)}{\sqrt{T_{C_j}^2(A_m) + F_{C_j}^2(A_m) + I_{C_j}^2(A_m)}\sqrt{T_{C_j}^2(A^*) + F_{C_j}^2(A^*) + I_{C_j}^2(A^*)}} \tag{6}$$

Next, to identify the degree of the ideal object under intensity conditions, a similarity score is calculated as given in Eq. (7).

$$S_{C_g}(P(x,y), A^*) = \frac{T_{C_g}(x,y)T_{C_g}(A^*) + F_{C_g}(x,y)F_{C_g}(A^*) + I_{C_g}(x,y)I_{C_g}(A^*)}{\sqrt{T_{C_g}^2(x,y) + F_{C_g}^2(x,y) + I_{C_g}^2(x,y)}\sqrt{T_{C_g}^2(A^*) + F_{C_g}^2(A^*) + I_{C_g}^2(A^*)}}$$

(7)

The calculated similarity score is sensitive to noise on the image. In order to make the calculated similarity score robust against the noise, the neutrosophic domain image representation equations need to be updated by considering the local mean intensity criterion C_m and the local homogeneity criterion C_h, respectively. Thus, Eqs. (1)–(3) are rewritten as the following;

$$T_{C_m}(x,y) = \frac{g_m(x,y) - g_{m\min}}{g_{m\max} - g_{m\min}}$$

(8)

$$g_m(x,y) = \frac{1}{w^2} \sum_{m=x-w/2}^{x+w/2} \sum_{n=y-w/2}^{y+w/2} g(m,n)$$

(9)

$$F_{C_m}(x,y) = 1 - T_{C_m}(x,y)$$

(10)

$$I_{C_m}(x,y) = 1 - \frac{Gd_m(x,y) - Gd_{m\min}}{Gd_{m\max} - Gd_{m\min}}$$

(11)

as Eq. (9) shows the mean filtering operation and $g_m(x,y)$ and $Gd_m(x,y)$ are the intensity and gradient magnitude values at the position of (x, y).

In addition, the neutrosophic domain image representation functions are updated under the local homogeneity criterion as given in Eqs. (12)–(15), respectively.

$$T_{C_h}(x,y) = \frac{H(x,y) - H_{\min}}{H_{\max} - H_{\min}}$$

(12)

$$F_{C_h}(x,y) = 1 - T_{C_h}(x,y)$$

(13)

$$I_{C_m}(x,y) = 1 - \frac{Gd_h(x,y) - Gd_{h\min}}{Gd_{h\max} - Gd_{h\min}}$$

(14)

$$H(x,y) = \text{TEM}(g(x,y))$$

(15)

where $H(x,y)$ shows the homogeneity value at the spatial location (x,y) and $H_{\min}$ and $H_{\max}$ show the minimum and maximum $H(x,y)$ values, respectively. $H(x,y)$ is obtained after filtering with the TEM filters (Guo et al., 2014). $Gd_h(x,y)$ is the gradient value on $H(x,y)$.

$$S_{C_m}(P(x,y),A^*) = \frac{T_{C_m}(x,y)T_{C_m}(A^*) + F_{C_m}(x,y)F_{C_m}(A^*) + I_{C_m}(x,y)I_{C_m}(A^*)}{\sqrt{T_{C_m}^2(x,y) + F_{C_m}^2(x,y) + I_{C_m}^2(x,y)}\sqrt{T_{C_m}^2(A^*) + F_{C_m}^2(A^*) + I_{C_m}^2(A^*)}}$$

(16)

$$S_{C_h}(P(x,y),A^*) = \frac{T_{C_h}(x,y)T_{C_h}(A^*) + F_{C_h}(x,y)F_{C_h}(A^*) + I_{C_h}(x,y)I_{C_h}(A^*)}{\sqrt{T_{C_h}^2(x,y) + F_{C_h}^2(x,y) + I_{C_h}^2(x,y)}\sqrt{T_{C_h}^2(A^*) + F_{C_h}^2(A^*) + I_{C_h}^2(A^*)}}$$

(17)

The average value of S_{C_g}, S_{C_m}, and S_{C_h} is finally calculated as the Neutrosophic Similarity Score, as shown in Eq. (18)

$$NSS = \frac{(S_{C_g} + S_{C_m} + S_{C_h})}{3}$$

(18)

2.3 Features extraction

The obtained color images are decomposed into R, G, and B color channels. A two-dimensional (2D) sliding window is employed on each color channel to calculate the local entropy values. The local entropy of a given window is calculated as;

$$\sum_{m=x-w/2}^{x+w/2} \sum_{n=y-w/2}^{y+w/2} -p(m,n)\log_2(p(m,n))$$

(19)

where $p(m,n)$ shows the probability of the pixel gray tone located on the (m,n) position. As the calculated entropy values constitute the feature vectors for all color channels, the final feature vector is constructed by concatenation of these feature vectors from all colors.

2.4 Proposed method

Fig. 1 shows the proposed method. As seen in Fig. 1, the segmentation of the input EEG signal constitutes the first step of the proposed method. A fixed length of the window is considered for segmentation of the input EEG signals. The segmentation of the EEG signals is carried out randomly as shown in Fig. 1. The segmentation window is located on the input signal randomly to cover a part of the signal. The second step of the proposed method covers the signal-to-image transformation.

The TF transformation is applied to convert the segmented EEG signals into EEG images. The STFT method is considered in the TF transformation. The obtained images are called spectrogram images. The spectrogram images are saved as color images.

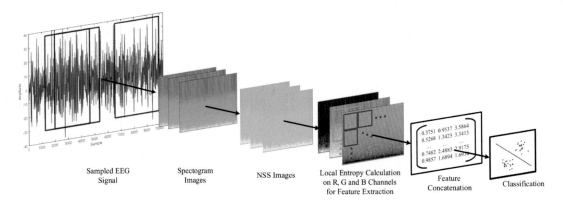

Sampled EEG   Spectogram   NSS Images   Local Entropy Calculation   Feature   Classification
Signal   Images   on R, G and B Channels   Concatenation
                                               for Feature Extraction

Fig. 1 The proposed F-EEG and NF-EEG signals classification system.

The obtained color images are then decomposed into R, G, and B color channels. The NSS images are computed on each of the R, B, and G channels after the spectrogram images are generated. Local entropy features are extracted from the color channels of NSS images and then combined to form a feature vector. For local entropy feature extraction, a nonoverlapping sliding window is used. The size of the window is chosen to acquire the local textural features. The features are concatenated that are calculated from each location of the sliding window. DT, k-NN, SVM, and EL methods are used in classification.

3 Experimental works and results

3.1 Focal and nonfocal EEG dataset

The proposed method is evaluated on the Bern-Barcelona EEG dataset (Andrzejak et al., 2012). Five epilepsy patients admitted for a surgical operation were used to acquire the F-EEG and NF-EEG signals. These patients were suffering from drug-resistant and longstanding temporal lobe epilepsy. There are 7500 EEG signals in the dataset where 3750 pairs of them are from the F-EEG category and the other 3750 pairs are from the NF-EEG category. EEG signals were recorded randomly by the adjacent channel (x and y) pairs. The first column is the x-signal and the second column is the y-signal. The difference of both columns is processed with sampling frequency of the recorded EEG signals is 512 Hz, and their durations are about 20 s. Fig. 2 shows F-EEG and NF-EEG signals. Sample F-EEG and NF-EEG signals are given in Fig. 2A and B, respectively.

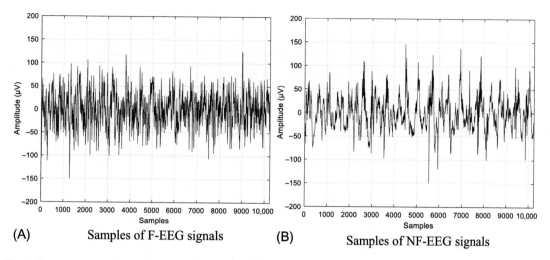

(A) Samples of F-EEG signals

(B) Samples of NF-EEG signals

Fig. 2 Illustration of the EEG signals. (A) Samples of F-EEG signals and (B) samples of NF-EEG signals.

3.2 Experimental settings and results

As mentioned earlier, the Bern-Barcelona EEG dataset is used in experimental works. The experimental works are conducted on MATLAB software with a computer having an Intel Core i7-4810MQ CPU and 32-GB memory. A 10-fold cross-validation (CV) test is considered in the evaluation of the experimental works and the average accuracy scores are recorded. A hamming window width 120 ms and overlap of 100 ms and the number of the FFT is chosen as 256 for spectrogram image formation. These values are selected heuristically. The initial spectrogram images are $875 \times 656 \times 3$ and are resized to $512 \times 512 \times 3$ for convenience. Fig. 3 shows sample spectrogram images from both the F-EEG and NF-EEG signals. The spectrogram images for the F-EEG signals are located in the first row of Fig. 3 and the spectrogram images for the NF-EEG signals are given in the second row of Fig. 3, respectively. Fig. 4 also shows the corresponding NSS images of Fig. 3. As seen in Fig. 4, the color of the input spectrogram images is changed after the NSS procedure. In data augmentation, the length of the segmentation window is chosen as 7500 samples. Other window lengths such as 5000 and 10,000 samples are also considered in the experimentation, but these window lengths did not bring any improvement.

The MATLAB classification learner tool (MCLT) is used in the classification of F-EEG and NF-EEG signals (Sengur, Turhan, & Karabatak, 2018). MCLT contains various classifiers such as decision trees, discriminant analysis, k-NN, SVM, and EL (Turhan et al., 2018). Six SVM-based classifiers—linear SVM

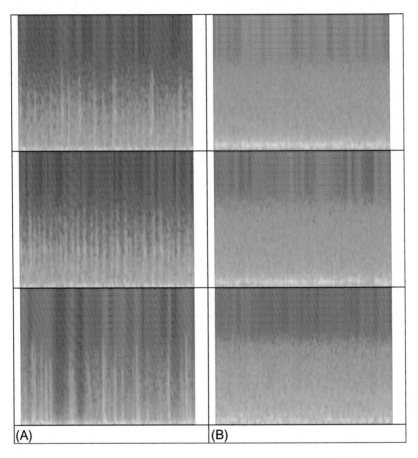

Fig. 3 Generated spectrogram images. (A) The spectrogram images for F-EEG signals. (B) The spectrogram images for NF-EEG signals.

(L-SVM), quadratic SVM (Q-SVM), cubic SVM (C-SVM), fine Gaussian SVM (FG-SVM), medium Gaussian SVM (MG-SVM), and coarse Gaussian SVM (CG-SVM)—are presented by MCLT. The default setting parameters are used for SVM-based classifiers because tuning them did not produce any significant improvement in accuracy. The k-NN-based techniques, which are presented in MCLT, are fine k-NN (F-kNN), medium k-NN (M-kNN), coarse k-NN (CR-kNN), cosine k-NN (CS-kNN), cubic k-NN (CB-kNN), and weighted k-NN (W-kNN), respectively. The number of neighbor k is chosen as 1 in the F-kNN technique. And, for the M-kNN and C-kNN techniques, the numbers of neighbors are selected as 10 and 100. The cosine and cubic distance metrics are used in CS-kNN and CB-kNN approaches and the numbers of the neighbors are set to 10 for both the CS-kNN

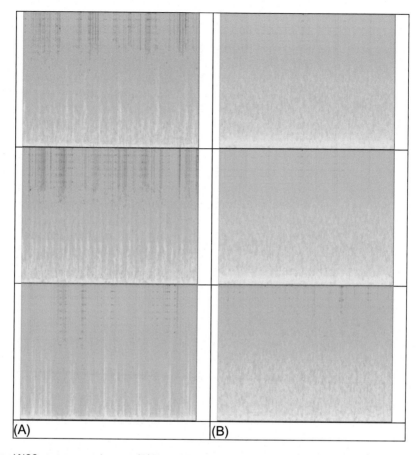

Fig. 4 Generated NSS spectrogram images. (A) The NSS spectrogram images for F-EEG signals. (B) The NSS spectrogram images for NF-EEG signals.

and CB-kNN techniques. A weighted distance function is used in the W-kNN classifier and k is set to 10. Other k values such as 3, 5, 7, etc., were used in experiments, but we did not get any improved results. MCLT presents five ensemble learner techniques—boosted trees (BT-Trees), bagged trees (BG-Trees), subspace discriminant (SD), subspace k-NN (S-kNN), and RUSBoost trees (RB-Trees). The AdaBoost ensemble method is employed in the boosted trees technique and the random forest ensemble method is employed in the BG-Trees technique. Subspace with discriminant learners and nearest neighbor learners are used in subspace discriminant and S-kNN methods and RB tree learners are used in the RB tree method.

The initial experiments are conducted on the given dataset without any data augmentation. Thus, the effect of the data augmentation will be investigated. Without data augmentation, 7500 F-EEG and NF-EEG signal images are used in experiments. The local entropy features are extracted based on a 128×128 window on three channels (red, green, and blue) of the input spectrogram images. We also applied other window sizes such as 64×64 and 256×256 but did not get any improved results. Thus, a 7500×48 dimensional data matrix is produced. The obtained results are presented in Table 1. As seen in Table 1, the best accuracy score of 74.8% is obtained with the MG-SVM classifier. The L-SVM classifier obtains a 71.7% accuracy score, which is the second-best accuracy score in all SVM classifier achievements. The FG-SVM technique produces the worst accuracy score with a recorded accuracy score of 66.2. The average accuracy score of the SVM technique achievements is 72.0%. The CS-kNN technique produces a 71.4% accuracy score, which is the best accuracy score among the kNN method achievements. F-kNN produces a 65.3% accuracy score, which is the worst among all classifiers. The average accuracy of the kNN methods is 69.6%. The S-kNN

Table 1 F-EEG versus NF-EEG signal classification results without data augmentation.

	Classifier type	Accuracy
SVM	L-SVM	71.7
	Q-SVM	74.3
	C-SVM	73.2
	FG-SVM	66.2
	MG-SVM	**74.8**
	CG-SVM	71.8
kNN	F-kNN	65.3
	M-kNN	70.2
	CR-kNN	71.0
	CS-kNN	71.4
	CB-kNN	69.2
	W-kNN	70.5
Ensemble	BT-Trees	71.6
	BG-Trees	73.2
	SD	70.7
	S-kNN	73.7
	RB-Trees	67.9

The bold case shows the best accuracy.

ensemble technique produces a 73.7% accuracy score, which is the highest in ensemble techniques. The worst accuracy score of 67.9% is produced by the RB-Trees classifier. The average accuracy score of the ensemble methods is 71.42%. When the average accuracy scores of the SVM, kNN, and ensemble methods are considered, it is observed that SVM classifiers are more successful than the kNN and ensemble methods. In addition, the ensemble methods are more accurate than the kNN techniques.

In our second experiment, we augmented the dataset by constructing 15,000 spectrogram images. As mentioned earlier, the data augmentation is obtained by random sampling of all EEG categories with a window of 7500 samples, as shown in Fig. 1. A total of 7500 of the constructed spectrogram images is from the F-EEG category and the rest are from the NF-EEG category.

Table 2 shows the obtained accuracy scores for each classifier. Accuracy scores are calculated as the ratio of a number of correctly classified samples to the total number of samples. As seen in Table 2, the produced accuracy scores are in the range of

Table 2 F-EEG versus NF-EEG signal classification results with data augmentation.

	Classifier type	Accuracy
SVM	L-SVM	71.7%
	Q-SVM	80.0%
	C-SVM	91.1%
	FG-SVM	97.1%
	MG-SVM	80.7%
	CG-SVM	72.3%
kNN	F-kNN	96.9%
	M-kNN	76.8%
	CR-kNN	73.7%
	CS-kNN	78.2%
	CB-kNN	75.6%
	W-kNN	97.4%
Ensemble	BT-Trees	74.0%
	BG-Trees	97.5%
	SD	70.9%
	S-kNN	**97.6%**
	RB-Trees	70.1%

A total of 15,000 spectrogram images are used in the experiments. The bold case shows the best accuracy.

70.1%–97.6%. The best accuracy score of 97.6% is produced by the S-kNN ensemble technique and the worst accuracy score of 70.1% is produced by RB-Trees. The BG-Trees ensemble technique produced the second-best accuracy score where the recorded accuracy is 97.5%. SD produced one of the worst results where the accuracy score is 70.9%. The W-kNN and F-kNN methods produced 97.4% and 96.9% accuracy scores, respectively. These scores are the best scores in all the kNN methods. The CR-kNN technique produces the worst accuracy score in all the kNN techniques. The best accuracy score of 97.1% is produced by the FG-SVM method, which has the best accuracy among all the SVM techniques. The C-SVM technique also produced an accuracy score of 91.1%. The worst accuracy score of 71.7% is produced by the L-SVM technique, which is the worst among all the SVM techniques. The average accuracies of the SVM, kNN, and Ensemble techniques are 82.15%, 83.10%, and 82.02%, respectively. According to these average accuracy scores, the kNN methods produce better results than the other methods.

We replicated our experiment with more EEG signal samples, where a total of 22,500 EEG signals of length 7500 samples were used. Half the EEG dataset (11,250) is produced for F-EEG signals and the other half is produced for NF-EEG signals. After applying the standard methodology (Fig. 1) of our work, a feature matrix is obtained. The dimension of the feature matrix is $22,500 \times 48$. The experimental work is conducted based on the 10-fold cross-validation test and the obtained results are given in Table 3.

As seen in Table 3, data augmentation improves the classification accuracy where the highest accuracy score is 99.8%. The obtained highest accuracy score is 2.2% better than the highest accuracy score of the first experiment. The F-kNN and W-kNN classifiers of the kNN and the S-kNN classifier of the ensemble yield the best accuracy scores of 99.8% for the second experiment. The worst classification result of 67.0% is produced by the RB-Trees (Ensemble) method. A 99.7% accuracy score is produced by the BG-Trees method, which is classified in ensemble methods. In kNN methods, except F-kNN and W-kNN, all other kNN methods produce accuracy scores below 80%. The FG-SVM technique obtains a 99.6% accuracy score, which is the best among all SVM technique achievements. Another successful achievement is obtained by the C-SVM technique, where the recorded accuracy score is 92.2%. If the average accuracy scores of each classifier title (SVM, kNN, and Ensemble) are calculated, the calculated average accuracy scores are 82.75%, 85.07%, and 81.40%, respectively. It is seen that the kNN method achievement is higher than other classification titles.

Table 3 F-EEG versus NF-EEG signal classification results with data augmentation.

	Classifier type	Accuracy
SVM	L-SVM	69.9%
	Q-SVM	82.0%
	C-SVM	92.2%
	FG-SVM	99.6%
	MG-SVM	81.7%
	CG-SVM	71.1%
kNN	**F-kNN**	**99.8%**
	M-kNN	78.5%
	CR-kNN	74.5%
	CS-kNN	79.5%
	CB-kNN	78.3%
	W-kNN	**99.8%**
Ensemble	BT-Trees	71.6%
	BG-Trees	99.7%
	SD	68.9%
	S-kNN	**99.8%**
	RB-Trees	67.0%

A total of 22,500 spectrogram images are used in experiments. The bold case shows the best accuracy.

We also investigate the effect of NSS on classification accuracy. To do that, the NSS procedure is canceled in the proposed method and the rest of the methodology is applied. The augmented dataset is used in this new experiment and the obtained accuracy scores are tabulated in Table 4. As observed in Table 4, the highest accuracy score of 99.4% is obtained by the F-kNN, W-kNN, and s-kNN methods, respectively. The worst result of 67.1% is produced by the SD and RB-Trees ensemble methods. The FG-SVM method produces the 99.3% method, which is the best accuracy score among the SVM method achievements. With a 90.8% accuracy score, the C-SVM method obtains the second-best performance. The average accuracy score of the SVM methods is 82.25%. The CR-kNN method produces the worst accuracy score where the recorded accuracy score is 74.5%. The M-kNN, CS-kNN, and CB-kNN methods produce 78.1%, 79.4%, and 78.0% accuracy scores, respectively. The average achievement of the kNN methods is 84.8%, which is better than the SVM method

Table 4 F-EEG versus NF-EEG signal classification results without the NSS procedure (with data augmentation).

	Classifier type	Accuracy
SVM	L-SVM	69.6%
	Q-SVM	81.2%
	C-SVM	90.8%
	FG-SVM	99.3%
	MG-SVM	81.6%
	CG-SVM	71.0%
kNN	**F-kNN**	**99.4%**
	M-kNN	78.1%
	CR-kNN	74.5%
	CS-kNN	79.4%
	CB-kNN	78.0%
	W-kNN	**99.4%**
Ensemble	BT-Trees	71.3%
	BG-Trees	99.3%
	SD	67.1%
	S-kNN	**99.4%**
	RB-Trees	67.1%

A total of 22,500 spectrogram images are used in experiments. The bold case shows the best accuracy.

performances. The average accuracy score for the ensemble methods is 80.84%, which is worse than the SVM and kNN methods. The best performance is obtained by the SB-kNN ensemble method, where the accuracy score is 99.4%. When we compare the results with NSS and without NSS approaches, it is seen that the highest accuracy score with the NSS approach is 99.8%. In addition, the highest accuracy score without the NSS method is 99.4%. Moreover, the average accuracy score with the NSS approach is 83.17% and the average accuracy without the NSS approach is 82.74%. This shows that NSS improves the accuracy by 0.43%.

A further performance comparison of obtained accuracy scores of the proposed method with some of the existing method's achievements is conducted and the related comparisons are given in Table 5. The comparison has been done on the basis of the feature extraction method, the features, the classifier, and the dataset

Table 5 Performance comparison of the proposed method with existing methods on the same dataset.

Authors (year)	Methods and features	Classifier	No of signals	Accuracy (%)
Zhu et al. (2013)	DPE	SVM	F: 50 NF: 50	84
Sharma et al. (2014)	EMD, entropy	LS-SVM	F: 50 NF: 50	87
Sharma, Pachori, and Rajendra Acharya (2015)	DWT, entropy	LS-SVM	F: 50 NF: 50	84
Sharma, Pachori, and Acharya (2015)	EMD, entropy	LS-SVM	F: 50 NF: 50	87
Rai et al. (2015)	EMD, AvgBratio	Unsupervised learning	F: 750 NF: 750	89.06
Das and Bhuiyan (2016)	EMD, DWT, log energy entropy	KNN	F: 50 NF: 50	89.4
Deivasigamani et al. (2016)	DT-CWT	ANFIS	F: 50 NF: 50	89
Gupta et al. (2017)	FAWT, various entropies	LS-SVM	F: 3750 NF: 3750	94.41
Bhattacharyya et al. (2017)	TQWT, fuzzy entropy	LS-SVM	F: 50 NF: 50	84.67
Sharma et al. (2017b)	TQWT	LS-SVM	F: 50 NF: 50	95
Sharma et al. (2017a)	Wavelet filter bank, Entropy features	LS-SVM	F: 3750 NF: 3750	94.25
Bajaj et al. (2017)	Rhythm-based correlation features	LS-SVM	F: 750 NF: 750	99.2
Fasil et al. (2018)	Differential operation, entropy and energy	SVM	F: 3750 NF: 3750	88.14
Bhattacharyya et al. (2016)	EMD, central tendency measure	LS-SVM	F: 50 NF: 50	90
Sharma and Pachori (2018)	BEMD	LS-SVM	F: 50 NF: 50	85.1
Acharya et al. (2018b)	Nonlinear features	LS-SVM	F: 3750 NF: 3750	87.93
Taran and Bajaj (2018)	CVMD	ELM	F: 3750 NF: 3750	96
Raghu and Sriraam (2018)	Neighborhood component analysis	SVM	F: 3750 NF: 3750	96.1
Proposed approach	TF images, NSS, and entropy	DT, SVM, kNN, and ensemble	F: 3750 NF: 3750	**99.8**

used in the evaluation accuracy of the proposed method. In Zhu et al. (2013), Fasil et al. (2018), Acharya et al. (2018b), and Raghu and Sriraam (2018) methods, the features are directly extracted for EEG signals. In Sharma et al. (2014), Deivasigamani et al. (2016), and M. Sharma et al. (2017) methods, the features are extracted for the wavelet decomposition. In Prilipko et al. (2005), Sharma, Pachori, and Rajendra Acharya (2015), Sharma, Pachori, and Acharya (2015), Rai et al. (2015), Das and Bhuiyan (2016), Bajaj et al. (2017), and Bhattacharyya et al. (2016) methods, the features are extracted from the EMD. In Bhattacharyya et al. (2017) and R. Sharma et al. (2017) methods, the features are extracted from TQWT. In Gupta et al. (2017) method, the features are extracted from FAWT. In most of the methods, the EEG signals decompose into different bands. Time-frequency image-based features will provide more inside information on EEG signals. It can observed from Table 5 that most of the methods generally prefer the LS-SVM classifier. In the proposed method, different variants of the three classifiers SVM, k-NN, and ensemble have been explored for better comparison. The proposed methods have been tested on a small dataset and a large dataset. The method used in the larger dataset is a more promising method for identification of F-EEG signals.

As seen in Table 5, researchers generally prefer SVM classifiers and multiresolution technique-based feature extraction in their works. The obtained accuracy scores are in the range of 84%–96.1%. In Zhu et al. (2013), the authors used the DPE and SVM classifier and obtained an 84% accuracy score. In Sharma et al. (2014), the authors used EMD, entropy, and LS-SVM for F and NF-EEG classification and obtained an 87% accuracy score. In Sharma, Pachori, and Rajendra Acharya (2015), the DWT, entropy, and LS-SVM classifiers were considered for F and NF-EEG classification. Authors reported an 84% accuracy score. That author group also used EMD, entropy, and LS-SVM and obtained an 87% accuracy score (Sharma, Pachori, & Acharya, 2015). Later, the authors used FAWT, TQWT, wavelet filter banks, rhythm-based features, BEMD, CVMD, and nonlinear features for F-EEG and NF-EEG discrimination. Until this work, the highest accuracy was reported by Bajaj et al. (2017), where that score was 99.2%. So it is seen that this work improves the performance of the F-EEG versus NF-EEG classification task. In addition, from Table 5, it is seen that the number of signals affects the classification accuracy. When the number of signals for both F and NF is 50, the accuracy is around 87%, but with 3750 signals, the obtained accuracy is around 96%.

4 Conclusions

In this work, a novel compact methodology is proposed for discrimination of the F-EEG and NF-EEG signals. The proposed method uses a random sampling window of length 7500 samples for a sampling of the F-EEG and NF-EEG signals. The sampled F-EEG and NF-EEG signals are then transformed into color images by the STFT method. The constructed F-EEG and NF-EEG signals are further processed with NSS methodology for enhancing the EEG images. Local entropy in a 128×128 window is used as the feature. Various classifiers in MCLT are used in classification. The obtained results show that the proposed method is outperformed. The obtained accuracy score is 99.8%. The following conclusions are worth mentioning: (1) The proposed approach is quite efficient in F-EEG and NF-EEG signal classification where the highest accuracy score so far is obtained. Various experiments are conducted to validate the efficiency of our proposal. (2) Both the traditional dataset and the augmented dataset are used in the experiments. It is observed that the data augmentation highly improves the classification accuracy, as more samples increase the learning ability of the machine-learning techniques. (3) In addition, we performed experiments with and without the NSS operation. The results show that the NSS approach also improves the classification results when compared to that without NSS results.

In future works, the proposed method will be applied to other EEG datasets. The alcoholic brain EEG dataset, which covers drowsiness and awake states, is a potential one for future works. Moreover, EEG-based emotion detection is a potential application for future studies. Various TF methods will be investigated in future works. Especially, continuous WT, Hilbert-Huang, and Wigner-Ville will be potential TF methods where many of their applications can be seen in the literature. Furthermore, various membership degree calculation functions can be used in NSS procedures. Traditional fuzzy membership functions can be used to calculate the truth, indeterminacy, and falsity memberships.

References

Acharya, U. R., et al. (2018a). Deep convolutional neural network for the automated detection and diagnosis of seizure using EEG signals. *Computers in Biology and Medicine, 100,* 270–278.

Acharya, U. R., et al. (2018b). Characterization of focal EEG signals: A review. *Future Generation Computer Systems, 91,* 290–299.

Andrzejak, R. G., Schindler, K., & Rummel, C. (2012). Nonrandomness, nonlinear dependence, and nonstationarity of electroencephalographic recordings from epilepsy patients. *Physical Review E—Statistical, Nonlinear, and Soft Matter Physics*, (4), 86.

Bajaj, V., & Pachori, R. B. (2012). Classification of seizure and nonseizure EEG signals using empirical mode decomposition. *IEEE Transactions on Information Technology in Biomedicine, 16*(6), 1135–1142.

Bajaj, V., & Pachori, R. B. (2013). Epileptic seizure detection based on the instantaneous area of analytic intrinsic mode functions of EEG signals. *Biomedical Engineering Letters, 3*(1), 17–21.

Bajaj, V., et al. (2017). Rhythm-based features for classification of focal and nonfocal EEG signals. *IET Signal Processing, 11*(6), 743–748.

Bhattacharyya, A., Pachori, R. B., & Acharya, U. R. (2017). Tunable-Q wavelet transform based multivariate sub-band fuzzy entropy with application to focal EEG signal analysis. *Entropy, 19*(3).

Bhattacharyya, A., et al. (2016). A novel approach for automated detection of focal EEG signals using empirical wavelet transform. *Neural Computing and Applications, 29*(8), 47–57.

Das, A. B., & Bhuiyan, M. I. H. (2016). Discrimination and classification of focal and non-focal EEG signals using entropy-based features in the EMD-DWT domain. *Biomedical Signal Processing and Control, 29*, 11–21.

Deivasigamani, S., Senthilpari, C., & Yong, W. H. (2016). Classification of focal and nonfocal EEG signals using ANFIS classifier for epilepsy detection. *International Journal of Imaging Systems and Technology, 26*(4), 277–283.

Dwivedi, A. R., et al. (2016). Analysis of focal and non-focal EEG signals using bivariate empirical mode decomposition. In *2016 IEEE Students' Conference on Electrical, Electronics and Computer Science (SCEECS)* (pp. 1–3).

Fasil, O. K., Rajesh, R., & Thasleema, T. M. (2018). Influence of differential features in focal and non-focal EEG signal classification. In *5th IEEE Region 10 Humanitarian Technology Conference 2017, R10-HTC 2017* (pp. 646–649).

Gehlot, M., et al. (2015). EMD based features for discrimination of focal and non-focal EEG signals. In *Advances in Intelligent Systems and Computing* (pp. 85–93).

Guo, Y., Şengür, A., & Ye, J. (2014). A novel image thresholding algorithm based on neutrosophic similarity score. *Measurement: Journal of the International Measurement Confederation, 58*, 175–186.

Gupta, A., Singh, P., & Karlekar, M. (2018). A novel signal modeling approach for classification of seizure and seizure-free EEG signals. *IEEE Transactions on Neural Systems and Rehabilitation Engineering, 26*(5), 925–935.

Gupta, V., et al. (2017). Automated detection of focal EEG signals using features extracted from flexible analytic wavelet transform. *Pattern Recognition Letters, 94*, 180–188.

Huang, H., et al. (2018). Epileptic seizure detection in EEG signals using sparse multiscale radial basis function networks and the Fisher vector approach. *Knowledge-Based Systems, 164*, 96–106.

Li, Y., et al. (2018). Epileptic seizure classification of EEGs using time-frequency analysis based multiscale radial basis functions. *IEEE Journal of Biomedical and Health Informatics, 22*(2), 386–397.

Pachori, R. B., & Bajaj, V. (2011). Analysis of normal and epileptic seizure EEG signals using empirical mode decomposition. *Computer Methods and Programs in Biomedicine, 104*(3), 373–381.

Pathak, A., et al. (2018). Automatic seizure detection by modified line length and Mahalanobis distance function. *Biomedical Signal Processing and Control, 44*, 279–287.

Prilipko, L., et al. (2005). Atlas: Epilepsy care in the world. *Buch, 129*, 17. Available at: http://apps.who.int/iris/handle/10665/43298%5Cnhttp://books.google.com/books?id=ZJfku__6BKMC&pgis=1.

Raghu, S., & Sriraam, N. (2018). Classification of focal and non-focal EEG signals using neighborhood component analysis and machine learning algorithms. *Expert Systems with Applications, 113*, 18–32.

Rai, K., Bajaj, V., & Kumar, A. (2015). Novel feature for identification of focal EEG signals with k-Means and fuzzy c-means algorithms. In *International conference on digital signal processing, DSP* (pp. 412–416).

Ren, D., et al. (2018). Epileptic seizure detection in long-term EEG recordings by using wavelet-based directed transfer function. *IEEE Transactions on Biomedical Engineering, 65*(11), 2591–2599.

Şengür, A., Guo, Y., & Akbulut, Y. (2016). Time–frequency texture descriptors of EEG signals for efficient detection of epileptic seizure. *Brain Informatics*, Available at: http://link.springer.com/10.1007/s40708-015-0029-8.

Sengur, D., Turhan, M., & Karabatak, S. (2018). Prediction of the school administrators, who attended an action learning course, based on their conflict-handling styles: A data mining approach. *International Online Journal of Educational Sciences, 10*(4).

Sharma, R., & Pachori, R. B. (2018). Automated classification of focal and non-focal EEG signals based on bivariate empirical mode decomposition. In: *Biomedical signal and image processing in Patient Care* (pp. 13–33): IGI Global.

Sharma, R., Pachori, R. B., & Acharya, U. R. (2015). Application of entropy measures on intrinsic mode functions for the automated identification of focal electroencephalogram signals. *Entropy, 17*(2), 669–691.

Sharma, R., Pachori, R. B., & Gautam, S. (2014). Empirical mode decomposition based classification of focal and non-focal seizure EEG signals. In *Proceedings—2014 international conference on medical biometrics, ICMB 2014* (pp. 135–140).

Sharma, R., Pachori, R. B., & Rajendra Acharya, U. (2015). An integrated index for the identification of focal electroencephalogram signals using discrete wavelet transform and entropy measures. *Entropy, 17*(8), 5218–5240.

Sharma, M., et al. (2017a). An automatic detection of focal EEG signals using new class of time–frequency localized orthogonal wavelet filter banks. *Knowledge-Based Systems, 118*, 217–227.

Sharma, R., et al. (2017b). Decision support system for focal EEG signals using tunable-Q wavelet transform. *Journal of Computational Science, 20*, 52–60.

Siuly, S., et al. (2018). Exploring Hermite transformation in brain signal analysis for the detection of epileptic seizure. *IET Science, Measurement & Technology, 13*(1), 35–41.

Smarandache, F. (2003). *A unifying field in logics: Neutrosophic logic. Neutrosophy, neutrosophic set, neutrosophic probability: Neutrosophic logic: Neutrosophy, neutrosophic set, neutrosophic probability, Infinite study.* .

Taran, S., & Bajaj, V. (2018). Clustering variational mode decomposition for identification of focal EEG signals. *IEEE Sensors Letters, 2*(4), 1–4.

Truong, N. D., et al. (2018). Convolutional neural networks for seizure prediction using intracranial and scalp electroencephalogram. *Neural Networks, 105*, 104–111.

Tsiouris, K. M., et al. (2017). A robust unsupervised epileptic seizure detection methodology to accelerate large EEG database evaluation. *Biomedical Signal Processing and Control, 40*, 275–285.

Turhan, M., et al. (2018). Neutrosophic weighted support vector machines for the determination of school administrators who attended an action learning course based on their conflict-handling styles. *Symmetry, 10*(5).

Tzimourta, K. D., et al. (2018). Epileptic seizures classification based on long-term EEG signal wavelet analysis. In *Precision medicine powered by pHealth and connected health* (pp. 165–169: Springer.

Walde, S., et al. (2016). Time frequency Image based features for detection of focal EEG signals. In *2016 International conference on signal processing and communication (ICSC)* (pp. 358–362).

Zhu, G., et al. (2013). Epileptogenic focus detection in intracranial EEG based on delay permutation entropy. In *AIP conference proceedings* (pp. 31–36).

13

Neutrosophic multiple deep convolutional neural network for skin dermoscopic image classification

Yanhui Guo*, Amira S. Ashour[†]

*Department of Computer Science, University of Illinois at Springfield, Springfield, IL, United States. [†]Department of Electronics and Electrical Communications Engineering, Faculty of Engineering, Tanta University, Tanta, Egypt

1 Introduction

Skin diseases are critical, common, and widespread worldwide, and can be considered the initial sign for other diseases (Havlickova, Czaika, & Friedrich, 2008). Skin cancer has several types, including melanoma, melanocytic, seborrheic keratosis, basal cell carcinoma, and nevus (Kennedy, Willemze, de Gruijl, Bavinck, & Bajdik, 2003). Melanoma is considered one of the most fatal forms. It can be visually examined and detected as it appears on the skin surface (Brady et al., 2000). Different clinical rules, such as the ABCDE (asymmetry, border, color, diameter, and evolving) rule and CASH (color, architecture, symmetry, and homogeneity) were used to enable an accurate distinction between melanomas and nevi (Campos-do-Carmo & Ramos-e-Silva, 2008; Lin, Koga, Takata, & Saida, 2009). Such clinical-based diagnosis methods rely on the visual experience of dermatologists to detect and distinguish the suspicious lesions (Gachon et al., 2005).

Nevertheless, manual visual examination by dermatologists is insufficient to accurately detect all the melanoma cases. This gives high impact to using imaging devices, namely dermoscopy to reduce the skin's surface reflection for deep visualization of the skin layers using optical magnification (Kapsokalyvas et al., 2013; Mullani, 2006, 2016). To make a translucent contact area, dermoscopy uses either cross-polarized or low-angle-of-incidence

Neutrosophic Set in Medical Image Analysis. https://doi.org/10.1016/B978-0-12-818148-5.00013-8

lighting with liquid immersion, which visualizes the subsurface structures easily compared to traditional clinical images (Argenziano et al., 2002). However, for less experienced dermatologists, dermoscopy may reduce the diagnostic accuracy.

Subsequently, developing advanced computer-aided diagnosis systems becomes critical to guarantee accurate early detection and classification of melanoma to improve the diagnosis performance (Vestergaard, Macaskill, Holt, & Menzies, 2008). These systems provide a second independent diagnostic opinion for prescreening and follow-up of patients to help clinicians. Additionally, the advancements in communication technologies direct studies and scientists to implement algorithms. These techniques are applied for dermoscopic image screening and assessment to improve melanoma diagnosis and discrimination in different skin lesion types and further improve the patient's healthcare.

Therefore, numerous classifiers have been designed for dermoscopy image classification, including the bag-of-features model (Barata, Marques, & Mendonça, 2013; Barata, Marques, & Rozeira, 2013; Barata, Ruela, Mendonça, & Marques, 2014; Situ, Yuan, Chen, & Zouridakis, 2008), the artificial neural network (Carrara et al., 2007; Rubegni et al., 2002; Veredas, Mesa, & Morente, 2010), ensemble classification (Drucker, Cortes, Jackel, LeCun, & Vapnik, 1994; Xie et al., 2017), and the support vector machine (Wahba, Ashour, Guo, Napoleon, & Elnaby, 2018; Wahba, Ashour, Napoleon, Elnaby, & Guo, 2017). However, skin lesion dermoscopy images have challenging characteristics, including the irregularity and complexity of the skin lesion structures, the different lesion colors in the same region, the fine-grained inconsistency in the skin lesion appearance, and the existence of dense hair (Ashour, Hawas, Guo, & Wahba, 2018; Oliveira et al., 2016). Moreover, other artifacts can affect the captured dermoscopic image, such as air bubbles, illumination variations, and noise (Ashour, Guo, Kucukkulahli, Erdogmus, & Polat, 2018; Guo, Ashour, & Smarandache, 2018).

Generally, machine-learning procedures can be classified into unsupervised/supervised learning procedures. A neural network (NN), one of the supervised learning methods, is considered the basis of deep-learning methods, where an NN of multiple hidden layers (layers between the input and output) is considered a "deep" neural network. Deep belief networks and stacked autoencoders are complex due to their layer-by-layer unsupervised pretraining way that precedes the supervised fine tuning of the stacked network. Accordingly, to simplify the training process, trained end-to-end approaches that have supervised learning procedures can be used. Such approaches include the recurrent neural network (RNN) and the CNN.

Subsequently, deep-learning (DL) procedures, particularly convolutional neural networks (CNN) that have an imperative role in medical analysis and classification, were employed for skin lesion detection and classification (Codella et al., 2017; Demyanov, Chakravorty, Abedini, Halpern, & Garnavi, 2016; Esteva et al., 2017; Haenssle et al., 2018; Nasr-Esfahani et al., 2016; Yuan, Chao, & Lo, 2017). Typically, CNN encloses several layers to transform the input with convolution filters. CNN has a significant role in numerous image classification applications due to its conceptual structure, including sharing weights and dominant discrimination ability as well as using both the time domain and the down-sampling space (Krizhevsky, Sutskever, & Hinton, 2012; Lee, Grosse, Ranganath, & Ng, 2009; Schmidhuber, 2015). Typically, CNN has different designed networks, including AlexNet, U-Net, Inception-V3, QuocNet, BNInception-V2, and Inception (GoogleNet) (Celebi, Iyatomi, Schaefer, & Stoecker, 2009; Hoo-Chang et al., 2016; Hu, Xia, Hu, & Zhang, 2015; Rastegari, Ordonez, Redmon, & Farhadi, 2016; Xiao et al., 2015).

Furthermore, deep convolution neural networks (DCNNs) are applied in several image classification applications (Dong, Loy, He, & Tang, 2014; Hoo-Chang et al., 2016; Hu, Huang, Wei, Zhang, & Li, 2015). Nevertheless, the DCNN model is time consuming, where it suffers from poor performance with the limited training cases and processes. Recently, researchers have designed multiple DCNN models to enhance the CNN/DCNN individual model performance and reduce the training time using fewer epochs. In the DCNN, an incremental learning strategy is used during the training process, where the classification results are attained using a voting procedure (Guo, Budak, & Şengür, 2018). From another point of view, CNN with a reinforcement sample learning approach has attained better results in comparison with the CNN and the DCNN in terms of the required iteration number in the training process leading to less training time (Guo, Budak, Vespa, Khorasani, & Şengür, 2018).

Consequently, in the present chapter, a novel multiple convolution neural network model (MCNN) is designed to classify dermoscopy images. In the MDCNN, transfer learning was applied for training multiple models on different samples. These samples are chosen according to the performance of their scores in the previous models, where the neutrosophic reinforcement sample learning strategy (NRSL) was used during the training process between the used DCNN models to prepare the samples that will be used further in the next DCNN in the whole MDCNN. To assess the proposed classification procedure performance for classifying the two skin lesion classes, selected images from the ISIC2016 dataset of 900 training images and 379 validation and testing images were used.

In the following sections, Section 2 reports different related studies for classification of skin lesion dermoscopic images. Section 3 introduces the methods employed in the proposed method. Section 4 demonstrates the experimental results with extensive discussion. Lastly, Section 5 includes conclusions and suggested future work.

2 Related work

For skin lesion dermoscopy image recognition and classification, Yu, Chen, Dou, Qin, and Heng (2017) designed a melanoma recognition approach using very deep convolutional neural networks of more than 50 layers. A fully convolutional residual network (FCRN) was constructed for precise segmentation of skin cancer, where residual learning was applied to avoid overfitting when the network became deeper. In addition, for classification, the used FCRN was combined with the very deep residual networks. This guarantees the acquirement of discriminative and rich features for precise skin lesion detection using the classification network without using the whole dermoscopy images.

Codella et al. (2015) used the deep-learning method through two parallel paths, namely the transfer of CNN features learned from the natural photograph domain and using sparse coding for unsupervised feature learning of dermoscopy images. These pretrained CNNs extracted deep features for atypical melanoma lesion classification. Afterward, classifiers were trained based on nonlinear support vector machines, and their average scores were used for final fusion results.

Codella et al. (2017) integrated DL with machine-learning procedures to design ensembles of methods for segmenting skin lesions to detect melanoma in dermoscopic images available from the ISIC 2016 benchmark dataset of 900 training and 379 test images. A combination of support vector machines, sparse-coding methods, and hand-coded feature extractors with fully convolutional neural networks (FCNN) and deep residual networks into ensembles was evaluated. The experimental results emphasized that the integrated multitude of machine-learning methods achieved improved performance compared to using these methods individually. This ensemble had 76% accuracy,

62% specificity, and 82% sensitivity when evaluated on a subset of 100 test images.

Afterword, Kawahara, BenTaieb, and Hamarneh (2016) generalized CNN pretrained filters on natural images to classify dermoscopic images with converting a CNN into an FCNN. For accurate classification of dermoscopy images, the following frameworks were applied, including normalization using mean subtracted images, feature extraction using pooled multiscale, and finally pooling of augmented feature space where aggregating features improves the prediction performance. Thus, the standard AlexNet CNN was used for feature extraction rather than using CNN from scratch to reduce time consumption during the training process.

A further study was conducted by Esteva et al. (2017) to classify 129,450 skin lesion clinical images using a pretrained single CNN GoogleNet inception-V3 structure. During the training phase, the input of the CNN network was pixels and disease labels only. For evaluation, biopsy-proven images were involved to classify melanomas versus nevi as well as benign seborrheic keratoses (SK) versus keratinocyte carcinomas. Previously, Blum et al. (2004) fulfilled a deep residual network (DRN) for classification of skin lesions using more than 50 layers. An ImageNet dataset was employed to pretrain the DRN for initializing the weights and deconvolutional layers.

Additionally, González-Díaz (2017) incorporated the knowledge of dermatologists to CNNs for skin lesion diagnosis using several networks for lesion identification and segmentation. Matsunaga, Hamada, Minagawa, and Koga (2017) proposed an ensemble of CNNs that were fine tuned using the RMSProp and AdaGrad methods. The classification performance was evaluated on the ISIC 2017, including melanoma, nevus, and SK dermoscopy image datasets. The prior studies indicated the impact of using pretrained deep-learning models in the classification applications with the necessity to speed up the MDCNN model.

3 Methodology

CNN emerged as a dominant classification procedure in several applications compared to the traditional classification methods. For example, CNNs require much fewer parameters and connections with easier training processes compared to feedforward neural networks of similar-sized layers. Typically, the conventional neural network's ability is controllable by varying its breadth and depth to provide a strong description of the image nature, including the pixel locale and the stationarity of the statistics.

In the present chapter, the MDCNN is trained to classify melanomas and nevi, where a neutrosophic reinforcement sample learning (NRSL) procedure was employed to accelerate the training process of the MDCNN. Multiple networks in the MDCNN were trained to fine tune the learning samples for different DCNN models.

3.1 Deep convolution neural networks

In the proposed model, the whole image was input into the CNN for further output classification results. To construct the DCNN network, five types of layers were used for classification, namely the convolution, ReLU (rectified linear unit), pooling, softmax, and classification layers.

All neurons in the convolutional layer apply the convolution operator to the inputs for feature extraction. Convolution reserves the spatial relation between pixels using small squares (filters) of input data to learn the image features. Thus, in the convolutional layer, the filter size is considered the most significant factor in a convolutional neuron, where each of the different layers has a different size of the filter. At the layer $l-1$, assume $x^{l-1}(m)$ is the mth input feature while $W^l(m, n)$ is the filter's weight that connects the nth feature of the output layer to the mth feature of the input layer. The value $x^l(n)$ in the lth convolutional layer is given by:

$$x^l(n) = f\left(\sum_m \left(x^{l-1}(m) * W^l(m, n) + b^l(n) \right) \right) \qquad (1)$$

$$f(x) = \frac{1}{1 + e^{-x}} \qquad (2)$$

where $b^l(n)$ is the bias, f is a nonlinear sigmoid function, and * is the convolutional operation. The filter's weights $W^l(m, m)$ were initialized randomly for further updating using the back propagation algorithm.

The nonlinear ReLU operation is used after every convolution operation, which is applied per pixel to replace the negative pixel values by zero. In the ReLU layer, a thresholding operation is performed *on each element of the input,* using the following formula:

$$f(x) = \begin{cases} x & x \geq 0 \\ 0 & x < 0 \end{cases} \qquad (3)$$

Afterward, a spatial pooling operator, which is usually a downsampling process, is used for dimensionality reduction on the feature map and still retaining the significant information. *Moreover, the pooling layer can improve the number of network parameters and avoid the overfitting issue. In* the pooling layer *l*, $x^l(n)$ values can be calculated using the following formula:

$$x^l(n) = \text{pool}\left(x^{l-1}(n)\right) \qquad (4)$$

where $\text{pool}(\cdot)$ is a sampling function that might be average or maximum functions where the average pool function is used in the proposed model.

Afterward, because the convolutional and pooling layer outputs represent the high-level features of the input image, a fully connected (FC) layer is employed to use these features to classify the input image into different classes based on the training dataset. Generally, the *FC layer is considered to flatten the feature map as well as to connect them to the output layer.* It is a multilayer perceptron where every neuron in any layer is linked to every neuron in the succeeding layer. In the output layer, a softmax activation function is used. Hence, the *input is multiplied by a weight matrix in* this layer, *and then a bias vector is added* where the softmax activation *function is defined as:*

$$P(y = 1 \mid x; w) = \frac{1}{1 + e^{-w^T x}} \qquad (5)$$

where w and y are the weight and the class label, respectively.

In the model training stage, transfer learning was applied with multiple pretrained CNN models to speed up the training stage, where a neutrosophic reinforcement sample learning (NRSL) strategy is proposed in the MDCNN. Generally, in a single DCNN training, the NRSL is not used while the NRSL is applied in the proposed model to prepare the samples for the next DCNN in the MDCNN model.

3.2 Neutrosophic reinforcement sample learning strategy

The main role of reinforcement learning strategies in deep neural network training is to maximize rewards over time. Their concept repeatedly trains the network on the samples having poor performance in the previous training iteration (Guo, Budak, Vespa, et al., 2018). Typically, a traditional DCNN has a fixed learning procedure where all the samples are trained the same number of times regardless of the classification performance on this sample. However, in the DCNN training process, the sample classification results might vary during each training epoch.

The present work proposed an NRSL scheme that trains the samples with adaptive times based on their performance to reinforce the training of the poor performance samples with extra times inconsistent with their performance. At the same time, it trains/tunes the samples of high performance with fewer times, which speeds up the training process. Hence, the key to the reinforcement sample learning strategy is the amount of reinforced training time, which is adaptive based on the training performance on the sample. In NS, three subsets are defined, namely T, I, and F, which are the truth, indeterminacy, and falsity degrees, respectively (Ansari, Biswas, & Aggarwal, 2011; Broumi & Smarandache, 2013; Guo et al., 2013; Guo, Cheng, & Zhang, 2009; Guo, Şengür, & Ye, 2014; Maji, 2012; Majumdar & Samanta, 2014; Nguyen, Son, Ashour, & Dey, 2017; Salama & Alblowi, 2012; Smarandache & Vlăduțescu, 2013; Ye, 2015). This motivates the use of a neutrosophic set (NS) to determine the reinforced training number according to the classification performance during the training process due to the NS capability to interpret the indeterminacy information. For the first DCNN training results, T, I, and F are defined along with the Neutrosophic Similarity Score (NSS) to decide which samples will be used again in the training process in the succeeding (second) DCNN and so on.

The whole training set is used to train the first network for limited iterations for accelerating the training process, where the training samples were randomly divided into several batches. Then, the DCNN network is trained on all batches in an epoch. The first network's performance on each sample batch is defined using the neutrosophic set components. During the training process, the accuracy for each batch in each epoch can be defined as:

$$T_m(i) = \overline{S_m}(i) \tag{6}$$

$$I_m(i) = S_m^h(i) - S_m^l(i) \tag{7}$$

$$F_m(i) = S_m^l(i) \tag{8}$$

where $\overline{S_m}(i)$, $S_m^h(i)$, and $S_m^l(i)$ are the average, highest, and lowest scores of the sample batch i for the mth model. Hereafter, for N samples in the batch, the difference between the mean of T_i in each epoch and the mean for all batches T_m is calculated using the following formula:

$$l_i = T_i - \frac{1}{N} \sum_{m=1}^{N} T_m \tag{9}$$

Because the neutrosophic set similarity measure (NSSM) provides information about the degree of similarity between each of the NS intervals (NSI) (Ye, 2013), in the present chapter, a Neutrosophic Similarity Score (NSS) (Guo, Şengür, & Ye, 2014) was applied. This NSS procedure is used to link the similarity degree of the ideal sample with the best performance using the following formula:

$$NSS = T_i(1 - l_i)(1 - T_i) \tag{10}$$

The values of NSS are then used to determine the reinforced training number during the training process, where the batches with poor accuracies in each epoch are determined. Thus, for a batch of samples, the lower the NSS value, the less the reinforced number will be engaged in the training of this batch and vice versa.

Afterward, the DCNN is tuned using the batches having a more reinforced training number based on their NSS value. This process is repeated for each epoch to determine the reinforced training number using NSS until all epochs are completed. Consequently, the classification process using the designed DCNN is terminated.

To increase the classification accuracy and improve the final classification performance, the preceding steps of the classification using DCNN are then repeated on other DCNNs to form the proposed multiple DCNNs (MDCNN), where the NRSL is used between the MDCNN models but not inside the DCNN.

3.3 Multiple deep convolution neural networks

An MDCNN structure is assembled by cascading multiple networks of the same constructions. For Q, the total number of DCNNs in the proposed model, the MDCNN can be expressed as:

$$MDCNN = \{CNN_1, CNN_2, ..., CNN_Q\} \tag{11}$$

An extra learning strategy is used in this work for the training of the MDCNN, which is the incremental learning strategy. Hence, in the MDCNN, each DCNN is trained using the samples of the preceding DCNN model that have poor performance. Accordingly, the succeeding DCNN will overwhelm the poor sample performance from the preceding DCNN using the following formula:

$$SP_{q+1} = \{SP_q, ReInSP_q\} \tag{12}$$

where SP_q and SP_{q+1} are the sample for the qth DCNN and $(q+1)$th DCNN, respectively, and $ReInSP_q$ is the reinforcement sample for the $(q+1)$th DCNN. Then, from the classification results using DCNN in the MDCNN, the samples of poor classification performance results are identified to include them in the next DCNN model for further training to improve their performance repeatedly, where the sample set for the $(q+1)$th model is given by:

$$ReInSP_q = \{SP_q(i)|P_q(i) < Tr^*\} \tag{13}$$

$$P_q(i) = T_q(i)*T_q(i)*(1 - T_q(i)) \tag{14}$$

where the trial-and-error procedure was applied to determine the threshold Tr^*, which was found to be 0.9 in the present work. In addition, on sample patch i, $P_q(i)$ is the qth DCNN's classification performance, which is defined using the neutrosophic subset T to measure the performance in most samples in this patch that were not affected by the noisy classification score.

This incremental learning strategy-based training process is performed iteratively until all the DCNN models in the MDCNN are trained using the additional samples of poor performance from the previous models in each iteration.

In the test phase, the input image was classified by sequential MCNN models, which are involved in the MDCNN. The final classification result of each sample is determined based on the model with the highest performance score that can be given by:

$$L(i) = \arg\max_n\left\{S_q^n(i)\right\} \tag{15}$$

where $S_q^n(i)$ is the prediction score to sample n of the qth model.

3.4 Voting scheme-based final classification

The final classification result is obtained by using a voting scheme (Guo, Budak, & Şengür, 2018) on the MDCNN's results. Thus, for a sample i, consider $y_q(i)$ as the classification result of this sample from the qth DCNN model, thus, the final classification $C(i)$ can be expressed as:

$$C(i) = \text{Vote}\left(y_1(i), y_2(i), ..., y_Q(i)\right) \tag{16}$$

where $y_q(i)$ is the classification result of the qth DCNN model.

4 Experimental results

The public ISIC2016 dataset from the ISIC archive was engaged in the present work. This dataset includes 900 and 379 skin lesion images in the training and testing sets, respectively (https://challenge.kitware.com/#phase/5667455bcad3a56fac786791). Two sample images from each class in the ISIC 2016 dataset are shown in Fig. 1.

A total of 900 skin lesion images were engaged to train the proposed model, and the 379 images from the test set were engaged

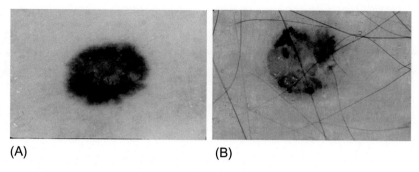

(A)   (B)

Fig. 1 Sample images from the ISIC 2016 dataset: (A) benign (nevus) (B) malignant (BCC).

to assess the proposed NMDCNN model performance to classify the dermoscopy images.

4.1 Experiments on classification

Statistical analysis was measured to assess the proposed NMDCNN model for classifying the two skin lesion classes, namely melanoma (malignant) and nevi (benign). Such final classification evaluation was executed by measuring different evaluation metrics, such as the accuracy, sensitivity, area under the receiver operating characteristic (ROC) curve, and specificity. In classification, specificity is the percentage of properly classified nevi lesions in the dermoscopy images. In addition, the sensitivity is the percentage of the correctly classified melanomas in the dermoscopy images. These performance metrics are expressed as follows:

$$Accuracy = \frac{T_P + T_N}{T_P + T_N + F_P + F_N} \qquad (17)$$

$$Specificity = \frac{T_N}{T_N + F_P} \qquad (18)$$

$$Sensitivity = \frac{T_P}{T_P + F_N} \qquad (19)$$

where T_P represents the number of BCC malignant images that are correctly classified, and T_N is the number of nevus images that are properly classified. In addition, F_N and F_P represent the number of nevus images that are wrongly classified as BCC, and the counts for the number of nevus images that are wrongly classified, respectively. Furthermore, the ROC curve is a graphical representation showing the diagnostic capability of the classifier to

Table 1 Evaluation metrics of the NMDCNN.

	Specification (%)	Sensitivity (%)	Accuracy (%)
Training set	97.4	99.4	97.78
Testing set	86	77.1	85.22

distinguish between the melanoma and nevi by measuring the area under the ROC curve (AUC) (Fawcett, 2006).

In the training stage, five ResNet50 networks have been used to transfer learning and be trained for five epochs using the NRSL strategy. From the confusion matrix of the proposed classification procedure on training and testing sets, respectively, we calculated the specification and sensitivity values on the training set as 97.4% and 99.4%, respectively, where the achieved accuracy during the training phase was 97.78%. In the testing set, the specification and sensitivity values are calculated showing 86% and 77.1%, respectively, with an obtained 85.22% accuracy. These detailed outcomes are reported in Table 1 as follows.

These results show that the proposed classification model has the ability to classify the two classes efficiently. However, it is suggested to increase the dataset to solve any misclassifications in future works.

5 Conclusion

Skin lesion classification is a complex process caused by the characteristic limitations of the dermoscopic image along with the produced artifacts during the capturing process. Generally, skin lesions have numerous types that can be categorized as cancerous (malignant), such as melanoma, or benign (nonmalignant), such as nevi, BCC, and SCC. However, melanoma is often fatal, which requires a prompt and accurate diagnosis of such malignancy to increase the recovery chances. This inspired researchers to develop new classifiers using deep learning to exploit their prevailing discrimination ability. Recently, in vivo dermoscopic devices have been incorporated with different machine-learning procedures to provide dominant computer-aided diagnosis systems with efficient accuracy for diagnosis of early skin cancer.

In the present chapter, a neutrosophic multiple deep convolutional neural network (NMDCNN) was proposed for classifying two types of skin lesions in dermoscopy images, namely, melanoma and nevi. The ISIC2016 dataset was engaged to train and evaluate the proposed NMDCNN model. In each DCNN network, the proposed neutrosophic reinforcement sample learning strategy-based transfer learning was proposed to train each DCNN model on the different samples. The neutrosophic theory using the neutrosophic similarity score was applied to determine the amount of reinforced training time, which varies based on the performance on the sample. This process was repeated with each DCNN in the MDCNN, where the samples were selected based on their scores' performance at the previous model. Typically, in each DCNN, traditional training was employed while the incremental learning was used to generate samples for the next DCNN using Eq. (12). The final classification result was obtained using the voting scheme. The results demonstrated the impact of the proposed NMDCNN model with 97.78% training accuracy and 85.22% accuracy of the testing phase.

References

Ansari, A. Q., Biswas, R., & Aggarwal, S. (2011). Proposal for applicability of neutrosophic set theory in medical AI. *International Journal of Computer Applications, 27*(5), 5–11.

Argenziano, G., Soyer, H. P., De Giorgi, V., Piccolo, D., Carli, P., & Delfino, M. (2002). *Dermoscopy: A tutorial* (p. 16). EDRA Medical Publishing & New Media.

Ashour, A. S., Guo, Y., Kucukkulahli, E., Erdogmus, P., & Polat, K. (2018). A hybrid dermoscopy images segmentation approach based on neutrosophic clustering and histogram estimation. *Applied Soft Computing, 69*, 426–434.

Ashour, A. S., Hawas, A. R., Guo, Y., & Wahba, M. A. (2018). A novel optimized neutrosophic k-means using genetic algorithm for skin lesion detection in dermoscopy images. *Signal, Image and Video Processing*, 1–8.

Barata, C., Marques, J. S., & Mendonça, T. (2013). Bag-of-features classification model for the diagnose of melanoma in dermoscopy images using color and texture descriptors. In *International Conference Image Analysis and Recognition, June (pp. 547–555)*. Berlin, Heidelberg: Springer.

Barata, C., Marques, J. S., & Rozeira, J. (2013). The role of keypoint sampling on the classification of melanomas in dermoscopy images using bag-of-features. In: *Iberian Conference on Pattern Recognition and Image Analysis, June*, Berlin, Heidelberg: Springer, pp. 715–723.

Barata, C., Ruela, M., Mendonça, T., & Marques, J. S. (2014). A bag-of-features approach for the classification of melanomas in dermoscopy images: the role of color and texture descriptors. In *Computer vision techniques for the diagnosis of skin cancer* (pp. 49–69). Berlin, Heidelberg: Springer.

Blum, A., Hofmann-Wellenhof, R., Luedtke, H., Ellwanger, U., Steins, A., Roehm, S., ... Soyer, H. P. (2004). Value of the clinical history for different users of dermoscopy compared with results of digital image analysis. *Journal of the European Academy of Dermatology and Venereology, 18*(6), 665–669.

Brady, M. S., Oliveria, S. A., Christos, P. J., Berwick, M., Coit, D. G., Katz, J., & Halpern, A. C. (2000). Patterns of detection in patients with cutaneous

CHAR

CHAR

CHAR

CHAR

CHAR

CHAR

CHAR

CHAR

CHAR

CHAR

CHAR

CHAR

CHAR

CHAR

CHAR

CHAR

CHAR

CHAR

CHAR

CHAR

CHAR

CHAR

CHAR

CHAR

CHAR

CHAR

CHAR

CHAR

CHAR

CHAR

CHAR

CHAR

CHAR

CHAR

CHAR

CHAR

CHAR

CHAR

CHAR

CHAR

CHAR

CHAR

CHAR

CHAR

CHAR

melanoma: implications for secondary prevention. *Cancer: Interdisciplinary International Journal of the American Cancer Society, 89*(2), 342–347.

Broumi, S., & Smarandache, F. (2013). Correlation coefficient of interval neutrosophic set. In *Vol. 436. Applied mechanics and materials* (pp. 511–517): Trans Tech Publications.

Campos-do-Carmo, G., & Ramos-e-Silva, M. (2008). Dermoscopy: basic concepts. *International Journal of Dermatology, 47*(7), 712–719.

Carrara, M., Bono, A., Bartoli, C., Colombo, A., Lualdi, M., Moglia, D., … Santinami, M. (2007). Multispectral imaging and artificial neural network: mimicking the management decision of the clinician facing pigmented skin lesions. *Physics in Medicine & Biology, 52*(9), 2599.

Celebi, M. E., Iyatomi, H., Schaefer, G., & Stoecker, W. V. (2009). Lesion border detection in dermoscopy images. *Computerized Medical Imaging and Graphics, 33*(2), 148–153.

Codella, N., Cai, J., Abedini, M., Garnavi, R., Halpern, A., & Smith, J. R. (2015). Deep learning, sparse coding, and SVM for melanoma recognition in dermoscopy images. In: *International workshop on machine learning in medical imaging, October* (pp. 118–126). Cham: Springer.

Codella, N. C., Nguyen, Q. B., Pankanti, S., Gutman, D. A., Helba, B., Halpern, A. C., & Smith, J. R. (2017). Deep learning ensembles for melanoma recognition in dermoscopy images. *IBM Journal of Research and Development, 61*(4) 5-1.

Demyanov, S., Chakravorty, R., Abedini, M., Halpern, A., & Garnavi, R. (2016). Classification of dermoscopy patterns using deep convolutional neural networks. In: *Biomedical imaging (ISBI), 2016 IEEE 13th international symposium on, April* (pp. 364–368): IEEE.

Díaz, I. G. (2017). *Incorporating the knowledge of dermatologists to convolutional neural networks for the diagnosis of skin lesions.* arXiv preprint arXiv:1703.01976.

Dong, C., Loy, C. C., He, K., & Tang, X. (2014). Learning a deep convolutional network for image super-resolution. In *European conference on computer vision, September* (pp. 184–199). Cham: Springer.

Drucker, H., Cortes, C., Jackel, L. D., LeCun, Y., & Vapnik, V. (1994). Boosting and other ensemble methods. *Neural Computation, 6*(6), 1289–1301.

Esteva, A., Kuprel, B., Novoa, R. A., Ko, J., Swetter, S. M., Blau, H. M., & Thrun, S. (2017). Dermatologist-level classification of skin cancer with deep neural networks. *Nature, 542*(7639), 115.

Fawcett, T. (2006). An introduction to ROC analysis. *Pattern Recognition Letters, 27*(8), 861–874.

Gachon, J., Beaulieu, P., Sei, J. F., Gouvernet, J., Claudel, J. P., Lemaitre, M., … Grob, J. J. (2005). First prospective study of the recognition process of melanoma in dermatological practice. *Archives of Dermatology, 141*(4), 434–438.

Guo, Y., Ashour, A. S., & Smarandache, F. (2018). A novel skin lesion detection approach using neutrosophic clustering and adaptive region growing in dermoscopy images. *Symmetry, 10*(4), 119.

Guo, Y., Budak, Ü., & Şengür, A. (2018). A Novel Retinal Vessel Detection Approach Based on Multiple Deep Convolution Neural Networks. *Computer Methods and Programs in Biomedicine, 167*, 43–48.

Guo, Y., Budak, Ü., Vespa, L. J., Khorasani, E., & Şengür, A. (2018). A retinal vessel detection approach using convolution neural network with reinforcement sample learning strategy. *Measurement, 125*, 586–591.

Guo, Y., Cheng, H. D., & Zhang, Y. (2009). A new neutrosophic approach to image denoising. *New Mathematics and Natural Computation, 5*(03), 653–662.

Guo, Y., Şengür, A., & Ye, J. (2014). A novel image thresholding algorithm based on neutrosophic similarity score. *Measurement, 58*, 175–186.

Guo, Y., Zhou, C., Chan, H. P., Chughtai, A., Wei, J., Hadjiiski, L. M., & Kazerooni, E. A. (2013). Automated iterative neutrosophic lung segmentation for image analysis in thoracic computed tomography. *Medical Physics, 40*(8).

Haenssle, H. A., Fink, C., Schneiderbauer, R., Toberer, F., Buhl, T., Blum, A., ... Uhlmann, L. (2018). Man against machine: diagnostic performance of a deep learning convolutional neural network for dermoscopic melanoma recognition in comparison to 58 dermatologists. *Annals of Oncology, 29*(8), 1836–1842.

Havlickova, B., Czaika, V. A., & Friedrich, M. (2008). Epidemiological trends in skin mycoses worldwide. *Mycoses, 51*, 2–15.

Hoo-Chang, S., Roth, H. R., Gao, M., Lu, L., Xu, Z., Nogues, I., ... Summers, R. M. (2016). Deep convolutional neural networks for computer-aided detection: CNN architectures, dataset characteristics and transfer learning. *IEEE Transactions on Medical Imaging, 35*(5), 1285.

Hu, W., Huang, Y., Wei, L., Zhang, F., & Li, H. (2015). Deep convolutional neural networks for hyperspectral image classification. *Journal of Sensors, 2015.*

Hu, F., Xia, G. S., Hu, J., & Zhang, L. (2015). Transferring deep convolutional neural networks for the scene classification of high-resolution remote sensing imagery. *Remote Sensing, 7*(11), 14680–14707.

Kapsokalyvas, D., Bruscino, N., Alfieri, D., de Giorgi, V., Cannarozzo, G., Cicchi, R., ... Pavone, F. S. (2013). Spectral morphological analysis of skin lesions with a polarization multispectral dermoscope. *Optics Express, 21*(4), 4826–4840.

Kawahara, J., BenTaieb, A., & Hamarneh, G. (2016). Deep features to classify skin lesions. In *Biomedical imaging (ISBI), 2016 IEEE 13th international symposium on, April* (pp. 1397–1400): IEEE.

Kennedy, C., Willemze, R., de Gruijl, F. R., Bavinck, J. N. B., & Bajdik, C. D. (2003). The influence of painful sunburns and lifetime sun exposure on the risk of actinic keratoses, seborrheic warts, melanocytic nevi, atypical nevi, and skin cancer. *Journal of Investigative Dermatology, 120*(6), 1087–1093.

Krizhevsky, A., Sutskever, I., & Hinton, G. E. (2012). Imagenet classification with deep convolutional neural networks. In *Advances in neural information processing systems* (pp. 1097–1105).

Lee, H., Grosse, R., Ranganath, R., & Ng, A. Y. (2009). Convolutional deep belief networks for scalable unsupervised learning of hierarchical representations. In: *Proceedings of the 26th annual international conference on machine learning, June* (pp. 609–616): ACM.

Lin, J., Koga, H., Takata, M., & Saida, T. (2009). Dermoscopy of pigmented lesions on mucocutaneous junction and mucous membrane. *British Journal of Dermatology, 161*(6), 1255–1261.

Maji, P. K. (2012). A neutrosophic soft set approach to a decision making problem. *Ann Fuzzy Math Inform 3*(2), 313–319.

Majumdar, P., & Samanta, S. K. (2014). On similarity and entropy of neutrosophic sets. *Journal of Intelligent Fuzzy Systems, 26*(3), 1245–1252.

Matsunaga, K., Hamada, A., Minagawa, A., & Koga, H. (2017). Image classification of Melanoma, Nevus and Seborrheic Keratosis by deep neural network ensemble. In *International skin imaging collaboration (ISIC) 2017 challenge at the international symposium on biomedical imaging (ISBI).*

Mullani, N. A. (2006). *US Patent No. 7006223.* Washington, DC: U.S. Patent and Trademark Office.

Mullani, N. (2016). *US Patent No. 9458990.* Washington, DC: U.S. Patent and Trademark Office.

Nasr-Esfahani, E., Samavi, S., Karimi, N., Soroushmehr, S. M. R., Jafari, M. H., Ward, K., & Najarian, K. (2016). Melanoma detection by analysis of clinical images using convolutional neural network. In *Engineering in medicine and biology society (EMBC), 2016 IEEE 38th annual international conference of the, August* (pp. 1373–1376): IEEE.

Nguyen, G. N., Son, L. H., Ashour, A. S., & Dey, N. (2017). A survey of the state-of-the-arts on neutrosophic sets in biomedical diagnoses. *International Journal of Machine Learning and Cybernetics*, 1–13.

Oliveira, R. B., Mercedes Filho, E., Ma, Z., Papa, J. P., Pereira, A. S., & Tavares, J. M. R. (2016). Computational methods for the image segmentation of pigmented skin lesions: a review. *Computer Methods and Programs in Biomedicine, 131*, 127–141.

Rastegari, M., Ordonez, V., Redmon, J., & Farhadi, A. (2016). Xnor-net: imagenet classification using binary convolutional neural networks. In *European Conference on Computer Vision, October* (pp. 525–542). Cham: Springer

Rubegni, P., Burroni, M., Perotti, R., Fimiani, M., Andreassi, L., Cevenini, G., ... Barbini, P. (2002). Digital dermoscopy analysis and artificial neural network for the differentiation of clinically atypical pigmented skin lesions: a retrospective study. *Journal of Investigative Dermatology, 119*(2), 471–474.

Salama, A. A., & Alblowi, S. A. (2012). Neutrosophic set and neutrosophic topological spaces. *IOSR Journal of Mathematics, 3*(4), 31–35.

Schmidhuber, J. (2015). Deep learning in neural networks: an overview. *Neural Networks, 61*, 85–117.

Situ, N., Yuan, X., Chen, J., & Zouridakis, G. (2008). Malignant melanoma detection by bag-of-features classification. In *Engineering in medicine and biology society, 2008. EMBS 2008. 30th annual international conference of the IEEE, August* (pp. 3110–3113): IEEE.

Smarandache, F., & Vlăduțescu, Ș. (2013). *Communication vs information, an axiomatic neutrosophic solution*. Infinite Study.

Veredas, F., Mesa, H., & Morente, L. (2010). Binary tissue classification on wound images with neural networks and bayesian classifiers. *IEEE Transactions on Medical Imaging, 29*(2), 410–427.

Vestergaard, M. E., Macaskill, P. H. P. M., Holt, P. E., & Menzies, S. W. (2008). Dermoscopy compared with naked eye examination for the diagnosis of primary melanoma: a meta-analysis of studies performed in a clinical setting. *British Journal of Dermatology, 159*(3), 669–676.

Wahba, M. A., Ashour, A. S., Guo, Y., Napoleon, S. A., & Elnaby, M. M. A. (2018). A novel cumulative level difference mean based GLDM and modified ABCD features ranked using eigenvector centrality approach for four skin lesion types classification. *Computer Methods and Programs in Biomedicine, 165*, 163–174.

Wahba, M. A., Ashour, A. S., Napoleon, S. A., Elnaby, M. M. A., & Guo, Y. (2017). Combined empirical mode decomposition and texture features for skin lesion classification using quadratic support vector machine. *Health Information Science and Systems, 5*(1), 10.

Xiao, T., Xu, Y., Yang, K., Zhang, J., Peng, Y., & Zhang, Z. (2015). The application of two-level attention models in deep convolutional neural network for fine-grained image classification. In *Proceedings of the IEEE conference on computer vision and pattern recognition*, (pp. 842–850).

Xie, F., Fan, H., Li, Y., Jiang, Z., Meng, R., & Bovik, A. (2017). Melanoma classification on dermoscopy images using a neural network ensemble model. *IEEE Transactions on Medical Imaging, 36*(3), 849–858.

Ye, J. (2013). Multicriteria decision-making method using the correlation coefficient under single-valued neutrosophic environment. *International Journal of General Systems, 42*(4), 386–394.

Ye, J. (2015). Trapezoidal neutrosophic set and its application to multiple attribute decision-making. *Neural Computing and Applications, 26*(5), 1157–1166.

Yu, L., Chen, H., Dou, Q., Qin, J., & Heng, P. A. (2017). Automated melanoma recognition in dermoscopy images via very deep residual networks. *IEEE Transactions on Medical Imaging, 36*(4), 994–1004.

Yuan, Y., Chao, M., & Lo, Y. C. (2017). Automatic skin lesion segmentation using deep fully convolutional networks with jaccard distance. *IEEE Transactions on Medical Imaging, 36*(9), 1876–1886.

14

Neutrosophic set-based deep learning in mammogram analysis

Guanxiong Cai*, Yanhui Guo†, Weiguo Chen‡, Hui Zeng‡, Yuanpin Zhou*, Yao Lu*

*School of Data and Computer Science, Sun Yat-sen University, Guangzhou, People's Republic of China. †Department of Computer Science, University of Illinois at Springfield, Springfield, IL, United States. ‡Department of Diagnostic Radiology, Nanfang Hospital, Guangzhou, People's Republic of China

1   Introduction

Breast cancer (BC) is the most frequent cancer type that may lead to death among females. According to recent statistics (Bray et al., 2018), there were about 2,088,849 new cases and 626,679 deaths from BC that occurred worldwide during 2018. The etiology of BC is still controversial, and prevention of the disease is thus challenging. One of the main symptoms in the early stage of BC is the appearance of microcalcifications (MCs), whose diameters range from 0.1 to 1 mm. This has been widely used in clinical practice for BC detection (Wang et al., 2016).

Recently, full-field digital mammograms (FFDMs) have been widely used in the prescreening of BC. Such modality provides 12–14 bits of gray-level information with 0.07-mm pixel size as spatial resolution (Nishikawa, Giger, Doi, Vyborny, & Schmidt, 1995; Sahli, Bettaieb, Abdallah, Bhouri, & Bédoui, 2016). However, manual interpretation of clinical MCs is a tiring and time-consuming task due to their fuzzy nature and low distinguishability from their surroundings (Cheng, Cai, Chen, Hu, & Lou, 2003). Accordingly, clustered MCs (MCCs) are considered an early sign of BC, and take 30%–50% among BC patients (Sahli et al., 2016). The high correlation between the presence of clustered MCs and BC has attracted widespread attention from academia (Cheng et al., 2003). Numerous studies have been conducted on how to utilize computer-aided

Neutrosophic Set in Medical Image Analysis. https://doi.org/10.1016/B978-0-12-818148-5.00014-X

detection (CADe) and diagnosis (CADx) in the clinical practice of BC (Pereira, Ramos, & Nascimento, 2014).

A CADe system can be considered the second reader by emphasizing suspicious MCC lesions for additional review or interpretation by radiologists (Dromain et al., 2013). The traditional procedures of the CAD system can be grouped into three categories, namely basic digital image enhancement methods, multiscale decomposition methods, and machine-learning/pattern-recognition methods. Typically, image enhancement methods are employed to improve the contrast between MCs and backgrounds, and then a thresholding technique can be applied to separate them. Bankman, Nizialek, Simon, and Gatewood (1997) developed a hill-climbing algorithm for the segmentation of compact intensity hills, which achieved lower computational complexity in comparison with the multitolerance region growing procedure as well as active contours. Dengler, Behrens, and Desaga (1993) implemented a two-phase procedure for spot detection and shape extraction based on the difference of Gaussians (DoG) to detect MCs. Multiscale decomposition methods are mainly based on the difference in frequency content of the bright MC spots compared to their surrounding backgrounds. Yoshida, Doi, and Nishikawa (1994) applied a decimated wavelet transform to increase the signal-to-noise ratio of MCs. First, the wavelet transform was applied to decompose the digitized mammograms, which were then reconstructed from the transform coefficients modified at several levels in the transform space. Strickland and Hahn (1996, 1997) applied an undecimated biorthogonal wavelet transform and optimal subband weighting for detecting and segmenting clustered MCs. Several studies employed machine-learning and pattern-recognition methods for MC detection. Zhang et al. (1994) implemented a shift-variant artificial neural network (ANN) to detect MCCs. Each region of interest (ROI) was classified as a positive ROI if the total number of MCs detected in the ROI was greater than a certain number; otherwise, the ROI was classified as a negative ROI. Chan, Lo, Sahiner, Lam, and Helvie (1995) used a difference-image technique to detect MCs on FFDMs, and further classified detected findings using a convolution neural network (CNN). Bazzani et al. (2001) proposed an MC detection method using multiresolution filter analysis, where an SVM classifier was applied to reduce false positive MCs. Valvano et al. (2017) applied a deep convolution neural network to segment MCs and obtained an accuracy of 83.7% compared to the 58% of the traditional method.

A CADx system aims to automatically differentiate benign from malignant MCCs. De Santo, Molinara, Tortorella, and Vento (2003) proposed an approach for recognizing malignant clusters based on multiple classifier systems that use simultaneous evidence obtained from the malignancy of single MCs and of the MCC. Lo, Gavrielides, Markey, and Jesneck (2003) developed an ensemble model using the combination of local models constructed by image-processing features, radiologist features, morphology features, and the patient's age. Kallergi (2004) selected 13 morphology features of the individual MCs and the distribution of the cluster and combined that with the patient's age to build an artificial neural network.

Individual MC detection on mammograms is a challenging task because the morphology of MCs varies greatly. On the one hand, obvious MCs and subtle MCs always appear at the same time. On the other hand, subtle MCs are susceptible to noise interference. Recently, the NS theory has been used in image processing of noisy images with indeterminant information by defining an element using a degree of truth, indeterminacy, and falsity, called T, I, and F (Guo, Şengür, & Tian, 2016; Guo, Şengür, & Ye, 2014). The NS procedure deals with the nature, origin, and scope of neutralities as well as their interactions with different spectra (Guo & Şengür, 2015).

From the preceding studies, this chapter proposes a novel NS-based deep-learning technique for the analysis of digital mammograms. At first, the FFDM is mapped into the NS domain, which is represented by T, I, and F along with a Neutrosophic Similarity Score (NSS) approach. Then, in combination with the deep convolution neural network (DCNN), lesion detection, false positive (FP) reduction, regional clustering, and classification experiments are conducted on our dataset.

The remaining sections are organized as follows. Section 2 includes materials and proposed methods of the proposed CAD system. Sections 3 and 4 present the experimental results and discussion. Lastly, the conclusion is depicted in Section 5.

2 Materials and methods

The block diagram of this study is demonstrated in Fig. 1, and it mainly consists of five stages: (1) Neutrosophic domain transformation; (2) MC coarse detection stage; (3) MC classification using a DCNN1 classifier; (4) Regional clustering of MCs; and (5) MCC classification using a DCNN2 classifier. During the DCNN1 training procedure, the classifier is trained using a newly proposed scheme, a neutrosophic reinforcement sample learning (NRSL)

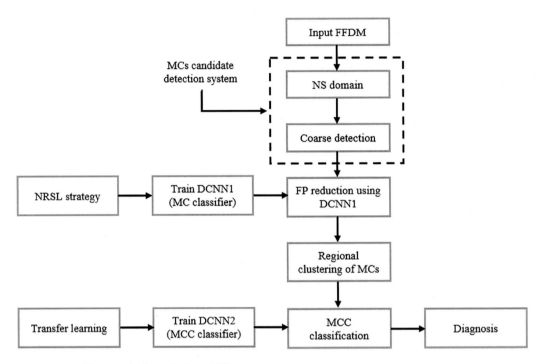

Fig. 1 The block diagram of this study for a CAD system.

strategy, to speed up the training and improve the DCNN1 performance.

The detailed description of each part in the proposed system is given as follows.

2.1 Neutrosophic domain transformation

In the preprocessing stage, the breast region is automatically determined using Otsu's method (Otsu, 1979). Otsu's algorithm calculates a global threshold to binarize the input mammogram, and an eight-connectivity labeling technique is applied to find the largest connected region as the breast area. All the following operations are constrained in the breast area.

Then, NS is specified into the mammogram domain, where I_o is the preprocessed image and I_{NS} is the processed image of the NS domain. Each pixel $P(x, y)$ in I_o mapped to the NS domain can be expressed as $P_{NS}(x, y) = \{T(x, y), I(x, y), F(x, y)\}$. $T(x, y)$, $I(x, y)$, and $F(x, y)$ represent the memberships belonging to the obvious MC (*OMC*) pixel set, the indeterminate set (subtle MCs or uncertain noise), and the nonobvious MC pixel set, respectively. These membership values are defined under two different conditions.

First, based on the gray-level intensity value conditions C_g, they are defined as (Guo et al., 2016):

$$T_{C_g}(x, y) = \frac{GL(x, y) - GL_{\min}}{GL_{\max} - GL_{\min}} \tag{1}$$

$$OMC(x, y) = DctS(g(x, y)) \tag{2}$$

$$I_{C_g}(x, y) = g(x, y) \backslash OMC(x, y) \tag{3}$$

$$F_{C_g}(x, y) = 1 - T_{C_g}(x, y) \tag{4}$$

where $g(x, y)$ and $GL(x, y)$ are the pixel value at position (x, y) on the preprocessed image and the image after Laplacian of Gaussian (LoG) filtering, respectively. $OMC(x, y)$ is the pixel value at position (x, y) in the obvious MC pixel set of the preprocessed image, and is obtained by using the MC detection system (noted as $DctS(\cdot)$) in our previous study (Cai et al., 2018) with a preprocessed image $g(x, y)$ as the input. Thus, $I_{C_g}(x, y)$ means replacing OMC in the preprocessed image with the corresponding pixel value of the local background.

Second, for robust domain transformation to noise, a new local mean intensity condition C_m is used to define the mapping from the pixels of the mean filtered image to the NS domain as:

$$T_{C_m}(x, y) = \frac{GL_m(x, y) - GL_{m}\min}{GL_m\max - GL_{m}\min} \tag{5}$$

$$OMC_m(x, y) = DctS(g_m(x, y)) \tag{6}$$

$$I_{C_m}(x, y) = g_m(x, y) \backslash OMC_m(x, y) \tag{7}$$

$$F_{C_m}(x, y) = 1 - T_{C_m}(x, y) \tag{8}$$

where $g_m(x, y)$ and $GL_m(x, y)$ are the pixel value at position (x, y) on the mean filtered image and the LoG filtered image. $OMC_m(x, y)$ is the intensity value at position (x, y) in the obvious MC pixel set of $g_m(x, y)$, and is obtained by using the MC detection system $DctS$ with mean filtered image $g_m(x, y)$ as the input. $I_{C_m}(x, y)$ means replacing $OMC_m(x, y)$ in the mean filtered image $g_m(x, y)$ with the pixel value of the local background.

Afterward, similarity scores are computed to identify the degree to the ideal object under the two different conditions (Guo et al., 2016):

$$S_{C_g}(P(x, y), A^*) = \frac{T_{C_g}(x, y)A_T + I_{C_g}(x, y)A_I + F_{C_g}(x, y)A_F}{\sqrt{T_{C_g}^2(x, y) + I_{C_g}^2(x, y) + F_{C_g}^2(x, y)} \times \sqrt{A_T^2 + A_I^2 + A_F^2}} \tag{9}$$

$$S_{C_m}(P(x,y),A^*) = \frac{T_{C_m}(x,y)A_T + I_{C_m}(x,y)A_I + F_{C_m}(x,y)A_F}{\sqrt{T_{C_m}^2(x,y) + I_{C_m}^2(x,y) + F_{C_m}^2(x,y)} \times \sqrt{A_T^2 + A_I^2 + A_F^2}}$$

(10)

The value of A^* denotes the best alternative of A, and under the two conditions are the same as $A^* = (A_T, A_I, A_F) = (1,0,0)$, which are constant vectors obtained by trial and error. The final NS map of the mammogram is defined as:

$$I_{NS}(x,y) = \frac{S_{C_g}(x,y) + S_{C_m}(x,y)}{2}$$

(11)

2.2 MC coarse detection stage

In the coarse detection stage, potential MCs are determined with an adaptive thresholding procedure. In this procedure, the purpose is to segment individual MC candidates. First, the gray-level histogram inside the breast area of the NS domain image I_{NS} is analyzed to calculate an initial global threshold, and the threshold is used as a feature to obtain a series of initial seed points. At the position (x,y) of each seed point, a locally adaptive gray level thresholding technique (Gurcan, Chan, Sahiner, Hadjiiski, & Petrick, 2002) is applied for extracting all the connected pixels above a local threshold LT_{xy} that can be defined as follows:

$$LT_{xy} = m_{xy} + k\sigma_{xy}$$

(12)

where m_{xy} and σ_{xy} represent the local mean pixel value and the root mean square (RMS) value, respectively, in the current window centered at position (x,y), and k is a constant factor. When k is relatively large, the threshold value will be strict, which corresponds to fewer false positives and lower detection sensitivity. Conversely, the threshold will be loose, corresponding to more false positives and higher detection sensitivity. The locally adaptive thresholding technique is given by:

$$\phi(x,y) = \begin{cases} 1 & I_{NS}(x,y) > LT_{xy} \\ 0 & I_{NS}(x,y) \leq LT_{xy} \end{cases}$$

(13)

where $I_{NS}(x,y)$ is the input mammogram, and $\phi(x,y)$ is the output mammogram. The local window size is chosen as 41×41 to give a proper estimate of the local background fluctuation (Ge et al., 2006). Then, the global threshold changes iteratively until the final total number of obtained candidates falls within a predefined range (Chan et al., 1987).

The connected component analysis is taken on the obtained binary image to calculate characteristics of components, such as area and locations, and components of a small size (an area smaller than three pixels) considered a subtle noise point are first excluded. The potential candidates will be classified as either a true positive (TP) or a false positive (FP) MC in the next step.

2.3 MCs classification using DCNN1 classifier

The potential MCs containing a large number of FP MCs are then screened by a DCNN1. The proposed DCNN1 is designed to extract features from the input images automatically and has a dramatic effect on the identification of MCs. In this model, the input to the DCNN1 is a patch with a size of 32×32 pixels cropped from the original mammograms, either a true or false MC is located at the center of the patch, and the output of the DCNN1 is a probability value between 0 and 1. A total number of 6490 MCs are selected randomly from 115 cases of the INbreast database (Moreira et al., 2012) and then divided into three groups. The first group (88 cases with 4970 patches) is used as a training set, the second group (15 cases with 800 patches) is selected as a testing set, and the third group (12 cases with 720 patches) is selected as a testing set. The three sets are mutually independent from each other. As for the negative cases, 7249 negative patches are selected for training, with 800 negative patches for validation and 784 negative patches for testing. Negative patches are selected using our MC candidate detection system. After been detected in the candidate detection stage, the detected signals are determined as TP or FP by comparison with the coordinates of the ground truth. Signals that are at least 23 pixels (to ensure true MCs are eliminated from negative patches) away from the location of the ground truth are selected as our FP signals for the negative patches. Fig. 2 lists the number of patches with true and false MCs used to train, validate, and test the DCNN1 classifier.

In contrast to handcrafted features designed in traditional approaches, DCNN1 is able to automatically learn and extract hierarchical features by training the parameters of a multilayer feedforward structure. In this way, low-level features are constructed to high-level features to form a representation of pyramidal levels, which provides greater robustness to intraclass variability.

As shown in Fig. 3, the input patch with a size of 32×32 is first convolved with 64 filters of 3×3 pixel weight kernels, and the convolution results are stored in the corresponding nodes of

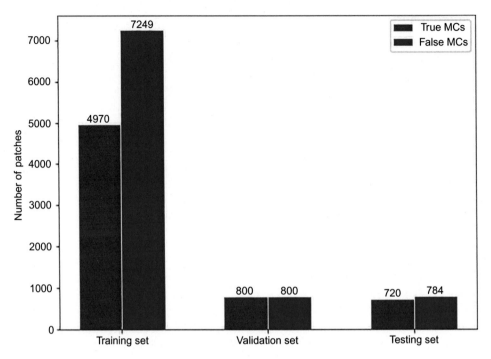

Fig. 2 The number of patches with true and false MCs.

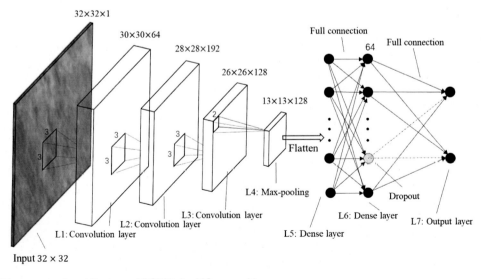

Fig. 3 The proposed architecture of DCNN1 for MC recognition.

the input layer. These will be activated by the rectified linear units (ReLU) (Krizhevsky, Sutskever, & Hinton, 2012) activation function in the first layer, and 64 feature maps will be obtained. Those 64 feature maps of the first layer are then convolved with 192 filters of 3×3 pixel kernels to obtain 192 feature maps in the second layer. Similarly, 128 feature maps are obtained in the third layer. The function of convolutional layers is to further extract features from the input patch or the feature maps of former layers with different kernels, and then the activation function will operate on the convolved results to produce the feature maps. The fourth layer is a max-pooling layer with a 2×2 window size. Multidimensional input is transformed into one dimension in the first dense layer. The dense layer is a fully connected layer. A dropout technique is imposed to randomly disconnect a certain percentage (rate) of the input neurons at each update during training time, which is used to prevent overfitting. The last layer is also a dense layer with two nodes as output. To clarify how the neural network is computed, we use the following notations. L_k denotes the kth hidden layer, x_m^{k-1} denotes the mth feature map of layer L_{k-1}, the connecting weight kernel between the nth feature map of the output layer and the mth feature map of the input layer is denoted as W_{mn}^k, and the bias of the nth feature map is denoted as b_n^k. Then, the obtained feature map in layer L_k is computed as:

$$x_n^k = f\left(\sum_m x_m^{k-1} \otimes W_{mn}^k + b_n^k \right) \tag{14}$$

where $\otimes$ is the operation of convolution, and $f(\cdot)$ is a nonlinear mapping ReLU function (Krizhevsky et al., 2012).

$$f(x) = \begin{cases} x & x \geq 0 \\ 0 & x < 0 \end{cases} \tag{15}$$

The weight kernel W_{mn}^k is randomly initialized, trained using a back propagation (BP) algorithm (Hirose, Yamashita, & Hijiya, 1991), and further optimized with a stochastic gradient descent (SGD) (Bottou, 2010).

In the fully connected layer, the output feature vector of the former layer will be fed to the softmax function as input. The output of the softmax function yields the probabilities of prediction results. The hypothesis is formulated as:

$$P(y = 1 \mid x, w, b) = \frac{\exp(w \cdot x + b)}{1 + \exp(w \cdot x + b)} \tag{16}$$

$$P(y = 0 \mid x, w, b) = \frac{1}{1 + \exp(w \cdot x + b)} \qquad (17)$$

where y is the class target, $x \in R^{N \times 1}$ is a N dimensional feature vector, $w \in R^{N \times 1}$ is the weight parameter, and b is a bias term.

A binary cross-entropy function is used to compute the binary cross-entropy (BCE) between predictions and targets, and worked as the loss function as follows:

$$BCEL = -\frac{1}{N_0} \sum_{i=1}^{N_0} [t_i \log(p_i) + (1 - t_i) \log(1 - p_i)] \qquad (18)$$

where N_0 is the total number of training samples; p_i is the prediction result of each sample, which is the sigmoidal output of the DCNN; and t_i is the target in $\{0, 1\}$, which corresponds to the value of truth label. This empirical loss function returns an expression for the element-wise binary cross-entropy as the loss function value. From the perspective of information theory, the BCE loss function is equivalent to the cross-entropy between the trained model (distribution) and the real model (distribution), and the value of this cross-entropy measures the gap between them. The smaller the cross-entropy is, the closer the model is to the real distribution. Compared with the mean square error (MSE) loss function, BCE can slow down the gradient dispersion and speed up the training process.

In traditional DCNN, the learning process is fixed, and all the samples are trained the same number of times. We proposed a neutrosophic reinforcement sample learning (NRSL) strategy during the training stage of DCNN1, which trains the samples with adaptive times. The main idea of the NRSL strategy is to reinforce training the poor performance samples with more times according to their performance while the samples with high performance are not tuned as much. In this way, the training procedure is more target-oriented and will be sped up.

The amount of reinforced training time is a key in reinforcement sample learning, which is obtained using a metric neutrosophic similarity score due to its ability to interpret the indeterminacy information during training. We use NS to determine the reinforced training number, different from Section 2.1 that applied NS in image processing of noisy images with indeterminant information. For each epoch in training, we have accuracy for each batch to be defined as T_i' and $F_i' = 1 - T_i'$. Then, we calculate the mean of T_i' in this epoch for all batches as T_m' and let

$$l_i = T_i' - T_m' \qquad (19)$$

Table 1 Detailed steps of NRSL training algorithm

Step 1: Randomly split the training samples into m batches
Step 2: Train DCNN1 on all batches in an epoch
Step 3: Find batches with poor accuracies in the current epoch
Step 4: Tune the DCNN1 using these batches with a more reinforced training number according to their NSS value
Step 5: Go to step 2 to train the network until all the epochs are finished

where N denotes the number of patch samples in this batch.

We define NSS_i as the similarity degree to the ideal sample with the best performance in the ith batch:

$$NSS_i = T_i'(1 - l_i)F_i' \qquad (20)$$

The reinforced training number is determined using a strategy based on the previous NSS_i values. The basic idea is that the higher the NSS_i, the more reinforced number will be imposed to train that batch of patch samples.

In this study, for each epoch, the repeated reinforced training number is determined by a piecewise function on NSS_i. The whole NRSL training procedure is summarized in Table 1. After the classification by the designed DCNN1, potential MCs will be divided into two classes: true MCs and false MCs.

2.4 Regional clustering of MCs

Final MCCs are identified by a regional clustering algorithm based on a basic assumption that MCs of clinical interest always emerge in clusters on FFDMs (Ge et al., 2006). In this study, a density-based spatial clustering of applications with a noise (DBSCAN) algorithm (Ester, Kriegel, & Xu, 1996) is then performed on those true MCs to form the final MCCs. The main advantages of the DBSCAN algorithm are the number of clusters does not need to be specified in advance, and the algorithm has good adaptability to noise objects.

In this DBSCAN algorithm, the data points are classified as core points, which are represented by the subset $\widetilde{T}$, the boundary points set $\widetilde{I}$, and the noise points set $\widetilde{F}$. A point p is considered as belonging to $\widetilde{T}$ if at least M points (including p) are within a given distance ε of point p. Those points are in fact directly reachable from point p because a point q is defined to be directly reachable from point p if point q is within a distance ε from the point p,

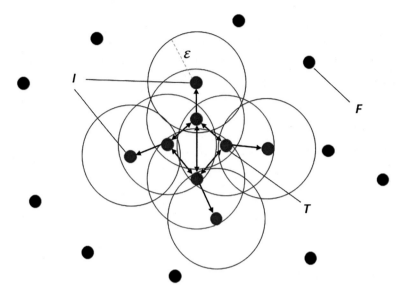

Fig. 4 An illustration of the DBSCAN algorithm.

and the point p must belong to set $\widetilde{T}$. A point q is considered as belonging to set $\widetilde{I}$, if q is directly reachable from some core point p of set $\widetilde{T}$. All the remaining points not directly reachable from any core point are considered as belonging to set $\widetilde{F}$. As illustrated in Fig. 4, red points belong to set $\widetilde{T}$, blue points belong to set $\widetilde{I}$, and black points belong to set $\widetilde{F}$. The parameter M is set as 4.

2.5 MCC classification using DCNN2 classifier

Another DCNN (DCNN2) for MCCs is trained on 197 cases (138 malignant and 59 benign cases) from Nanfang Hospital, Guangzhou, China (NFH, 394 clinical high-resolution FFDMs); these contain only relatively small biopsy-proven benign or malignant MCCs. The network is then validated in 70 cases (29 benign and 41 malignant cases) and tested on 71 cases (29 benign and 42 malignant cases). This network is the main classification process to classify the abnormal regions while the DCNN1 in Section 2.3 is used during the MC detection process. Note that the validation set and testing set may contain large-scale distributed MCCs, and these mammograms are not suitable for training. However, the overall ground truth of malignancy of the whole cases is known. Hence, we divide them into validation and testing sets, instead of the training set. The size of the input patch is 224×224 pixels, and each MCC is fully located at the center of the patch. A total of 2421 patches are selected from the 197 training cases and divided into three groups; the number of patches of

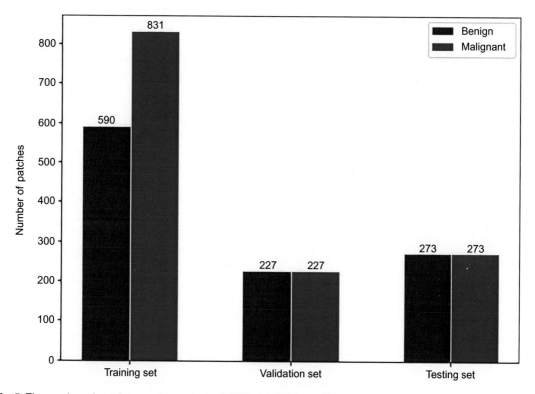

Fig. 5 The number of patches used to train the DCNN2 for MCC classification.

each group is shown in Fig. 5. The first group containing 1421 patches (590 benign and 831 malignant) is used as a training set. In addition, the second group containing 454 patches (227 benign and 227 malignant) is selected as a validation set, and the third group containing 546 patches (273 benign and 273 malignant) is used as a testing set. Each group is completely independent of each other. An augmentation method using random rotation and adding Gaussian noise is performed on the training set to expend training data volume for reducing overfitting. Note that digital mammograms are always coupled with noise, especially Gaussian noise (Lashari, Ibrahim, & Senan, 2015), so a method of adding Gaussian noise is used to expand the data volume.

The structure of this second DCNN2 used for the classification of MCCs is illustrated in Fig. 6. This second DCNN2 mainly contains one input layer, five blocks, two fully connected layers, and one output layer. Each block consists of 2–3 convolution layers and one max-pooling layer. The architecture mainly follows from VGG16 (Simonyan & Zisserman, 2014), and a transfer learning

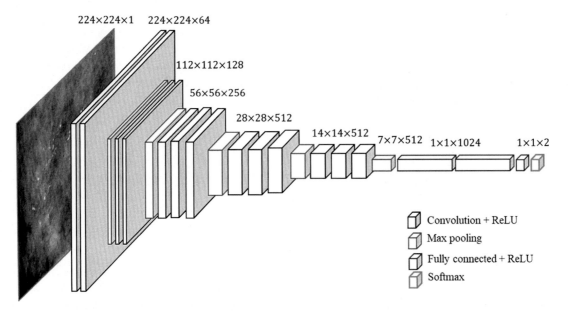

Fig. 6 The computerized architecture of DCNN2 for the classification of MCCs.

method (Bengio, 2012) is imposed to accelerate the training process.

2.6 Automated diagnosis of MCC

The goal of this study is to build an automatic and robust system in a seamless methodology that yields detection as well as the probability of malignancy. For each detected MCC on the validation and testing sets, a rectangular bounding box region containing the MCC is cropped from the original mammogram and put into the pretrained DCNN2 to predict, and each input MCC region will be classified as either benign or malignant. If all regions containing the detected MCCs in a given mammogram are classified as benign, then the whole mammogram is considered benign while if at least one region containing the detected MCC in a given mammogram is classified as malignant, the whole mammogram is considered malignant. For case-based evaluation, we weight sum the maximal CNN malignancy output value of each view together (note as P_{CC}, P_{MLO}), and if the obtained value is greater than a certain threshold, then this case is considered to be malignant; otherwise it is benign. This weighted sum can be expressed as:

$$P = w_1 \cdot P_{CC} + w_2 \cdot P_{MLO} \tag{21}$$

where $w_1 + w_2 = 1$, and if there is no prior information, we assume that the accuracy of the CC and MLO view in predicting the malignancy of the entire case is independent of each other, thus w_1, w_2 are both equal to 0.5.

3 Experimental results

In this study, FFDMs of only MCs were mainly collected from Nanfang Hospital (NFH), Guangzhou, China, and the publicly available INbreast database (Moreira et al., 2012), respectively. The NFH dataset is used for this research with permission from the NFH ethics committee. This dataset contains 338 cases with 676 mammograms. The annotations of the MCCs of the NFH dataset are made by an experienced radiologist and validated by another radiologist. The same procedure was followed with all annotations of individual MCs and MCCs of the INbreast dataset. A total of 154 cases concerning MCs are selected from the INbreast database. The acquisition equipment is the Mammo-Novation Siemens FFDM, with a solid-state detector of amorphous selenium, a pixel size of 70 μm (microns), a 14-bit contrast resolution, and an image matrix of 2560×3328 or 3328×4084 pixels. All cases include two mammographic views, namely the cranio-caudal (CC) view and the mediolateral oblique (MLO) view. The results of all cases have been proven by biopsy, which is used to evaluate the classification performance of the proposed system. However, compared with Western women, the breasts of Asian women generally tend to be denser, and MCs are often obscured by those dense glands, making mammographic screening of BC more challenging.

All detailed results are demonstrated in this section. In the preprocessing stage, the input image is processed to obtain an MC-enhanced image, where the low frequency background was removed. Fig. 7 illustrates a comparison of the original MC lesions and the corresponding enhanced results.

In the MC candidate detection stage, an average of 90% true MCs is truly extracted, and the other 10% subtle MCs are missed on average; examples are shown in Fig. 8.

To validate the performance of the NRSL strategy, we compare it with the traditional training strategy on performances of accuracy and epochs. Fig. 9 shows a comparison of accuracies on training and validation sets between traditional DCNN1 and DCNN1 with the NRSL strategy. The red lines are the accuracies of DCNN1 with a traditional training strategy, and the blue lines are the accuracies of DCNN1 with the NRSL strategy. The solid

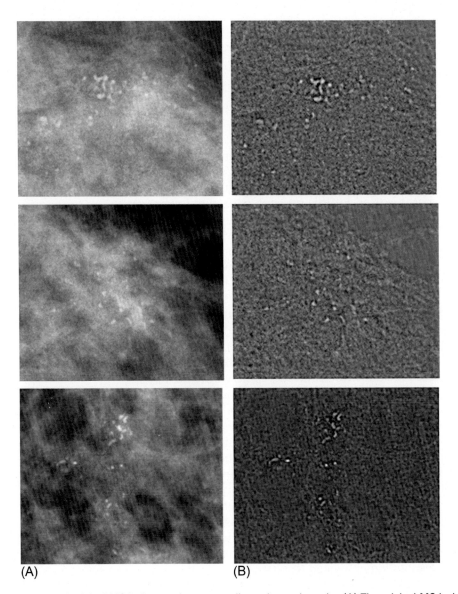

(A)   (B)

Fig. 7 A comparison of original MC lesions and corresponding enhanced results: (A) The original MC lesions, and (B) MC-enhanced image with the proposed method.

lines represent the accuracies on the training set, and the dotted lines stand for the accuracies on the validation set.

Fig. 9 demonstrates that after using the proposed NRSL strategy, the accuracy curve converges faster and goes relatively higher compared with the traditional DCNN at the same epochs. Also, an early stopping scheme is imposed during the training process,

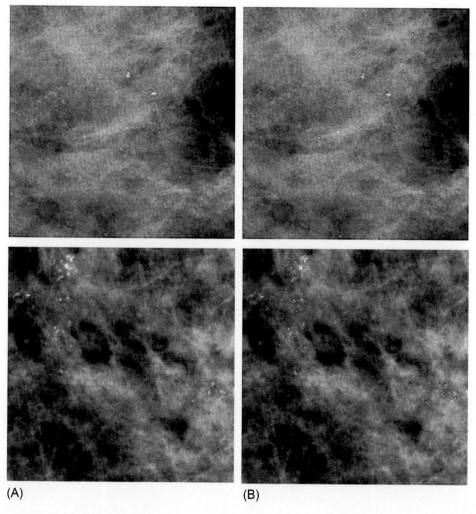

(A)   (B)

Fig. 8 Example images of MC detection results: (A) original MC lesions, and (B) final MC detection results, where detected MCs are highlighted by *red circles*.

where the training process is chosen to stop at the 40th epoch. In this study, the accuracies on training, validation, and testing sets are 99.87%, 95.12%, and 93.68% for the proposed method after 40 epochs, but 98.03%, 93.49%, and 92.36% for the traditional method, respectively. Furthermore, Fig. 10 demonstrates examples of the automatically detected MCCs. Fig. 10A and C are the original mammograms while Fig. 10B and D are their corresponding detection results. The red solid lines are the manual contours drawn by expert radiologists, the red points are the detected MCs, and the blue rectangles are the detected MCCs by our algorithms.

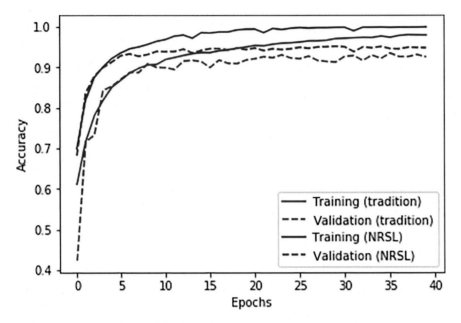

Fig. 9 Classification accuracy on the number of epochs.

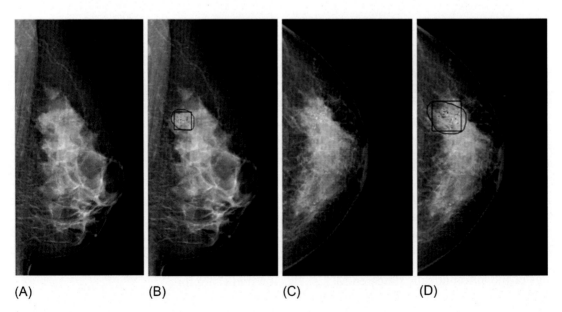

(A)   (B)   (C)   (D)

Fig. 10 MCC detection results: (A) and (C) original mammogram while (B) and (D) are the corresponding detection results of (A) and (C), respectively.

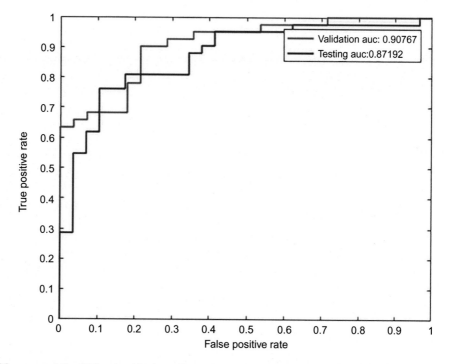

Fig. 11 ROC curves of the CADx algorithm's performance on the validation and testing sets.

Subsequently, the rectangular bounding box of the detected MCC was compared to the polygon drawn by expert radiologists. If the ratio of the intersection area to either the rectangular bounding box or the polygon area is larger than 40%, then the MCC lesion is considered to be detected successfully. For evaluating the cluster-based MCC detection process, a 92.5% sensitivity value is obtained at 0.50 FPs per image.

The final diagnosis on the basis of automatic detection is performed, and the ROC curves of the CADx algorithm's performance on the validation and testing sets are shown in Fig. 11.

The AUCs on the validation and testing sets are 0.908 and 0.872 for the proposed DCNN2, and the case-based classification accuracies on the validation and testing sets are 0.855 and 0.813, respectively.

4 Discussion

This study aims to develop a robust and seamless MCC detection and classification system using NS-based DCNN methods to help radiologists automatically identify suspicious MCC lesions as benign or malignant. Thus, fewer unnecessary biopsies for true benign cases can be conducted clinically.

MC detection is an important step in CADe on FFDMs. This study combined obvious and subtle MC information using an NS domain transformation technique to develop an automatic CADe system, and used a newly proposed NRSL strategy to speed up the training process of DCNN. To obtain MCCs, a DBSCAN algorithm is performed on clustering in this study. We also tried mean-shift clustering in the experiment, but the result was not better than the DBSCN algorithm. Therefore, it seems that the difference in clustering methods is not the key to this problem. However, the DBSCAN algorithm does not need to specify the number of clusters in advance, and the algorithm has good adaptability to noise points (isolated MCs). In the MCC detection evaluation, there are 234 cases (117 malignant and 117 benign cases) randomly selected from the NFH dataset included in the test abnormal set. For the test negative set, 101 cases that are free of MCs and might have some other symptoms are used to calculate the false positive rate (FPR), which is defined as the average number of FPs per image.

Fig. 12 illustrates a comparison of the ROC curves on the validation and testing set. The green line represents the

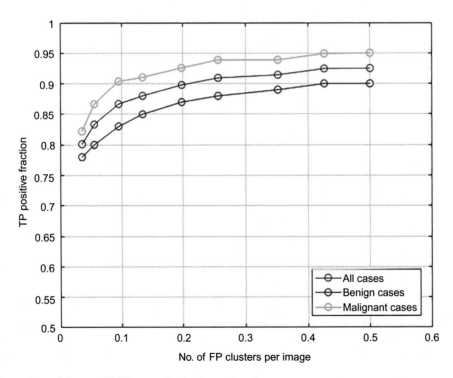

Fig. 12 Comparison of the test FROC curves for benign and malignant cases.

free-response ROC (FROC) curve of malignant cases while the blue curve stands for benign cases and the red line is the FROC curve of all cases. The FROC curve is plotted by adjusting the clustering parameter ε from 30 to 158 at intervals of 16. When the value of ε is small, there are often more FPs and a higher detection sensitivity of MCC. When the value of ε is large, there will be fewer FPs and the detection sensitivity of MCC may also decline.

As for the CADx scheme, a robust diagnosis classifier is built on the basis of automatic detection in a seamless methodology. Especially for Asian women, their breasts tend to be very dense, which makes detection and diagnosis very challenging. In addition, it is found that the cases that are misclassified by the proposed algorithm are exactly the ones that radiologists find difficult to diagnose, and they usually belong to the BI-RAD category 4. Because our research is conducted on our own dataset, it is hard to compare results directly with the other literature.

5 Conclusions

In mammograms, MCs are very subtle and very hard to detect in Asian women. This chapter implemented an automatic detection method using NS domain transformation, then the similar procedure as in a traditional CAD system was performed in the NS domain. A DCNN1 classifier was specially trained to recognize individual MCs and served as the FP MC reduction step. A novel adaptive NRSL strategy based on NS theory was applied to speed up the learning process. In the MCC detection scheme, a sensitivity of 92.5% was achieved at 0.50 FPs per image for cluster-based evaluation. Then, a robust DCNN2 classifier was built for diagnosis on the basis of automatic detection in a seamless methodology, and the AUCs on the validation and testing sets are 0.908 and 0.872 for the proposed DCNN2. Additionally, the case-based classification accuracies on the validation and testing sets are 0.855 and 0.813, respectively. The obtained results demonstrated that the proposed method plays a significant role in improving the performance for the automatic detection and classification of MCCs on FFDMs.

Acknowledgments

This research is supported by the Ministry of Science and Technology of China under grant 2016YFB0200602, the National Science Foundation of China under grant 11401601, the Guangdong Province Frontier and Key Technology Innovative

Grants 2015B010110003 and 2016B030307003, the Guangdong Cooperative and Creative Key Grant 201604020003, and the Guangzhou Science and Technology Creative Key Grant 2017B020210001. The authors thank Dr. Yanhui Guo and Dr. Amira Ashour for their helpful comments on the revision.

References

Bankman, I. N., Nizialek, T., Simon, I., & Gatewood, O. B. (1997). Segmentation algorithms for detecting microcalcifications in mammograms. *IEEE Transactions on Information Technology in Biomedicine, 1,* 141.

Bazzani, A., Bevilacqua, A., Bollini, D., Brancaccio, R., Campanini, R., Lanconelli, N., Riccardi, A., & Romani, D. (2001). An SVM classifier to separate false signals from microcalcifications in digital mammograms. *Physics in Medicine and Biology, 46,* 1651.

Bengio, Y. (2012). Deep learning of representations for unsupervised and transfer learning. In *Proceedings of ICML workshop on unsupervised and transfer learning* (pp. 17–36).

Bottou, L. (2010). Large-scale machine learning with stochastic gradient descent. In *Proceedings of COMPSTAT'2010* (pp.177–186): Physica-Verlag HD.

Bray, F., Ferlay, J., Soerjomataram, I., Siegel, R. L., Torre, L. A., & Jemal, A. (2018). Global cancer statistics 2018: GLOBOCAN estimates of incidence and mortality worldwide for 36 cancers in 185 countries. *CA: A Cancer Journal for Clinicians, 68,* 394–424.

Cai, G., Guo, Y., Zhang, Y., Qin, G., Zhou, Y., & Lu, Y. (2018). A fully automatic microcalcification detection approach based on deep convolution neural network. *Proceedings of SPIE.*

Chan, H. P., Doi, K., Galhotra, S., Vyborny, C. J., Macmahon, H., & Jokich, P. M. (1987). Image feature analysis and computer-aided diagnosis in digital radiography. I. Automated detection of microcalcifications in mammography. *Medical Physics, 14,* 538–548.

Chan, H. P., Lo, S. C., Sahiner, B., Lam, K. L., & Helvie, M. A. (1995). Computer-aided detection of mammographic microcalcifications: pattern recognition with an artificial neural network. *Medical Physics, 22,* 1555.

Cheng, H. D., Cai, X., Chen, X., Hu, L., & Lou, X. (2003). Computer-aided detection and classification of microcalcifications in mammograms: a survey. *Pattern Recognition, 36,* 2967–2991.

De Santo, M., Molinara, M., Tortorella, F., & Vento, M. (2003). Automatic classification of clustered microcalcifications by a multiple expert system. *Pattern Recognition, 36*(7), 1467–1477.

Dengler, J., Behrens, S., & Desaga, J. F. (1993). Segmentation of microcalcifications in mammograms. *IEEE Transactions on Medical Imaging, 12,* 634–642.

Dromain, C., Boyer, B., Ferré, R., Canale, S., Delaloge, S., & Balleyguier, C. (2013). Computer-aided diagnosis (CAD) in the detection of breast cancer. *European Journal of Radiology, 82,* 417–423.

Ester, M., Kriegel, H. P., & Xu, X. (1996). A density-based algorithm for discovering clusters a density-based algorithm for discovering clusters in large spatial databases with noise. In *International conference on knowledge discovery and data mining* (pp. 226–231).

Ge, J., Sahiner, B., Hadjiiski, L. M., Chan, H. P., Wei, J., Helvie, M. A., & Zhou, C. (2006). Computer aided detection of clusters of microcalcifications on full field digital mammograms. *Medical Physics, 33,* 2975.

Guo, Y., & Şengür, A. (2015). NCM: neutrosophic c-means clustering algorithm. *Pattern Recognition, 48*, 2710–2724.

Guo, Y., Şengür, A., & Tian, J. W. (2016). A novel breast ultrasound image segmentation algorithm based on neutrosophic similarity score and level set. *Computer Methods and Programs in Biomedicine, 123*, 43–53.

Guo, Y., Şengür, A., & Ye, J. (2014). A novel image thresholding algorithm based on neutrosophic similarity score. *Measurement, 58*, 175–186.

Gurcan, M. N., Chan, H. P., Sahiner, B., Hadjiiski, L. M., & Petrick, N. (2002). Optimal neural network architecture selection: effects on computer-aided detection of mammographic microcalcifications. *Medical Imaging*, 1325–1330.

Hirose, Y., Yamashita, K., & Hijiya, S. (1991). Back-propagation algorithm which varies the number of hidden units. *Neural Networks, 4*(1), 61–66.

Kallergi, M. (2004). Computer-aided diagnosis of mammographic microcalcification clusters. *Medical Physics, 31*, 314–326.

Krizhevsky, A., Sutskever, I., & Hinton, G. E. (2012). ImageNet classification with deep convolutional neural networks. In *International conference on neural information processing systems* (pp. 1097–1105).

Lashari, S. A., Ibrahim, R., & Senan, N. (2015). De-noising analysis of mammogram images in the wavelet domain using hard and soft thresholding. In: *Information & communication technologies.*

Lo, J. Y., Gavrielides, M. A., Markey, M. K., & Jesneck, J. L. (2003). Computer-aided classification of breast microcalcification clusters: merging of features from image processing and radiologists. In *Vol. 5032 Medical Imaging 2003: Image Processing* (pp. 882–890). International Society for Optics and Photonics.

Moreira, I., Amaral, I., Domingues, I., Cardoso, A., Cardoso, M., & Cardoso, J. (2012). INbreast: toward a full-field digital mammographic database. *Academic Radiology, 19*, 236–248.

Nishikawa, R. M., Giger, M. L., Doi, K., Vyborny, C. J., & Schmidt, R. A. (1995). Computer-aided detection of clustered microcalcifications on digital mammograms. *Medical & Biological Engineering & Computing, 33*, 174.

Otsu, N. (1979). A threshold selection method from gray-level histograms. *IEEE Transactions on Systems, Man, and Cybernetics, 9*, 62–66.

Pereira, D. C., Ramos, R. P., & Nascimento, M. Z. (2014). Segmentation and detection of breast cancer in mammograms combining wavelet analysis and genetic algorithm. *Computer Methods and Programs in Biomedicine, 114*, 88–101.

Sahli, I. S., Bettaieb, H. A., Abdallah, A. B., Bhouri, I., & Bédoui, M. H. (2016). Detection and segmentation of microcalcifications in digital mammograms using multifractal analysis. In *International Conference on Image Processing Theory, TOOLS and Applications* (pp. 180–184).

Simonyan, K., & Zisserman, A. (2014). *Very deep convolutional networks for large-scale image recognition.* arXiv preprint, arXiv: 1409.1556.

Strickland, R. N., & Hahn, H. I. (1996). Wavelet transforms for detecting microcalcifications in mammograms. *IEEE Transactions on Medical Imaging, 15*(2), 218–229.

Strickland, R. N., & Hahn, H. I. (1997). Wavelet transform methods for object detection and recovery. *IEEE Transactions on Image Processing, 6*, 724–735.

Valvano, G., Latta, D. D., Martini, N., Santini, G., Gori, A., Iacconi, C., Ripoli, A., Landini, L., & Chiappino, D. (2017). Evaluation of a deep convolutional neural network method for the segmentation of breast microcalcifications in Mammography Imaging. In *EMBEC & NBC 2017* (pp. 438–441): Springer.

Wang, J., Yang, X., Cai, H., Tan, W., Jin, C., & Li, L. (2016). Discrimination of breast cancer with microcalcifications on mammography by deep learning. *Scitific Reports, 6.*

Yoshida, H., Doi, K., & Nishikawa, R. M. (1994). Automated detection of clustered microcalcifications in digital mammograms using wavelet processing techniques. *Proceedings of SPIE, 2167,* 868–886.

Zhang, W., Doi, K., Giger, M., Wu, Y., Nishikawa, R., & Schmidt, R. (1994). Computerized detection of clustered microcalcifications in digital mammograms using a shift-invariant artificial neural network. *Medical Physics, 21,* 517–524.

Challenges and future directions in neutrosophic theory

15

Challenges and future directions in neutrosophic set-based medical image analysis

Deepika Koundal, Bhisham Sharma

Department of Computer Science and Engineering, Chitkara University School of Engineering and Technology, Chitkara University, Himachal Pradesh, India

1   Introduction

Smarandache (2005) presented the idea of neutrosophic sets (NS). In the neutrosophic set, the indeterminacy by the evident is measured unambiguously. In this condition, membership, indeterminacy, and nonmembership functions are not dependent on each other. NS, one division of neutrosophy theory, can solve real-world challenges such as medical image analysis. In image processing, this is an emerging area to generalize the fuzzy-based methods to neutrosophy-based ones. Neutrosophic theory was introduced in 1998 by Florentin Smarandache, and was oriented toward real-world engineering and scientific applications. As the world consists of imperfect knowledge and indeterminacy that can be observed from real world problems, also initiate vagueness. However, this theory is mostly discussed in mathematics (Smarandache, 2002). Neutrosophic theory offers an even mathematical framework for reasoning, decision making, and knowledge representation, and can be applied to various domains for solving real-world issues to remove indeterminacy (Mohan, Chandra, Krishnaveni, & Guo, 2013; Mohan, Krishnaveni, & Guo, 2013a, 2013b). Neutrosophic theory is widely used for medical image processing problems due to its ability to deal with imprecision and uncertainty. Diagnosis is one of the difficult tasks because of the occurrence of fuzziness and the restricted subjectivity of the experts using medical images. Therefore, to perform

Neutrosophic Set in Medical Image Analysis. https://doi.org/10.1016/B978-0-12-818148-5.00015-1

accurate diagnosis using medical images, various neutrosophic theory-based image-processing methods such as denoising, segmentation, and classification have been investigated to interpret the inherent ambiguity, vagueness, and uncertainty. It has been found that the results using NS are much superior to fuzzy sets, as NS can consider imprecise information in a better way due to its handling capability of indeterminate information.

In this chapter, neutrosophy-based schemes are discussed that are applied to deal with the uncertainty of medical images. Some new areas and the main research are emphasized and investigated.

2 Medical image analysis

This is the branch of investigating medical problems based on different imaging modalities and image analysis techniques. Many works have been performed on the analysis of different types of medical images. Computer-aided diagnosis (CAD) systems were an important research topic in diagnostic radiology and medical imaging. Various categories of CAD systems have been presented for the characterization and detection of several lesions found in medical imaging. The above-mentioned imaging technologies utilize ultrasound (US), magnetic resonance imaging (MRI), computed tomography (CT), radiography, etc. It is essential to use efficient image-processing techniques in various CAD phases to obtain high accuracy and performance for computerized diagnosis (Aswathy & Jagannath, 2017).

Nowadays, the usage of the technology and its applications is not restricted to "native" digital methods such as MRI and CT, but is also extended to imaging modalities such as radiography and endoscopy. The aim of CAD is to deliver a useful additional judgment to support radiologists in interpreting images by increasing the precision and reliability of radiological diagnosis, including the reduction of image understanding time. It is vital to use efficient image analysis techniques in a CAD system to achieve a high-quality image. Several researchers have highlighted the various improvements in CAD systems in various medical domains. Medical images in CAD are a collection of pixels to which discrete color values or brightness is allocated. Analysis of medical images is generally carried out in a methodical order in which steps are employed for abstract interpretation as well as quantitative measurements of biomedical images (Fig. 1). They need existing information on the content and nature of the images that must be integrated into the algorithms on a high point of notion.

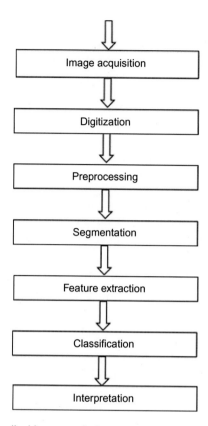

Fig. 1 Stages of medical image analysis.

Therefore, the execution of a biomedical image is very explicit, and a method for one application domain can be shifted hardly straight into others.

3   Image modalities

Medical imaging is an efficient method to determine patient diseases as well as to suggest treatments without any destructive side effects. It is also able to understand what is going on inside a body without the need for an operation or other aggressive actions (medical imaging procedures, 2018). In relation to diagnosis, the most-needed imaging categories include CT (Hsieh, 2009), MRI (Ishioka et al., 2018), ultrasound (Yap et al., 2018), and X-rays (Al-antari, Al-masni, Choi, Han, & Kim, 2018).

3.1 Ultrasound

US is one of the more cost efficient and harmless forms of medical imaging and has an extensive variety of applications. It has no injurious effect and uses sound waves instead of ionizing radiation. With the transmission of frequent soundwaves to the body from the probe through the conducting gel, those waves then bounce back after hitting various body parts to generate an image for diagnosis. US images suffer from speckle noise, which tends to degrade contrast and resolution, thus reducing the diagnostic accuracy. The texture information is often interpreted as noisy pixels and thus get smoothed inadvertently instead of being preserved. Therefore, to preserve indeterminate texture pixels and to deal with uncertain information, neutrosophic sets are used with truth membership, false membership, and indeterminacy membership.

3.2 Magnetic resonance imaging

MRI scans use radiowaves and a high magnetic field to produce images of the body that cannot be clearly seen using CT scans or X-rays. MRI creates diagnostic images without using harmful radiation. It is mostly used to observe the inner body parts to detect tumors, strokes, brain function, spinal cord injuries, and aneurysms. Rician noise is presented in MR images, which makes other image-processing tasks such as segmentation, classification, reconstruction, and registration difficult. Therefore, neutrosophy-based approaches are becoming more popular in handling Rician noise and indeterminate pixels.

3.3 X-ray imaging

X-rays are one of the oldest and most commonly used imaging types. They are a form of electromagnetic radiation. Generally required for detecting problems with the skeletal system, X-rays can be used to diagnose cancer through mammography and gastric issues through barium swallows and enemas. The neutrosophic set is also becoming popular in the diagnosis of dental problems using X-ray images.

3.4 Computer tomography

It is the type of X-ray that generates a three-dimensional (3D) image for diagnosing diseases. X-rays are used to produce cross-sectional images of various parts of the body. CT provides better quality as compared to traditional X-rays with complete images of the bones, blood vessels, internal organs, and soft tissues of the body. The use of a CT scan avoids the need for exploratory surgery. The neutrosophic set considers the noise as an indeterminate component to handle the indeterminacy; lesions are true components and other areas are considered false components for analysis of abnormalities and diseases in CT.

4 Neutrosophy-based medical image analysis

NS is related to human rationality as it elaborates imprecise information (Guo, Cheng, & Zhang, 2009). Subsequently, the medical data derived from various patients related to illness is variable, incomplete, imprecise, imperfect, and vague. Therefore, there is no static treatment system, precise drug practice, or modalities of treatment. Commonly, medical analysis necessitates big volumes of information processing, wherever huge part of which is calculable including fast insensible data processing, thus the complete method provides low inter- and intra-observer variability. Consequently, indeterminacy, discrepancy, inconsistencies, and fuzziness should be resolved. Therefore, accurate analysis of medical images is very important for superior understanding and diagnosis. NS has an important role in the medical domain. The performance of NS systems is near medical reality in a better way as compared to their fuzzy counterparts. These neutrosophic methods are comprehensive logic sets that can have all the essential qualities to encode medical data and gather medical input. NS delivers a novel start to link the gap among various advanced medical schemes and expert systems. It can deal with the medical systems by acquiring data, producing information, fact, indeterminacy and the inaccuracy (Nguyen, Ashour, & Dey, 2019).

Ye (2015) used the improved cosine-related actions of a simplified NS for medical diagnosis. It implemented the NS for medical diagnosis on the basis of dice metrics and trapezoidal numbers of NS. Pramanik and Mondal (2015) introduced an NS-based medical diagnostic technique. Guo et al. (2013) presented the NS-based image analysis technique for lung segmentation. Further studies based on NS in medical diagnosis are explained in Koundal, Gupta, and Singh (2012), Mohan, Krishnaveni, and Guo (2012a), and Qi, Liu, and Xu (2016).

4.1 Preprocessing of medical images

One type of indeterminate information is noise, which is usually presented in medical images. Therefore, the image denoising research domain is becoming a very active area of research to remove this indeterminate information in the form of noise. The images in the NS domain due to its indeterminacy-handling capability help in achieving superior performance during image denoising. Several noise removal methods based on neutrosophic sets for eliminating Gaussian, salt and pepper, Rician, and speckle noise are listed in Table 1, as reported in the literature (Bajger, Ma, & Bottema, 2009; Guo et al., 2013; Koundal et al., 2012; Koundal et al., 2016a; Koundal, Gupta, & Singh, 2018; Mohan, Chandra, et al., 2013; Mohan, Chandra, Krishnaveni, & Guo, 2012; Mohan, Krishnaveni, & Guo, 2012a, 2012b, 2012c; Mohan, Krishnaveni, & Guo, 2013a; Qi et al., 2016).

Table 1 Literature of various neutrosophic-based medical image denoising methods

Refs.	Dataset	Method	Noise	Metrics	Limitations
Koundal, Gupta, and Singh (2016a)	Synthetic and thyroid images	Neutrosophic-based method	Speckle	SNR = 24.26 UQI = 0.8606 FSIM = 0.8790 EPI = 0.8718 MSSIM = 0.809 VIF = 0.3565	Computationally complex
Mohan, Krishnaveni, and Guo (2012a)	MRI of brain	NS-median filter	Rician	PSNR = 24.56	Number of images used for experimentation is not mentioned
Mohan, Chandra, et al. (2013); Mohan, Krishnaveni, and Guo (2013a, 2013b)	MR images	NS Wiener	Rician	PSNR = 27.68 SSIM = 0.9802	Spatially varying noise level in parallel imaging MRI has not been considered
Mohan, Krishnaveni, and Guo (2012b)	MRI datasets	w-Wiener	Rician	PSNR = 37.5 SSIM = 13.88	More metrics need to be evaluated
Mohan, Krishnaveni, and Guo (2013b)	MRI of brain	Nonlocal neutrosophic set (NLNS) approach of Wiener	Rician	PSNR = 24.08 SSIM = 0.9682 QILV = 0.9882	Spatial information has not been incorporated

Unit of PSNR and SNR is dB. Others are unit-less metrics. *UQI*, universal quality index; *SSIM*, structural similarity index; *EPI*, edge preservation index; *PSNR*, peak-signal-to-noise ratio; *QILV*, quality index-based on local variance; *VIF*, visual information fidelity; *MSSIM*, multiscale structural similarity index metric.

4.1.1 Ultrasound

For denoising, images are mapped to the neutrosophic set domain and a filter called the γ-median has been presented for reducing indeterminacy and noise. The experimental results have been performed on various types of natural images with diverse levels of noise (Mohan, Chandra, et al., 2012). Further, Mohan et al. have presented the NS-based denoising method for removing Gaussian and salt and pepper noise with several variances (Mohan, Chandra, et al., 2013; Mohan, Krishnaveni, & Guo, 2012b; Mohan, Krishnaveni, & Guo, 2013a, 2013b).

Furthermore, neutrosophic-based KUAN (NKUAN) and neutrosophic-based LEE methods (NLEE) have been presented for speckle noise reduction (Koundal et al., 2012). The experiments have demonstrated that neutrosophic set methods performed well as compared to KUAN and LEE on simulated artificial images that were corrupted by multiplicative noise (speckle) with various noise levels. The qualitative results also revealed that NKUAN and NLEE preserved the edges and suppressed the speckle noise well as compared to KUAN and LEE. Further, a neutrosophic domain nonconvex speckle reduction method based on gamma noise statistics has been introduced to maintain a good balance between texture preservation and speckle suppression (Koundal et al., 2016a). From the literature, it is observed that most of the work is done for the removal of Rician, Gaussian, and salt and pepper noise. Moreover, the work is generally performed on two or three images by simulating noise on same. There is a need for large image datasets on which neutrosophic-based techniques can be applied so that method performance can be evaluated extensively. Moreover, it is also observed that only the performance metric such as peak signal-to-noise ratio (PSNR) is mostly computed to evaluate these techniques. Therefore, there is a need for other evaluation metrics such as structural similarity index metric (SSIM), universal quality index (UQI), and edge preservation index (EPI) to be evaluated on these images in order to determine noise removal as well as edge preservation.

Another method known as the neutrosophic domain Nakagami total variation (NNTV) approach has been presented. In the neutrosophic domain, the NNTV method transformed the image and employed the neutrosophic filtering operation for speckle noise removal. The performance of NNTV has been measured quantitatively and qualitatively by performance evaluation measures using synthetic images and real US images. Moreover, visual examination by medical experts was carried out and the mean opinion score has been computed on real US images (Koundal et al., 2018).

4.1.2 Mammograms

Bajger et al. (2009) utilized the neutrosophic-based denoising methods for the denoising of mammograms. The study revealed that automated tuning of the minimum spanning tree (MST) segmentation method is done by a degree of entropy for locating mass-like objects in mammograms for CAD systems. It is proficient for different manufacturers to increase the mass detection ratio by producing very limited failures. This is a serious problem; subsequently the result of the segmentation will be an input for further CAD tasks such as registration techniques. A shortcoming of the presented technique is that every single image has to be segmented a number of times before the finest segmentation can be selected.

4.1.3 Magnetic resonance imaging

Different types of approaches for removing Rician noise using MRI have been reported. In the literature, a neutrosophic-based Wiener filter has been introduced for Rician noise and indeterminacy removal. The experimental results were carried out on clinical MR images and simulated MRIs from the brain web database (Mohan, Krishnaveni, & Guo, 2012c). From the results, it has been noticed that the neutrosophic-based Wiener filter is able to suppress noise and preserve edges. Mohan et al. presented a neutrosophic-based image denoising method with a Wiener filter and entropy to evaluate the fuzziness. Various noisy images were used with various noise levels to perform the experiments. The experiment results have shown that the technique can efficiently eliminate the noise from diverse categories of noisy images with several noise levels without classifying the noise type (Mohan, Chandra, et al., 2013; Mohan, Krishnaveni, & Guo, 2013a).

Another method introduced is neutrosophic-based median filtering (Mohan, Chandra, et al., 2012; Mohan, Krishnaveni, & Guo, 2012a). The neutrosophic-based median filter has been used for removing noise and indeterminacy. The experimental results have shown that the introduced filter outperformed other filters at different levels of noise. In (Mohan, Krishnaveni, & Guo, 2013b), another method called the nonlocal neutrosophic set (NLNS) was presented based on a Wiener filter for Rician noise removal from MR images. The experiments have revealed that the NLNS Wiener filter has improved on denoising in comparison to other filters. In Guo et al. (2013), a neutrosophic-based filtering approach is introduced with a level set. The experimental results have shown that the method carried out the segmentation well due to its ability to handle indeterminacy.

4.2 Segmentation of images

Presently, researchers are paying much attention toward neutrosophy-based methods to solve image segmentation problems due to their capability of handling indeterminate information. In the literature, a number of authors have reported different types of NS-based image segmentation methods (Guo & Cheng, 2009; Guo & Şengür, 2013; Zhang, Zhang, & Cheng, 2010b).

4.2.1 Ultrasound

Another neutrosophic L-means (NLM) clustering method has been presented for breast ultrasound images. The NLM has obtained improved accuracy with fair computational speed. The major constraints of NLM are that it cannot segment more than one lesion while it also failed under the severe shadowing effect (Shan, 2011). Furthermore, a Neutrosophic Similarity Score (NSS) method is presented with the integration of a level set for breast tumor segmentation on ultrasound images (Guo, Şengür, & Tian, 2016). The ultrasound image was mapped to the neutrosophic set domain through membership subsets. Afterward, NSS was utilized to quantify the membership degree of the true region. Eventually, the level set is applied for segmentation of the tumor in breast ultrasound images. The experiments showed that NSS can segment the breast tumor accurately and effectively.

The neutrosophic set of methods is used for mapping an image to a binary image. Then, the watershed method has been employed for segmenting mapped images to locate a tumor in a segmented area. The introduced watershed method is completely automatic, robust, and efficient (Zhang, Zhang, & Cheng, 2010a). Another automated segmentation method is introduced that combines the spatial neutrosophic clustering with level sets for segmenting thyroid nodules using ultrasound images. The results have shown that it can delineate more than one nodule effectively and accurately (Koundal, Gupta, & Singh, 2016b). Lotfollahi, Gity, Ye, and Far (2018) introduced a neutrosophic-based semiautomatic segmentation using a region-based active contour that allows for additional accurate breast segmentation of ultrasound images with power in homogeneity. Nonlocal means filters have been used for speckle reduction and the fuzzy logic method has been used for contrast enhancement. This technique is not restricted only to the breast ultrasound images, but can be tailored to different ultrasound images of diverse organs. Classification of lesions into benign or malignant has not been done. In another work, an effort has been made to perform a comparative analysis of neutrosophic C-means (NCM) and intuitionistic fuzzy C-means (IFCM) clustering, including spatial information for medical image segmentation (Koundal, Anand, & Bhat, 2017).

Guo, Ashour, and Sun (2017); Guo, Budak, Şengür, and Smarandache (2017); Guo, Du, Xue, Xia, and Wang (2017); Guo et al. (2017) presented a neutrosophic graph cut (NGC) image segmentation method that is used to locate the qualified rendering of thyroid ultrasound images. Subsequent to indeterminacy filtering, an energy function is presented with the neutrosophic values in the NGC method and the segmentation results are generated by the maximum flow method. Experimental results have shown that the NGC method is proficient in locating the eligible rendering frame with better accuracy for the additional diagnosis of thyroid cancer (Guo, Jiang, et al., 2017).

Further, a technique called information gain-based neutrosophic L-means (IGNLM) clustering has been presented. The technique incorporated the information gain calculated from the local area of every pixel to revise the membership values in the NLM clustering process. For clustering decisions about a pixel, the existing NLM method considered only its membership value and distance from the cluster center, but it ignored the important characteristics in an image that the neighboring pixels have similar characteristics and their possibility of belongingness to the same cluster is high. This neighborhood information has been exploited in the technique by using a concept of entropy called information gain. It has been subsequently used to improve the segmentation capability of the NLM clustering process. From the results, it has been analyzed that the IGNLM method is robust to the shadowing effect as it produced homogeneous clustering, even in the presence of shadow regions and fully automatic (Lal, Kaur, & Gupta, 2018a, 2018b). A normalization algorithm using fuzzy C-means and neutrosophic clustering has been presented for the enhancement and segmentation of images. The method has achieved better performance in segmentation of a breast nodule with normalization than without normalization (Nugroho, Rahmawaty, Triyani, & Ardiyanto, 2017). Further, an approach is presented to categorize the features of the breast nodule into bounded and nonbounded classes. Seven applicable characteristics have been extracted from the nodule by NS and breaking point methods. These experiments specify that the approach effectively categorizes the margin features of the breast ultrasound nodule. A scheme for categorization of breast nodule margin features using ultrasound images has been introduced. The watershed method and the neutrosophic set are used to automatically segment the nodule. Out of nine extracted features, seven relevant features are used to enhance the performance of the categorization method (Nugroho, Triyani, Rahmawaty, & Ardiyanto, 2017).

Koundal (2017) introduced an image segmentation method by considering the texture information. The method can handle the indeterminate information that arose while creating the membership function. Then, the center of the cluster has been updated by including the texture information in the objective function. The method resulted in efficient and accurate segmentation of objects, even in the case of low contrast and vague edge images. The existing state-of-the-art NS methods are not able to incorporate any features that result in poor results on complex textures, noise, and unclear edges.

4.2.2 Histology

An automatic mitosis detection method has been introduced to detect mitosis cells having similar characteristics with lymphocytes and noncancerous cells. A Gaussian filter was implemented to the image for removing noise and enhancing the image. After that, every pixel of the improved image was transformed to the NS domain and the true image from every channel was improved by morphology operations. Several features were extracted and selected from every candidate mitosis and used to feed the classification and regression tree (CART) to categorize every candidate as mitosis or nonmitosis (Sayed & Hassanien, 2017).

4.2.3 Magnetic resonance imaging

Neutrosophic-based segmentation was carried out for tumor detection in MRI images. An NS-based clustering method was presented as a modified nonlocal fuzzy C-means (MNLFCM). The cancer was segmented in an MRI brain image using modified level sets (MLS); therefore, the method is called NS-MNLFCM-MLS. The results have shown that the method extracted the tumor better and was less sensitive to noise on the MRI (Elnazer, Morsy, & Abo-Elsoud, 2016).

4.2.4 Computed tomography

Another method called iterative neutrosophic lung segmentation (INLS) for lung and rib segmentation has been introduced on the basis of expectation maximization analysis and morphological operations (EMM) (Guo et al., 2013). Based on lungs and ribs, the EMM segmentation is initialized using INLS to get a final segmentation of the lung regions. The experiments have demonstrated that with or without diseases in the lung, CT images are segmented accurately. Another segmentation scheme is presented for computed tomography angiography (CTA) images in which coronary arteries are correctly and automatically segmented. The scheme automatically obtained the seed point of a 3D region growing by obtaining the difference between two adjacent slices due to the small changes of the aorta. Then, the possible position of coronary arteries was initially searched by 3D region growing and then dilated by three voxels. After dilation of the probable location, 3D neutrosophic transformation to the CTA volume and 3D discrete wavelet transformation (DWT) was performed for detecting coronary arteries (Chen et al., 2015). A neutrosophic set-based 3D skeleton method for the identification of the skeleton on a 3D volume has been introduced (Guo & Sengur, 2015). A 3D distance transform is used to obtain a distance map and define a ridge point set. Subsequently, a cost function is determined for each ridge point on the basis of indeterminate value and true value of NS. Lastly, the lowest cost path is obtained as a skeleton between different ridge points. The introduced method got high accuracy.

Furthermore, an unsupervised texture-color image segmentation method with an effective indeterminacy reduction operation has been presented, which integrated the nonsubsampled contourlet transform (NSCT) and the NS. The NSCT domain features and color channels of the texture-color image are mapped into the NS domain and then K-means clustering was applied for image segmentation (Heshmati, Gholami, & Rashno, 2016). A neutrosophic-based fuzzy C-means scheme was introduced for the segmentation of an abdominal CT image. A connected component algorithm is required for segmenting the abdominal CT image and for selecting liver parenchyma (Sayed, Ali, Gaber, Hassanien, & Snasel, 2015). A preprocessing and segmentation approach using neutrosophy was presented for extracting blood vessels. The method integrated the neutrosophic set with the adaptive histogram equalization algorithm, the morphological reconstruction scheme for the enhancement of contrast, and the Wiener filter for reduction of noise. The method helped in the correction of vessel information for improved accuracy (Sharma & Rani, 2016).

Rashno et al. (2018) developed an automatic segmentation method for segmentation of cysts/fluids using optical coherence tomography (OCT) of the retina with diabetic macular edema (DME) pathology based on NS and graph shortest paths. An accurate delineation of DME biomarkers is significant because it can present a quantitative measure for the analysis of DME. The efficiency of the method is improved by testing it on three OCT datasets with DME. The segmentation results revealed that the segmented images generated by the algorithm are not in close conformity with the manual segmentations of the two ophthalmologist experts, although they also accomplished enhanced performance with respect to dice, precision, and coefficient comparison criterion as compared to other methods. The limitation is that fine tuning of the algorithm is required for OCT images generated from other manufacturers. At last, a consistent study among segmentation subsequent repeat imaging can leads to another research challenge.

Siri and Latte (2017a) designed a segmentation method for liver CT scan images. NS is explored for generating the speed function and eliminating the adjacent structures of the liver. A fast-marching method is useful to get a periphery of the liver, automatically locating the initial points in the speed function. It can be applied for locating the volume and area of the liver, which assists the doctor in the identification of liver disease and liver transplantation. It can be pragmatic to find different structures of the stomach such as the spleen and kidneys with minor modifications. Rashno et al. (2017) presented an automatic segmentation method based on NS, the graph shortest path, and the graph cut for segmenting 3D fluid volume in terms of exudative age-related macular degeneration (EAMD) pathology. The results showed that fluid volumes generated from the method closely interrelated to the ground truths given by ophthalmologists and accomplished improved results in comparison to other methods using precision measures, dice coefficients, and sensitivity in 2D individual scans. Fine tuning of the algorithm for OCT images has not been introduced.

Lee, Nishikawa, Reiser, and Boone (2017) introduced the neutrosophic approach for segmenting the lesions in breast CT images. The NS reflected the properties of neutrality that are neither true nor false. The image noise is considered as indeterminate element whereas the breast lesion and different breast areas are considered as true and false elements. Every voxel of the image in the NS domain can be defined as its association in true, false, and indeterminate sets. Procedures α-mean, β-enhancement, and γ-plateau are iteratively smoothened and improved the contrast of an image by reducing the noise level of the true set. Further, Lee, Nishikawa, Reiser, and Boone (2018) presented an approach to segment lesions in breast CT images. Its segmentation and associated classification performances are statistically better than the previous method. Although the method is tested on one segmentation algorithm, it can be worked as a preprocessing step such that it can be combined with other segmentation algorithms. Further research with larger datasets is required to extend the finding to other imaging modalities, such as MRI.

In this, a scheme is presented to change an abdominal CT scan image into an NS domain that is able to eradicate adjoining tissues of liver and offer an estimated liver tissue. This method is designed to provide an initial contour within the liver which evolves superficially to find the boundary of liver using Chan-Vese model. It can be a model for detecting the area and volume of the liver that helps the physician to easy diagnoses and liver transplantation. It is also useful for the detection of additional anatomical structures of the abdomen such as the spleen, kidney, etc., with slight changes (Siri & Latte, 2017b). Further, the neutrosophic set expert maximum fuzzy-sure entropy (NS-EMFSE) method has been reported for detecting the boundaries of tumors in brain MRI images. The method was compared with support vector machine (SVM), NS-Otsu, fuzzy C-means (FCM), and particle swarm optimization (DPSO) approaches. It has been noticed from results that NS-EMFSE obtained superior edge detection performance of the tumor as compared to the other four methods (Sert & Avci, 2019).

Further, a fully automatic 3D method is presented for extracting vessel branches in computed tomographic angiography (CTA). A 3D Frangi filter and neutrosophic transform are introduced to identify lung vessels more correctly based on lung region segmentation with gray-level thresholding and morphological operations (Chen & Lee, 2017). In addition, an enhanced segmentation method for an abdominal CT liver tumor based on NS, PSO, and the fast fuzzy C-mean algorithm (FFCM) is introduced. The median filter approach was used for enhancing the contrast, high frequencies, and intensity values of the CT liver. The entropy is used to determine the indeterminacy after that transformation of the abdominal CT image to the NS domain that is defined with three subsets, that is, the percentage of true T, indeterminate I, and false F. Subsequently, FFCM with PSO is optimized by passing the NS image for the optimization of clusters results and segmentation of the liver from the abdominal CT. Then, segmented livers are provided to the PSO-FCM method to segment the tumors. The solution generated on the basis of the analysis of the Jaccard index, the dice coefficient, and the variance (ANOVA) technique results explain that the overall correctness presented by NS is accurate, noise robust, less time consuming, and performs well on nonuniform CT images (Anter & Hassenian, 2018).

4.2.5 X-ray

An automatic approach for the segmentation of jaw lesions in X-ray images was introduced. It involved noise removal and a neutrosophic set-based hybrid fuzzy C-means approach

(NFCM). NFCM detected the jaw lesion accurately but increased the computation time in comparison to other methods (Alsmadi, 2018). Ali, Khan, and Tung (2018) introduced a fuzzy clustering method on the basis of neutrosophic orthogonal matrices to segment dental X-ray images. It converted the images into NS and then computed the interior products of the cutting matrix of input. It transformed each and every pixel of the input image into the NS to calculate the neutrosophic similarity matrix (NSM). NSM is used for the generation of a cutting matrix that adds shapes to the pixel's clusters. The method is validated beside the appropriate techniques with reference to the calculation time and cluster value. The method overcame the limitations of the existing methods, thus enhancing the quality of service and diagnosis.

4.2.6 Digital retinal images

Guo, Budak, et al. (2017) used indeterminacy filtering and shearlet transform to present a retinal vessel detection method. An indeterminacy filter is required for the eradication of vague information and a line-like filter is required for the improvement of vessel regions. Lastly, the vessel is recognized using a neural network classifier. The relationship with different methods also explained that the technique yielded the maximum evaluation metric value and defined the effectiveness and correctness of the method.

4.2.7 Dermoscopy images

Ashour, Hawas, Guo, and Wahba (2018) designed a genetic algorithm (GA)-based skin lesion detection technique with NS operation for decreasing the uncertainty of dermoscopy images. After that, K-means clustering has been employed for the segmentation of skin lesion regions. The comparison outcomes developed the supremacy of the technique with 99.3% accuracy over the K-means and γ-K-means methods for the segmentation and detection of diverse shape, size, skin surface roughness, color, and consistency of the skin lesion. The approach resulted in greater advantage and can be compared with the deep learning-based approaches. Further, detection of the skin lesion depends on integration of the neutrosophic clustering with the adaptive region growing algorithm using dermoscopic images, and is known as the adaptive region growing and neutrosophic clustering. Initially, the dermoscopic images are transformed into the NS domain with the shearlet transform. The images are described by these relationships: true, indeterminate, and false. For the reduction of indeterminacy in the images, an indeterminate filter is used in NS. To segment the dermoscopic images, the neutrosophic C-means (NCM) clustering method is implemented. The skin lesions are recognized accurately using an adaptive region growing with clustering method (Guo, Ashour, & Smarandache, 2018).

Moreover, a skin lesion detection method known as histogram-based clustering estimation neutrosophic C-means (HBCENCM) has been presented using the histogram-based clustering estimation (HBCE) method for finding the essential cluster numbers in the NCM method. In the experimentation work, 900 images were used for training and 379 images were used for testing. The histogram method was used for determining the required cluster number for further segmentation of dermoscopic images. The HBCENCM method is trained and tested using the International Skin Imaging Collaboration (ISIC) 2017 dataset. A total of 200 images were used for training and 700 images were used for testing in random order. The assessment metrics recognized the advantage of the HBCENCM with a horizontal-vertical process for segmenting and detecting the skin lesion (Ashour, Guo, Kucukkulahli, Erdogmus, & Polat, 2018).

4.2.8 Microscopic images

Shahin, Amin, Sharawi, and Guo (2018); Shahin, Guo, Amin, and Sharawi (2018) presented the Neutrosophic Set Similarity Score (NSS) for the enhancement of color images. The NSS is used to derive the improved RGB coefficients wherever every channel coefficient is computed separately. Then, the resulting coefficients were used to scale the input image. The experimental results have shown that the comparative analysis of image enhancement methods for diverse pathology. It seemed to be an effective method for the enhancement of pathology color images by improving contrast, brightness, and color appearance using NSS. The presented method improved the images and did not perform any background distortion. A clear change among every blood color component is determined visually and made the segmentation task.

A fully automated glomerular basement membrane (GBM) image segmentation technique for abnormalities and kidney diseases in microscopic images was established on the basis of shearlet transform and NS (Guo, Ashour, & Sun, 2017). A K-means clustering algorithm is used to segment the neutrosophic image in the shearlet domain. The designed technique is verified using the dataset of a rat's renal corpuscle images that was accomplished by light microscope. The technique using the shearlet characteristics and NS is used to enhance the accuracy of the

GBM method. Additional work is ongoing to enhance an automatic CAD system by using the advanced segmentation results.

4.2.9 Other medical images

In this method, the integration of NS and a multiscale similarity measure is presented for detecting white blood cells (WBCs) in the blood smear images. To determine the similarity among diverse color components of the blood smear image, the NS similarity score is used. The segmentation method is carried out without any morphological operations. At some point in the future, the whole CAD system will be developed for WBC identification and the connected blast cells will be isolated in order to recognize the staining artifacts, accelerate and enhance the projected method as it worked under multi-criteria that consumed more time (Shahin, Amin, et al., 2018; Shahin, Guo, et al., 2018). A neutrosophic active contour model (NACM) has been presented for the detection and segmentation of the myocardium region in the short-axis left ventricle of the myocardial contrast echocardiogram (SLVMCE) image (Guo, Du, et al., 2017). The similarity value in NS has been well defined through homogeneity, which has features to interpret the fuzziness such as low contrast, speckle noise, and a vague boundary on MCE. The myocardium region is lastly found by evolving the curve. The solution defined in the presented NACM technique can find and segment the LVMCE images rapidly and correctly (Guo, Ashour, & Sun, 2017; Guo, Budak, et al., 2017; Guo, Du, et al., 2017; Guo, Jiang, et al., 2017). In another work, an improved neutrosophic graph cut scheme is presented for cervical cancer detection. It is used for the extraction of nuclei and cytoplasmic boundaries of the Pap smear cells. This segmentation system improved the classification rate of cervical cancer detection with an indeterminacy filter to lower the indeterminacy value of spatial information and the extracted intensity values of the preprocessed cancer cell images (Devi, Sheeba, & Joseph, 2018).

4.3 Image classification

The neutrosophic classification is gaining popularity due to its utilization of simple rules. A neutrosophic classifier utilizes neutrosophic logic to handle the stochasticity acquisition errors and indeterminacy.

4.3.1 Ultrasound

A neutrosophic set-based feature extraction method was introduced for tumor classification using a support vector machine (SVM) in breast ultrasound images (BUS), which combined the morphological and statistical features. The BUS images are converted into the NS and then the set of features is extracted. The chi-squared feature selection method was employed for the reduction of the dimension of features pool. The experimental results explained that the accuracy offered by the presented novel features is higher (Amin, Shahin, & Guo, 2016). A neutron connectedness and neutrosophic subsets were defined to model the intrinsic indeterminacy and uncertainty of the images. The experiments have been carried out on a breast ultrasound image. The method is robust and accurate in segmented tumors (Xian, Cheng, & Zhang, 2014).

Kraipeerapun and Fung (2009) presented medical binary classification via ensemble neural networks (NN) depending on interval neutrosophic sets (INS) and the bagging method. In this, every module consists of a pair of NNs trained to forecast the false and truth membership degree. The indeterminacy function was determined for characterization and evaluation of the indeterminate information. An INS is designed by accumulating the three membership functions. The result of an ensemble was dynamically weighted and summed for joining and categorizing the outputs from components in the ensemble. The presented technique has been verified with three datasets, i.e., the ionosphere, liver, and pima. The projected ensemble enhanced the performance of classification related to the simple averaging methods and majority vote. The results illustrated that the INS is able to represent the uncertain information and supported the classification well. Another scheme called the hierarchical self-organizing map (HSOM) was introduced for the segmentation of images using color and texture features. The training samples are selected on the basis of homogeneity properties. A diverse density SVM (DDSVM) framework extended the multiple-instance learning (MIL) scheme for image categorization tasks. In this, the image is viewed as a bag of instances corresponding to the image regions achieved from segmentation. Then, in the new bag space, the neutrosophic SVM (N-SVM) is used as the classifier (Ju & Cheng, 2013).

4.3.2 Thermograms

A CAD system has been designed for breast cancer classification using thermograms. The method consists of automatic segmentation and classification. In the segmentation stage, the neutrosophic set-based fast-FCM (F-FCM) method was introduced. Moreover, a postsegmentation scheme has been presented for the segmentation of breast parenchyma using thermogram images. In addition for breast parenchyma classification, diverse kernel functions were used in SVM. The results showed that the system diagnosed breast cancer well with 100% accuracy (Gaber et al., 2015).

4.4 Image retrieval

The image retrieval system is used for retrieving images related to the user request from the database. In the presented image retrieval system, the set of texture features was extracted and incorporated into the NS domain to represent image content in the training dataset (Eisa, 2014). Another technique called unsupervised learning image classification has been introduced, and it is based on the integration of optimization linear programming and neutrosophic sets (Salama, Eisa, ElGhawalby, & Fawzy, 2016). In this, texture features are presented for embedding images in the neutrosophic domain. This set of features is used for image retrieval using the neutrosophic domain.

4.5 Recommender system

An effective way to enhance the accuracy and efficiency of medical diagnosis is to include the NS into other tools. Various recommender systems (RS) have been frequently used on the basis of patient preferences to make recommendations in medical diagnosis (Thanh & Ali, 2017). In this work, a hybrid system is established that consists of NS with RS on the basis of a neutrosophic algebraic measure known as the neutrosophic recommender system (NRS) to improve the accuracy of previous standalone medical diagnosis systems. This method was experimentally tested and established a benefit over the associated methods. A clustering method for NRSs is also introduced. New algebraic structures in the NRS such as Brouwerian algebra, Kleen algebra, De Morgan algebra, lattices, and Stone algebra are introduced. Neutrosophic-based algebraic structures are used to define the λ-cutting matrix for NRS clustering. Lastly, the experiments were conducted on the benchmark medical datasets for comparing the method with other methods in terms of computational time and accuracy. The limitation is that the computational time is higher as compared to other methods. In order to reduce the computational time, a Bayesian-based approach is designed to automatically estimate the parameters of the NRS and clustering method for extending the NRS for multicharacteristic contexts and for applying the multicriteria NRS to resolve the complicated problems (Ali, Thanh, & Van Minh, 2018).

5 Discussion on challenges and the future scope in neutrosophic set-based medical image analysis

As per the above literature, it is evident that the neutrosophic set has a significant function in medical image analysis tasks in terms of decision making and diagnosis. To date, the neutrosophic set is employed for image denoising, segmentation, and classification in numerous domains, together with medical image analysis. Table 2 lists different types of neutrosophic-based denoising methods, whereas, in the future, other clustering techniques can be integrated to the neutrosophic set. Tables 3 and 4 list the different types of neutrosophic-based denoising and clustering methods, respectively.

However, future research is ongoing with other image-processing applications such as image registration, fusion, and compression. Therefore, it has been suggested to use NS methods in such tasks related to existing techniques. Most of the neutrosophic integrated clustering techniques are based on FCM. Therefore, in the future, other clustering techniques can be integrated to the neutrosophic set.

Moreover, several classification techniques can be integrated with a neutrosophic set to solve various classification problems. In addition, it is suggested to discuss the subsequent studies on NS in addition to the fuzzy set that can be functional in medical and diverse application domains. Furthermore, NS approaches can be used in numerous studies of breast cancer for further developments. Also, integration of NS with other mathematical models has attracted the interest of many new researchers. Moreover, various challenges have been discussed such as a requirement for image analysis that can efficiently be revised for a definite clinical task. Effective generation of ground truth annotations is required to match the growing necessities on reliability and robustness commercially. Methods for evaluating more heterogeneous images will allow the further extensive acceptance of postprocessing applications of MRI, in addition to novel applications, for example, those associated with big data analytics as well as the creation of complete organs and anatomical models with the least manual interaction. Moreover, medical image analysis gives life to medical imaging when integrated with virtual/augmented reality.

Table 2 Various neutrosophic-based image denoising methods with their advantages and drawbacks

Refs.	Method	Modality	Drawback	Advantage
Mohan, Krishnaveni, and Guo (2012a, 2012b, 2012c); Mohan, Chandra, et al. (2012)	γ-Median	General images	Edges are not preserved, medical images are not explored	Handle indeterminacy and noise Remove Gaussian noise
Koundal et al. (2012)	NKUAN NLEE	Thyroid US	Removes multiplicative noise well	Edges and details are not preserved Caused blurriness
Koundal et al. (2016a, 2016b)	NS-based nonconvex speckle reduction method	Thyroid US	Not able to preserve details effectively	Removed the speckle noise Based on gamma noise statistics
Koundal et al. (2018)	NNTV	Thyroid US	High computational time	Based on Nakagami noise statistics Maintains a good balance between texture preservation and speckle suppression
Bajger et al. (2009)	NS-based denoising methods	Mammograms	Every single image has to be segmented a number of times before the finest segmentation can be selected	Automated tuning of minimum spanning tree (MST) segmentation
Mohan, Krishnaveni, and Guo (2012a, 2012b, 2012c); Mohan, Chandra, et al. (2012)	NS-based Wiener filter	**Brain MRI**	Number of images should be high in dataset	Rician noise and indeterminacy removal
Guo et al. (2013)	Nonlocal neutrosophic set (NLNS)			

Table 3 Neutrosophic-based image segmentation techniques with their drawbacks and benefits

Refs.	Methods	Images	Drawback	Benefits
Shan (2011)	NLM	Breast US	Cannot segment more than one lesion as well as failed under severe shadowing effect	Improved accuracy with fair computational speed
Guo et al. (2016)	NSS-based LS	Breast US	Automatic generation of suitable initial contour is very difficult and the deformation procedure is very time consuming	Can segment malign and benign cases with different tumor size and shape
Zhang et al. (2010b)	NS-based watershed	Breast US	Sensitive to noise and inhomogeneity	Fully automatic, robust and efficient No seed is needed. Resulting regions are connected
Koundal et al. (2016a, 2016b)	SNDRLS	Thyroid US	Fails to delineate isoechoic images	Can find optimal boundaries Can delineate more than one nodule
Lotfollahi et al. (2018)	NS-based region-based active contour	Breast US	Semiautomatic segmentation	Not restricted to breast ultrasound images and can be tailored for different ultrasound images of diverse organs
Guo, Jiang, et al. (2017)	NGC	Thyroid elastography	Requires further diagnosis on thyroid cancer	Locate the eligible rendering frame with better accuracy
Nugroho, Rahmawaty, et al. (2017)	FCM and neutrosophic clustering-based normalization algorithm	Breast nodule US	Accuracy is less and can be improved	Segment the nodule accurately with normalization
Lal et al. (2018a)	IGNLM	Breast US	Human intervention is there	Fully automatic, robust to shadowing effect
Koundal (2017)	NS-based texture method	Medical US images	Computational time is more	Efficient and accurate segmentation of objects, even in case of vague edges and low contrast images
Sayed and Hassanien (2017)	NS and moth-flame optimization (MFO)	Breast histology for mitosis detection	Fewer images used Accuracy is required to be improved	Fast, robust, efficient, and coherent

Reference	Method	Image type	Disadvantage	Advantage
Elnazer et al. (2016)	MNLFCM	MRI brain	Accuracy is less	Extract the tumor better; Less sensitive to noise
Guo et al. (2013)	EMM-based INLS	Lung CT	May fail to segment if the intensity distributions of the diaphragm and the chest wall are changed substantially due to the presence of invasive disease	Accurate and automatic segmentation of lungs and ribs
Chen et al. (2015)	NS-based 3D DWT	Coronary arteries CTA	No evaluation of intra- and interreader variabilities; Fewer datasets are used	Detect coronary pathologies accurately and automatically
Sayed et al. (2015)	NS-based FCM	Liver abdominal CT	Extract tumor but its diagnosis is not done; Images used are less	Extract only liver
Rashno et al. (2018)	NS-based Graph shortest paths	(OCT) retina	Sensitivity is less; Fine tuning of method is not done; Segmentation of fluid-filled regions is not done	Segment the fluid/cyst accurately; Appropriate number of clusters is computed automatically from the estimated fluid/cyst regions
Sharma and Rani (2016)	NS with adaptive histogram equalization	Retinal images	Recognition of diseases such as diabetic retinopathy, glaucoma, hypertension	Extract blood vessels accurately
Rashno et al. (2017)	NS-based graph shortest paths	OCT scan images for liver	Fine tuning of the algorithm is not done for OCT images that are generated from other manufacturers	Automatic segmentation
Siri and Latte (2017a)	NS-based fast marching method	CT scan images for liver	Initialization is required	Pragmatic to find different structures of the stomach such as spleen and kidneys with minor modifications
Lee et al. (2018)	NS-based method	Breast CT	Larger image datasets are not used to extend the finding to other imaging modalities, such as MRI	Segmentation and classification performance is better
Siri and Latte (2017b)	NS-based Chan-Vese model	Abdominal CT scan	Suffers from noise	Detect accurate area and volume of liver
Sert and Avci (2019)	NS-EMFSE	Brain MRI	Computationally complex	Detect the edges of brain tumors
Chen and Lee (2017)	3D Frangi filter and neutrosophic transform	CTA	Number of images in dataset is not mentioned	Extract vessel branches

Continued

Table 3 Neutrosophic-based image segmentation techniques with their drawbacks and benefits—cont'd

Refs.	Methods	Images	Drawback	Benefits
Anter and Hassenian (2018)	NS-based FFCM	Abdominal CT scan	More theoretical analysis of performance and convergence properties are not explored	Accurate, noise robust, less time consuming and performs well on nonuniform CT images
Alsmadi (2018)	NFCM	Jaw lesions in X-ray images	Requires real time deployment	Detected the jaw lesion accurately
			Computation time increased	
Ali, Khan, and Tung (2018)	Neutrosophic orthogonal matrices-based fuzzy clustering	Dental X-ray images	Dental related diseases are not explored	Accurate segmentation of dental images
Guo, Budak, et al. (2017)	Indeterminacy filtering and shearlet transform	Retinal images	Requires postprocessing methods to improve the quality of vessel detection	Automatic retinal vessel detection and classification
Ashour, Hawas, et al. (2018)	NS-based GA for skin lesion detection	Dermoscopy images	Comparison with deep learning-based methods is required	Detection of diverse size, shape, color, skin surface roughness, and consistency of the skin lesion
			Computationally complex	Solves the optimization problem
Guo et al. (2018)	NCARG	Dermoscopy images	More accurate automated diagnosis and clinical decision support is required	95.3% accuracy achieved with different shape, size, color, uniformity, skin surface roughness, light illumination during the image capturing process and existence of air bubbles
Ashour, Guo, et al. (2018)	HBCENCM	Skin lesion dermoscopic images	Characterized by dark black border of the image, dark small lesion within brighter region, or very small bright lesion	Skin lesion detection based on intensity and morphological features. Histogram-based cluster estimation has been used to find the cluster numbers in image

Reference	Method	Application		
Shahin, Amin, et al. (2018); Shahin, Guo, et al. (2018)	Pathological images enhancement based on NSS under multicriteria	Microscopic images	Required more processing time, which needs to be optimized and accelerated	Effective method for contrast, brightness, and color appearance improvement Does not comprise any background distortion Low complexity Adaptive with different resolution and lighting conditions
Guo, Ashour, and Sun (2017)	Shearlet transform and NS	Kidney diseases in microscopic images	More enhancement is needed in automatic CAD system	Accurate extraction of glomerular basement membrane (GBM) regions
Shahin, Amin, et al. (2018); Shahin, Guo, et al. (2018)	NS and multiscale similarity measure	Blood smear images	Consumed more time	Detect white blood cells without any morphological binary methods
Guo, Du, et al. (2017)	Neutrosophic active contour model (NACM)	Echocardiography images	Detect and delineate left ventricular myocardium on contrast echocardiography images quickly and accurately	Not a fully automatic method to measure myocardial perfusion, and infarct size in apical long-axis images
Devi et al. (2018)	Neutrosophic graph cut-based segmentation (NGCS)	Pap smear cells for cervical cancer detection	Minimized the computation overhead, improved the rate of classification accuracy, specificity, and sensitivity as compared to benchmarked graph cut-based methods	High time complexity as compared to non graph cut methods

Table 4 Neutrosophic-based image classification methods with their limitations and benefits

Refs	Methods	Images	Advantages	Disadvantages
Amin et al. (2016)	NS-based feature extraction method	Breast ultrasound images	Classification accuracy is increased by combining texture, morphologic, and neutrosophic score features	Significant types of features are not well optimized Tested only smaller set of images
Xian et al. (2014)	NS-based neutron-connectedness	Breast ultrasound image	Robust and accurate in segmenting tumor	Requires human intervention
Gaber et al. (2015)	NS-FFCM	Thermograms	Automatic classification for thermogram to normal and abnormal	Reliability is not tested on large size of the image datasets
Salama et al. (2016)	NS-based image retrieval system		NS image retrieval improved the quality and made the retrieval easier and more effective	Only small set of images is tested
Thanh and Ali (2017)	NRS	Medical images	NRS for accurate medical diagnosis	Computational time is slower
Ali, Thanh, and Van Minh (2018)	Bayesian-based approach NRS	Medical images	Reduced the computational time	Algorithm based on similarity measures was designed for medical diagnosis

6 Conclusion

In this research, numerous image analysis methods are presented for the quantification of medical images. The past few years have brought an enormous volume of work linked to image analysis. The key requirement of this research was to attempt to include the variety of methods for texture, shape, and parametric explanation, and offer a guide that physicians can utilize for additional investigation. That will be important for the expansion of CAD systems for more accurate prognosis and diagnosis. Several real-world decision-making challenges are comprised of imprecision, uncertainty, indistinctness, unreliability, incompleteness, and indeterminacy. Therefore, logic and NS are achieving important consideration to resolve such issues. This measures the indeterminacy, trueness, and falsehood. On the contrary, the NS is clearly measuring the indeterminacy, although the indeterminacy, truth, and falsity memberships are self-determining. These features are very important in numerous applications such as image fusion, which is used to merge the data from diverse sensors for additional biomedical diagnoses problems. Recently, NS has become a very popular research area in decision-making systems for medical diagnosis. Mostly, NS is used widely in numerous applications of medical diagnosis due to the handling of inadequate and unreliable data where a patient's data for decision making are unavailable to model the medical information base. Subsequently, the present work highlights the requirement of the NS in diverse medical diagnosis applications to support scholars and attract experts with the NS applications. Subsequently, the medical image is to be characterized in the neutrosophic set domain. This alteration is achieved by manipulating the three membership sets. Formerly, the entropy of the indeterminate subset is designed. So as to accomplish superior performance for the medical image procedure under concern, the value of the indeterminate subset is to be lessened. Furthermore, due to the superior role of NS in image segmentation, denoising, and clustering for effective medical diagnosis, registration, fusion, and classification are not described or handled by NS without any strong purpose. Therefore, researchers are suggested to make use of NS with such errands specifically for accurate medical diagnosis.

References

Al-antari, M. A., Al-masni, M. A., Choi, M. T., Han, S. M., & Kim, T. S. (2018). A fully integrated computer-aided diagnosis system for digital X-ray mammograms via deep learning detection, segmentation, and classification. *International Journal of Medical Informatics, 117*, 44–54.

Ali, M., Khan, M., & Tung, N. T. (2018). Segmentation of dental X-ray images in medical imaging using neutrosophic orthogonal matrices. *Expert Systems with Applications, 91*, 434–441.

Ali, M., Thanh, N. D., & Van Minh, N. (2018). A neutrosophic recommender system for medical diagnosis based on algebraic neutrosophic measures. *Applied Soft Computing, 71*, 1054–1071.

Alsmadi, M. K. (2018). A hybrid fuzzy C-means and neutrosophic for jaw lesions segmentation. *Ain Shams Engineering Journal, 9*(4), 697–706.

Amin, K. M., Shahin, A. I., & Guo, Y. (2016). A novel breast tumor classification algorithm using neutrosophic score features. *Measurement, 81*, 210–220.

Anter, A. M., & Hassenian, A. E. (2018). Computational intelligence optimization approach based on particle swarm optimizer and neutrosophic set for abdominal CT liver tumor segmentation. *Journal of Computational Science, 25,* 376–387.

Ashour, A. S., Guo, Y., Kucukkulahli, E., Erdogmus, P., & Polat, K. (2018). A hybrid dermoscopy images segmentation approach based on neutrosophic clustering and histogram estimation. *Applied Soft Computing, 69,* 426–434.

Ashour, A. S., Hawas, A. R., Guo, Y., & Wahba, M. A. (2018). A novel optimized neutrosophic k-means using genetic algorithm for skin lesion detection in dermoscopy images. *Signal, Image and Video Processing, 12*(7), 1311–1318.

Aswathy, M. A., & Jagannath, M. (2017). Detection of breast cancer on digital histopathology images: present status and future possibilities. *Informatics in Medicine Unlocked, 8,* 74–79.

Bajger, M., Ma, F., & Bottema, M. J. (2009). Automatic tuning of MST segmentation of mammograms for registration and mass detection algorithms. In *Digital image computing: Techniques and applications* (pp. 400–407).

Chen, S. T., & Lee, D. (2017, November). Improving the segmentation of lung vessel trees by reducing the uncertainty in neutrosophic transform. In: *4th international conference on systems and informatics (ICSAI)* (pp. 1229–1233).

Chen, S. T., Wang, T. D., Lee, W. J., Huang, T. W., Hung, P. K., Wei, C., et al. (2015). Coronary arteries segmentation based on the 3D discrete wavelet transform and 3D neutrosophic transform. *BioMed Research International,* 1–9. Article ID 798303.

Devi, M. A., Sheeba, J. I., & Joseph, K. S. (2018). Neutrosophic graph cut-based segmentation scheme for efficient cervical cancer detection. *Journal of King Saud University-Computer and Information Sciences* (in press).

Eisa, M. (2014). A new approach for enhancing image retrieval using neutrosophic sets. *International Journal of Computer Applications, 95*(8), 12–20.

Elnazer, S., Morsy, M., & Abo-Elsoud, M. E. A. (2016). Brain tumor segmentation using hybrid of both neutrosophic modified nonlocal fuzzy C-mean and modified level sets. *International Journal of Science and Research, 5*(2), 1908–1914.

Gaber, T., Ismail, G., Anter, A., Soliman, M., Ali, M., Semary, N., Hassanien, A. E., & Snasel, V. (2015). Thermogram breast cancer prediction approach based on neutrosophic sets and fuzzy c-means algorithm. In: *2015 37th annual international conference of the IEEE engineering in medicine and biology society (EMBC)* (pp. 4254–4257).

Guo, Y., Ashour, A., & Smarandache, F. (2018). A novel skin lesion detection approach using neutrosophic clustering and adaptive region growing in dermoscopy images. *Symmetry, 10*(4), 119.

Guo, Y., Ashour, A. S., & Sun, B. (2017). A novel glomerular basement membrane segmentation using neutrsophic set and shearlet transform on microscopic images. *Health Information Science and Systems, 5*(1), 15.

Guo, Y., Budak, Ü., Şengür, A., & Smarandache, F. (2017). A retinal vessel detection approach based on shearlet transform and indeterminacy filtering on fundus images. *Symmetry, 9*(10), 235.

Guo, Y., & Cheng, H. D. (2009). New neutrosophic approach to image segmentation. *Pattern Recognition, 42*(5), 587–595.

Guo, Y., Cheng, H. D., & Zhang, Y. (2009). A new neutrosophic approach to image denoising. *New Mathematics and Natural Computation, 5*(03), 653–662.

Guo, Y., Du, G. Q., Xue, J. Y., Xia, R., & Wang, Y. H. (2017). A novel myocardium segmentation approach based on neutrosophic active contour model. *Computer Methods and Programs in Biomedicine, 142,* 109–116.

Guo, Y., Jiang, S. Q., Sun, B., Siuly, S., Şengür, A., & Tian, J. W. (2017). Using neutrosophic graph cut segmentation algorithm for qualified rendering image selection in thyroid elastography video. *Health Information Science and Systems, 5*(1), 8.

Guo, Y., & Şengür, A. (2013). A novel image segmentation algorithm based on neutrosophic filtering and level set. *Neutrosophic Sets and Systems, 1*, 46–49.

Guo, Y., & Sengur, A. (2015). A novel 3D skeleton algorithm based on neutrosophic cost function. *Applied Soft Computing, 36*, 210–217.

Guo, Y., Şengür, A., & Tian, J. W. (2016). A novel breast ultrasound image segmentation algorithm based on neutrosophic similarity score and level set. *Computer Methods and Programs in Biomedicine, 123*, 43–53.

Guo, Y., Zhou, C., Chan, H. P., Chughtai, A., Wei, J., Hadjiiski, L. M., & Kazerooni, E. A. (2013). Automated iterative neutrosophic lung segmentation for image analysis in thoracic computed tomography. *Medical Physics, 40*(8).

Heshmati, A., Gholami, M., & Rashno, A. (2016). Scheme for unsupervised colour–texture image segmentation using neutrosophic set and non-subsampled contourlet transform. *IET Image Processing, 10*(6), 464–473.

Hsieh, J. (2009, November). *Computed tomography: Principles, design, artifacts, and recent advances.* Bellingham, WA: SPIE.

Ishioka, J., Matsuoka, Y., Uehara, S., Yasuda, Y., Kijima, T., Yoshida, S., Yokoyama, M., Saito, K., Kihara, K., Numao, N., & Kimura, T. (2018). Computer-aided diagnosis of prostate cancer on magnetic resonance imaging using a convolutional neural network algorithm. *BJU International, 122*(3), 411–417.

Ju, W., & Cheng, H. D. (2013). A novel neutrosophic logic Svm (N-Svm) and its application to image categorization. *New Mathematics and Natural Computation, 9*(01), 27–42.

Koundal, D. (2017). Texture-based image segmentation using neutrosophic clustering. *IET Image Processing, 11*(8), 640–645.

Koundal, D., Anand, V., & Bhat, S. (2017). Comparative analysis of neutrosophic and intuitionistic fuzzy set with spatial information on image segmentation. In *2017 fourth international conference on image information processing (ICIIP)* (pp. 1–5).

Koundal, D., Gupta, S., & Singh, S. (2012). Speckle reduction filter in neutrosophic domain. In: *International conference of biomedical engineering and assisted technologies* (pp. 786–790).

Koundal, D., Gupta, S., & Singh, S. (2016). Speckle reduction method for thyroid ultrasound images in neutrosophic domain. *IET Image Processing, 10*(2), 167–175.

Koundal, D., Gupta, S., & Singh, S. (2016b). Automated delineation of thyroid nodules in ultrasound images using spatial neutrosophic clustering and level set. *Applied Soft Computing, 40*, 86–97.

Koundal, D., Gupta, S., & Singh, S. (2018). Neutrosophic based Nakagami total variation method for speckle suppression in thyroid ultrasound images. *IRBM, 39*(1), 43–53.

Kraipeerapun, P., & Fung, C. C. (2009). Binary classification using ensemble neural networks and interval neutrosophic sets. *Neurocomputing, 72*(13–15), 2845–2856.

Lal, M., Kaur, L., & Gupta, S. (2018). Modified spatial neutrosophic clustering technique for boundary extraction of tumours in B-mode BUS images. *IET Image Processing, 12*(8), 1338–1344.

Lal, M., Kaur, L., & Gupta, S. (2018b). Automatic segmentation of tumors in B-mode breast ultrasound images using information gain based neutrosophic clustering. *Journal of X-ray Science and Technology*, 1–17.

Lee, J., Nishikawa, R.M., Reiser, I. and Boone, J.M., 2017. Neutrosophic segmentation of breast lesions for dedicated breast CT. In Medical imaging 2017: Computer-aided diagnosis (Vol. 10134, p. 101340Q). (International Society for Optics and Photonics).

Lee, J., Nishikawa, R. M., Reiser, I., & Boone, J. M. (2018). Neutrosophic segmentation of breast lesions for dedicated breast computed tomography. *Journal of Medical Imaging, 5*(1).

Lotfollahi, M., Gity, M., Ye, J. Y., & Far, A. M. (2018). Segmentation of breast ultrasound images based on active contours using neutrosophic theory. *Journal of Medical Ultrasonics, 45*(2), 205–212.

medical imaging procedures. (2018). https://www.cdc.gov/features/medical-imaging-procedures/index.html.

Mohan, J., Chandra, A. T. S., Krishnaveni, V., & Guo, Y. (2012). Evaluation of neutrosophic set approach filtering technique for image denoising. *The International Journal of Multimedia & Its Applications, 4*(4), 73.

Mohan, J., Chandra, A. T. S., Krishnaveni, V., & Guo, Y. (2013). Image denoising based on neutrosophic wiener filtering. In *Advances in computing and information technology* (pp. 861–869). Berlin, Heidelberg: Springer.

Mohan, J., Krishnaveni, V., & Guo, Y. (2012a). Validating the neutrosophic approach of MRI denoising based on structural similarity. In: *IET conference on image processing (IPR 2012)* (p. 2012).

Mohan, J., Krishnaveni, V., & Guo, Y. (2012b). Performance analysis of neutrosophic set approach of median filtering for MRI denoising. *International Journal of Electronics and Communication Engineering & Technology, 3*, 148–163.

Mohan, J., Krishnaveni, V., & Guo, Y. (2012c). Performance comparison of MRI denoising techniques based on neutrosophic set approach. *European Journal of Scientific Research, 86*(3), 307–318.

Mohan, J., Krishnaveni, V., & Guo, Y. (2013a). A new neutrosophic approach of Wiener filtering for MRI denoising. *Measurement Science Review, 13*(4), 177–186.

Mohan, J., Krishnaveni, V., & Guo, Y. (2013b). MRI denoising using nonlocal neutrosophic set approach of Wiener filtering. *Biomedical Signal Processing and Control, 8*(6), 779–791.

Nguyen, G. N., Ashour, A. S., & Dey, N. (2019). A survey of the state-of-the-arts on neutrosophic sets in biomedical diagnoses. *International Journal of Machine Learning and Cybernetics, 10*(1), 1–13.

Nugroho, H. A., Rahmawaty, M., Triyani, Y., & Ardiyanto, I. (2017). Neutrosophic and fuzzy C-means clustering for breast ultrasound image segmentation. In *2017 9th international conference on information technology and electrical engineering (ICITEE)* (pp. 1–5).

Nugroho, H. A., Triyani, Y., Rahmawaty, M., & Ardiyanto, I. (2017). Breast ultrasound image segmentation based on neutrosophic set and watershed method for classifying margin characteristics. In *2017 7th IEEE international conference on system engineering and technology (ICSET)*, (pp. 43–47).

Pramanik, S., & Mondal, K. (2015). Cosine similarity measure of rough neutrosophic sets and its application in medical diagnosis. *Infinite Study.*

Qi, X., Liu, B., & Xu, J. (2016). A neutrosophic filter for high-density salt and pepper noise based on pixel-wise adaptive smoothing parameter. *Journal of Visual Communication and Image Representation, 36*, 1–10.

Rashno, A., Koozekanani, D. D., Drayna, P. M., Nazari, B., Sadri, S., Rabbani, H., & Parhi, K. K. (2018). Fully automated segmentation of fluid/cyst regions in optical coherence tomography images with diabetic macular edema using neutrosophic sets and graph algorithms. *IEEE Transactions on Biomedical Engineering, 65*(5), 989–1001.

Rashno, A., Nazari, B., Koozekanani, D. D., Drayna, P. M., Sadri, S., Rabbani, H., & Parhi, K. K. (2017). Fully-automated segmentation of fluid regions in exudative age-related macular degeneration subjects: Kernel graph cut in neutrosophic domain. *PLoS One, 12*(10).

Salama, A. A., Eisa, M., ElGhawalby, H., & Fawzy, A. E. (2016). Neutrosophic features for image retrieval. *Image, 34*, 35.

Sayed, G. I., Ali, M. A., Gaber, T., Hassanien, A. E., & Snasel, V. (2015, December). A hybrid segmentation approach based on neutrosophic sets and modified watershed: a case of abdominal CT Liver parenchyma. In *2015 11th international computer engineering conference (ICENCO)* (pp. 144–149).

Sayed, G. I., & Hassanien, A. E. (2017). Moth-flame swarm optimization with neutrosophic sets for automatic mitosis detection in breast cancer histology images. *Applied Intelligence, 47*(2), 397–408.

Sert, E., & Avci, D. (2019). Brain tumor segmentation using neutrosophic expert maximum fuzzy-sure entropy and other approaches. *Biomedical Signal Processing and Control, 47*, 276–287.

Shahin, A. I., Amin, K. M., Sharawi, A. A., & Guo, Y. (2018). A novel enhancement technique for pathological microscopic image using neutrosophic similarity score scaling. *Optik, 161*, 84–97.

Shahin, A. I., Guo, Y., Amin, K. M., & Sharawi, A. A. (2018). A novel white blood cells segmentation algorithm based on adaptive neutrosophic similarity score. *Health information science and systems, 6*(1), 1.

Shan, J. (2011). *A fully automatic segmentation method for breast ultrasound images.* (Doctoral dissertation, Utah State University).

Sharma, A., & Rani, S. (2016, April). An automatic segmentation & detection of blood vessels and optic disc in retinal images. In *2016 international conference on communication and signal processing (ICCSP)* (pp. 1674–1678).

Siri, S. K., & Latte, M. V. (2017a). A novel approach to extract exact liver image boundary from abdominal CT scan using neutrosophic set and fast marching method. *Journal of Intelligent Systems*, 1–16. https://doi.org/10.1515/jisys-2017-0144.

Siri, S. K., & Latte, M. V. (2017b). Combined endeavor of neutrosophic set and Chan-Vese model to extract accurate liver image from CT scan. *Computer Methods and Programs in Biomedicine, 151*, 101–109.

Smarandache, F. (2002). *Neutrosophy, a new branch of philosophy.* [Infinite Study].

Smarandache, F. (2005). Neutrosophic set-a generalization of the intuitionistic fuzzy set. *International Journal of Pure and Applied Mathematics, 24*(3), 287.

Thanh, N. D., & Ali, M. (2017). A novel clustering algorithm in a neutrosophic recommender system for medical diagnosis. *Cognitive Computation, 9*(4), 526–544.

Xian, M., Cheng, H. D., & Zhang, Y. (2014). A fully automatic breast ultrasound image segmentation approach based on neutro-connectedness. In *2014 22nd international conference on pattern recognition* (pp. 2495–2500).

Yap, M. H., Pons, G., Martí, J., Ganau, S., Sentís, M., Zwiggelaar, R., Davison, A. K., & Martí, R. (2018). Automated breast ultrasound lesions detection using convolutional neural networks. *IEEE Journal of Biomedical and Health Informatics, 22*(4), 1218–1226.

Ye, J. (2015). Improved cosine similarity measures of simplified neutrosophic sets for medical diagnoses. *Artificial Intelligence in Medicine, 63*(3), 171–179.

Zhang, M., Zhang, L., & Cheng, H. D. (2010). A neutrosophic approach to image segmentation based on watershed method. *Signal Processing, 90*(5), 1510–1517.

Zhang, M., Zhang, L., & Cheng, H. D. (2010b). Segmentation of ultrasound breast images based on a neutrosophic method. *Optical Engineering, 49*(11).

Further reading

Cheng, H. D., & Guo, Y. (2008). A new neutrosophic approach to image thresholding. *New Mathematics and Natural Computation, 4*(03), 291–308.

Index

Note: Page numbers followed by *f* indicate figures, *t* indicate tables, and *b* indicate boxes.